BUILDING THE NATION

Portrait of N.F.S. Grundtvig, 1872, by Christian Adolph Barfod Lønborg. The Royal Library, Copenhagen.

Building the Nation

N.F.S. Grundtvig and Danish National Identity

Edited by

JOHN A. HALL, OVE KORSGAARD,

AND OVE K. PEDERSEN

McGill-Queen's University Press
Montreal & Kingston • Ithaca

ISBN 978-0-7735-4405-5 (cloth)
ISBN 978-0-7735-4406-2 (paper)
ISBN 978-0-7735-9631-3 (ePDF)
ISBN 978-0-7735-9632-0 (ePUB)

Legal deposit first quarter 2015
Bibliothèque nationale du Québec

Published simultaneously in the United Kingdom, Eire, and Europe in paperback by Djøf Publishing, Copenhagen.

Printed in Canada on acid-free paper that is 100% ancient forest free (100% post-consumer recycled), processed chlorine free

Publication of this book has been supported by funding received from the Grundtvig Study Center.

McGill-Queen's University Press acknowledges the support of the Canada Council for the Arts for our publishing program. We also acknowledge the financial support of the Government of Canada through the Canada Book Fund for our publishing activities.

Library and Archives Canada Cataloguing in Publication

Building the nation : N.F.S. Grundtvig and Danish national identity / edited by John A. Hall, Ove Korsgaard, and Ove K. Pedersen.

Co-published by: DJØF Publishing Copenhagen.
Includes bibliographical references and index.
Issued in print and electronic formats.
ISBN 978-0-7735-4405-5 (bound). – ISBN 978-0-7735-4406-2 (pbk.). –
ISBN 978-0-7735-9631-3 (ePDF). – ISBN 978-0-7735-9632-0 (ePUB)

1. Grundtvig, N. F. S. (Nicolai Frederik Severin), 1783–1872 – Political and social views. 2. Grundtvig, N. F. S. (Nicolai Frederik Severin), 1783–1872 – Influence. 3. Denmark – Intellectual life – 19th century. 4. Denmark – Social conditions – 19th century. 5. Denmark – History – 19th century. 6. Philosophers – Denmark – Biography. 7. Authors, Danish – 19th century – Biography. 8. Lutheran Church – Denmark – Clergy – Biography. I. Hall, John A., 1949–, editor II. Korsgaard, Ove, 1942–, editor III. Pedersen, Ove Kaj, 1948–, editor

DL249.G78B83 2014   948.9'04092   C2014-906834-4
C2014-906835-2

Typeset by Jay Tee Graphics Ltd. in 10.5/13 Sabon

Contents

Acknowledgments

Finding the scholars able to deal with this aspect of Grundtvig's polymathic oeuvre has been a very pleasurable experience for the editors, and they wish to thank all the contributors. We have met on several occasions, most recently at the Centre for European Studies; we are indebted to its staff and above all to its director, Professor Grzegorz Ekiert, for warmth and efficiency. We benefited early on from the advice of scholars who do not appear in this volume, with particular contributions coming from Grzegorz Ekiert, Sinisa Malesevic, Brendan O' Leary, Juliane Englehardt, and Jes Fabricius Møller. But beyond these particular acknowledgments lie three foundations. First, we have benefited from the help of Edward Broadbridge, the great translator of Grundtvig into English and the translator of several of the papers in this volume. Second, we thank the Grundtvig Centre for funding and for endless enthusiasm, brilliantly organized by Michael Schelde, the leader of the centre. Third, three superb research students – Kalyani Thurairajah, Jason Jensen, and Sara Hall – helped enormously, checking facts and references, organizing conferences, and standardizing texts. Life would have been impossible for one of the editors without their help, and the thanks due are very great. Finally, it has been a great pleasure to work with Wilfried Roloff at Danmarks Jurist- og Økonomforbund Publishing in Copenhagen. Very special thanks go to Kyla Madden, our incisive and charming editor at McGill-Queen's University Press. We also thank Joanne Richardson for her superb copyediting skills.

BUILDING THE NATION

Introduction

JOHN A. HALL AND OVE KORSGAARD

It is very hard to question what seems natural. This certainly applies to the sense of belonging to a nation, so totally taken for granted in modern times – particularly by the Danes. But any sustained reflection on the historical record mandates awareness of the presence of alternative identities, mostly local, sometimes religious or military or imperial for the elites of the pre-industrial world. Hence the nation is best seen as a project, a category of practice as much as a universal reality inscribed in the souls of men and women throughout the historical record (Brubaker 2002). To make this point less abstract, consider censuses. German was the language of social mobility in the Hapsburg Empire, and census returns – always political acts – sought to maximize the number of "Germans" in Cisleithenia (the "rump" of the empire once the Magyars gained autonomy in 1867) by considering ethnicity in terms of language of daily use. But this method was bitterly contested by the Czechs, who wanted to enhance their numbers by measuring "mother tongue." In contrast, *independantists* in contemporary Montreal like to measure nationality in terms of mother tongue as this gives the impression that French is threatened – which is, in fact, nonsense as most immigrants use French in daily life. But if the nation is a contested project, it is equally important to stress that it is a project that has, in large part, been successful (Wimmer and Min 2006). All opinion polls within the European Union, for instance, show the nation to be the primary focus of identity, albeit with interesting variations by country and by social class (Fligstein 2008; Medrano 2009). Still, there is complexity here, and this must be highlighted. The most famous definition of nationalism, that of Gellner (1983), insists that a nation needs its own state – to which one can equally add the desire of many states to rule over a single nation. That definition stresses the importance of homogeneity, and it has enormous descriptive power. But it has been challenged, in theory and in reality, for there are occasions when different nations are content, especially when cultural rights are protected, to live under a single political roof. So we need to treat the connection between nation and state as contingent rather than as inevitable. Nowhere is this more true than in Denmark, so homogeneous as to be nearly completely unaware of the manner in which its national identity was created.

Our knowledge of the ways in which nations are built remains imperfect, with absurdly little being understood about the role of great nation builders, as Anthony Smith, Francis Fukuyama, and Michael Böss note at the start of this volume. Fukuyama (2011, 265) is certainly correct to stress that a great individual can have an enormous impact:

> Certain historical events are catalyzed by individuals and cannot be explained without reference to their particular moral qualities. The investiture conflict was one such movement. Gregory had a titanic and inflexible will, and was once addressed by one of his associates in the papal party as 'my holy Satan.' Like Martin Luther four centuries later, he had a grand vision for a reformed church and its role in society. He could not be intimidated and was willing to see the conflict with the emperor escalate into outright war.

But he goes on to say that "this historical conflict cannot be explained simply as a matter of individual will" and turns immediately to "critical background conditions" that allowed an individual to have such an impact. This collection has both sides of this equation in mind in adding to the understanding of national construction by focusing on one such figure, the polymathic N.F.S. Grundtvig (1783–1872), at once Lutheran priest, writer, and philosopher. Our first task must be to present basic biographical information on a figure properly seen as the Moses of the Danish nation.

Nikolai Frederik Severin Grundtvig was born on 8 September 1783, the last of five surviving children, in the village of Udby, ninety-seven kilometres south of Copenhagen. His father, Johan Grundtvig, preached a pietistic Lutheran Christianity; his mother, Marie Bang, was a strong-willed and practical woman, who traced her lineage back to the famous Danish warrior Skjalm Hvide (ca. 1040–1113). After private tutoring in the vicarage, the young Grundtvig was sent away to Jutland at the age of nine to be prepared for Aarhus Grammar School by a family friend.

Academically he went from success to success, gaining a first-class degree in theology from Copenhagen in 1803 at only twenty years of age. From 1805 to 1808, while in-house tutor to Carl, the young son of Constance Steensen-Leth, Grundtvig conceived a barely suppressed passion for the lady of the manor. He sublimated his feelings by studying Nordic mythology, along with German literature and aesthetics, and, with the publication of *Nordic Mythology* in 1808 he entered the Copenhagen literary scene. When his aging father then called him back to Udby as curate in 1810, Grundtvig was so torn between a literary career in the city and family duty in the country that the resulting existential crisis brought about his first nervous breakdown. He chose to help his father until the latter's death in 1813, whereupon Grundtvig moved back to Copenhagen and eked out an existence as an occasional preacher. His fiery temperament hindered his appointment to any vacant benefice, and in resignation he withdrew to a marginalized position for the next ten years in Copenhagen, supported by a small royal grant, and only later gaining a benefice in Copenhagen.

Grundtvig read and wrote widely and developed a new philosophy of life that found expression in his literary masterpiece, *New Year's Morning* (1824). The long poem can be read as a reflection on Grundtvig's own life so far, as an expression of his powerful will for self-interpretation, and as a coherent philosophy of life that included mythology and Christianity. Sensing, somewhat precociously, that he carried within him a whole new epoch, he called himself "Luther the Little" in the poem. The following year, in response to a major work on church history by Professor H.N. Clausen, Grundtvig published a vitriolic attack, *The Church's Retort*, which brought a libel case down on his head. When he lost this and was placed under life-long censorship he resigned his living and gratefully received a further royal grant to study in England during the summers and autumns of 1829, 1830, and 1831, respectively. These trips proved crucial to Grundtvig's views on life, society, and education. He believed the Nordic spirit had survived in England, where he was astounded by the practical energy he witnessed – just as he was dismayed by the negative effects of industrialization. His experiences translated into his most influential work, *Nordic Mythology* (1832), a wake-up call to build a new society based on the common experience of being a citizen of Denmark, with a common history and language rather than a common faith. Here, too, are his famous words in defence of freedom for *all* people: "Freedom for Loki as well as for Thor." On this canonical work rests the "People's High School," or "Folk High School," movement (these terms are used interchangeably throughout this volume).

In 1837, Grundtvig published the first volume of his *Hymns for the Danish Church*, his monumental task being to renew the Danish hymnbook. Especially in his songs and hymns, Grundtvig inculcated his view of popular character and social philosophy, as expressed in the Danish language, with formulations that have become almost proverbial. One of his hymns from 1837 he entitled "First a Man, Then a Christian" (Grundtvig 1948). His most famous political-poetic statement is from the song "Far Higher are Mountains" from 1820: "In this lies our wealth, on this tenet we draw: / that few are too rich, and still fewer too poor" (Grundtvig 1916).

In 1837, Grundtvig's censorship was revoked, and, in 1838, he gave a series of public lectures entitled "Within Living Memory." This series addressed Danish history of the past half century as seen from a European perspective. This series was so successful that a new series followed in 1844–45 on Greek and Nordic myths. In 1839, Grundtvig became pastor of Vartov Church in central Copenhagen and gathered around him a congregation of like-minded Christians, including royalty, who turned him into something of a cult figure until his death at the age of eighty-eight in 1872.

Grundtvig witnessed enormous change during his long life, much of it at a personal level. With his first wife Lise Blicher, whom he married in 1818, he had three children in the 1820s: Johan, Svend, and Meta. In the same year that Lisa died, 1851, he married Marie Toft, a widow thirty years his junior – much to the outrage of his supporters. Marie died in 1854 after giving birth to son Frederik. In 1858, Grundtvig then married the wealthy widow Countess Asta Reedtz, who was forty-three years his junior. At the age of seventy-six he fathered his last child, Asta, born in 1860. More important than his personal life was his participation in fundamental social and political change. His contribution to politics, as actor and as theorist, has often been neglected. Although Grundtvig did not participate in the mass march on the Danish royal palace on 21 March 1848, which led to the end of absolute monarchy and the introduction of democracy, he became a voluble member of the assembly that drew up the new Constitution. He then served almost continuously in Parliament from 1849 to 1858 before retiring at the age of seventy-five. However, Denmark's disastrous defeat at the hands of Bismarck in 1864, and the subsequent loss of the duchies of Schleswig and Holstein, persuaded him to return to politics. He was re-elected as upper chamber member for East Jutland in 1866 at the age of eighty-three, his prime aim being an ultimately unsuccessful campaign to repeal new restrictions that appeared in the revised Constitution that year and that were directed against farmers.

The reason Grundtvig is given credit for so many apparently conflicting views is that, during a long life, he both experienced and contributed to one of the greatest processes of transformation in the history of Europe, variously involving rationalism, romanticism, nationalism, revolution, and industrialization. We regard the nation-state, democracy, and a constitution as the foundation of all political theory, but this was not the case in Grundtvig's day: these forms were established during his lifetime as Denmark moved from a united monarchy to a nation-state and from autocracy to democracy. Just as the fall of the Iron Curtain and the collapse of Communism in 1989 forced political thinkers to face up to new challenges, so did the transformations of the nineteenth century force Grundtvig to rethink the positions he had adopted earlier in life, including his fear of a democratic parliament without educated members.

The impact of Grundtvig – and the Grundtvigians who followed him – has been so comprehensive in Denmark that he is a fundamental and inescapable reference point whenever themes such as people, nation, democracy, freedom, church, and education are to be discussed. In stages, *Building the Nation* investigates the role of Grundtvig in the making of modern Denmark, and the remainder of this introduction offers particular comments on individual chapters. After three theoretical chapters on the nature of nationalism, we turn to the conditions that enabled Grundtvig to have such a major impact. We then turn to key elements of Grundtvig's social and political theory. Several chapters then help us to better understand Grundtvig by placing him in a comparative perspective. If the realization that there were other icons of nationalism makes him seem less unique, it also helps us to understand the peculiarities of his position. The section that follows emphasizes the distinction already made between Grundtvig and the use that the Grundtvigian movement made of his work. There is much overlap between the two, but the Grundtvigians had their own particular position. A final section reflects on some of the key legacies of Grundtvig and the Grundtivgian movement before a conclusion draws together the findings of the whole volume.

NOTES ON NATION BUILDING

The study of nationalism has undergone both renaissance and development since the 1980s, in part driven, of course, by the break-up of the last great land empire of the modern world. While it is not possible to survey the whole of this intellectual field, something can be said about the elements that contribute to the nation and about the varied routes to national autonomy. Concentration on these factors is not accidental. To the contrary, the intent is to underline categories that allow the Danish case to be understood. And this case, it should be noted immediately, has special features that, in turn, illuminate and advance our general understanding.

Layers and Stages

In what follows, it is useful to bear in mind the famous claim of Tom Marshall (1963), which is that citizenship developed in three stages, from legal to political to social. This view is based on, and accurately describes, British historical development. But the ordering of these variables can be totally different, with Bismarck famously seeking to integrate the working class by granting social citizenship rights before granting democracy, with the avowed purpose of avoiding popular incursion into elite decision making. The elements that go into the construction of nations can be, and indeed were, played out in diverse order, not least in Denmark. In a nutshell, layers can have different stadial formations.

A particularly important early layer of nations in Europe is that of religion. For one thing, there is the clear push for religious homogenization that took place in so many European countries beginning in the sixteenth century (Marx 2003). Key historical events include the expulsion of the Huguenots from seventeenth-century France and that of the Moriscos from Spain, together with that country's forcible assimilation of Jews. For another, there is the much more important introduction of confessional politics during the Reformation and Counter-Reformation, the "disciplinary revolution" that made the countries of Northwest Europe far more homogeneous than, in particular, the Ottoman Empire, whose diversity was enshrined in its millet system (Gorski 2003). It is as well to remember in this connection that the earliest form of British nationalism was anti-Catholic in character (Colley 2005).

A second early layer of nations is state building. In England and Wales the incremental development of justice over time, and its increasing penetration throughout the territory, led to linguistic uniformity. It is hard for most English speakers to read Chaucer but not at all difficult for them to read Shakespeare, whose famous proto-nationalist statements in *Richard II* highlight the development of the nation. Very different processes are involved here. If some come, at least in part, from below, as in the English case, others are top-down – notably, the instance when the French revolutionaries insisted on linguistic unification, killing many in the Vendée to ensure that this took place (Balibar and Laporte 1974; Tilly 1964). Their success was only partial: one great study of nation building points out that it took conscription in the late nineteenth century to turn peasants into Frenchmen (Weber 1976).

Still, there is general recognition that the national question came to the fore only since the late eighteenth century. Gellner's (1983) classic account stresses the link between the awakening of nations and industrialization. This needs to be amended by linking nationalism to modernization, taken in a more generic sense, and with references to eighteenth- as well as to nineteenth-century developments. For one thing, the commercialization of agriculture could disrupt traditions as much as could the creation of industry – as was the case in Denmark. For another, the increase in national sentiment in France and Britain in the eighteenth century followed from sustained geopolitical competition. Increased rates of fiscal extraction and military participation led "the people" to ask which "nation" they were fighting for (Mann 1992). In this connection it is appropriate to recall Max Weber's belief that national belonging is born from participation in war. There is an obvious link here to "democratization." Popular politics follows from the disruption of stable agrarian conditions, of course, but it equally follows from changes in a political regime, with participation enhancing the sense of belonging to the nation. But great care must be taken here, for "democratization" can have two meanings: (1) the elite's mobilization of the people and (2) the people's control of political power through electoral processes. Nationalism has often been touted (and can serve) as an alternative to formal democratic process, even though it is a powerful force that can lend the latter support.

Membership of the nation was completed in many European countries, particularly after the Second World War. The disasters of the Great Depression and total war led to the destruction of extreme right and extreme left, thereby leading to historic class compromise within Europe. National reconstruction came through the provision of generalized welfare. Loyalty to the nation came when the state did much for society, when it provided a people's home. This development was of course Janus-faced. To offer so much to the nation went hand-in-hand with offering less to outsiders, who were ever more excluded within European polities (Wimmer 2002).

Either/Or

With these stages in mind, let us consider historic patterns, best placed within two broad categories: (1) those that emerged before the rise of nationalist self-consciousness and (2) those that were part of the development of nationalist self-consciousness.

The slow, organic, and incremental consolidation of the nation-state within Europe is apparent in the English case already discussed. What matters here is the measured increase in state power, best seen in the endless ways in which the infrastructural reach of the state increased over time. The nation is simply the result of caging so very many activities – religious, legal, educational – within the borders of a particular territory whose centre gained ever greater powers. The great sociologist of this route is Michael Mann (2005), who argues that the nation developed because the state was so powerful.

The second category of historic patterns, however, is that in which national movements gain self-consciousness. If a neat way to characterize English or French developments is to stress that state came before nation, this second category reverses that causation. It is important to remember that there is diversity here. German nationalism (and, to a lesser extent, that of the Italian peninsula) is that of a cultural zone marked by extremely varied polities seeking unification under a single, newly created state. But the better-known form of nationalism is that of secession. This is the world of such composite monarchies as those of the Hapsburgs and Romanovs. Here there was a single state, but the territory had never been rationalized and centralized, with the rulers characteristically holding several titles and swearing on accession to respect the liberties of the different geographical areas in question. The "nations" within these social formations – often in the earliest stages not much more than social movements largely made up of professors – were able to resist the assimilation that had overwhelmed and destroyed so many groups and languages within the first type because they gained their own educational rights. It is very important to note, however, that active nation building was involved here. Consider the great frustration of the intellectual nation builders of Cisleithenia at the end of the nineteenth century, irritated by their own putative members, often bilingual and passively opposed to being caged within a single identity (Judson 2006). Resistance to their project also, of course, came from those who had an imperial ethnicity – the officer corps, the socialists, and the Jews in Austro-Hungary, for example (Darwin 2010). But the empires themselves often tried to increase their power and to control movements from below by seeking to turn themselves into nation-states, something which often bred reactive nationalist awakenings (Anderson 1983; Kumar 2010; Lieven 2000).

The central analytic question here is whether this world of national awakening was bound to destroy composite monarchies. Here there is real complexity. Gellner certainly thought that destruction was inevitable, and the core of his view can be seen at work in Lange's (2012) superb treatise on education and ethnic violence. Social dynamite is released when a newly educated majority finds itself faced with minorities in control of the most important jobs and statuses. Nonetheless, it is certainly not the case that every awakened nation always wants to separate. No Czech national leader, for instance, demanded independence before 1914, fearing for the future (given the presence of Germany and Russia on either side). In a sense, this is to argue that geopolitics kept Austro-Hungary together and that it took defeat in war, and the corresponding weakening of the state, to allow secession to take place (Hiers and Wimmer 2013; Wimmer and Feinstein 2010). Still, the dreams of many small nations were for political decompression, for the creation of liberal empires – or, perhaps more accurately, for constitutional monarchies – in which an increased voice would make exit unnecessary (Hirschman 1970). But the brutal fact of the matter is that every composite monarchy in nineteenth-century Europe did break up, none managed to turn itself into a more liberal entity within which several nations could prosper. But if nationalism within empires had a significant role in the demise of this political form, it remains necessary to note that this failure in the politics of transition does not rule out the possibility that multinational democracies can be created and can prosper.

CREATING DENMARK

Denmark is not much studied, and this for the most terrible of reasons: it is seen as small, successful, peaceful, and insignificant. A moment's reflection makes one realize that there is everything to be said for studying the way in which a small nation was created, has survived, and now prospers – a matter to which this volume in fact contributes a great deal. In this connection it is important, as noted, for Danes to realize that their current condition is novel, certainly not the distillation of some eternal essence. For Denmark most certainly has not always been a markedly homogeneous nation-state. Nor has it been insignificant historically.

In early modern Europe it was one of the greater powers, possessing a fiscal base in tolls levied at the entrance to the Baltic because it ruled over southern Sweden. Even after the loss of Scania in 1658 it remained a great power, not least due to its possession of a huge navy, such a threat to Great Britain that the British navy attacked Copenhagen in 1801 (and again in 1807 when it took the Danish fleet), thereby driving neutral Denmark into an alliance with Napoleon. As a consequence of this involvement, the four-hundred-year-old United Monarchy was dissolved in 1814 as Norway came under Swedish sovereignty. But the state remained a multinational, multilingual composite affair consisting of the Kingdom of Denmark and the duchies of Schleswig, Holstein, and Lauenburg; the north Atlantic isles (Iceland, Greenland, and the Faroes); and a few small colonies throughout the world. The majority of the population in the kingdom spoke Danish, though in Holstein they spoke German, and in Schleswig half the population spoke Danish and the other half German. So the Oldenburg dynasty was very much of the same world as were the Romanovs and Hapsburgs. But collapse came much earlier, with modern Denmark taking a very particular form.

Grundtvig witnessed the collapse of the United Monarchy, and he did a very great deal, as did his followers and those who acted in his name, to create modern Denmark. But a distinction must be made. He participated in debates that led to the collapse of the dynasty, but his role in that process was relatively minor even though it is of considerable interest. In contrast, his impact (and that of "Grundtvigianism") on the highly homogenous state territory that remained after the defeat by Prussia and Austria in 1864 was very great indeed. Political simplification created the conditions in which his ideas and the institutions he created could have a determinate effect. Let us take these two periods in turn.

Simplification

The first layer of the nation (noted above) has great salience in the Danish case. Grundtvig grew up in an absolutist society based on common religion. Lutheranism was not only the foundation of the church but also the ideological and moral foundation of the state. But there is also a link to the third layer of the nation – modernization. In chapter 7 of this volume, Tine Damsholt points out that Danish absolutism was in a sense limited, far more contractual than its ideological apparatus suggests. Crucially, the state pushed through agrarian reforms that did something to mobilize society. So there was a good deal of movement in the society, the beginnings of the entry of the people onto the political stage. This movement is particularly apparent in the religious revival described by Hanne Sanders in chapter 4 (this volume). Grundtvig plays a large part here, becoming the leading advocate for a new view of the role of religion. Grundtvig helped revise Denmark's Lutheran basis insofar as it was not Christianity but the people's language that was to be the basis of state and school. Thus, after 1825, Grundtvig criticized three fundamental Lutheran dogmas: (1) the dogma of the scripture, (2) the dogma of human nature as fundamentally sinful, and (3) the dogma of the state church. The church's alliance with the state since Constantine the Great was, to Grundtvig, nothing short of the fall of the church, with which Luther had not done away. The transformation from a Christian prince-state to a popular polity necessitated a clarification of the relationship between religion, state, and politics. What was the ideological and moral foundation of society if not Christianity? The apple of discord was the catechism teachings. In contrast to Rasmus Sørensen (1799–1865), a leading lay preacher who wanted to continue the teaching of the catechism in the schools, Grundtvig wanted this abolished, arguing that only as a free endeavour could Christianity serve as a pillar for society. Grundtvig became the leading advocate for freedom of religion. In 1827, he wrote: "If I was a statesman, then at least religious freedom might be my solution" (Grundtvig 1907).

But the second layer of the nation, mentioned above in connection with English development, had no relevance in the Danish case. No organic process had turned different linguistic and ethnic groups into a common core. Still, bourgeois elements with different linguistic backgrounds shared an interest in demanding enlightenment reforms through patriotic societies brilliantly described by Juliane Englehardt (2010). The failure of the empire to allow for reform, Jason Jensen and John Hall (chap. 6, this volume) suggest, is a key background factor that explains the rise of competing nationalisms. Perhaps this was always likely. The loss of Norway had unbalanced the situation dramatically, as Uffe Østergård (chap. 5, this volume; see also Østergård 2013) notes, leaving a minority of German-speakers, often upper-class and territorially concentrated in the south, faced with a majority of Danish speakers. There had been tension between the two communities for some time, and this intensified rapidly from about 1830. Intellectuals from the universities of Kiel and Copenhagen produced competing nationalisms, demanding special rights for Germans and for Danes, with visceral conflict arising over the fact that both sides laid claims to Schleswig. Key questions arose. Could one, in a single process, allow for the people to enter politics and still keep the United Monarchy together? The problematic consisted in whether popular politics could be implemented in a United Monarchy or whether the implementation of the new political system required an alteration of state form. If the latter were to be the case, what should the guiding principles of this alteration be? Democracy's problem is that it requires a *demos* – that is, a people. But who were the people of the United Monarchy? Did the people correspond to population? Or were there several peoples within the state? The process of advancing towards democracy, however, was not calm. A civil war broke out, ending in 1851 without solving the fundamental question: Who belongs to the Danish people? In the years after the war the National Liberals in Copenhagen tried, unsuccessfully, to Danify Schleswig.

From 1851 to 1864, the main question was still whether it was possible or desirable to keep the United Monarchy together. In 1850, the lawyer and civil servant A.S. Ørsted tried to reason with his fellow countrypeople by warning them against new nationalistic movements in the kingdom as well as in the duchies. He published a historical and state-juridical writing entitled *For the Sake of the Danish State's Preservation in Its Entirety*. Ørsted (1850, iii) knew that the odds of reasoning with the two parties, the Danes and the Schleswig-Holsteinians, had not improved with the events that had "caused dissension and finally civil war in our previously happy fatherland." Indeed, they had done quite the opposite. To solve the Gordian knot, the Danish Parliament decided in November 1863 to include Schleswig in the Kingdom of Denmark. This decision led to war. Bismarck attacked Denmark in early 1864 and took both Holstein and Schleswig.

This is the general context in which Grundtvig developed his ideas. Uffe Jonas's important contribution (chap. 8, this volume) captures the flavour of Grundtvig's approach to life as a whole – its concern with love and enlightenment, its base in an organic view of society, and its desire to capture almost everything (religion, state, family, and people) in a single related frame. Tine Damsholt (chap. 7, this volume) places this general metaphysic within the field of political theory. She notes the rather idiosyncratic character of Danish absolutism, stressing the contractual nature of the link between people and monarch. It is this that explains Grundtvig's seemingly odd relationship to democracy. He was more than prepared to allow progress for the people to come from above, not least as the events of the French Revolution were seen in terms of an abuse of democracy. This attitude stayed with him throughout his life. Nonetheless, there was substantial change, as Ove Korsgaard makes clear in chapter 9 (this volume). Grundtvig's earliest writings show him concerned to raise the standards of the people, seen as a category within an estates society. But his three trips to England between 1829 and 1831, together with the pressure of events, moved him to a new position, in which the sovereignty of the people was vested in the nation (see Korsgaard 2004). In this context, it is important to note the difference between Grundtvig and the National Liberals. The latter wanted to build the nation by means of a state nationalism from above, in which popular forces would have limited power within the electoral process. Grundtvig stood a little closer to the great liberal thinkers in England, keen to extend the vote but only once the populace was enlightened (Harvie 1976). But there was a considerable difference between the English and Danish situations, the latter gaining a tinge of populism that was wholly absent in the island nation.

The nature of Grundtvig's contribution is better understood when we look at it through a comparative lens. After elucidating the meaning of "the people," Per Øhrgaard (chap. 10, this volume) makes much of the similarities between Fichte and Grundtvig. Both follow Herder in placing language at the centre of their theories, and both are initially moved to theorize, at least in part, in accordance with geopolitical disasters that had struck their respective homelands. But the differences between them tell us still more. Fichte's position is highly abstract and intellectual, and his concern with educating the people rests on his view of their immaturity and, hence, on the need for children to be taken away from their parents so as to be turned into material fit for the new nation. Grundtvig's world is entirely different. Most important, everything centres on God, with the Danish nation being best seen as a proper receptacle for his message. More generally, Grundtvig has much greater trust in the people than does Fichte, and he most certainly opposes the idea of sending children from their homes.

The basic image of community identified by Øhrgaard is at the centre of Katrine Baunvig's contribution (chap. 11, this volume). The most obvious link between the great French sociologist Émile Durkheim and Grundtvig is their shared concern with education, albeit the former sought to take over and reform the state system whereas the latter stood in opposition to that system. But what is much more important is the very striking similarity between the two thinkers when they speak of community. The French theorist famously sought the origins of religion in moments of "collective effervescence." People gathered together under the influence of dance, song, and alcohol create society – that is, society is an "emergent property," a blessing that takes us out of ourselves into something larger, something that is certainly more than a mere assemblage of separate individuals. This was the origin of religion, and Durkheim saw ritual as the re-enactment of such moments of solidarity. This is the link to Grundtvig, a wholly practical figure, as one would expect. The singing of powerful and moving hymns has mattered enormously in Denmark, and it is best seen in Durkheimian terms (Buckser 1996). Of course, Durkheim himself was a secular sociologist, explaining religion's creation and maintenance in terms of solidarity – as society worshipping itself. Grundtvig would not have accepted this: solidarity for sure but, in his case, with absolute belief in God.

After Øhrgaard's comparison of Grundtvig and Fichte, and Baunvig's of Grundtvig and Durkheim, Ole Vind (chap. 12, this volume) sheds light on similarities and differences between British liberalism and Grundtvig's particular Nordic conception of freedom by comparing Grundtvig with Adam Smith and Adam Ferguson. Arguing for free competition and rejecting all state regulation and welfare measures, Grundtvig can be considered a staunch economic liberal. However, a key question – or the Gordian knot – for Grundtvig as well as for Smith and Ferguson concerned the balance between individual self-interest and the common good. All three tried to solve this fundamental problem by preaching enlightenment and moral education. For Ferguson, Smith, and Grundtvig the Gordian knot of economic liberalism had been tied as a historical necessity and could be loosened by enlightenment and moral education. However, they differ in that Ferguson and Smith believed in the efficacy of science and knowledge, whereas Grundtvig believed both of these to be marked by a materialist, spiritless rationalism. Grundtvig's original contribution to the debate was to loosen the Gordian knot through applying a new form of moral education and popular education for all: "This new enlightenment was to be 'historical and poetic' in order to illuminate the close link between 'the life of the individual, the nation, and the whole human race'" ... [I]t would thereby allow the individual to see himself as duty-bound not only to his fellow citizens but also, and not least, to both his forefathers and his unborn successors" (Vind, chap. 12, this volume, 262).

Through reference to East Central Europe, Peter Bugge (chap. 13, this volume) casts light on Grundtvig and on his importance for others. One part of his argument places Grundtvig in the company of many intellectuals of the time, from Marx to Mazzini, who contended that the "awakening" of the Slavs was, so to speak, a mistake: such peasant nations would be better off losing their languages and adopting German, a truly world historical language. But Grundtvig did not apply this approach to Denmark; rather, he sought to build a nation on a language, whose antiquity and importance his work on Norse myths had (at least in his eyes) made apparent. Interestingly, Bugge notes that the lack of sympathy with "awakeners" might well have resulted from the fact that Denmark had a state tradition: occupation of a pre-existing entity was the name of the game, not the invention of something new. The second part of Bugge's argument gives an amusing and detailed account of the admiration shown by Czechs for the achievement of the Grundtvigians. And this latter point could easily be extended: visitors from as far apart as Wales and India wrote about the People's High Schools and even tried to adapt them to their national circumstances.

Troels Nørager's (chap. 14, this volume) discussion of Grundtvig and Emerson finds a remarkable similarity between the two thinkers in their opposition to established religion, which is prone to force its message upon the people. Only freedom will allow belief to prosper, and only through freedom can the human spirit expand. Nørager traces the impact of this shared view on the People's High Schools and, in Emerson's case, on the more diffuse demand for the virtuous citizens needed for the American republic. He ends his discussion with reflections on the continuing relevance of the moral sentiments for the reconstruction of our own era.

Comparisons need not concern different cultures. Matias Dalsgaard (chap. 15, this volume) offers a comparison within Denmark between Grundtvig and Søren Kierkegaard, his wholly different but equally great contemporary. After laying out the differences between the two thinkers, Dalsgaard moves in an extremely interesting direction: he explains a similarity between the two thinkers – a similarity that marks Danish mentality to this day.

Intensification

With the loss of Holstein, Schleswig, and Lauenburg, Denmark was close to fulfilling the ideal requirements of the nation-state envisaged by Gellner – that is, being a homogeneous entity based on the co-extension of state, language, culture, and territory.[1] This dramatic change led to a fundamental change in political thought and cultural life. Danish perceptions of themselves and of the rest of the world were entirely altered.

It is crucial, at all times, to bear in mind the geopolitical situation. With the war against Denmark in 1864, Prussia, under the leadership of Bismarck, started on a road of expansionist politics, attacking Austria in 1866 and France in 1870–71. These three wars altered the geopolitical situation in Europe and put Denmark in the following dilemma: Should the country be defended to the last person standing or should Denmark surrender the moment it was attacked by a major power? It was an extremely sensitive question. The majority of the population regarded Germany as the enemy, but it was nevertheless a hard geopolitical fact that Denmark, with its 2 million inhabitants, at this point was a neighbour of Europe's – and therefore the world's – strongest power. Rousseau's *Considerations on the Government of Poland* (1772) may indirectly shed some light on the Danish situation. With Russia, Austria, and Prussia as neighbours, Poland was surrounded by states with superior military capacity: "She has no strongholds to stop their incursions. Her depopulation makes her almost entirely defenceless" (Rousseau 1991, 167). What is Rousseau's advice to the Poles? Mainly, it is to ground the Polish republic in the hearts of the Polish people. "I can see only one way to give her the stability she lacks ... it is to establish the Republic so firmly in the hearts of the Poles that she will maintain her existence there in spite of all the efforts of her oppressors" (167–8). Exactly the same sentiment became prevalent in the Danish insistence that "what has been outwardly lost must be inwardly gained." In addition, Rousseau advised the Poles on how to sow the republic in the hearts of the Polish people through a national system of education. Poland needed a new type of defence as well: "Poland is surrounded by warlike powers which constantly maintain large standing armies which she herself could never match without soon exhausting herself" (182).[2]

It is also important to note that rather different social forces were involved in the creation of a new Danish identity. Crucially, the National Liberals were blamed for the defeat of 1864, thereby allowing a new social group – namely, the peasants and their cultural shock troops (the so-called Grundtvigians) – to influence this development to a degree unparalleled in the rest of Europe. In the power vacuum that appeared in the wake of the fall of the National Liberals, the Grundtvigianism of the populace was the only movement with a fairly broad appeal. The movement possessed an impressive self-awareness, allowing it to modify, translate, and institutionalize Grundtvig's ideas. According to Ove Korsgaard (chap. 16, this volume, 321): "The 'popular' became understood as a counterpoint to the state." The most immediate transmission came through schooling. Korsgaard continues: "Grundtvigians criticized the state educational system (the common school, the Latin school, and the university), hoping to create an alternative, more 'popular,' system with private schools (for children) and People's High Schools (for young adults)." After the defeat in 1864, Grundtvig's popular elite came to dominate the People's High School movement. From 1864 to 1872, more than fifty new People's High Schools were set up, most of them by Grundtvigians. As Korsgarrd says: "According to Grundtvigianism, the public school could not, due to its ties to the state, be regarded as truly popular. Only the 'free' school could be popular. By virtue of this liberal streak, the notion of the popular had become almost synonymous with what was outside the state. And, in this manner, in Denmark the notion of the popular came to be equated with the liberal notion of 'voluntarism'" (321). While the Danish political elite continuously bestowed significance on state institutions, on the building of the nation, the Grundtvigians relied more on institutions outside the state. It is this that lends an air of populism to Danish political culture, seen at its best in Denmark's rescue of the Jews during the Second World War (Buckser 2001).

But the impact of Grundtvigianism went well beyond educational matters. In the first half of the nineteenth century religious revivalism was part of the great transition from an absolutistic and feudal society into a democratic and modern society, a move completed by the guarantee of religious freedom in the Constitution of 1849. The main element of Danish revivalism was that of religious meetings – "conventicles" – in private houses, led by a member of the laity rather than by a clergyman. In the second half of the century revivalist practices became part of the Grundtvigian movement and the Inner Mission movement. Andy Buckser (chap. 17, this volume) follows the Grundtvigian movement in the island of Mors. The Grundtvigian "free" church still stands there: "And its large and active membership still sees itself as a key centre of Grundtvigianism in Denmark. They think this, in part, because of their theological outlook, which, though it has changed somewhat over time, remains inspired by what they see as the essential elements of Grundtvig's thought. Even more so, however, they think this because of a continuity of experience, a sense in which the practice and aesthetic of the congregation remain rooted in Grundtvigian culture. The hymns they sing, the societies they join, the exercises they do, and the environment that surrounds them maintain a continuity with Grundtvigian practice" (Buckser, chap. 17, this volume, 332).

Henning Eichberg (chap. 18) makes an important contribution to this volume. Gymnastics and sports in general not only increased communal solidarity but also helped turn peasants into physically fit, fully functioning citizens. Still, the most obvious way in which popular education affected Danish society was through the cooperative movement, which, through no fewer than 699 cooperative dairies, dominated milk and butter production by 1890. Hans Henrik Hjermitslev (chap. 19, this volume) describes the growth of the cooperatives, and makes us realize something absolutely crucial: Grundtvigianism was not opposed to scientific advance.[3] It was this background that allowed, for instance, for the invention of the Maglekilde centrifuge in 1879, which was able to effectively extract cream in central dairies rather than on large estates. Further, such cooperatives were fundamentally democratic: voting procedures were normally by head and not by size of holdings. It is very important to realize that the craft traditions developed in the countryside were later transferred to the cities – and back again in times of depression – as is made clear in the brilliant discussion of Kristensen and Sabel (1997). It is sometimes hard for political economists to understand wherein the wealth of modern Denmark is to be found. The shortest answer is that there is no place: rather, the craft tradition derived from Grundtvigianism allows Danes to change jobs endlessly and so enabled them to occupy interstices in the market.

Korsgaard (chap. 16, this volume) usefully reminds us of the final stages of Danish nation building. The years after 1864 were, in many ways, confused: the conservatives remained in power, even though crucial developments occurred in civil society, and the Liberal Party (*Venstre*) gained a majority in Parliament. The election in Denmark on 3 April 1901 was epoch-making in that the Liberal Party's demand for parliamentarianism was finally heard. One of the new government's goals was to alter and democratize the ecclesiastical and educational systems so that these old bastions of general education came to reflect the popular revolution, which, on the political level, had resulted in cabinet responsibility. Though Denmark was neutral during the First World War, geopolitical uncertainty played its part in key political changes. First, a new constitution was agreed upon, giving the vote to women and servants. Second, a system of proportional representation was introduced – at once a symbol of basic national consensus in the face of vulnerability and a mechanism that did much to enhance it. The growth of the labour movement from the beginning of the century allowed the Social Democrats to come into power in 1924–26 as a minority government and again from 1929 to 1940, together with the Social Liberal Party (*Radikale Venstre*). Ever since the First World War, the strategy of the Social Democrats in Denmark, and in Scandinavia in general, has been to work towards grounding socialism on national soil. It was the Swedish social democrat Per Albin Hansson (1885–1944) who, in 1928, made "the People's Home" (*Folkhemmet*) a key notion in the party's ideology. In Denmark, the ideological motto among Social Democrats under the leadership of Prime Minister Thorvald Stauning (1873–1942) became "Denmark for the people" (*Danmark for folket*), which was used as the title of a new party manifesto in 1934.

Stauning's greatest political achievement was the so-called Kanslergade settlement, whereby the leading parties entered into a historic settlement on a series of social reforms intended to counter the social consequences of the Great Depression. The settlement's importance was thrown into further relief by the fact that it was signed on 30 January 1933, the very day that Hitler was appointed Reich Chancellor in Berlin. In contrast to the racist interpretation of the term "people" adopted by National Socialism, the Social Democracy Party developed a social democratic interpretation. By turning the notion of people into a core concept, Stauning took a position that approached that of Grundtvig.

In *Plague over Europe*, Hartvig Frisch (1893–1950), a leading social democratic thinker, insisted that there should be a clear front against communism, fascism, and Nazism. Frisch argued that all three were antidemocratic. In particular, he devoted considerable attention to the labour movement's position in the ideological struggle. For the working class in Denmark, it was a matter of holding firmly onto Nordic democracy, whose essence, according to Frisch (1933, 10), was the nation seen as the starting point for cooperation between workers, farmers, and other groups: "It was the peasant farmers in the Nordic countries that had led parliamentarianism to victory and created political democracy – it is to their credit. It is the labour movement that has built on this platform and forged the foundation for social democracy."

A key element in the social democratic model is the concept of the "friendly state," which stands in contrast to Grundtvigian state scepticism. But, during and following the Second World War, a number of Grundtvigians, such as Hal Koch (1904–63), began to approach the social democratic perspective of the state. The establishment of the welfare state did not lead to a complete abandonment of liberal ideas, however. Unlike a totalitarian system, the welfare state was ultimately based on a liberal view of the state (Pedersen 1994, 125). During the Second

World War, the liberal and social democratic views became more integrated, and, after the war, the establishment of the Danish welfare state became a more or less common project. It was Hal Koch who made the greatest contribution to formulating a national compromise, uniting the liberal and the social democratic conceptions of the state, nation, people, and democracy. In the postwar period this compromise became the foundation for the creation of the welfare state, which was governed by socialist as well as by liberal ideas.

Part 5 concludes with two chapters that discuss the diffusion of Grundtvigian ideas in Denmark today. Esben Lunde Larsen (chap. 20, this volume) wittily demonstrates the extent to which these ideas have become the property of very different political parties, each able to extract from Grundtvig's huge oeuvre something to their taste. It is precisely this pervasive influence that matters in explaining the notable success of Denmark within the contemporary world economy. John Campbell and John Hall (chap. 21, this volume) provide clear evidence that the cohesion of a markedly homogeneous society – also present in Kevin O'Rourke's (2006) discussion of nineteenth-century Danish cooperatives – has had very great benefits for competitiveness, measured not just in terms of economic growth but also in terms of human capital. There is no sign that this is fading.

CONCLUSION

When we look back at the impact of Grundtvig on Danish history, a simple conclusion leaps to the fore. Not all, indeed not many, small nations survive and prosper (Davies 2011). The popular and cohesive will of the Danes has most certainly rested on this firm foundation, without which the pattern of the past may well have been different. In the Conclusion to this volume, Ove K. Pedersen's reflections offer thoughts along these lines. The five theses he offers note and highlight the underlying thrust of the volume as a whole.

But it is probable that all opportunities have their costs. Denmark today faces the difficulty of allowing immigrants and new Danes (who, according to "out-marriage" statistics, are "in" but are not assimilated) into its society. This is necessary given that its fertility rate is slightly below replacement level. In any case, arguments have been made suggesting that, in the future world economy, innovation will matter more than imitation. Nation building never ends, and Denmark's new challenge may be to allow for greater diversity.

NOTES

1 There were, however, two elements that disturbed the idyllic image. One of these was that the North Atlantic isles could not, without further ado, be regarded as a part of the Danish nation-state. The other – and far more crucial – problem was that 200,000 Danes fell under German rule. The last matter did not get straightened out until the reorganization of Europe after the First World War, which, in 1920, led to a plebiscite in Schleswig and the subsequent division of the old duchy. The northern half was incorporated into Denmark, while the southern part remained German.

2 A hundred years later, in a debate over Danish defence, some on the left put forward a number of points similar to those of Rousseau. Where conservatives proposed a standing army as the key element in the country's defence, the left advocated a defence based on arming the people. Grundtvig had already vehemently opposed the idea of a standing army in 1848 because he saw it as suppressing the peasant class. Therefore, just as Rousseau had advised the Poles, so Grundtvig (1909, 174) advised the Danes: "Men of Denmark, as truly as we all constitute a freeborn royal people; no ordinary military service of bondage, but an arming of the people in freedom." And in the defence commission of 1866, nearly all of Balthazar Christensen's (1802–82) many contributions defended the idea of a "people's army," a "national guard," or an "arming of the people." To the left, this was a matter of securing the people's autonomy even in matters of national defence (Nielsen 1979, 77).

3 Furthermore, they were far from opposed even to Darwinian theory (Hjermitslev 2011).

REFERENCES

Anderson, B. 1983. *Imagined Communities: Reflections on the Origin and Spread of Nationalism*. London: Verso.

Balibar, R. and D. Laporte. 1974. *Le Français National*. Paris: Hachette.

Brubaker, R. 2002. "Ethnicity without Groups." *European Journal of Sociology* 43 (2): 163–89.

Buckser, A. 1996. *Communities of Faith: Sectarianism, Identity and Social Change on a Danish Island*. Providence: Berghahn Books.

– 2001. "Rescue and Cultural Context during the Holocaust: Grundtvigian Nationalism and the Rescue of the Danish Jews." *Shofar* 19 (2): 1–25.

Colley, L. 2005. *Britons: Forging the Nation, 1707–1837*, 2nd ed. New Haven, CT: Yale University Press.

Darwin, J. 2010. "Empire and Ethnicity." *Nations and Nationalism* 16 (3): 383–401.

Davies, N. 2011. *Vanished Kingdoms: The History of Half-Forgotten Europe.* New York: Penguin.

Engelhardt, J. 2010. *Borgerskab og Fællesskab: De patriotiske selskaber i den danske helstat 1769–1814* [Citizenship and community: The patriotic societies in the Danish United Monarchy, 1769–1814]. Copenhagen: Museum Tusculanum Press.

Fligstein, N. 2008. *Euroclash: The EU, European Identity, and the Future of Europe.* Oxford: Oxford University Press.

Frisch, Hartvig. 1933. *Pest over Europa* [Plague across Europe]. Copenhagen: Forlaget Fremad.

Fukuyama, F. 2011. *The Origins of Political Order: From Prehuman Times to the French Revolution.* New York: Farrar, Straus and Giroux.

Gellner, E. 1983. *Nations and Nationalism.* Oxford: Blackwell.

Gorski, P. 2003. *The Disciplinary Revolution: Calvinism and the Rise of the State in Early Modern Europe.* Chicago: University of Chicago Press.

Grundtvig, N.F.S. 1907. "Om Religions-Frihed" [On religious freedom]. In *Udvalgte Skrifter, bd. 5* [Selected writings, vol. 5]. Copenhagen: Nordisk.

– 1909: "Dansk Rigsdags-Tale imod den saakaldte 'almindelige Værnepligt'" [Speaking Danish in the parliament against the so-called 'ordinary conscription]. *Udvalgte Skrifter, bd. 9* [Selected writings, vol. 9]. Copenhagen: Nordisk.

– 1916. *Digte i Udvalg* [Selected poems]. Edited by F. Rønning. Copenhagen: Gad.

– 1948. *Grundtvigs Sang-Værk* [Grundtvig's songwork]. Copenhagen: Det danske Forlag.

Harvie, C. 1976. *The Lights of Liberalism: University Liberals and the Challenge of Democracy, 1860–86.* London: Allen Lane.

Hiers, W., and A. Wimmer. 2013. "Is Nationalism the Cause or Consequence of the End of Empire?" In *Nationalism and War*, ed. J.A. Hall and S. Malesevic. Cambridge: Cambridge University Press.

Hirschman, A.O. 1970. *Exit, Voice, and Loyalty: Responses to Decline in Forms, Organizations, and States.* Cambridge, MA: Harvard University Press.

Hjermitslev, H.H. 2011. "Protestant Responses to Darwinism in Denmark, 1859–1914." *Journal of the History of Ideas* 72: 279–303.

Judson, P. 2006. *Guardians of the Nation: Activists on the Language Frontiers of Imperial Austria.* Cambridge, MA: Harvard University Press.

Korsgaard, O. 2004. *Kampen om folket* [The struggle for the people]. Copenhagen: Gyldendal.

Kristensen, P.H., and C. Sabel. 1997. "The Small-Holder Economy in Denmark: The Exception as Variation." In *World of Possibilities: Flexibility and Mass Production in Western Industrialization*, ed. C. Sabel and J. Zeitlin, 344–78. Cambridge: Cambridge University Press.

Kumar, K. 2010. "Nation-States as Empires, Empires as Nation-States: Two Principles, One Practice?" *Theory and Society* 39: 119–43.

Lange, M. 2012. *Educations in Ethnic Violence: Identity, Educational Bubbles, and Resource Mobilization*. New York: Cambridge University Press.

Lieven, D. 2000. *Empire: The Russian Empire and Its Rivals*. London: John Murray.

Mann, M. 1992. "The Emergence of Modern European Nationalism." In *Transition to Modernity: Essays on Power, Wealth, and Belief*, ed. J.A. Hall and I.C. Jarvie. Cambridge: Cambridge University Press.

– 2005. *The Dark Side of Democracy: Explaining Ethnic Cleansing*. Cambridge: Cambridge University Press.

Marshall, T.H. 1963. "Citizenship and Social Class." In T.H. Marshall, *Sociology at the Crossroads and Other Essays*, 67–127. London: Heinemann.

Marx, A. 2003. *Faith in Nation: Exclusionary Origins of Nationalism*. Oxford: Oxford University Press.

Medrano, J.D. 2009. *Framing Europe: Attitudes to European Integration in Germany, Spain and the United Kingdom*. Princeton, NJ: Princeton University Press.

Nielsen, Johs. 1979. *Genrejsningshåb og undergangsangst: Dansk forsvarspolitik mellem 1864 og 1870 og folkestyrets første forsvarsordning* [Hope of recovery and anxiety of doom. Danish defence policy between 1864 and 1870]. Odense: Odense Universitetsforlag.

O'Rourke, K.H. 2006. "Late 19th-Century Denmark in an Irish Mirror: Land Tenure, Homogeneity and the Roots of Danish Success." In *The State of Denmark: Small States, Corporatism and the Varieties of Capitalism*, ed. J.L. Campbell, J.A. Hall, and O.K. Pedersen, 159–96. Montreal and Kingston: McGill-Queen's University Press.

Ørsted, A.S. 1850. *For den danske Stats Opretholdelse i dens Helhed* [To maintain the Danish state in its entirety]. Copenhagen: Gyldendal.

Østergård, U. 2014. "Nation-Building and Nationalism in the Oldenburg Empire." In *Nation-Building in the Core of Empires: A Comparative Perspective*, ed. S. Berger and A. Miller. Manchester: Manchester University Press.

Pedersen, O.K. 1994. *Demokratiets lette tilstand* [Democracies at Ease]. Copenhagen: Spektrum.

Rousseau, J.J. 1991 [1772]: "Considerations on the Government of Poland." In *Rousseau on International Relations*, ed. S. Hoffman and D.P. Fidler, 162–96. Oxford: Clarendon Press.
Tilly, C. 1964. *The Vendée: A Sociological Analysis of the Counter-Revolution of 1793*. Cambridge, MA: Harvard University Press.
Weber, E. 1976. *Peasants into Frenchmen: The Modernization of Rural France, 1870–1914*. Stanford, CA: Stanford University Press.
Wimmer, A. 2002. *Nationalist Exclusion and Ethnic Conflicts: Shadows of Modernity*. Cambridge: Cambridge University Press.
Wimmer, A., and B. Min. 2006. "From Empire to Nation-State: Explaining Wars in the Modern World, 1816–2001." *American Sociological Review* 71 (6): 867–97.
Wimmer, A., and Y. Feinstein. 2010. "The Rise of the Nation-State across the World, 1816–2001." *American Sociological Review* 75 (5): 764–90.

PART ONE

Theoretical Groundwork

1

Nation Building and State Building

FRANCIS FUKUYAMA

The significance of an individual like N.F.S. Grundtvig must be seen in terms of the building of a modern Danish nation, which was, in turn, critical to the success of the modern Danish state. Nation building is critical to the success of state building. The state consists of tangible institutions like armies, police, bureaucracies, and the like, while the nation has to do with shared traditions, symbols, historical memories, language, and other cultural points of reference. The reason that nation building is key to state building reaches to the core meaning of the state: as the organizer of legitimate violence, the state periodically calls upon its citizens to risk their lives on its behalf. They will never be willing to do so if they feel that the state as such is unworthy of this ultimate sacrifice. Political stability is bolstered enormously if citizens feel the emotions associated with patriotism.

In the first part of this chapter I discuss theories of national identity and nationalism, and explain why nationalism is closely linked to the process of modernization. National identity has been understood as the byproduct of underlying structural factors, but it is also socially constructed by human agents. Both the structural and constructivist understandings are correct; the actual national identities that eventually emerge result from the confrontation of constructed ideas with power politics and economic imperatives. In the second part of the chapter I illustrate this interplay with reference to three cases: Russia, Indonesia, and Denmark.

Nationalism is one specific form of national identity that found its first major expression in the French Revolution. It is based on the view that the political boundaries of the state ought to correspond to a cultural boundary, one defined primarily by shared language and shared culture (Gellner 2006).

Nationalism developed a terrible reputation in the twentieth century because it took on militarily aggressive forms and fed the passions underlying the two World Wars. National identity does not have to be defined in ethnic or narrow cultural terms, however. Countries like Switzerland, India, and Canada recognize multiple languages and cultural communities, and base their national identity instead on other types of shared values and institutions. Since the rise of political Islam in the late twentieth century, many Islamist groups have argued that identity should be based on religion rather than on nation or language. American national identity has always been built around the US Constitution and founding democratic principles and has, therefore, accommodated immigrants from diverse cultural backgrounds.[1]

National identity is one form of the even larger phenomenon of identity, plain and simple. Key to the idea of identity is the notion that there can be a disjunction between one's inner, authentic self and the social norms or practices that are required by the surrounding society. Identity becomes problematic, and a source both of personal anxiety and political contestation, because of a perceived gap between the inner self and outward social practice.

NATIONAL IDENTITY AND MODERNIZATION

The modern notion of identity, understood as a conflict between inner and outer selves, does not really exist as a problem in premodern societies. In either a hunter-gatherer or agrarian economy, there is a differentiation of social identities – between hunters and gatherers, men and women, peasants, priests, warriors, and bureaucrats – but there is so little social mobility and such a restricted division of labour that one does not have much choice in one's associations. All of a person's important life choices – where to live, what to do for a living, what religion to practise, whom to marry – were all determined by the surrounding tribe, village, or caste. Consequently, individuals in agrarian societies did not spend a lot of time sitting around asking themselves, "Who am I, really?"

According to Benedict Anderson (1983), all of this began to change with the emergence of commercial capitalism in the sixteenth century, powered by the invention of the printing press and the growth of a market for books. The printing press sharply reduced the price of written communication and thus made possible the publication of books in vernacular languages. The emergence of a vernacular print-language facilitated, for the first time, the emergence of what Anderson calls an "imagined community" of speakers and readers. In this respect, Martin Luther, whose German-language writings were widely circulated among the German states, was a father of German identity. The later advance of newspapers, read by emerging educated middle-class readers, had an even more dramatic effect on building national consciousness in the nineteenth century. By reading, people who had never travelled beyond the confines of their little village could all of a sudden perceive a connection to other people in other isolated villages.

Ernest Gellner dates nationalism at a somewhat later point and roots it in the transition from agrarian to industrial societies. In agrarian societies, there is no uniformity of culture: in virtually all of them, language and ritual separated the different classes of society. As Gellner (1987, 15–16) explains, the requirements for an industrial society are very different:

> A society that lives by growth needs must pay a certain price. The price of growth is eternal innovation. Innovation in turn presupposes unceasing occupational mobility, certainly as between generations, and often within a single life-span. The capacity to move between diverse jobs, and incidentally to communicate and cooperate with numerous individuals in other social positions, requires that members of such a society be able to communicate in speech and writing, in a formal, precise, context-free manner …
>
> This is the general profile of a modern society: literate, mobile, formally equal with a merely fluid, continuous, so to speak atomised inequality, and with a shared, homogeneous, literacy-carried, and school-inculcated culture. It could hardly be more sharply contrasted with a traditional society, within which literacy was a minority and specialised accomplishment, where stable hierarchy rather than social mobility was the norm, and culture was diversified and discontinuous.

The expanding division of labour brought on, first, by expanding trade and commerce, and then by the process of industrialization, brings in its train increased specialization, urbanization, requirements for higher levels of education, and recruitment on the basis of skills and talent rather than inherited status. This economic transformation thus prepares the ground for modern nationalism, where language-based culture becomes the central unifying source of social cohesion (see also Gellner 2006).

Social mobility fostered by an expanding division of labour immediately opens up the question of identity in an acute fashion. At one moment I am a peasant in a small village in Saxony; the next moment I'm working in a large Siemens factory in Berlin. In the early twenty-first century, similar migrations are occurring throughout China as peasants leave their villages for job opportunities in the industrial sector. The fixed, intimate, and limited social world that was defined by the peasant village is replaced by the large, anonymous, and diverse cosmopolis of the modern city. This shift – the classic transition from Gemeinshaft to Gesellschaft first elaborated by Ferdinand Tönnies – not only involves a change in identities from one social occupation to another but also opens up the question of identity itself: wherein the question "Who am I?" has all of a sudden become real and pressing. This shift is experienced as a crisis or trauma, and it produces a condition that Émile Durkheim labels "anomie."

Nationalism had other and different sources in the former colonial world than it did in Western Europe. If these countries did not industrialize on a Western European pattern, they nonetheless acquired a new stratum of modernized elites who confronted the totally different cultures of their colonizers. These elites felt enormous pressures to conform to the culture and mores of the colonial power, and many indeed got sucked into that power structure. But this created for them a crisis of identity as they were separated from their families and compatriots by language and Westernization. This was the crisis that struck the young, British-trained lawyer Mohandas Karamachand Gandhi while practising in South Africa and led him eventually into the struggle for Indian independence. It was also the crisis that created the concept of "Négritude."[2]

This meant, however, that nationalism took on a very different form in the former colonial world. In Western Europe, the preeminent nationalist movement was that of the Germans, which sought to unite all German speakers under a single sovereignty. In places like India, Kenya, or Burma, nationalism could not be built around language since these were ethno-linguistically fragmented societies with no dominant group that could unite the whole country around its culture. Indeed, in many countries the language of the colonizer remained the lingua franca because, first, it was regarded as a more neutral choice than any of the languages of the ethnic subgroups and, second, it connected the former colony to the wider global economy better than any indigenous language.

ROUTES TO NATIONHOOD

Most scholars, like Gellner, studying the phenomenon of national identity assert that it is "socially constructed." In doing so they contest the view of many nationalists that nations are primordial, biologically based groupings that have existed since time immemorial. Others would go further, unmooring national identity from its connection to large social forces like industrialization and making it a product of the creativity of artists and poets. Another school influenced by economics argues that identities are essentially coordinating mechanisms used by political entrepreneurs to promote underlying economic interests.[3]

It is certainly correct that nationalism was a byproduct of modernization and that specific national identities were socially constructed. But the social constructivist view gives rise to a number of important questions: Who is it that constructs new national identities? Is it the result of a top-down or bottom-up process? Some national identities, once created, become incredibly durable, while others fail to stick. The Soviet Union, for example, spent seventy years trying to create a "new Soviet man" that would be class conscious, cosmopolitan, and above categories like ethnicity and religion. And yet, the USSR broke up into its different union republics in 1991 as much older national identities, thought to be long dead, reasserted themselves. Similarly, the European Union has been trying to construct a postnational sense of European citizenship since the 1950s, a project that has demonstrably failed in the wake of the euro crisis that began in 2009. What are the limits and possibilities of nation building?

Far from being an open-ended process of social construction, national identity is formed through four basic processes, which can be used separately or in combination with one another. Some are overtly top-down and political, requiring the power of states to enforce. Others are more bottom-up, the results of spontaneous actions by populations. There must be some complementarity between the top-down and the bottom-up processes, otherwise identities won't stick.

The four basic processes are: (1) the defining of political borders to fit populations, (2) the moving or physical elimination of populations to fit existing borders, (3) the cultural assimilation of subpopulations into the dominant culture, and (4) the modification of the concept of national identity to fit what is politically feasible, given the social and physical endowments of the society. Most successful national identity projects have resulted from the interaction of all four approaches.

Moving Borders to Fit Posited National Identities

Dynastic polities around the world, from the Roman and Mauryan to the Ottoman and Austro-Hungarian Empires, were constructed without regard to cultural identity. As the nationalist principle began to take hold from the French Revolution onward, the large extant political units began to break apart into more ethno-linguistically homogenous ones. Thus Turkey was reduced to its Turkish-speaking core in Anatolia, and Austria-Hungary fragmented into the myriad small nations of the Balkans. The most recent of these imperial dissolutions was that of the former Soviet Union.

Moving or Eliminating Populations to Create More Homogeneous Political Units

This is what, during the Balkan wars following the breakup of the former Yugoslavia, came to be known as "ethnic cleansing." Ethnic cleansing was, in a sense, the natural concomitant to the shift in legitimating principle from dynastic rule to a nationalist principle. The great agrarian polyglot empires were compatible with both impersonal administration and rule of law. Indeed, they depended on such universalistic institutions in order to function since they thrived on the interactions of ethnically and linguistically diverse people. At the height of the Roman Empire in the second century AD, travellers moving from Britain to North Africa to Syria or Asia Minor could expect to find similar administrative structures, laws, and roads. Fin de siècle Vienna was one of the most liberal and cosmopolitan cities in the world, which was one of the reasons it became an intellectual fountainhead of modernism in so many fields.

When multiethnic empires broke apart into states organized on a nationalist principle, various minority populations were left stranded in them. They could have been accommodated had the new national states adopted a liberal rule of law, but the power of ethno-nationalist self-assertion guaranteed that this seldom happened. The result was huge movements of populations as various minority groups were forced out of the new would-be nation-states or traded for minorities in neighbouring countries. The Second World War was triggered, in some sense, by stranded populations like the Sudeten Germans in Czechoslovakia and the Baltic Germans in Poland. The end of the war in 1945 saw huge transfers of populations (as well as substantial redrawing of borders) between Germany, Poland, Ukraine, Czechoslovakia, and other countries. Ethnic cleansing in the Balkans was thus not an invention of the post-Cold War period. As some observers pointed out at the time, the postwar stability of modern Western Europe was built on ethnic cleansings that had taken place in earlier historical periods, which modern Europeans had simply chosen to forget.

Cultural Assimilation

Subordinate populations can adopt the language and customs of the dominant group or, in some cases, intermarry to the point of disappearing as a distinct minority. Assimilation can happen voluntarily as minorities decide that it is in their self-interest to conform to the dominant culture. The reduction in the number of regional languages in France and the adoption of Parisian French as a national standard is an example. Similarly, most immigrant groups arriving in the United States learned English and took on American customs because that was a route to upward social mobility.

We should not underestimate the degree of power and often outright coercion that has been required to bring about cultural assimilation. Choice of a national language is a political act on the part of those who speak it. Few minorities voluntarily give up their mother tongues, particularly if they themselves are concentrated in a particular region where they have lived for generations. The primary instrument of cultural assimilation is either the public education system or the choice of language in public administration. Control over the school system is thus a hugely contested issue and the central objective of would-be nation builders.

Adjusting Posited National Identities to Fit Political Realities

All nation-building projects eventually run into practical obstacles to achieving correspondence between idea and reality, and it is often the idea that, in the face of simple power politics, gives way first. The identity question cannot be separated from the territorial question. Ideas can be adjusted in a variety of ways: territorial claims can be scaled back; identity can be shifted from ethnicity or religion to secular ideology or a more flexible concept of culture; or entirely new concepts of identity can be introduced to supersede existing ones.

There is a constant interplay between changing borders, moving populations, assimilating cultures, and adjusting ideas. The term "nation building" is misleading insofar as it suggests that building a nation is an activity similar to building a house. It is true that human agency is involved in both activities. But with house building, there is an architect and a general contractor in charge. No one is so clearly in charge of the nation-building project; rather, it emerges from the agency of disparate actors who are often working at cross-purposes. We can see in greater detail the interaction of these four routes to national identity through the cases of Russia, Indonesia, and Denmark.

SMALL RUSSIA

When Russian nationalism first emerged early in the nineteenth century it was hardly a monolithic movement. The first generation of Slavophiles, writers like A.S. Khomyakov, Ivan Kire'evskiy, Konstantin and Ivan Aksakov, and the like were all well-educated people familiar with the culture and traditions of Europe. Most accepted the universalism of Christianity and were not haters of the "world civilization" created in the West; what they sought was to define Russia's place in world history and the specific contributions it could make to a larger whole (Berdyaev 1979, 44).

This early generation of Slavophiles should be contrasted with those of the last third of the nineteenth century, who, in conditions of growing competition with a unified Germany, took an increasingly chauvinistic, xenophobic, and imperialist line. The early Slavophiles were interested in defining Russia's cultural uniqueness and paid little attention to external affairs; the later generation, by contrast, was quite explicit in justifying an expansionist foreign policy based on pan-Slavism. For example, Nikolay Danilevskiy rejected the Christian universalism of Khomyakov in favour of a Spenglerian view of a world dominated by distinct and self-regarding civilizations (Utechin 1963, 86; Yanov 2000, 34; Berdyaev 1979, 65). In the second half of the nineteenth century, Slavophilism began to merge with or develop into pan-Slavism, which had a more overt foreign policy focus of protecting Slavic populations outside of Russia. The initial impetus behind pan-Slavism came from the Western or Southern Slavs who sought Russian help in liberating themselves from Ottoman or Austrian rule. The Russians, however, understood pan-Slavism more as a kind of pan-Russianism, where the Slavs outside of Russia would be used as spearheads for Russian imperial influence.[4] Russian support for Serbia during the wars of the 1990s can be seen as a continuation of this tradition.

Russian nationalism disappeared as a legitimating principle after the Bolshevik Revolution in 1917 and was replaced by Marxism-Leninism as the Soviet Union's official ideology. It nonetheless lived on in the form of National Bolshevism, a nationalist movement that saw Communism as a convenient tool for the promulgation of Russian influence. The power of the Russian idea was evident during the Second World War, when Stalin downplayed Marxist themes in favour of Russian ones in order to secure the loyalty of citizens fighting the Germans. During the Brezhnev years, nationalists could express themselves obliquely on issues like the decline of traditional moral values, alcoholism, hostility to Western liberalism, and environmental issues (e.g., protection of Lake Baikal).

As Mikhail Gorbachev introduced the reform slogans of perestroika and glasnost in the 1980s, Russian nationalists could express themselves more freely, but they also became fearful of the spread of nationalist ideas in the other Union Republics, like Estonia and Ukraine. They were particularly dismayed by the rise of Aleksandr Yakovlev, the liberal party secretary in charge of culture, who took an overtly anti-nationalist line.[5] The conservative nationalists made a critical mistake, however, by aligning themselves with the neo-Stalinist conservatives within the Communist Party during the attempted coup against Gorbachev in August 1991. The coup's failure discredited both groups and led directly to the referendum in which Ukraine and other republics voted to leave the USSR.

The moment of the breakup of the Soviet Union represented a uniquely open-ended moment in the history of nation building. The new Russian Federation that emerged as an independent state could define itself in any number of ways, and there were a full range of visions for a new Russian identity on the table. There were, of course, residual hard-line conservatives who wanted to restore the former USSR intact (a group that may likely include Vladimir Putin). The great novelist Aleskandr Solzhenitsyn took a position echoing that of earlier Slavophiles like Konstantin Aksakov when he argued that the core of Russian identity was an inner spiritual one that could not be expressed through external institutions like liberal political rights. On the territorial issue he was perfectly happy to see the non-Russian nationalities like the Balts and Central Asians depart, but he argued in favour of a Slavic union between Russia, Ukraine, and Belarus. He attracted some sympathy for this territorial vision from a number of Russian liberals, like Yuriy Karyakin, Galina Starovoitova, Alla Latynina, Father Gleb Yakunin, and others (Tolz 1990).

But Solzhenitsyn's pan-Slavism put him at odds, surprisingly, with neo-fascist writers like Karem Rash, Eduard Volodin, and Aleksandr

Prokhanov who began arguing in favour of a "small Russia" – that is, a Russia free of entanglements not only with the non-Russian republics but also with the Slavic ones.[6] Volodin (1990) criticized the subsidies being paid by the centre to the non-Russian republics and noted: "We have hard work ahead of us for restoring the all-Russian economic ties and the market and the revival of the peasantry. We need a national program for the development of Central Russia. Life is being renewed here, Russia is being renewed, and the destiny of the homeland will be decided in this historical center of Russia." He concludes by saying that, in taking back its own name, "Russia is taking back her dignity and her own historical purpose" (1990). For his part, the militarist writer Prokhanov (1990) argued that few Russians were willing "to lay down even a single shaved Russian head" for the sake of keeping the empire together by force, even among those "indignant concerning the liberal appeasement of the national extremists."

In the late 1990s and early 2000s, it appeared that, under President Vladimir Putin, the Russian national identity question was largely settled in its territorial dimension in favour of the small Russia idea. The Russians were exhausted and impoverished as a result of their own transition and had little enthusiasm for redrawing their borders. They showed no willingness to revive the Slavic Union idea, even when Belarus's dictator, Aleksandr Lukashenko, in effect offered his country up to them on a platter.

This situation changed abruptly in the second decade of the century, when Vladimir Putin began pressuring neighbouring states, and particularly Ukraine, to join a Eurasian customs union and to avoid further integration with the European Union. This culminated in the sudden forceful annexation of Crimea into the Russian Federation in the spring of 2014, after demonstrations in Kiev toppled Putin's ally Viktor Yanukovich. Following on more than a decade of steady economic growth, a more confident Russia seemed to reject the post-Cold War territorial settlement by in effect telling ethnic Russians outside of Russia that they could expect support from Moscow. Putin's reference to a historical *Novorossiya* that included parts of eastern Ukraine suggests that, for him, the question of the borders of the Russian Federation has been reopened.

LINGUA FRANCAS

If the Russian problem during the 1990s was to shrink their expansive idea of national identity to fit the realities of post–1991 borders, many former colonies faced exactly the opposite problem: the borders handed to them by the former colonial powers were way too large and did not correspond to a single ethnic, linguistic, or cultural community. In these cases the national idea had to be stretched in the opposite direction: it had to be expanded to encompass multiple diverse groups, which, in turn, would have to adapt to the new concept of identity. This is a task that Nigeria completely failed to accomplish, and this is what lies at the root of its stunted development. There were, however, certain countries that enjoyed greater success at identity building, among them Indonesia and Tanzania. But this success has come at a steep price – that of an authoritarian government.

Indonesia is comparable in many ways to Nigeria. Both are large, ethnically diverse former colonies that started national existences at comparable levels of poverty. Both found oil in the 1960s and 1970s. Both countries are notorious for their corruption and have clientelistic political systems, but relative levels matter. Indonesia has done far better than Nigeria in using its resources not just to increase per capita incomes but also to reduce poverty, improve public health, and educate its population. One of the reasons for this is the greater coherence, capacity, and autonomy of the Indonesian state compared to its Nigerian counterpart. And part of this coherence is due, in turn, to Indonesia's stronger sense of national identity.

Prior to the twentieth century, the country of Indonesia did not exist. Stretching over an archipelago containing more than eleven thousand islands, the area known variously as the Indian Archipelago, the Indies, the Tropical Netherlands, or the Dutch East Indies consisted of a wide variety of sultanates, tribes, trading posts, and ethnic groups speaking hundreds of different languages. Few of the indigenous inhabitants were aware of a world much beyond their village or, at most, island (Elson 2008, 1–4).

This all began to change at the end of the nineteenth century and the beginning of the twentieth as the Dutch extended their political control and trading networks outwards from Batavia (the location of present-day Jakarta), the headquarters of the Dutch East India Company. Regular steamship travel gave people a sense of the archipelago as a whole, as did the possibility of making the Hajj to Mecca, which reconnected Indonesian Muslims to the broader Muslim community. A very small indigenous elite with access to European education emerged and began to adopt concepts like nationalism and Marxism from the West (Taylor 2003, 238–9).

By the third decade of the twentieth century, there were quite a lot of ways in which identity could have been defined. Since a large majority of the inhabitants of the colony were Muslim, they could have defined themselves as a Muslim state, as Pakistan was to do. The Communist Party of Indonesia (PKI) wanted a class revolution that would link it to the global Communist International, like the Chinese and Vietnamese parties had done. And there were many regional and local identities that could have supported their own regional political units, especially on the larger islands of Java and Sumatra. There were also racial ideas circulating at the time, though how race could be defined in a racially diverse archipelago was not clear.

Instead, a completely new idea for a country to be called Indonesia emerged during the second half of the 1920s with the creation of the Indonesian National Association (PNI), the Congress of Indonesian National Political Associations, and a nationalist youth group known as Young Indonesia. The second Indonesia Youth Congress meeting in Batavia in October 1928 adopted a national anthem, "Indonesia Raya" (one of the first public uses of the word "Indonesia") and declared Bahasa Indonesia as the national language (Elson 2008, 64–5).

The adoption of Indonesian was a critical element of identity-formation for the nascent country. Indonesian is a standardized version of classical Malay, one that had been in use for many centuries as a lingua franca of traders and travellers operating within the archipelago. It was the first language of only a relatively small number of the archipelago's inhabitants, the vast majority of whom continued to speak Javanese, Sundanese, or, for the educated elite, Dutch. It was also a more egalitarian language than Javanese, lacking the latter's elaborate system of registers reflecting the relative status of the speaker and those spoken to. Many of the early youth nationalists could not speak Indonesian or could not speak it well. But after Indonesian was taught in the school system over many years, the number of its speakers rose steadily and today approaches 100 percent of the population (Elson 2008, 65).

One of the most important formulators of the idea of Indonesia was the country's first post-independence president, Sukarno, who published a short pamphlet in 1927 entitled *Nationalism, Islam, and Marxism*. In it he took on the three major intellectual currents at the time and sought to argue that there was no fundamental inconsistency between them that would prevent the creation of a broad political front against Dutch rule. The one political principle Sukarno was not interested in including in his synthesis was Western liberalism, precisely because this doctrine did not provide a justification for a strong state that would play an integrative role in formulating identity or engage in the redistributionist policies he felt necessary for "social justice." These ideas from 1927 were articulated as the "Five Pillars" in a speech given in 1945 to the Investigating Committee, and they were to become the Pancasila doctrine that underlay the independent Indonesian state (Dahm 1969, 340–1; Sukarno 1969).

Sukarno's concept could not be implemented, however, except in the context of an increasingly authoritarian state. Indonesia's original Constitution on independence in 1950 provided for multiparty democracy and sidelined President Sukarno as a weak figurehead. After the first general elections in 1955, Sukarno began an attack on parliamentary democracy as such, and, with the outbreak of ethnic rebellions on the outer islands, martial law was declared in March 1957. Backed by the army and the PKI, Sukarno crushed the liberal opposition and created a national front named Nasakom that represented the three forces of his 1927 pamphlet – nationalism, religion, and Communism. Increasingly dependent on support from the Communists and, externally, from China and the Soviet Union, Sukarno used the state to mobilize mass support on the basis of his Pancasila ideology (Dahm 1969, 331–5).

Sukarno ultimately failed because he could not in fact synthesize his three pillars, particularly the nationalist one represented by the army and the Marxist one represented by the PKI. These two sources of support became increasingly suspicious of one another during the early 1960s. An attempted coup by Sukarno's presidential guard and the murder of a number of generals led the army, led by General Suharto, to strike back, forcing Sukarno out of power and leading to the bloody purge in which the PKI was decimated and anywhere from 500,000 to 800,000 people were killed. The resulting New Order of General Suharto dropped the Marxist part of Sukarno's program but retained his reliance on a strong, centralized state as a guarantor of national unity along with his Pancasila ideology as the source of national identity. Indonesia's small Chinese minority, from which the PKI recruited heavily, was forced to take Indonesian names and assimilate into the broader population (Hughes 1967; Taylor 2003, 356–60).

Indonesian national identity was entrenched, in a way that Nigerian national identity would never be, through articulation of a clear integrative ideology, establishment of a national language, and enforcement by authoritarian power based on a national army. The limits of this integrative process were made clear, however, in places like Timor Leste, West Papua (the former West New Guinea), Ambon, and Aceh, which never accepted the national narrative coming out of Jakarta. West Papua and Timor Leste are both Melanesian by ethnicity, largely non-Muslim, and were annexed by Indonesia only in 1963 and 1975, respectively. The Indonesian government moved transmigrants from Java and other parts of Indonesia into both places in an effort to change the ethnic balance, taught Indonesian and promoted Pancasila ideology through the school system, and relied on outright force to retain sovereignty in both places in the face of armed local insurgencies. Timor Leste nonetheless voted for independence in a 1999 referendum and became, in the face of terrible violence provoked by pro-Indonesian militias, an independent country in 2002. West Papua has remained within Indonesia, but there has been a continuing low-level insurgency and independence movement there.

Despite the clear limits to the radius of the national identity that the Indonesian state has been able to impose, however, the government has been able to achieve a remarkable degree of national integration for a region that was not remotely a single nation one hundred years earlier. Indeed, Indonesian identity by the 1990s had become sufficiently secure that, when the country as a whole transitioned to democracy after the Asian financial crisis in the late 1990s, it was able to permit a substantial devolution of power to its provinces and localities without worrying that this would stimulate further fragmentation. Indonesia remains a highly fractured country, as communal violence against the Chinese and Christian communities continues. Levels of corruption remain high as well. But all success is relative: given the kind of ethnic, religious, and regional fractionalization with which the country started, its nation-building success is quite remarkable.[7]

GETTING TO DENMARK

The first two cases of identity-formation discussed here involved illiberal and/or authoritarian governments; in the Indonesian case, authoritarian power was necessary to produce a national culture. The Danish case is interesting because a strong national identity emerged as the result of a bottom-up process in a country that was liberal and democratizing.

At the beginning of the nineteenth century, the country now known as Denmark was part of a multinational empire that included Norway, Iceland, Greenland, the Faroe Islands, and the predominantly German-speaking duchies of Schleswig and Holstein. In slightly more than half a century, this extensive empire would be stripped down to a rump Danish-speaking core, a process that culminated in the traumatic loss of Schleswig and Holstein as a result of the war with Prussia in 1864. Denmark lost a third of its population and territory, with a good number of Danish-speakers stranded on the German side of the border.[8] Confined to the northern part of the Jutland peninsula, the Danes nonetheless went on to consolidate a prosperous and coherent democracy that today is one of the most successful modern countries in the world. This became possible only because of the reorientation of Danish national identity that occurred in the years prior to the trauma of 1864. This would not have been possible without the work of a Lutheran priest, N.F.S. Grundtvig.

Grundtvig's ideas were highly eclectic. He read British liberals like John Locke, Adam Smith, and John Stuart Mill, but he also delved into German idealists and romantics like Herder, Hegel, and Fichte. He expressed himself less in systematic treatises than in speeches as a parliamentarian and in songs and poems. Grundtvig's writings were critical in positing the idea of a Danish folk, or people, who were united by their use of a common language across the class lines established by the feudal system of estates. He was not, however, a believer in democracy in the contemporary sense of the term. He argued that the Danish king (who since 1660 had ruled as an absolute monarch) did not derive his powers from God but from an implicit social contract with his people. Consistent with his view of the need for a linguistically based common culture, he made the following critical argument with respect to the territorial issue: "The land of the Danes goes only so far as they speak Danish and no further than where they continue to speak Danish, in other words, somewhere in the middle of the duchy of Schleswig" (Grundtvig quoted in Korsgaard, chap. 9, this volume).

The most important of Grundtvig's ideas, however, had to do not with politics but with education. Returning from a trip to England in 1831 when he visited Trinity College, Cambridge, he conceived the idea of a "People's High School" that would recreate the atmosphere of fellowship and collegiality that he had witnessed there. He distinguished between the "masses" and the "people" and saw education as a means of transforming the one into the other. And he believed that the language of instruction should be the language of the peasants – Danish – and not Latin, as was still the case for much of European elite education at the time. The new People's High School was to be complemented by a Nordic university in Gothenberg, and the two would link the teaching of practical skills with the kind of higher academic education needed to link Denmark to the rest of the world (Grundtvig 2011).

Grundtvig was not himself able to realize his educational plans, but, after the Prussian defeat, a popular movement based on his ideas spread and led to the establishment of some fifty Grundtvigian high schools. The curriculum of these schools incorporated the telling of stories of Danish national identity. It is notable that these schools sprang out of civil society rather than being sponsored by the state; more than that, they were built around an ideology that argued that the people themselves should take responsibility for their own education and advancement. These schools had a major economic effect when Danish agriculture was challenged by imports of cheap American grain in the 1870s: rather than retreating into protectionism, farmers organized themselves into cooperatives to improve their productivity and technological sophistication. Politically, the Grundtvigian movement was associated with the peasants' United Left Party, which, after 1864, displaced the discredited (and more elite) National Liberals as the dominant party in Parliament (see Korsgaard, chap. 16, this volume).

Grundtvig and his movement are of interest because they present a case of a strong national identity being formed from the bottom up rather than by a top-down state builder using authoritarian methods. They also present a case of a strong national identity being defined in a way that is compatible with democracy and a non-aggressive foreign policy. It stands in sharp contrast to the kind of chauvinistic nationalism being cultivated to the south in Germany at the time. Of course, the Danes had little choice with regard to their international position since Bismarck had stripped them of Schleswig and Holstein and undercut any pretentions Denmark might have had of being a great power. Nonetheless, Danish identity took an inclusive and tolerant form and was important in building consensus behind modern Danish democracy.

DEMOCRACY AND HISTORICAL AMNESIA

National identities are articulated by writers, artists, philosophers, journalists, or, in the case of N.F.S. Grundtvig, priests. But the actual identities that eventually take hold are formed in a crucible in which ideas collide with power politics. The importance of political power to identity-formation means that national identity will always exist in a continuous tension with liberal democracy. As the political theorist Pierre Manent (1997, 98) points out: "The world of democratic nations was formed when the principle of consent was adopted by political bodies that had been constituted in accord with other principles, both political and religious. Now that the principle of consent has banished every other principle, it is not clear how a new body could form and then subject itself to the principle of consent that constituted the democratic nation. The political molds are broken, and democratic vigilance inhibits their reconstruction."

There is no question that modern nationalism was born out of a fundamentally democratic impulse. As Liah Greenfeld (1992, 168–9) explains, as late as the time of Montesquieu in the early eighteenth century, it was common to associate the nation exclusively with elites – the nobles, clergy, and upper bourgeoisie – who held political power. The "people" were understood to be an unorganized rabble who somehow existed outside the body politic. The fundamental change in thinking that occurred in Europe from the beginning of that century until its end was the inclusion of non-elites – the peasantry, artisans, the urban poor – into the nation and its redefinition from a body based on class to one based on common language. It is no accident then that the French Revolution was both democratic *and* nationalist.

But while nationalism was democratic, it was not necessarily liberal. Nations were often defined in terms of ethnicity, race, religion, or culture in a strong sense (e.g., mandatory use of a national language) that invariably excluded certain individuals living within the nation-state's territory. We do not need to be reminded of the impact of nationalism on twentieth-century European history.

However, even when the nation was defined in relatively non-exclusive terms, establishment of a common identity required a high degree of social homogenization as competing identities, languages, and local allegiances were squeezed out. This could be done through outright repression or it could be done semi-coercively, as when a government mandates a particular educational curriculum or language. In either case, nation building often required authoritarian methods. As Manent (2006) suggests, modern European liberal democracies were beneficiaries of nation-building projects that well antedated their emergence as liberal democracies.

This is no less true in the contemporary developing world, as the example of Indonesia indicates. Indonesia's Pancasila doctrine was not based on exclusivist racial or ethnic identities, nor was it religiously grounded, except in the most general terms (i.e., monotheism). Indeed, Indonesian identity was deliberately constructed to suppress ethnic identities and to promote broad inclusion. Nonetheless, it is not clear that this nation-building project could have succeeded had Indonesia been a full democracy at independence.

There are, of course, happier cases, like those of the United States, Canada, Switzerland, India, or Denmark, where democratic governments did not resort to highly coercive means to promulgate national identity. In these cases, the democratic political order could itself become a source of identity. In today's de facto multicultural societies, identity based on purely political criteria – what Alfred Stepan and Juan Linz (2010) call "state-nations" – is in fact the only route to avoiding violent identity politics.

It is important to remember, however, that, even if these "state-nations" did not themselves deliberately employ violence to form national identity, their identities were beneficiaries of violence wrought by others. Modern Switzerland was born in a civil war; India could become a secular democracy only as a result of the separation of Pakistan and the communal violence that accompanied partition; and the United States needed to fight a bloody civil war to establish consensus over how the principle of equality enunciated in the Declaration of Independence would be understood. The father of modern Danish identity was in some sense as much Bismarck as Grundtvig: had Prussia not forcefully annexed Schleswig in 1864, Denmark would have remained a multinational, multilingual society with plenty of reasons for continuing cultural conflict. The fact that many contemporary new democracies seem to see no way of building strong national identities remains one of their great weaknesses.

Identity-building projects that seek to create territorial nations are critical from the standpoint of state building and political order. But they are also extremely contentious because the world never consisted of compact, homogenous "nations" ready to be turned into political units. As a result of conquest, migration, and trade, all societies were complex mixtures of ethnicities, classes, religions, and regions. Any idea of a nation inevitably implied the conversion or exclusion of individuals deemed to be outside its boundaries; if they didn't want to do this peacefully, they had to be coerced. That coercion could be accomplished from the top down by states, but it could also take the form of communal violence, as one community killed or drove off their neighbors. The twenty-five or so nations that existed in Europe by the middle of the twentieth century were the survivors of the five hundred or more political units that had existed there at the end of the Middle Ages.

Ernest Renan, one of the first writers to describe the phenomenon of modern nationalism, spoke of a historical amnesia that accompanied the process of nation building. According to him: "Forgetting, I would even say historical error, is essential to the creation of a nation, which is why the advance of historical study often poses a threat to nationality. Historical inquiry, in effect, brings to light the violent events that are at the source of all political formations, even those whose consequences have been beneficial" (Renan 1996, 19). He argues that this amnesia extended all the way back to the original barbarian conquests of Europe, in which wifeless warriors, having subdued the decadent remnants of the Roman Empire, married the local women and adopted their customs. Historical amnesia continued through the centuries, and we have forgotten once proud and independent entities like Burgundy, the Grand Duchy of Parma, Prussia, and Schleswig, all of which now exist only as regions subordinate to larger territorial states or as mere memories.

Renan was simply echoing Niccolò Machiavelli. Writing about the early beginnings of Rome in the *Discourses on the First Ten Books of Livy*, Machiavelli notes that the great city's founding was based on a fratricide – the killing of Remus by Romulus. He makes a broader observation that all just enterprises originate in a crime. So, too, with the founding of modern democracies in places like the United States, Canada, Australia, Argentina, and Chile. These were not countries of "new settlement," as they are sometimes described, in which Europeans entered a terra nullius. They were thinly occupied by indigenous tribal groups who had to be exterminated, moved, or driven off their lands into reservations, or reserves, to make way for the democratic institutions of the settlers. This didn't make the final outcome less democratic, but it also does not mean that the original crime was not a crime.

NOTES

1 The question of whether American identity was also shaped by "Anglo-American" cultural values was the subject of Samuel Huntington's last book (see Huntington 2004). For a longer discussion of this issue, see Fukuyama (2014).

2 "Négritude" was a term coined in the 1930s by three black writers from different French colonies, Aimé Césaire, Léon Damas, and Léopold Senghor, who sought the transvaluation of the meaning of the word "Négre," which, for white Frenchmen at the time, had an entirely pejorative and racist connotation.

3 The general point about the current constructivist consensus is made by Darden (2013). For different types of constructivist arguments, see Brubaker (1996, 2004) and Laitin (2007).
4 Thus, at the second pan-Slav conference held in Moscow in 1867, the Russian spokesmen (to the dismay of the non-Russians attending) argued in favour of the spread of the Russian language among Slavs and other forms of Russification (see Kohn 1960).
5 Yakovlev had been the CPSU secretary for ideology and published a long attack on Russian nationalism in 1972, which led to his dismissal and sidelining until the 1980s (see Dunlop 1985, 227–33; Yanov 1987, 120–3).
6 On Prokhanov and Rash as nationalist-militarist ideologists, see Galeotti (1990, 8–10).
7 On post-authoritarian Indonesia, see Emmerson (2004, 2012).
8 There were a substantial number of Danish-speakers, particularly in northern Schleswig, that part of the province returned to Denmark in 1920 after Germany's defeat in the First World War and a referendum in Schleswig.

REFERENCES

Anderson, B. 1983. *Imagined Communities: Reflections on the Origins and Spread of Nationalism*. London: New Left Books.

Berdyaev, N. 1979. *The Russian Idea*. Westport, CT: Greenwood Press.

Böss, M., ed. 2011. *Narrating Peoplehood amidst Diversity: Historical and Theoretical Perspectives*. Aarhus: Aarhus University Press.

Brubaker, R. 1996. *Nationalism Reframed: Nationhood and the National Question in the New Europe*. New York: Cambridge University Press.

– 2004. *Ethnicity without Groups*. Cambridge, MA: Harvard University Press.

Dahm, B. 1969. *Sukarno and the Struggle for Indonesian Independence*. Ithaca, NY: Cornell University Press.

Darden, K. 2013. *Resisting Occupation: Mass Schooling and the Creation of Durable National Loyalties*. New York: Cambridge University Press.

Dunlop, J. 1985. *The New Russian Nationalism*. New York: Praeger.

Elson, R.E. 2008. *The Idea of Indonesia*. New York: Cambridge University Press.

Emmerson, D.K. 2004. "Indonesia's Approaching Elections: A Year of Voting Dangerously?" *Journal of Democracy* 15 (1): 94–108.

– 2012. "Southeast Asia: Minding the Gap between Democracy and Governance." *Journal of Democracy* 23 (2): 62–73.

Fukuyama, F. 2014. *Political Order and Political Decay: From the Industrial Revolution to the Globalization of Democracy*. New York: Farrar, Straus and Giroux.

– 2011. "National Identity, American and Otherwise." In *Narrating Peoplehood amidst Diversity: Historical and Theoretical Perspectives*, ed. M. Böss, 303–5. Aarhus, DK: Aarhus University Press.

Galeotti, M. 1990. "The Soviet Army's New Interest in Imperial Traditions." *Radio Liberty Research Bulletin*. 28 December, 8–10.

Gellner, E. 1987. "Nationalism and the Two Forms of Cohesion in Complex Societies." In *Culture, Identity, and Politics*, 6–28. Cambridge: Cambridge University Press.

– 2006. *Nations and Nationalism*. Ithaca: Cornell University Press.

Greenfeld, L. 1992. *Nationalism: Five Roads to Modernity*. Cambridge, MA: Harvard University Press.

Grundtvig, N.F.S. 2011. *The School for Life: N.F.S. Grundtvig on Education for the People*. Trans. and ed. E. Broadbridge, co-ed C. Warren and U. Jonas. Aarhus: Aarhus University Press.

Hughes, J. 1967. *Indonesian Upheaval*. New York: David McKay Co.

Huntington, S.P. 2004. *Who Are We? The Challenges to America's National Identity*. New York: Simon and Schuster.

Kohn, H. 1960. *Pan-Slavism, Its History and Ideology*. New York: Vintage Books.

Laitin, D. 2007. *Nations, States and Violence*. New York: Oxford University Press.

Manent, P. 1997. "Democracy without Nations?" *Journal of Democracy* 8: 92–102.

– 2006. *A World Beyond Politics? A Defense of the Nation-State*. Princeton, NJ: Princeton University Press.

Prokhanov, A. 1990. "Essay and Current Affairs: Notes of a Conservative." *Nash Sovremennik* 5 (May).

Renan, E. 1996. *Qu'est-ce qu'une nation?* [What Is a Nation?]. Toronto: Tapir Press.

Stepan, A.C., and J. Linz. 2010. "The Rise of 'State-Nations.'" *Journal of Democracy* 21 (3): 50–68.

Sukarno. 1969. *Nationalism, Islam and Marxism*. With an Introduction by Ruth McVey. Ithaca, NY: Cornell University Press.

Taylor, J.G. 2003. *Indonesia: Peoples and Histories*. New Haven, CT: Yale University Press.

Tolz, V. 1990. "Democrats Start Their Own Discussion of Russian National Problems." *Radio Liberty Research Bulletin*, 30 March.

Utechin, S.V. 1963. *Russian Political Thought: A Concise History*. New York: Praeger.

Volodin, E. 1990. "The New Russia in a Changing World." *Literaturnaya Rossiya* 4 (January).

Yanov, A. 1987. *The Russian Challenge and the Year 2000*. Oxford: Basil Blackwell.

2

Icons of Nationalism

ANTHONY D. SMITH

The recent exchange between Marine Le Pen and President Sarkozy about the place of Jeanne d'Arc in French history and her significance for the French nation reminds us that heroines and symbols, even of a far-gone age, can have a profound resonance for later periods and modern generations. How much more so when it comes to more recent figures – a Napoleon, a Bolivar, or a Garibaldi! Or, for that matter, a Michelet, a Manuel Gamio, or a Mazzini. In one sense, it hardly matters, except to historians, what these figures intended or signified in their own times; what matters is that they continue to resonate, more or less, even today, that they represent one or more perceived aspects of that elusive but potent abstraction "the nation," and for that reason they partake of the charisma of nations.

In another sense, the content of their signification *does* matter. Alfred may not have burned any cakes, and Bar-Kosiba may not have been Bar-Kochba, the son of a Star, but the consequences of their actions, for good or for ill, helped to shape, in the minds of successive generations, the political and/or cultural community in which many members of the modern generation trace their putative descent, such that even millennia later, they continue to be regarded as "icons of the nation." This is not to say that they cannot cease to be icons; historical enquiry may demolish the legends that grew up about them to reveal a quite different and a much less attractive persona. Yet, even then, they retain an aura that suggests that it is not their (often misguided) policies and exploits but, rather, their relation to "the nation" that endows them with their iconic power.

Here I want to explore that iconic power in two ways: (1) historical and comparative and (2) theoretical. Before embarking on these discussions, we need to have an entry into the main lines of historical and sociological approaches to the study of nations and nationalism as well as a clearer idea of the concept and dimensions of "the nation" itself and the related concepts of "national identity" and "nationalism." This will allow us to provide a historical and comparative framework for different kinds of nationalist leaders and enable us to evaluate their roles and their iconic status and potency in both modern and premodern ages. Only then can we assess how far such an exploration can contribute to existing theories of nations and nationalism.

AGENCY AND PROCESS

Two main approaches have developed over a century or more in the study of nations and nationalism. On the one hand, there has been the cumulative historical study of nationalist ideologies and movements conducted mainly by historians and, to some extent, by political scientists. Here "text" and "context" reign supreme. The exemplar of this approach is probably the late Elie Kedourie who, in his *Nationalism* and *Nationalism in Asia and Africa*, argues, on the basis of selected writings of nationalist ideologues, that nationalism was a misguided ideology invented in Europe around 1800 and a political response by marginalized young men caught between tradition and modernity to the penetration of bureaucracy and the state in Europe and its imperial offshoots in Asia and Africa. Dreaming that they could create a perfect world on the ruins of a pulverized traditional order, the "marginal" young men came to believe in the power of the Kantian autonomous will to create a new type of society – the nation – typified by love and brotherhood. And, to this end, they embarked on "children's crusades" against both their obscurantist elders and the foreign oppressors in a spirit of chiliastic expectation that inevitably bred political violence. As a result, we should not be surprised that Kedourie's pages are filled with portraits of fanatical youthful leaders. Apart from the philosophical forbears – Rousseau, Kant, and Herder – we encounter the German romantics, notably Fichte, Arndt, and Jahn; their East European followers, from Korais and Mickiewicz to Palacký and Karadzic; and later non-European cultural leaders, from Gokalp and Edward Blyden to Shakib Arslan and Tilak (Kedourie 1960, 1971; Leerssen 2006).

At the opposite pole we find the many sociological approaches that explain the appeal of nationalism in terms of social structures, social change, and the often dramatic transition to modernity. Of these, the most cogent and comprehensive has been the theory advanced by Ernest Gellner, and perhaps its most influential exposition is to be found in his *Nations and Nationalism*. The nub of his argument is that modernity is "modular." That is to say, modernization requires unified literate "high" cultures, with their specialists, in place of the many spontaneous premodern "low cultures" because it can only be effective with a numerate and literate workforce. Hence, the overriding need for mass, standardized, academy-supervised, state-supported, and state-regulated education – something to which nationalists everywhere are strongly committed. At the same time, the transition to modernity is often stressful: it uproots the peasantry and drives them into ever-expanding cities, forcing "low" cultures to either become literate and standardized or perish. Nevertheless, a few cultures remain counter-entropic: in particular, those that are based on colour differences or on an ancient textual religion may not be easily absorbed into the new high cultures, and this can result in conflict. But, in general, Ruritanians and their "low" cultures must either be assimilated into the cultural empire of megalopolis or secede to establish a new high culture and polity. And this is where the story always ends: in the "nation," a unit marked by the congruence of cultural and political boundaries, and by an integrative system of mass education, which has become the norm throughout the modern (and modernizing) world (Gellner 1983).

At first glance, it may be thought that one of the key differences between these two approaches relates to the role of agency in the rise of nationalism, with Kedourie and many earlier historians magnifying the role of ideologists of nationalism and sociologists like Gellner focusing on the large-scale processes at the expense of individual agency and ideology. But closer inspection reveals that the difference is not as great as has been commonly thought. Not only does Gellner speak of the role of uprooted Ruritanians in the city but Kedourie treats his named ideologists not as individuals but, rather, as representatives of the category of "marginal men." And both are assigned a causal role in the genesis of nationalism, in the first case through sudden awareness of cultural difference and its effects on life-chances in the city, in the second through the alienation and ideological discontent of people caught between tradition and modernity. But in neither case – and this goes for the vast majority of approaches and theories in the field – is the role of the singular individual, either as individual or as symbol or both, thought worthy of notice per se. This is true even when, as Tom Nairn argues, the emphasis is placed on the role of romantic populism and intellectuals in the nationalist response to uneven development; or, as Eric Hobsbawm would have it, on the "invention of tradition" by the lesser "examination-passing" intellectuals; or, in Benedict Anderson's analysis, print capitalism and literary culture play a vital role in the formation of the "imagined community" of the nation. As a result, we find no attempt to incorporate an analysis of leadership, of cultural models and symbolic influence, and of different kinds of symbolic leader and inspiration into a broader approach to the rise and persistence of nations and nationalism. This means, inter alia, that, to this day, the pivotal role and inspiration of these leaders, so important not only in a crisis but also for the distinctive "qualities" of the nation they have helped to shape, is obscured to the extent that their influence cannot be assessed. This is undoubtedly an important lacuna in the theory of nations and nationalism, and it needs to be addressed. However, here I can only provide some prefatory remarks to, and some reflections upon, an analysis of symbolic and historical leadership, setting out some of the considerations and examples of what we might term their "iconic" status and highlighting their significance for a more general approach to, and theory of, nations and nationalism (Anderson 1991; Hobsbawm 1990; Hobsbawm and Ranger 1983, Introduction; Nairn 1977, chap. 2).

NATIONS AND THEIR "QUALITIES"

Any analysis should start from a definition of that most elusive of concepts, "the nation," or "national community." There are as many definitions as there are scholars of nationalism, but, for my purposes, a useful working definition might be: a named human community residing in a perceived homeland, whose members share a heritage of memories, myths, symbols, values, and traditions; disseminate a distinctive public culture; and observe common laws and customs. The related concept of "national identity" can be defined as: the continuous reproduction and reinterpretation by the members of a national community of the pattern of values, symbols, memories, myths, and traditions composing the distinctive heritage of nations, and the variable identification of its individual members with that heritage and its cultural elements. As for the concept of "nationalism," clarity requires that it be confined to an ideology, a movement, and a symbolic language and that it be defined as: an ideological movement for attaining and maintaining the autonomy, unity, and identity of a human community deemed by some of its members to constitute an actual or potential "nation." I should stress that these are only preliminary definitions, but they provide a starting point for analysis and serve to delimit the field.[1]

The obvious point of entry for leadership, historical and symbolic, is the nationalist movement, with its characteristic ideology of a world divided into nations, each with its own character, history, and destiny, to which primary allegiance is owed, in devotion to which individuals discover their true freedom, and which must therefore seek their fullest self-expression and autonomy. Only a world built on this basis, contend the nationalists, can provide peace with justice and liberty (Smith 1991, 73–4).

But where could the inspiration to build such an ideal world be found? For the nationalists, the answer was obvious: in "the people" – that is, the people on whose behalf they were campaigning, the people who, in their mind's eyes, either already formed a "nation" or would, as a result of the nationalists' own exertions, soon do so. But, even in those cases in which it was felt that the nation had already been formed, its members had to be made to "realize their nationhood": they must be made to feel that they constituted a territorialized, unified, autonomous, and unique culture community with a common symbolic heritage, a distinctive public culture, and common laws and customs. To these ends, they had to be socially and politically "mobilized." Not simply in the generic sense charted by sociologists like Karl Deutsch and Tom Nairn, who focus essentially on the uprooting of the peasantry and their mass migration to cities and towns, important as that process undoubtedly was. No, here mobilization had to have a strong cultural dimension; it had to mean vernacular mobilization, the entry of the middle and lower classes, urban and rural, into a shared and distinctive ethnic culture (however formed) and their reconstitution as an ethnic "people" of equals and, ultimately, a political "nation" on the basis of legal citizenship and a distinctive shared culture (Deutsch 1966; Nairn 1977, chap. 2; cf. Smith 2011).

This was a huge task, and it required not just the usual preconditions of economic and social development, and the instruments of state building and systematic education, but also the generation of powerful symbolic resources and strong motivations for popular sacrifice for the nascent national community. Without these, we might have a world of (more or less) strong states but not of national states or of national populations (more or less) committed to their "nation" and its sense of "national identity" – the nations of those states. But, to a large extent, we do have a world of national states, nations whose members have some sense (more or less) of their "national identity" and a global presumption of national autonomy and national self-determination (albeit hedged in by considerations of Realpolitik).

Whence came the widespread impetus for vernacular mobilization? How was it possible to integrate often disparate rural and urban populations in given areas, or even homogeneous but passive and scattered populations, into a single, dynamic, and all-embracing political nation on the basis of a more or less distinctive, indigenous ethnic culture? There are several reasons for this global movement and for its relative success. Here I want to focus on two interrelated factors: (1) the "charismatic" nature of nations and the national ideal and (2) the inspiration provided by national leaders, especially by national "educators" and the "cult of ancestors." Together, these factors go a long way to explaining the success of nationalism for over two centuries and to bridging the gulf between the historians' concerns for text and context, and the sociologists' focus on social structure and social change.

KEY ASPECTS OF THE NATION

We may start by noting three key aspects of nations, or national communities: (1) the nation as a set of collective projects, (2) the nation as a "palimpsest" of legacies, and (3) the nation as a community of "grace." The first aspect is relatively straightforward. Communities can be seen as products of collective action based either on notions of "tradition" or of some "rational" project involving a covenant or contract of mutual rights and duties. In the case of national communities, we are speaking of collective action periodically required for national vernacular mobilization in order to create, recreate, or maintain their distinctive societies and cultures. This is often achieved by means of symbolic projects of national and popular revival, unification, and redirection, which serve to focus the energies of the populace on the distinctive qualities of their community and its symbolic heritage. By and large, these projects of national and popular revival seek to attain the ideal of the nation held by the nationalists and others by including "the people" and educating them in the vernacular culture, thereby differentiating them even further from all neighbouring communities.

These projects on the part of individuals and groups take the form of revivalist circles, study groups, social movements, popular assemblies, and political institutions that reflect both the universal "requirements of modernity" and the languages, customs, memories, myths, and symbols of each community. Each of these projects expresses some interpretation of national history and culture and a particular conviction of the foreordained trajectory, or "destiny," of the nation. Of course, some of these revivalist projects compete with each other and conflict may ensue, as happened when the Westernizers in Russia clashed with the pan-Slav traditionalists. In a few cases, social revolution may undermine the basis of traditionalist projects, though rarely completely. More often, the rival projects are combined to some degree, if rather uneasily. This is what happened in nineteenth-century Greece, when the Greek diaspora Westernizers sought a return to the classical ideals of ancient Greece and were opposed by the traditionalists' yearnings for a restoration of the Orthodox Christian Byzantine Empire. In such cases, there occurs what John Hutchinson terms a "mythic overlaying," whereby later myths cover over, but do not obliterate, the earlier ethno-religious myths and traditions. For Hutchinson, mythic overlaying occurs in moments of crisis when nationalists offer a new mythology of national sacrifice, with themselves often cast, like Patrick Pearse in the Easter Rising of 1916, as martyrs for the nation, a mythology that overlays the older ethno-religious beliefs and is then gradually fused with them.[2] But it is not only through sacrifice, or in a crisis of war and revolution, vital though these may be, that such overlaying can occur. Rather, we may say that, with the mingling of populations through immigration and culture contact in the modern epoch, the laying down of later deposits over earlier ones has become so widespread that the modern nation must be viewed as a palimpsest: a complex cultural community and collective identity whose features, though often transformed, stem from the legacies of different epochs and their cultures. The result resembles a "mosaic nation," one in which different projects of cultural creativity from successive epochs can be located, and the extent to which their legacies have meshed gauged. Hence the relatively polyethnic character of many of today's nations, where typically the institutions and culture of a dominant ethnic have, in varying degrees, been overlaid by those of later waves of immigrants, while continuing to serve as the framework and grid of the national community. We see this layering in changes of language and idiom, in debates about the role of religion, and in the accumulation of new myths and traditions and the relegation of earlier memories and symbols (Smith 2007).

But it is a third aspect, the nation as a community of "grace," that is most germane to the significance and role of icons of nationalism. This stems from the dual conception of the nation, held by nationalists and others, as both the object of a cult and the subject of history. On the one hand, the nation embodies their vision of an ideal community characterized by "fraternity" and, latterly, also "sorority," one that is not only eternally "good" and pure, as Benedict Anderson argues, but also "magnetic" – that is, inspiring love and devotion and, ultimately, self-sacrifice by its members. In this conception, the nation is seen as charismatic, a community endowed with the gift of "grace," which in this case derives from the myth of divine election, such as inspired the covenanted Israelites at Sinai. In this sense, the nation can best be understood as a sacred communion of the citizens who partake of the gift of grace by virtue of kinship and divine election, and, as such, it becomes an object of worship and ardent devotion. In the words of Patrick Pearse, "they (the constitutional nationalists) have not recognised in their people the image and likeness of God. Hence the nation is not to them all holy, a thing inviolate and inviolable, a thing that a man dare not sell or dishonour on pain of eternal perdition" (cited in Lyons 1982, 85). This merely extends to a wider collectivity Paul's original notion of the holy "charisma" that dwelt within the small early Christian communities that he supported on his travels in Asia Minor, Greece and Italy. Unlike the Weberian concept of "charismatic authority," which is geared to exceptional individuals and to a form of legitimate domination, the Pauline conception emphasized the need for communal harmony for salvation and the possession of different kinds of charisma ("charismata") by each of the members working for the good of the community.[3] Similarly, in the nationalist conception of the nation, all the members of "the people" constitute an elect community and, therefore, partake of the nation's charisma, contributing each in his or her own way to the good of the commonwealth. But for nationalists, the charismatic nation is not simply the object of a cult, often symbolized by a powerful, usually female, figure of French Liberty or of Mother Russia, Germania, or Britannia, a figure who embodies the enduring essence of its "authenticity." The nation is equally felt to be an active dynamic force in history, a shining beacon whose radiant "fire" breaks out not only to warm and enlighten but also to consume and destroy, a fire whose irruption into history, as Weber understood, threatens havoc and destruction for tradition and bureaucracy alike.[4]

NATIONAL EDUCATORS

But, just as the flame of national ardour must be kept alive by its devotees, so must the charismatic nation itself be constantly renewed if its "grace" is to be imparted and its "fire" is to continue to inspire the members of the community. This means that the national community must not simply be revived: it must be made over anew. This task requires leaders who will to some extent embody the nation's charisma and, for that reason, are in a position to mobilize "the people" not just for resistance to an external oppressor but also, and more important, to rediscover themselves, their inner strength and "true" identity. That, in turn, requires that they engage in vernacular education, or re-education, as the case may be, a process of turning inwards to search for the distinctive elements and authentic qualities of "the people" in order to remake them as citizens of a unique culture community. Through the collective projects of vernacular mobilization, nationalists aim to reveal to their designated co-nationals the true worth of their membership in a unique and charismatic culture community, and to rouse them to participate in projects of cultural renewal that will authenticate and validate the nation.

The key figures in this process are what we may term "national educators" and artists: historians, poets, writers, musicians, and visual artists who, through their literary, philosophical, historical, musical, and artistic work, were able to open the way to an understanding in the minds of their co-nationals of the distinctive qualities and trajectory of the nation and inspire in their hearts an ardent love of the people and the homeland. Starting with Rousseau and Herder, there has been a succession of men and women who sought to reveal the true worth and inner life of the community. This was the case even when, to an outside observer, no such community existed and it was the educators themselves who called it into being. This only goes to confirm the abstract, idealized nature of the concept of the nation, which is to be "realized" concretely. For the national educator all that is required to forge or remake the national community is a vision of the nation in his or her mind's eye and some vernacular elements of language, religion, and customs; some shared memories, however shadowy; some myths, however embellished; some symbols and traditions, however partial or displaced from other universes of discourse, usually religious, in order to set in motion the task of national regeneration and moral renewal (Anderson 1991, chap. 5; Hutchinson 1992).

It is customary to identify political or military leaders as the primary agents of nationalist movements. The roll call here includes men like Ataturk in Turkey, Ben-Gurion in Israel, Venizelos in Greece, Garibaldi in Italy, Kossuth in Hungary, and, mutatis mutandis, Nelson and Churchill in Britain, Napoleon in France, and Bismarck for the creation of Germany. From the standpoint of the creation, or defence, of the (not always national) state, there is no doubting their centrality. But what of the nation? Concerned as they were with seeking the unity and independence of the nation in a state of its own, how far did these leaders seek to understand and rediscover the nation's "authenticity" and "identity"? Generally speaking, political leaders aimed to mobilize "the people" for resistance or war but not for self-expression or self-realization, the two main watchwords of the national educators. Of course, a few may have also devoted their energies to questions of national identity and self-realization; Masaryk certainly, and Herzl to some extent in his short life, wrote general philosophical or literary works exploring these themes. But this was not the focus of their national activity.

The struggles fought by national educators, on the other hand, were centred exactly on questions of national self-expression, self-realization, and self-determination. These were the concepts that were central to the thoughts of the "fathers" of nationalism, Rousseau and Herder, but they also preoccupied Herder's German followers, notably Fichte, Arndt, and Jahn. Elsewhere, it was Enlightenment influences that prevailed, an early example being the social philosopher, Adamantios Korais, whose intellectual impact was widely felt in early nineteenth-century Greece and who devoted his energies to reviving classical education as the best way of creating modern citizens in Greece. A century later, Ziya Gokalp, influenced by the sociology of Durkheim, also sought in national education the social solidarity necessary for making, or remaking, a Turkish nation.[5]

Among the national educators, national historians occupy a special place. Unlike contemporary professional historians who seek, with greater or less objectivity, to describe and analyze the causes and consequences of historical events and processes, the task of national historians was to create an "ethno-history" for the people and connect this "history" with the "destiny" of the nation, thereby infusing the members of the community (or community-to-be) with a sense of national identity and national purpose. There are many examples of such ethno-histories. Michelet retold the history of France from the standpoint of "the people"; Palacký's history sought to recall for oppressed Czechs their former glorious days; Paparrigopoulos's monumental history of Greece fused the ancient classical Greek with the Orthodox Byzantine ethnic narratives; George Petrie's archaeological researches revealed the artefacts of Ireland's early heroic ages; Elias Lönnrot aimed to provide subjugated Finns with a noble lineage and mythology going back to the pre-Christian Iron Age; while the histories of Heinrich Graetz and Simon Dubnow provided for the scattered Jewish communities a narrative of the ethnic trajectory of their medieval exile in both Western and Eastern Europe.[6]

Nor should we forget the vital role of visual artists in the creation of a "national art," one that drew upon, and imparted, national sentiments and ideals to successive generations of the educated classes. In some cases, the designation of "national artist" may have been part of the artists' intentions; in other cases, it was subsequently bestowed upon them. For all their undoubted patriotism, remaking the nation through a national art was hardly the primary aim of Turner or Constable, whereas that was undoubtedly a major part of the intention of Jacques-Louis David in his paintings before and during the Revolution and in his choreography of Revolutionary fetes, and, to a lesser extent, of Benjamin West in late eighteenth-century Britain and Akseli Gallen-Kallela in late nineteenth-century Finland. On the other hand, whatever their intentions, some of the works of these artists became part of the canon of a national art after generations, and, in that sense, David's *The Oath of the Horatii* (1785), Constable's *The Hay Wain* (1821), and Turner's *The Fighting "Temeraire"* (1838) became "iconic" for they seemed to endow the abstraction of the national ideal with a palpable reality and a memorable form that belied the remoteness of the "nation" from most people's immediate concerns (Daniels 1993; Reichardt and Kohle 2008; Smith 2011, 2013, chap. 4).

Literature, too, especially poetry, furnished another potent means of national renewal. The exemplars here are Pushkin for Russia, Mickiewicz for Poland and exile Poles, Burns for Scotland, Bialik for the Jews, Petöfi for Hungary, Lorca for Spain, Wordsworth and Tennyson for Britain, and Yeats for Ireland. The incorporation of popular ballads and folk tales, stimulated by the writings of Herder, brought Romantic poetry closer to what was deemed to be the "essence" of the nation, "the land and its people," their habitat, toil, mores, and customs. This provided the context, too, for the popularity of "rediscovered" (and sometimes forged) medieval epic poetry (so often thought to express the "true voice" of the people), which often ran into many editions across Europe, from Icelandic Eddic poetry and sagas to the Nibelungenlied, the Kalevala, and the Chanson de Roland, not to mention the "Ossianic lays" of James Macpherson. Other literary forms were equally influential in creating a sense of national identity and exploring the deep "roots" and varied tableaux of the nation. One thinks of the Grimm brothers' collection of

German fairy tales, Schiller's historical dramas, and, above all, the historical novels of Walter Scott, Flaubert, Tolstoy, and others that enjoyed such a vogue in Europe during the nineteenth century.[7]

Music, too, became a vital resource for national educators. This was not just a question of the unisonance engendered by the many choral societies that sprang up all over Europe and that opened up not just vocal music to the middle classes but also the concept and ideal of a national community that had so often provided the framework and setting of great choral works from Handel's *Israel in Egypt* to Sibelius's Kullervo Symphony and Walton's *Belshazzar's Feast*, not to mention the rousing choruses in Prokofiev's cantata *Alexander Nevsky*. In *The Triumph of Music*, Timothy Blanning sets out the many ways in which music, classical and later jazz and pop, became so influential in, even central to, the lives of all classes in society. If Handel's biblical oratorios were early exemplars, developments in opera from the early and mid-nineteenth century onwards, notably by Weber, Verdi, and Wagner, and in symphonic poems by Liszt, Smetana, Dvořák, Rimsky-Korsakov, and Sibelius, revealed the powerful influence of national ideals and sentiments. More important, they helped to distil and amplify those ideals not just in the subjects chosen (so often from national history, legend, and landscape) but also in their often free and passionate musical language and their increasing use of ethnic folk tunes and dances. Even the more restricted musical forms were affected, as we can see in Chopin's polonaises and mazurkas, the national dances that Tchaikovsky incorporated into his ballets, and the Hungarian and Rumanian folk dances that Bartok and Kodaly had researched.[8]

THE CULT OF THE ANCESTORS

Political and military leaders, national educators, musicians and artists: whatever their differences in aims and policies, the appearance of all these political and cultural figures in so many states and peoples at the epicentre of the cultural project of national "reawakening" has few parallels in history. But this efflorescence was in no way accidental. Quite apart from the social and political conditions that facilitated it, we tend to find this cultural project wherever there has been an ethno-cultural and historical basis for the subsequent emergence of nationalism; and the more distinctive and long-established that historical basis and cultural tradition, ceteris paribus, the more intense the subsequent national movement is likely to be.

An important dimension and symbol of this relationship between earlier cultural ties and recent vernacular mobilization is what Ernest Renan calls "the cult of the ancestors." Renan is usually credited with an unusually bold statement of a "voluntarist" ideology of nationalism; and it is undoubtedly true that, in the first part of his lecture, he dismisses the determinisms of language, religion, race, and geography in the definition and formation of nations. But later, when he reflects on what it is that constitutes the "essence" of the nation, it turns out to be something far more potent and directive than Will or the self-affirmation of a "daily plebiscite." The nation, for Renan, is a solidarity constituted by the memory of collective sacrifice. In his own words: "The nation, like the individual, is the culmination of a long past of endeavours, sacrifice and devotion. Of all the cults, that of the ancestors is most legitimate, for the ancestors have made us what we are. A heroic past, great men, glory (by which I understand genuine glory), this is the social capital upon which one bases a national idea. To have common glories in the past and to have a common will in the present, to have performed great deeds together, to wish to perform still more – these are the essential conditions for being a people" (Renan 1990, 19).

It is this "cult of the ancestors" that reappears so prominently in the cultural projects of national renewal and that will become yet another earlier "layer" in the palimpsest of the nation and the shared memories of its members. That is why, in the literature, art, music, and political thought of the educators, the example and exploits of certain heroic figures from an often distant past – leaders, warriors, saints, geniuses – are so often invoked for guidance and inspiration in the present. For not only have they "made us what we are" but the heroic ancestors also epitomise the underlying power and charisma of the "perennial" nation.

It is not difficult to think of examples of the cult of the ancestors and its continuing influence. Two such cults of early first millennium Irish ancestors were to play an influential role in modern Irish nationalism. The first was the legendary warrior hero of the ancient Irish sagas, Cuchulainn, whose triumph in death at the hands of his enemies was invoked, along with that of Christ's crucifixion, by Patrick Pearse to create the legend of Irish sacrificial martyrdom in the Easter Rising of 1916. The second, St Patrick, was a fifth-century British missionary who, through his untiring efforts to convert the pagan population, became the patron saint of Catholic Ireland and is venerated to this day both in the homeland and in the Irish diaspora (Lyons 1982, 85–95).

Equally influential for modern Swiss nationalism was the medieval figure of Wilhelm Tell and his associated legends. French plays and operas by Lemierre (1766) and Gretry (1791) and later by Rossini (1829), drawings by Füssli in England, and paintings by Schall and Vincent in Paris in the 1790s attest to the spread of his cult outside Switzerland, especially during the French Revolution, while Schiller's drama popularized his exploits in helping to defeat the encroachments of the Austrian Hapsburg rulers. Moreover, the discovery of the Bundesbrief of 1291, with its text of the Oath of the Rütli sworn by Stauffacher and his confederates from Uri, Schwyz, and Unterwalden on 1 August in that year in defence of their established rights, gave a new direction to the traditional ethnohistory of the chroniclers and of Johannes von Müller and inspired the sescentennial anniversary celebrations of 1891 (Detroit 1974, 604–5, under "Schall"; Kreis 1991; Zimmer 2003).

Nineteenth-century Danes, too, could look back to illustrious ancestors, despite, perhaps because of, the contraction of the Danish state and the reduction in its status and power. These ancestors included their early ruler, Harald Bluetooth, who forged a Danish kingdom and introduced Christianity to Denmark in 960; Queen Margrethe, who established the Union of Kalmar in 1397, which united Sweden and Norway under Danish rule; and the politically unsuccessful but culturally productive seventeenth-century king Christian IV, the architect king who was, inter alia, responsible for the rebuilding of Kronborg Castle and the commission to Dutch artists of large-scale paintings of glorious events in Danish history, several of which were subsequently carried off to Sweden in 1658 (Ferguson 2010, chap. 10; Jespersen 2004; Kronborg 2001, 58–61).

Nor is the cult of the ancestors confined to small nations or declining national states. Modern Russians have been inspired by early Muscovite kings like Dmitri Donskoy and Alexander Nevsky, whose defeat of the invading Teutonic Knights in the battle on the ice of Lake Peipius in 1242 was the subject of Sergei Eisenstein's celebrated 1938 anti-Nazi film set to memorable music by Sergei Prokofiev. Modern Russians have also looked to a succession of strong rulers such as Ivan IV Grozny, who was admired by Stalin and afforded another striking subject for a memorable two-part Eisenstein film; and Peter the Great, who was commemorated in Pushkin's great poem, "The Bronze Rider"; while others, especially the Old Believer settlements, turned to charismatic medieval Russian saints like St Sergius for their inspiration (Eisenstein 1989; Leyda 1974; Perrie 1998).

But perhaps the best-known figure in this cult of the ancestors is Jeanne d'Arc, later canonized as St Joan. Her reputation before the early nineteenth century was mixed. Condemned to be burned alive in Rouen in 1431 for heresy and cross-dressing, she was rehabilitated in the 1450s but assailed in subsequent centuries, notably by Voltaire, who wanted to discredit the Roman Catholic Church. It was the national educator Michelet in his great *History of France* (1841) who more than anyone established her modern cult, finding in her purity, innocence, and courage the lineaments of the "genuine nature" of the "French people" and the ancestress of the patriotic zeal of the Revolutionary soldiers of l'An II. By mid-century, the Roman Catholic Church sought to reclaim Jeanne for its own ideal of France as the "eldest daughter" of the church and saviour of the French, God's elect, the image that we see in Ingres' icon of her after the coronation of Charles VII at Rheims, painted in 1854. For Republicans, she was a purely secular figure whose aim was to free France of the English and to restore its national independence. Only after the Great War was a temporary consensus achieved between these conflicting interpretations of Joan, at the very moment of her canonization (Gildea 1994, 154–65; Warner 1983).

The cult of the ancestors included not only military and political figures but also great cultural luminaries, geniuses who partook of the nation's charisma, especially in those cases in which the nation (or nation-to-be) had for centuries lacked political unity or independence. For this reason, educated Italians harked back to the genius of Dante rather than Caesar, while Greeks looked to Homer, and Finns to their legendary shaman, Väinämöinen, the protagonist of the ballads of the Kalevala collected by Elias Lönnrot for the purpose of restoring to Finns a sense of historical dignity and self-worth. In other cases, cultural and religious heroes were joined to warriors and political leaders. This was the case in Germany, where, to the cults of Arminius (Hermann), who defeated the Roman legions in 9 AD in the Teutoberg Forest, and Frederick Barbarossa, who would rouse himself from his sleep under the Kyffhauser mountain to save Germany in her hour of need, were added those of Luther, the great religious genius who initiated the Reformation, and Albrecht Durer, whose cult as a prototype of German artistic genius became paramount during the nineteenth century. Indeed, in England, the genius of Shakespeare and Milton often outshone the inspiration of political heroes and heroines like Alfred, Henry V, and Elizabeth I, particularly from the late eighteenth century onwards. Even in a dispersed ethnic community like the Jews, cultural and religious figures like Isaiah, Rabbi Akiba, and Rashi were long revered as much as were David and Solomon; while among Armenians, to this day, early Armenian historians like Eghishe and Moses Khorenatsii come second only to the national hero, Vardan Mamikonian, the Armenian commander who, in 451 AD, fell as a national martyr in the battle of Avarayr against the Sasanian Persians.[9]

MAPPING THE ICONS

With such a profusion of cultural projects and national educators and ancestors, how are we to make sense of the national renewals in which they were embedded and of their roles and influence? Only by first mapping their place within an overall framework of national renewals can we hope to isolate the main features of these renewals in terms of collective action, overlaying of legacies, and charismatic "magnetism." And only then might we be able to broach wider issues of the role of agency within a general approach or theory of nations and nationalism.

Here I present a preliminary chart, or "map," of incumbents of the four main roles in national renewals: ancestors, political leaders, educators, and artists. The above relations between the ancestors and the roles of national renewal that they inspire can be presented schematically, as is shown in table 2.1.

This is, of course, a selective and incomplete map of key incumbents within these, mainly European, countries; and the choice of individual ancestors, leaders, educators, and artists can only be regarded as tentative. But a comparative framework that such preliminary mapping adumbrates may serve to alert us to some important features of national renewals, corresponding as they do to the attributes of nations, the collective action, overlaying, and magnetism that I describe. Here I have in mind:

1 commonalities in the role and functions of national renewal across countries and regions;
2 the key role of national educators in vernacular mobilization; and
3 the presence of artists and poets whose imagery often serves to make the nation appear "real" and appealing.

For nationalists, the formation or reconstruction of the nation requires the vernacular mobilization of large numbers of the designated co-nationals, and that, in turn, requires a clear conception of the nation or nation-to-be as well as one or more groups and organizations that

Table 2.1 Roles/incumbents of national renewal in selected countries

Country	*Ancestor*	*Leader*	*Educator*	*Artist*
USA	Washington/ Jefferson	Lincoln T. Roosevelt	Emerson	Cole/Copley
France	Joan of Arc	Napolean	Michelet	David/Hugo
England	Alfred/ Elizabeth I/ Shakespeare	Nelson/ Churchill	Carlyle/Arnold	Constable/Elgar
Ireland	Cuchulainn/ St. Patrick	Davis/Pearse	Petrie/Hyde	Yeats/Synge
Denmark	Harald/ Margarethe Christian IV	Christensen Christian X	Grundtvig	Nielsen/Købke
Norway	Trygvason/ Snorri	Bjornson	Wergeland	Ibsen/Grieg
Finland	Vainamoien	Snellman	Lonnrot/ Runeberg	Sibelius/ G-Kallela
Russia	Nevsky/Ivan IV	Peter/ Suvarov	Herzen/ Dostoevski	Pushkin/Tolstoy
Hungary	Arpad	Kossuth	Petofi	Bartok/Kodaly
Czechs	Wenceslaus/ Hus	Masaryk	Palacký	Smetana/Dvořák
Germany	Arminius/ Barbarossa	Bismarck	Herder/Fichte Arndt/Jahn	Wagner/ Grimm/Friedrich
Switzerland	Tell	Ochsenbein/ Lavater	von Muller	Keller
Italy	Dante	Garibaldi/ Cavour	Mazzini d'Azeglio	Verdi/Manzoni
Greece	Homer/Plato/ Alexander	Rhigas/ Venizelos	Korais/ Paparrigop-oulos	Cafavy
Turkey	Mehmet II/ Oguz Khan	Ataturk	Gokalp	
Israel	David/Akiba	Herzl/Ben Gurion	Ahad Ha'am/ Ben Yehuda	Bialik
Egypt	Ramses II/Saladin	Nasser	Abduh/Heikal	Mahfouz
Mexico	Moctezuma	Vasconcelos	Gamio	Rivera

can develop the national idea and draw upon wider strata for its realization. What is striking from the above schema is the regularity of the four kinds of role that we encounter in each case of national renewal: (1) the inspiration of the ancestors, (2) the politics of the leaders, (3) the cultural work of the educators, and (4) the image-making of the artists. One could hypothesize that all four roles are needed in the (re)making of nations and that deficiencies in any one of these types of role are likely to make it more difficult to create or reconstruct the national community. A "full" and "successful" national renewal, for the nationalists, would be one in which, inspired by a cult of ancestors, political leaders, educators, and artists would bring their talents and resources to the various collective projects of national reconstruction (Argyle 1976).

However, closer inspection of our chart reveals considerable variation and blurring of roles and their functions. For example, Theodor Herzl, the founder of "political Zionism," was actually a novelist, a highly secularized Viennese Jewish man of letters, whose success in convening the first Zionist Congress in Basel in 1897 on the basis of his analysis of the "Jewish question" in Europe (in his *The Jewish State* [1896]) turned him into an iconic political leader. Even then, he found time in his short life to write a novel entitled *Altneuland* (1902), outlining his ideas of the new national society of an independent Jewish state (Shimoni 1995; Vital 1980, pt. 3).

Artists, too, could straddle the educator role. This was often a function of their desire to make the abstract concept of the nation appear tangible, accessible, and "real." A well-known example is Richard Wagner, whose Gesamtkunstwerk at his theatre at Bayreuth was intended to serve the collective national purpose of German renewal. In particular, he wanted his rendering of the legends of the ancient Nibelungenlied in his Ring cycle of operas to bring Germans together in recognition of the essence of their underlying nationhood. In the same vein, Yeats hoped that his Abbey Theatre would provide an educational powerhouse for an Irish cultural renaissance. As John Hutchinson reminds us, by presenting the gods and heroes of the Irish epic cycles, especially the warrior-seer Cuchulainn, modern theatre could "perform for a literate age the equivalent of the ancient epics, whose communal recitations had bound older oral societies."[10]

Artists could also become involved in politics. An early case is that of the great French painter, Jacques-Louis David, celebrated for his memorable images of the French Revolution (*Oath of the Tennis Court*, 1791; *Death of Marat*, 1793). But his election to the National Convention as a Jacobin deputy helped to put him in charge of the design and choreography of the great fetes that marked the later stages of the Revolution, and his support for Robespierre led to his incarceration for a brief period after Thermidor. Few other artists were so directly involved. Mickiewicz and Chopin preferred to keep their distance from the revolutionary ferment in Poland, though they fervently supported it, and before 1848 Verdi was reluctant to be used by the radical Italian nationalists.[11]

Educators were more likely to try their hand at politics. Mazzini is an obvious example, though his political interventions proved fruitless. We have mentioned Ziya Gokalp's fruitful use of Durkheimain sociology for political education in the context of Ataturk's new Turkish Republic. Even more successful was the scholar and philosopher Thomas Masaryk, who updated Palacký's interpretation of Czech history and became president of the newly created Czechoslovakia after the First World War. But perhaps the outstanding case is that of the theologian Nikolai Grundtvig in Denmark. Almost single-handedly Grundtvig changed the moral, social, and educational content of subsequent Danish politics. Born in 1783, he came to manhood during the British invasion of Denmark and the subsequent contraction of the Danish-dominated conglomerate Oldenburg state. Perhaps in response to these disasters, Grundtvig wrote extensively about Denmark's distant, heroic past, with its Norse gods and heroes. In the 1830s, after some fruitful visits to England to study medieval English manuscripts, he began to formulate his liberal educational philosophy and, from 1838, developed his positive evaluation of the *folkelig*, or "popular," conception of religion, education, and social institutions. Jespersen explains that the Danish word *folkelighed*, which Grundtvig popularized, also has connotations of mutual obligation and commitment in a national community. It was this commitment that, in Grundtvig's eyes, made a "nation." Not only did he recommend freedom of association in worship, albeit within the Lutheran sphere, but he also inspired a network of "Folk High Schools" based on his liberal philosophy. When the national Constitutional Assembly was established in 1848–49 and, thereafter, the Parliament, following the dissolution of the absolutist state, Grundtvig was a powerful voice in favour of liberal laws on religion and education. Here the role of educator shifted imperceptibly into that of political leader, and to this day Grundtvig's inspiration and legacy for the values and ethos of the Danish welfare society model endures (Jesperen 2004, 103–13).

OUTWARD HARDENING, INWARD STRENGTHENING

It is true that the popularity of Grundtvig's value system and outlook was partly the result of the circumstances of Denmark's political decline, which was accentuated late in his life by the tragic defeat of the Danes by Bismarck's Prussians in the second Schleswig-Holstein War, 1864. These reverses and the loss of its former middle-power status had the effect of shearing off Denmark's multinational territories and confining the state of the kingdom to its largely Danish inhabitants (there was a German minority). It also had the broader effect of turning Danes "inwards," making them focus on the nature of the cultural, historical, and social bond of mutual obligation that held them together. It is hardly surprising that this concentration on the "national self" persisted in Denmark as well as in other small and compact national states that were created in the wake of the dissolution of older, polyethnic, and multinational empires. Nor was this inward-turning movement confined to Denmark even at the time. It was, after all, in part a product of the influence of the romanticism that Hegel defined as "absolute inwardness," an influence that, from the later eighteenth century, swept across Europe. But it was also the result of the growing compactness, or "hardening of space," of increasingly national states that emerged in the nineteenth and early twentieth centuries and that nationalism, by its drive for collective autonomy and ultimately sovereign independence, so powerfully encouraged and shaped (Blanning 2010; Jespersen 2004).

The national state, of course, had a longer history than its classic nineteenth-century form would suggest. It had emerged in the wake of the dissolution of Christendom in fifteenth-century Europe and the rise of national Reformed churches in the sixteenth century, with England, Holland, and Sweden early examples of a wider "covenantal" nationalism achieving state support. Nevertheless, before the onset of wider nationalist ideologies in the eighteenth century, a sense of national identity, or a "crown-centred patriotism," could only be attributed to a small cultural and political elite. The exigencies of the European inter-state system, both before and after Westphalia, and the incessant commercial and military rivalries of the European powers undoubtedly helped to fortify the bureaucratic penetration and territorial reach of an increasingly centralized state. But the question remained: Around which units of population should these states be formed, and what role, if any, should these populations have in the more compact state (Gorski 2000; Marx 2003; Smith 2008, chap. 5)?

The answers were to be supplied in large part by nationalists, though not, from their standpoint, without much travail and many setbacks. But nationalists did not forge their nations ex nihilo. They had two great models of statecraft and political culture before them. Already by the sixteenth century, if not earlier, parts of Europe were systemically divided into increasingly national states, in which ideas of the welfare, prestige, and independence of the nation exercised considerable influence on the outlook and policies of kings, elites, and governments, abetted by the classicizing patriotic discourse of honour of the legal scholars and humanists. After all, did not nationalism's view of the national units into which the world was divided parallel the system of nominally equal, multipolar polities and state-operated "locks" into which first Europe and then the world had long been, and would increasingly continue to be, organized? For this reason, the impact of nationalism could only be to harden the bureaucratic state's territorial space and make it yet more compact in opposition to the older, more diversified type of conglomerate states and empires. But, for the nationalists, that could hardly suffice. The outer shell of the national state might be fortified, but what of the population within? What was to be the nature of the bond that would both identify and unite them (Hirschi 2012, chap. 6)?

This was the point at which the exhortations of the national educators and their allies, the artists, made such a crucial difference. Their task was to set forth the ideal of the nation by searching out and selecting the legacies of memories, myths, symbols, and traditions among the populations that formed, or were to form, the cultural basis of the political nation. That entailed a focus on the cultural content, as opposed to the form, of the nation, usually through the discovery of a "usable" past and the fashioning of a single ethno-history out of the various traditions of "the people." Just as important was the discovery and standardization of a national language and literature that could stand comparison with earlier high cultures. But perhaps the most urgent task was to socialize the new generations of the designated co-nationals in "their" literary language, their literary canon, and their ethno-history, thereby forcing them to "look within" themselves and within the community for their new collective "self." By holding up the example of heroic ancestors from a "golden age" of culture and power, by bringing them and inculcating a vernacular literature and history, and by creating memorable and accessible images in paint and sound and stone, the national educators hoped to recreate the content of the culture and social bond of the national community. This meant that, in addition to the mass "exo-socialization" that Ernest Gellner thought so crucial, citizens required the more personal "endo-socialization" of vernacular mobilization that the national educators urged on them if "their" nations were to be (re)created and "their" national ideals realized.[12]

CONCLUSION

This brings us back to the theoretical divide between historians and social scientists with which I opened my discussion. There I focused on the second of the two models put forward by Ernest Gellner. However, in his first account in *Thought and Change* Gellner lays more emphasis on the role of literary culture and of its primary purveyors, the radical intelligentsia.

In contrast to his later account, Gellner's first theory affords an important role for "agency" – not only of the intelligentsia but also of the uprooted proletariat. But what even his first theory omits is, first, a detailed, historical account of the role and functions of the intelligentsia and their cultural projects and, second, an analysis of the "magnetism" they exercised over their followers as it derived from the charisma of the nation they sought to renew. Reinserting the actual historical figures of educators, artists, and political leaders, as well as the cult of the ancestors they invoked, is not to return us to some obsolete nineteenth-century view of the role of "great" men and women in history but, rather, to rescue the theory of nationalism from an ahistorical reductionism that would omit the considerable differences in the trajectories of nations and the manifold variety in their sources of inspiration, along with their cultural projects and movements for national renewal.

At the same time, it would reintroduce the analysis of historical sequence, which is often passed over in the recent work on popular nationalism or "everyday nationhood" and which tends to bypass the older "grand" theoretical narratives (Fox and Miller-Idriss 2008; Gellner 1964, chap. 7).

By placing the national educators, and their allies the artists, at the centre of any theory of nationalism, not only are we enabled to recognize their pivotal role in the vernacular mobilization of the period but we can also see how the ethos and features of national cultures and polities, to this day, have been infused with the spirit of their concerns and shaped by their agendas and achievements. By providing a framework for the comparative study of charismatic educators and artists, we can gauge both similarities and differences in their aims, methods, and achievements. This should enable us to provide a more nuanced and more historically grounded account of the trajectory of particular nations and of the emergence of nationalism, the ideological movement.

Educators as a category are not normally described as charismatic, but the case of "national educators," as I have tried to show, is different. For their charisma derives not from any claim to extraordinary personal qualities, be it of heroism or individual distinction (which they may or may not possess), but from their intimacy with and devotion to the nation they claim to represent. It is the "perennial" nation that is the perceived fount of charisma; the charisma of its devotees derives from their national mission, which is, as I said, to restore by their insight and ardour the "flame" of the nation and to keep it burning brightly. To this end, they look back to the ancestors in a golden age, both political leaders and cultural luminaries, and to their exempla virtutis, which, for Max Weber, exemplified his conception of personal charisma. Per contra, what matters to the national educators is not so much the personal heroism of the ancestors but the ways in which they symbolize the nation and embody its distinctive qualities; and what matters to later generations is not so much the personal qualities of the educators as the inspiration of their national mission and their devotion to the people.

But, in another, deeper, respect, the Weberian analysis of charisma is germane to our problem and needs to be incorporated into a theory of nations and nationalism. Weber claimed that "charisma" represented a force that irrupted periodically into history, breaking the transition from traditional to rational-bureaucratic legitimation of authority, the rationalization and disenchantment of all aspects of society, and even, at times, of the "iron cage" of modern capitalism. His model was the ancient Jewish emissary prophet sent by God to the people and speaking His words almost in spite of himself. His was a charisma of mission, of the Word in his ears. He might be a towering figure like Elijah or a man bowed down in sorrow like Jeremiah: all that mattered was the Word of God that he brought and that filled his being. Similarly, it was not the personal qualities of a Michelet, a Korais, or a Palacký that mattered but their exemplification of the national ideal, their devotion to the cause of the nation, which filled their being. This is what endowed them with charisma in the eyes of their followers and has raised them ever since to the status of "icons of the nation"; and this is the charisma that national educators like Nikolai Grundtvig and Giuseppe Mazzini exemplified (Weber 1965, chap. 4).

On a more general level, the national educators and their various cultural projects mark a historical caesura, a break with custom and tradition in the Weberian sense, and the beginnings of a new national, and inter-national, order. In that sense, we may speak of nationalisms as a series of charismatic revolutions in history, but revolutions above all in the spheres of morality, culture, and education, that lead to political change. Yet, as with many kinds of revolution, the break with the past that charismatic nationalism initiated was never complete. To remake the nation qua nation required a deep-ranging inquiry into the cultural palimpsest that made it unique. What transpired was certainly a break with what had gone before, but a selective one, with a new mythic layering, which could furnish the cultural basis for a remade nation. Just as the ancient prophets recalled the people to their covenant on Mount Sinai so as to re-establish the basis of a new Israel, so the national educators mobilized "the people" in their distinct historic languages, literatures, arts, and ethno-histories, which they themselves had selected and popularized. Hence, the nationalist revolution can be seen as a remoulding of what the educators genuinely felt to constitute the heritage of the community's past, but always in the light of their visions of the nation's destiny. Such is the complex and multifaceted revolution that charismatic nationalism wrought through the cultural work of its national educators.

NOTES

1 For a sample of earlier definitions of key terms like "nation" and "nationalism," see Deutsch (1966, chap. 1). For later definitions, see Connor (1994, chap. 4). For the rationale behind the definitions employed here, see Smith (2002); Smith (2010, chap. 1).

2 Hutchinson (2005, chaps. 2–3). For Russia, see Hosking (1997, esp. 67–74). On the divisions in Greece, see Kitromilides (1989); Roudometof (1998).

3 For Pearse's ideals, see Lyons (1982, 85–95). On the goodness of nations, see Anderson (1999). Paul's concept of charisma is outlined by Potts (2009, chaps. 2–3). And for Weber's conception of the role of charismatic authority, see Weber (1948, chap. 9).

4 See Weber (1968). For female symbolism of the nation, see Yuval-Davis (1997, 45). For the French use of Liberty, see Agulhon (1981); Reichardt and Kohle (2008).

5 For Korais, see Kedourie (1971, 37–47, 153–86). And for Gokalp, see Kedourie (1971, 50–2, 187–206); Lewis (1968, chap. 10).

6 For national historians in Western Europe, see the essays in Berger, Donovan, and Passmore (1999). And, more generally, see those in Carvalho and Gemenne (2009). On Paparrigopoulos, see Kitromilides (1998). For Palacký, see Zacek (1969, esp. 177–83).

7 On literary nationalism in Britain, see Trumpener (1997). For a comparison of Yeats and Bialik, see Aberbach and Hutchinson (1999). More generally, on nationalism and culture, see Leerssen (2006); Hutchinson (2005).

8 While there is as yet no general study of music and nationalism, see the interesting essays in Murphy and White (2001); as well as Blanning (2008). For nationalism and music in Russia, see Frolova-Walker (2007).

9 On Finnish nationalism, see Branch (1985). For the German monuments of resistance and liberation, see Mosse (1975, chap. 3). And for the cult of Durer, see Kuhlemann (2002). The Christian Armenian resistance and historians are discussed in Panossian (2006, 46–52).

10 See Brookner (1980) for a concise account of Jacques-Louis-David. For Chopin, see Zamoyski (2010). And for Verdi's relations with the early Risorgimento, see Korner (2009).

11 Hutchinson (2005, 56). On Pearse, see Lyons (1982, 47–51, 62–71). For the politics of Wagner's music dramas, see Arblaster (1992, chap. 5).

12 For the role of "exo-socialization" and general and specific education, see Gellner (1975, 1983). For the inspiration of "golden ages" for nationalists, see Smith (1997).

REFERENCES

Aberbach, D., and J. Hutchinson. 1999. "The Artist as Nation-Builder: William Butler Yeats and Chaim Nachman Bialik." *Nations and Nationalism* 5 (4): 501–21.

Agulhon, M. 1981. *Marianne into Battle: Republican Imagery and Symbolism, 1789–1880*. Cambridge, MA: Cambridge University Press.

Anderson, B.. 1991. *Imagined Communities: Reflections on the Origin and Spread of Nationalism*. 2nd ed. London: Verso.

– 1999. "The Goodness of Nations." In *Nation and Religion: Perspectives on Europe and Asia*, ed. P. van der Veer and H. Lehmann, 197–203. Princeton, NJ: Princeton University Press.

Arblaster, A. 1992. *Viva la Liberta: Politics in Opera*. London: Verso.

Argyle, W.J. 1976. "Size and Scale as Factors in the Development of Nationalism." In *Nationalist Movements*, ed. A.D. Smith, 31–53. London: Macmillan.

Berger, S., M. Donovan, and K. Passmore, eds. 1999. *Writing National Histories: Western Europe since 1800*. London: Routledge.

Blanning, T. 2008. *The Triumph of Music: Composers, Musicians and Their Audiences, 1700 to the Present*. London: Penguin.

– 2010. *The Romantic Revolution*. London: Phoenix.

Branch, M., ed. 1985. *The Kalevala, Land of Heroes*. London: Athlone.

Brookner, A. 1980. *Jacques-Louis David*. London: Chatto and Windus.

Carvalho, S., and F. Gemenne, eds. 2009. *Nations and Their Histories: Constructions and Representations*. Houndmills: Palgrave Macmillan.

Connor, W. 1994. *Ethno-Nationalism: The Quest for Understanding*. Princeton, NJ: Princeton University Press.

Daniels, S. 1993. *Fields of Vision: Landscape Imagery and National Identity in England and the United States*. Cambridge, MA: Polity.

Detroit. 1974. *French Painting, 1774–1830: The Age of Revolution*, Detroit, MI: Wayne State University Press.

Deutsch, K. 1966. *Nationalism and Social Communication*. 2nd ed. New York: MIT Press. Eisenstein, S. 1989. *Ivan the Terrible*. London: Faber.

Ferguson, R. 2010. *The Hammer and the Cross: A New History of the Vikings*. London: Penguin.

Fox, J., and C. Miller-Idriss. 2008. "Everyday Nationhood." *Ethnicities* 8 (4): 536–63.

Frolova-Walker, M. 2007. *Russian Music and Nationalism: From Glinka to Stalin*. New Haven, CT: Yale University Press.

Gellner, E. 1964. *Thought and Change*. London: Weidenfeld and Nicolson.

– 1975. "Scale and Nation." *Philosophy of the Social Sciences* 3: 1–17.

– 1983. *Nations and Nationalism*. Oxford: Blackwell.

Gildea, R. 1994. *The Past in French History*. New Haven, CT: Yale University Press.

Gorski, P. 2000. "The Mosaic Moment: An Early Modernist Critique of Modernist Theories of Nationalism." *American Journal of Sociology* 105 (5):1428–68.

Hirschi, C. 2012. *The Origins of Nationalism: An Alternative History from Ancient Rome to Early Modern Germany*. Cambridge, MA: Cambridge University Press.

Hobsbawm, E. 1990. *Nations and Nationalism since 1780*. New York: Cambridge University Press.

Hobsbawm, E., and T. Ranger, eds. 1983. *The Invention of Tradition*. Cambridge: Cambridge university press.

Hosking, G.A. 1997. *Russia: People and Empire, 1552–1917*. Cambridge, MA: Harvard University Press.

Hutchinson, J. 1992. "Moral Innovators and the Politics of Regeneration: The Distinctive Role of Cultural Nationalists in Nation-Building." In *Ethnicity and Nationalism: International Studies in Sociology and Social Anthropology*, vol. 60., ed. A.D. Smith, 101–17. Leiden: Brill.

– 2005. *Nations as Zones of Conflict*. London: Sage.

Jespersen, K. 2004. *A History of Denmark*. Houndmills: Palgrave Macmillan.

Kedourie, E. 1960. *Nationalism*. London: Hutchinson.

– ed. 1971. *Nationalism in Asia and Africa*. London: Weidenfeld and Nicolson.

Kitromilides, P. 1989. "'Imagined Communities' and the Origins of the National Question in the Balkans." *European History Quarterly* 19 (2): 149–92.

– 1998. "On the Intellectual Content of Greek Nationalism: Paparrigopoulos, Byzantium and the Great Idea." In *Byzantium and Modern Greek Identity*, ed. D. Ricks and P. Magdalino, 25–33. Aldershot: Ashgate Publishing.

Korner, A. 2009. "The Risorgimento's Literary Canon and the Aesthetics of Reception: Some Methodological Considerations." *Nations and Nationalism* 15 (3): 410–18.

Kreis, J. 1991. *Der Mythos von 1291: Zur Enstehung des Schweizerisches Nationalfeiertags* [The myth of 1291: The origin of Swiss national holidays]. Basel: Friedrich Reinhardt Verlag.

Kronborg. 2001. *Kronborg, the Castle and the Royal apartments*. Copenhagen: Palaces and Properties Agency.

Kuhlemann, U. 2002. "The Celebration of Durer in Germany during the Nineteenth and Twentieth Centuries." in *Albrecht Durer and His Legacy: The Graphic Work of a Renaissance*, ed. A.G Bartrum, n.p. London: British Museum Press.

Leerssen, J. 2006. *National Thought in Europe: A Cultural History*. Amsterdam: Amsterdam University Press.

Lewis, B. 1968. *The Emergence of Modern Turkey*. London: Oxford University Press.

Leyda, J., ed. 1974. Battleship Potemkin, October, and Alexander Nevsky by Sergei Eisenstein. London: Lorimer.

Lyons, F.S.L. 1982. *Culture and Anarchy in Ireland, 1890–1939*. Oxford: Oxford University Press.

Marx, A. 2003. *Faith in Nation: Exclusionary Origins of Nationalism*. Oxford: Oxford University Press.

Mosse, G. 1975. *The Nationalization of the Masses: Political Symbolism and Mass Movements from the Napoleonic Wars through the Third Reich*. Ithaca, NY: Cornell University Press.

Nairn, T. 1977. *The Break-Up of Britain: Crisis and Neo-Nationalism*. London: New Left Books.

Panossian, R. 2006. *The Armenians: From Kings and Priests to Merchants and Commissars*. London: Hurst.

Perrie, M. 1998. "The cult of Ivan the Terrible in Stalin's Russia." In *Russian Nationalism, Past and Present*, ed. G. Hosking and R. Service. Basingstoke: Macmillan.

Potts, J. 2009. *A History of Charisma*. Basingstoke: Palgrave Macmillan.

Reichardt, R., and H. Kohle. 2008. *Visualizing the Revolution: Politics and the Pictorial Arts in Late Eighteenth-Century France*. Edinburgh: Reaktion Books.

Renan, E. 1990 [1882]. *Qu'est-ce qu'une nation?* In *Nation and Narration*, ed. H. Bhabha, 8–22. London: Routledge.

Roudometof, V. 1998. "From Rum Millet to Greek Nation: Enlightenment, Secularisation and National Identity in Greek Society, 1453–1821." *Journal of Modern Greek Studies* 16 (1): 11–48.

Shimoni, G. 1995. *The Zionist Ideology.* Hanover NH: Brandeis University Press.

Smith, A.D. 1991. *National Identity.* Harmondsworth: Penguin.

– 1997. "The Golden Age and National Renewal." In *Myths and Nationhood*, ed. G. Hosking and G. Schopflin, 36–59. London: Routledge.

– 2002. "When Is a Nation?" *Geopolitics* 7 (2): 5–32.

– 2007. "Nations in Decline? The Erosion and Persistence of Modern National Identities." In *Nationalism in a Global Era: The Persistence of Nations*, ed. M. Young, E. Zuelow, and A. Sturm, 17–32. London: Routledge.

– 2008. *The Cultural Foundations of Nations.* Oxford: Blackwell.

– 2010. *Nationalism: Theory, Ideology, History.* 2nd ed. Cambridge, MA: Polity.

– 2011. "National Identity and Vernacular Mobilisation in Europe." *Nations and Nationalism* 17 (2): 223–56.

– 2013. *The Nation Made Real: Art and National Identity in Western Europe, 1600–1850.* Oxford: Oxford University Press.

Trumpener, K. 1997. *Bardic Nationalism: The Romantic Novel and the British Empire.* Princeton: Princeton University Press.

Vital, D. 1980. *The Origins of Zionism.* Oxford: Clarendon.

Warner, M. 1983. *Joan of Arc: The Image of Female Heroism.* Harmondsworth: Penguin.

Weber, M. 1948. *From Max Weber: Essays in Sociology.* Edited by H. Gerth and C.W. Mills. London: Routledge and Kegan Paul.

– 1965. *The Sociology of Religion.* London: Methuen.

– 1968. *On Charisma and Institution Building.* Edited by S.N. Eisenstadt. Chicago: University of Chicago Press.

White, H., and M. Murphy, eds. 2001. *Musical Constructions of Nationalism: Essays on the History and Ideology of European Musical Culture 1800–1945.* Cork: Cork University Press.

Yuval-Davis, N. 1997. *Gender and Nation.* London: Sage.

Zacek, J. 1969. "Nationalism in Czechoslovakia." In *Nationalism in Eastern Europe*, ed. P. Sugar and I. Lederer, 166–206. Seattle: University of Washington Press.

Zamoyski, A. 2010. *Chopin, Prince of the Romantics.* London: HarperCollins.

Zimmer, O. 2003. *A Contested Nation: History, Memory and Nationalism in Switzerland, 1761–1891.* Cambridge: Cambridge University Press.

3

Between Tradition and Modernity: Grundtvig and Cultural Nationalism

MICHAEL BÖSS

INTRODUCTION

On the last day of 1848, Grundtvig sat down at his desk in his home at Knabrostræde in inner Copenhagen to pen a sermon for New Year's Day after one of the most dramatic years in Danish history. The year had begun with the death of Grundtvig's protector, Christian VIII. It was followed by the outbreak of civil war in the duchies and the abolition of absolutism on 21 March after mass demonstrations and pressure from a broad political alliance. In the autumn, a general election for a constitutional assembly was held. In spite of his reservations about elective democracy, Grundtvig was one of those elected.

Noting the secular character of New Year's Day, Grundtvig granted himself permission to speak on secular matters on the following morning. He described 1848 as "peculiar" and "unforgettable" for, in that year, "chains, which did not tie the wicked but the good," had been broken around Europe, and "human life guided by the hand Providence" had made "a giant's step forward towards victory, freedom and enlightenment." And as for the smaller part of the world, Denmark and the Nordic countries, there was more reason to be thankful to "God the Father" and, "in the name of Jesus[,] to concede" that in no other place in the world had the year been so joyful. And this in spite of the fact that no other country had lost "such a good and wise king" and been caught up "in so dangerous and harmful a war"; and only in Denmark was "worse conceit, more obvious willfulness and blinder selfishness" to be found. What Grundtvig found reason to celebrate was that, even though the end of absolute monarchy had meant the breaking of the external bonds between the "ruler and his subjects and between high and low," his way of handling the people's petition had made the public realize that there had been an "internal bond, a bond of love between king and people and among us all as co-citizens [*medborgere*] from time immemorial and as children of the same mother." The "dangerous and harmful" war in the duchies – in which the kingdom, fatherland, mother tongue, honour, freedom, and independence of the people were at stake – had contributed to tightening these bonds. Indeed, they had awakened and nourished "a deep feeling among the Nordic peoples and realms" that they must "stand together and help each other against external enemies in order to live in honour and to pursue their great destiny." Grundtvig (1924, 218–19) was convinced that, far from causing harm, the present "unavoidable ferment and confusion among us" was only "a transition to a new order of things, far freer, more in harmony with the people [*folkelig*] and more human than we have seen for a long time, so that we may expect as genuine and blissful a peace as can be found in the realms of this world."

Grundtvig's New Year sermon in 1849 offers insight into his complex thoughts on history, society, humanity, freedom, justice, and divine providence. But it also expresses his personal perplexity at this watershed in Danish history and his own life. He was fully aware that Europe and Denmark had been utterly changed by the political and spiritual earthquake of 1848 and that a new age was dawning over his fatherland and people. But he was unsure about the implications. Against this background, passages of his sermon may be read as his dim vision of a prospective Denmark – a Denmark in the making but not yet clearly envisioned. Hence the discursive complexity of his sermon, in which elements from his thoughts and writings over the past twenty years are intertwined.[1]

Over the past decades, Grundtvig had adopted ideas from British liberalism, German idealism, and state theory as well as French and Italian political philosophy (Birkelund 2008; Grell 1988, 1992; Kaae 1986; Wåhlin 1989–90). He didn't fully subscribe to any one system of thought, probably because his deepest held convictions about the nature of liberty and the course of history were derived from his readings of the classical philosophers and the Bible (Birkelund 2008; Vind 1999). The New Year sermon reflects this complexity in its welding together of ideas of history, freedom, peoplehood, language, universal order, humanity, and citizenship in a rather idiosyncratic manner that causes confusion to those unfamiliar with his mind and habits of reading and writing.

Space does not allow me to unravel and expound on the various threads, which have been dealt with thoroughly by others. Instead, what I intend to do in this chapter is to offer a reading of another seminal text from this period, "The Transition Period in Denmark" (1849), an essay in which Grundtvig reflects on his vision of the "New Denmark" and his own contribution to nation building. My purpose is to characterize Grundtvig as a cultural nationalist. My argument is that Grundtvig was a typical cultural nationalist in so far as he mediated between the traditional and modernizing forces of his own time and saw himself as a spiritual nation builder. In order to demonstrate this, I draw on Calhoun, Hroch, and Greenfeld but especially Hutchinson. My argument, then, is as follows.

As a member of the new Danish Parliament, Grundtvig saw it as his principal task to promote what he called "the Danish cause." Central to this was to "enlighten" the common people – that is, to make them conscious of the values of their language and their cultural heritage so that they might take part in the rule of Denmark. Fully aware that he was not a politician and that politics was predicated on pre-political values, he did not have and did not subscribe to any political program. His sole objective was to help prepare Denmark for a glorious future in which the vernacular and the culture of the rural population would be respected. This meant the end of a period that had been dominated by modernizing urban elites, who had distanced themselves from the people and who had been steeped in Franco-German culture. Central to Grundtvig's cultural program – and this is where a postcolonial theoretical element enters my argument – was his conviction that the modernizing elites represented a foreign element in Danish society. Denmark, therefore, had to be restored.

The chapter consists of three sections. In the first section I briefly address theories relevant to understanding how modernization processes affected nineteenth-century nationalist discourse. In the second and major section I read Grundtvig's essay "The Period of Transition in Denmark" in light of Hutchinson's theory. In the last section I place Grundtvig in a wider historical and geopolitical context and conclude that he should be seen as a cultural nationalist in an age of transition.

THEORIES OF CULTURE AND NATIONALISM

As some scholars have pointed out (e.g., O'Day 1998), the factors that Anthony D. Smith (1991) lists as preconditions of national identity – the existence of a historic homeland; common myths and historic memories; a common, mass public culture; common legal rights and duties for all members; and, finally, a common economy with territorial mobility for members of the nation – do not arise at the same time. Nor do they always take the same form: their development and articulation are conditioned by particular political and social circumstances. Hence, in many of the old kingdoms of Europe, nation-building efforts may be traced hundreds of years back and should be seen as part of state building. Such kingdoms, I suggest, should therefore be distinguished from states that resulted from the fragmentation of empires and in which nation building was the product of nationalist movements and socially modernizing factors.

The followers of Ernest Gellner see nationalism as a product of modernization. So-called ethnosymbolists – the followers of Smith – agree that nationalism as an ideology is a modern phenomenon but argue that ideas of nationhood go back to the old kingdoms of Europe. A more controversial view, espoused by Liah Greenfeld (1992, 2006), sees modernization as a product of the rise of national awareness. Modern political nationalism thus presupposes pre-existing cultural and social identities. Greenfeld argues that, historically, the idea of the nation was always an effect of socio-political anomie; it took root among social groups who experienced a condition of "status inconsistency" in relation to elites, whether they be the aristocracy or colonial rulers. A related argument is found in Miroslav Hroch's (1968) account of the stages of nationalism. On the basis of his studies of the rise of nationalism in the empires of Central Europe, he shows how, in its first stage, nationalism took a cultural form prior to the rise of political movements. But since cultural nationalists lacked a political program, their ideas of nationhood did not have relevance to the mass population. It was not until socio-economic modernization made them relevant that they began to appeal to groups that found their social mobility hampered by existing social and political structures. In this context, the idea of the cultural nation became an instrument of political empowerment for marginalized groups in European empires who adopted the conviction that they were the legitimate inheritors of the homeland and that their own language, social values, and way of life were those of the true nation.

Cultural nationalism is a rather complex phenomenon, however, because it is connected to the process of modernization and the transition between traditional society and the values of modernity. Cultural nationalists would often use an emotional discourse characterized by a nostalgic yearning for an older and more traditional order, which had been violated by social change. But this should not be misread as a wish for social and political regression. Craig Calhoun (1997), emphasizing the discursive nature of nationalism, demonstrates how traditionalism, an ingredient of cultural nationalism, has frequently been a cover for rational political radicalism: the appeal to the tradition, language, and culture of the common people – usually the peasants – suggests that modernization caused by capitalist change threatened old social bonds and contracts. But it should not be seen as a rejection of new values and modernity as such (Calhoun 1983).

The celebration of allegedly authentic national values and traditions often reflected a resistance to the current political leadership and the way in which it administered social change. The discourse of "romantic nationalists" may thus sound irrational and motivated by fear of modernity and change, but it may, in real terms, express the demand of the rising farming middle class for a say in the governance of the new political order of their country. If change was perceived as coming from outside – from a dominant external and foreign power – this would not only make them turn towards political radicalism but also nationalism. It is in this context that N.F.S. Grundtvig should be seen: as a mediator between the values of two ages and as an intellectual who saw himself as one of the "friends" of farmers, who argued their case for membership in and moral leadership of the prospective Danish nation.

GRUNDTVIG IN BETWEEN TWO AGES

Grundtvig was fully aware of what British dominance had meant to Ireland, and he appears to have feared that Denmark might end up in a similar relation to Prussia. Like Irish nationalists, who argued that Ireland was suffering from British cultural dominance, Grundtvig was convinced that Danish culture was close to being extinguished by Germany and the "modern" culture it was imposing upon Denmark. In this section, I demonstrate this with special reference to "Overgangs-Tiden i Danmark" (The Transition Period in Denmark), an essay that Grundtvig published in *The Dane* in 1849.

Grundtvig began issuing his weekly journal, *The Dane*, from the very first week after the appointment of the new government on 22 March 1848, and he continued doing so over the following three years. It was to comprise 3,136 pages, mostly from Grundtvig's own hand. Grundtvig himself saw its purpose as saving "Danishness." He drew on his experiences and ideas from the public lectures he had given between 1838 and 1844. But he also used the journal to clarify thoughts that so far had been rather dim (not only to himself but also to others) about the nature of peoplehood and nationality, and the significance of expressing oneself in the vernacular (Lundgreen-Nielsen 1992). It was as a promoter of the mother tongue that, six months after the first issue, Grundtvig announced his candidacy for Parliament at a by-election in Præstø. His political candidacy was thus closely linked to his claim to be an interpreter of the peasant voice.

When Grundtvig decided to run for the election in his native town in November 1848, he did not see a strictly political role for himself. And he knew that many voters would wonder about it. "What will N.F.S. Grundtvig do in Parliament?" and "why did he want to be elected in Præstø and not Copenhagen where he had his home?" were the questions he was asked before the election. He admitted that he was driven neither by desire nor by honour. What he wanted was to represent "a Danish word in Parliament." The new assembly needed someone like him – someone who could and would, as he claimed, "dare" speak the language of the ordinary people. The very use of the term "Constitution" for "basic law" (*grundlov*) was, to Grundtvig, a dire forewarning of how a new dominant and paternalist "estate," consisting of public officials and their servants, threatened, first, to take power from the king; second, to limit the "Nordic spirit" of freedom; and third, to continue, with their abstract concepts and formal language (which he regarded as foreign to the true Danish nation), the repression of the ancient oral tradition of the common people. No matter the number of rights encoded in this Constitution, it would invariably lead to spiritual and cultural bondage. However "sensible" they might be, the new democratic institutions – general suffrage, an elected legislature, and responsible government – were inadequate guardians of the "popular spirit." This is because democracy presupposed "a common, progressive enlightenment about the conditions of human life in general and about the conditions of Danish popular life and the fatherland in particular." This kind of enlightenment, however, could only succeed if both "mouth and pen" were given unrestrained freedom. The "freedom of the word" depended on people's ability to speak their minds in their own mother tongue (Grundtvig 1848, 298–9).

The vernacular was thus vital to Grundtvig's "Danish cause." It was the vehicle of "enlightenment" and the "freedom of the [people's] heart," which was to put an end to the hegemony and paternalism of the state and replace it with the "hegemony of the people's spirit" (Grundtvig 1849, 323–4).

Grundtvig begins his essay by arguing that the "liberty of the word" – that is, freedom of expression – had been "tolerated" since the king's granting of a free constitution in March 1849. However, it had not been fully "admitted" (Grundtvig 1849, 322). Undoubtedly, liberty was the bright side of what had otherwise been an "excited, confused and turbulent time." But there was also a dark side: the remaining distrust in the beneficial effect of "the real freedom of the word" in the new national government and assembly (322). If this suspicion remained, he predicted, Danes would remain in chains, even if they succeeded in the ongoing war with the Germans. Only by granting freedom to the power of the "mouth and pen to express itself in the vernacular" would the "bewitchment" of "all the Nordic tribes, and especially the Danes" be lifted (323). Only through the vernacular could they be sufficiently enlightened about human life and the inner core of their life as a people to be able to rule their state. Grundtvig hoped, however, that the Danish people's deeply felt conviction of the need for this freedom would bring them through the transitional period "from death to life, from darkness to light, from night to day, from idleness to industry, from servitude to liberty, from caste system to equality in all public matters, and from secrecy to openness in all that concerns the interests of the whole and the common good!" (323). In other words, Grundtvig was worried that neither universal suffrage, nor eligibility, nor an elected assembly, nor responsible government would be enough in themselves to prevent the new system of rule from becoming the mere rule of the "raw and ignorant" masses. Even a form of responsible government, which could not be held "freely and [be] publicly accountable," would end up being carried out by "unconstitutional civil servants and paternalists of the worst and most dangerous kind" (324). However, if freedom of expression was granted, and if the people were spoken to in their own language, Grundtvig trusted that they would understand their own good and make the best out of the new conditions both in their private lives and in their roles of citizens.

To Grundtvig, "transition" was a universal phenomenon in human history – or the history of "Christendom," as he called it. It meant that history was passing from an "age of estates" to an "age of peoples." He saw this as "progress." But for progress to be achieved, it took more than electing a parliament: it took creating a people. As little as Rome could be built in one day, "as little can a whole people, even if it were born in one day, reach maturity at once" (Grundtvig 1849, 327). It required restoring the sense of peoplehood, which had been lost in the Middle Ages due to the rise of the three great estates: the clergy, the nobility, and the commoners. Grundtvig saw this rise as evidence of a Danish inferiority complex, which caused the Danes to imitate "Germans and other noble peoples" instead of trusting their own institutions and traditions (328). In Denmark – as in other parts of Europe – the estate system had made people forget their fatherland, their vernacular, and their ancient lore, indeed the very factors that constituted them as "a community with particular traits" and enabled to make "a common effort and perform great things" (329). In Denmark, where the higher estates were mostly made up of foreigners, freeholders, who had played a powerful role in medieval society, had been reduced to peasants.

As a result of social development – or "modernization," as we would call it today – new "artificial" estates had arisen and replaced the old ones: public officers, military men, businessmen – and in England also the "factory estate" – that is, industrialists ("but so far, thanks God, not in Denmark" Grundtvig [1849, 330] noted). He predicted that the old estates would ultimately disappear with the dawn of a society dominated by these new ones (e.g., officers of the army and state officers would replace the clergy). The new estates, he believed, gave no nourishment to society but, rather, appeared to lay it waste (e.g., the factory estate was "eating the soul out of people's lives" [Grudtvig 1849, 330]). So much greater was the danger of German dominance if Prussia were to win the war over the future state of the duchies, for Prussia represented the forces behind this development – the forces of modernization.

Defending Denmark against Germany was thus another way of defending the Danish vernacular and the values of the common people. Both threatened the dissolution of the kingdom and the end of the life of the people. When "the German will be our master," Danes will "in all likelihood only be allowed to speak Danish except in corners." Then they would have to accustom themselves to associating "popular" not with their own Danish "kind and inclination and sentiment" but, rather, with their "opposite" – namely, the "German," which was "foreign" and "inimical" (Grundtvig 1849, 331). If, on the other hand, Danes emerged victorious in the war for language and fatherland, the peoplehood of Danes would have "passed its test" and be able to sift the genuinely Danish from the foreign, including with regard to the "old estates." Furthermore, all the "un-Danish" aspects of the "new estates" – their "shopkeeper mentality" as well as their tyrannical and slavish elements – would be done away with without, however, forfeiting what might "serve to enlighten and straighten out Danish conditions, to protect and defend our Danish fatherland, or to promote and nourish any activity for the common good, which is beneficial in Denmark as well as in all other places" (321).

Grundtvig realized that this would require a new perception of the "people." Whereas the Danish word "people" used to be understood to refer, in a limited sense, to "the common people," it was wrong to speak of the new Parliament as though it were the embodiment of the people to whom all rights belonged. And even if the Danish people were defined as "all the estates and groups who feel and confess their commonality in birth and blood, mother tongue and fatherland, that is[,] all genuine Danes," it would be to no avail since no one would be able to tell "who they are and where they are." It would not say anything about their identity as a people. The only way they would grow into a people would be by drawing on – "pointing to" – the values and culture of the rural population. For, as Grundtvig (1849, 333) writes: "Our farmers descend from the people of old and know no other language than the mother language of the Danes." Since the farmers are "the only recognizable part of the population" that has preserved these qualities, "all the true friends of Denmark and Danishness, of fatherland and mother tongue are or ought to become decisive friends of the peasants."

The only problem was that, "although obviously the bottom layer of the Danish people and strength of the kingdom" and the potential "core around which all that pertains to peoplehood [should gather]," the farming estate had been neglected and abused for centuries by the dominating estates. For this reason, it approached the new system of government with a degree of ignorance that made it vulnerable to all kinds of new abuses. Besides, the peasants' grudge against the former estates might "tempt them to all kind of violence and justice." It was therefore important that they find "good friends among the more informed and educated compatriots" and that they have both "the humility and nobility of mind" to follow the "wise and well-intentioned advice" of such friends (Grundtvig 1849, 334). Of course, Grundtvig regarded himself as one of these friends.

As Grundtvig's essay demonstrates, in 1849 he was looking forward to the new age with both hope and trepidation. He was fully cognizant that Denmark – and the rest of Europe – stood on the verge of a new age, a modern age in which old social and economic structures would change and the former political regimes would be replaced by parliaments and constitutional governments responsible to the people, indeed, ruled by the people. The questions for him were, therefore: Who are the people? How can we avoid having the "new estates" take over the social and political power of the old estates and the monarch and thus bypass the people? What does it take to create a modern Denmark that reflects the identity and values of true Danish peoplehood?

Grundtvig's basic answer to these questions was that the social and political modernization of Denmark could only succeed if the social and cultural values of the Danish people – originating in a distant past characterized by freedom and social equality – were revived and made the basis of a new enlightened peoplehood in which individual liberty would serve the common good. For this to happen, the artificial, foreign culture that had been imposed on traditional society – with the effect of splitting people, marginalizing the farmers, and denigrating the vernacular – would have to be removed. What worried Grundtvig was that modernizing social forces might hinder Denmark's transition into the new "peoples' age." He identified these forces in the growing split between town and country, the increasing power of the centralized state bureaucracy, the formation of political parties based on social self-interests – and, not least, in the rationalism, materialism, and selfishness that he had castigated since his younger days. All these forces and social vices he regarded as foreign: as products of either French or German cultural dominance.

However, Grundtvig did not reject modernity as such; instead, he insisted upon the need to modernize Denmark on Danish terms. He saw it as his task to expound those terms. It was his task as a nation builder to make Danes masters in their own house by reminding them of their historical values and of the family-like character of their national community from time immemorial. This national community was not based on race; rather, it was a community bonded by loving devotion to fatherland and language, as he expressed it in his famous poem "*Folkeligt skal alt nu være*" (Everything will now have to be based on the people). Grundtvig was a traditionalist. But his traditionalism never took the anti-liberal character of much German nationalist thinking in this period. This may be explained not only as a result of his rejection of Fichte's ideas of German cultural and linguistic superiority but also as a result of his readings of Locke and his travels in England, which had convinced him of the virtues of Whiggish liberalism. And, not least, his Christian beliefs and his biblical view of the history of humankind prevented his philosophy of peoplehood from developing into an ethnocentric and quasi-religious nationalism.[2]

CONCLUSION

I conclude that Grundtvig should be seen as a mediator between the patriotism of the eighteenth century and the nationalism of the nineteenth century (Böss 2013). He surely regarded himself as living in an age of transition – between old and new, tradition and modernity. In this role, he contributed to the forging of an alliance between the mostly politically conservative but economically liberal class of middle farmers and the liberal urban middle class. Indeed, he saw himself as one of the so-called friends of the people (who included the more informed and educated of his compatriots from whom he urged the farmers to take advice. And because they actually did, the popular movements led by these farmers – most importantly in the form of cooperatives and the Folk High School movement inspired by Grundtvig and his followers – became highly significant in the modernization of Danish society.

Grundtvig should thus be seen as a typical cultural nationalist, as defined by John Hutchinson, mediating between the traditional social order – dominated by the estates and politically ruled by the monarch – and a new, market-oriented and increasingly more democratic order. Aware of the dangers of this social and political transition, Grundtvig warned against the social malaise and splits that modernization involved. He was also concerned that Denmark's new Constitution might lead either to mass rule or to the rule of the new privileged classes for their own gain. His solution was to recreate a lost sense of peoplehood and to replace the existing society of estates with a people's society characterized by freedom, equality, and the sense of a common good.

In *Zones of Conflict*, Hutchinson (2005) points out that nineteenth-century cultural nationalists were not always successful in reconciling the opposing interests of their own society. In many cases cultural nationalism not only led to social integration but also created "zones of conflict" and open division, especially in ethnically diverse and politically composite states. This was also what happened in the Kingdom of Denmark, and Grundtvig's campaign for Danishness – regardless of its alleged gentle and peaceful character – certainly added fire to the plan of the National Liberals to force the Germans living in the duchies into a Danish nation-state. Hence, his reconstructed concept of peoplehood should be understood within a larger geopolitical context. It demonstrates how new ideas and changing power relations in Europe not only made empires crumble but also sent intellectuals to the barricades to defend pre-political and premodern identities, which they saw as the moral core of the prospective nation-state.

NOTES

1 I concur with Tine Damsholt's and Vagn Wåhlin's interpretations (drawing on Lorenz Rerup) of Grundtvig's political development since the early 1830s. See, for example, Damsholt (1995); Rerup (1992); Wåhlin (1994).

2 Helge Grell, among many others, explains Grundtvig's rejection of nationalism as a product of his Christian faith and historical view.

REFERENCES

Birkelund, R. 2008. *Frihed til fælles bedste* [Freedom for the common good]. Aarhus: Aarhus University Press.

Böss, M. 2013. "Grundtvigs nationalisme i lyset af nationalismeteori" [The nationalism of Grundtvig in light of theories of nationalism]. In *Samfundsbyggeren* [Grundtvig as Nation Builder], ed. Ove Korsgaard and Michael Schelde, 57–87. Copenhagen: Anis.

Calhoun, C. 1983. "The Radicalism of Tradition: Community Strength or Venerable Disguise and Borrowed Language?" *American Journal of Sociology* 88: 886–914.

– 1997. *Nationalism*. Buckingham: Open University Press.

Damsholt, T. 1995. "'Jeg er en gammel Royalist, det ved De nok': Elementer i Grundtvigs politiske tækning" [I am an old Royalist, as you probably know: Grundtvig's political thought]. *Grundtvig Studier* 46: 140–62.

Greenfeld, L. 1992. *Nationalism: Five Roads to Modernity*. Cambridge, MA: Harvard University Press.

– 2006. "Nationalism and Modernity." In *Nationalism and the Mind: Essays on Modern Culture*, ed. L. Greenfeld, 64–92. Oxford: Oneworld.

Grell, H. 1988. *Skaberånd og folkeånd* [Creator spirit and spirit of the people]. Aarhus: Aarhus University Press.

– 1992. *England og Grundtvig* [England and Grundtvig]. Aarhus: Aarhus University Press.

Grundtvig, N.F.S. 1848 [1948]. "Hvad vil N.F.S. Grundtvig paa Rigsdagen" [What does N.F.S. Grundtvig want to do in the National Assembly?]. *The Dane* 1: 545–54. Reprinted in *Værker i Udvalg* [Selected works] vol. 5, 295–300. Ed. Georg Christensen and Hal Koch. Copenhagen: Gyldendalske Boghandel.

– 1849 [1948]. "Overgangsperioden i Danmark" [The transition period in Denmark], *The Dane* 2: 249–64. Reprinted in *Værker i Udvalg* [Selected works] vol. 5, 318–44. Ed. Georg Christensen and Hal Koch. Copenhagen: Gyldendalske Boghandel.

– 1924. "Nytårsdag." In *N.F.S. Grundtvigs Vartovs-prædikener* [The Vartov sermons of N.F.S. Grundtvig]. Copenhagen: Gyldendalske Boghandel.

Hroch, M. 1968. *Die Vorkämpfer der nationalen Bewegungen bei den kleinen Völkern Europas* [The champions of the nationalist movements of the small European peoples]. Prague: Universita Karlova.

Hutchinson, J. 2005. *Nations as Zones of Conflict*. London: Sage.

Kaae, L. 1986. "'Ikkun som voxne Menneske-Børn': Grundtvig og frihed" [Not only as grown-up children: Grundtvig and freedom]. In *Stykkevis og delt* [Parts and pieces], ed. T. Bekker-Nielsen, 75–122. Aarhus: Aarhus University Press.

Lundgreen-Nielsen, F. 1992. "Grundtvig og danskhed" [Grundtvig and Danishness]. In *Dansk identitetshistorie* [The history of Danish identity], vol.3, ed. O. Feldbæk, 9–187. Copenhagen: C.A. Reitzel.

O'Day, A. 1998. *Irish Home Rule, 1867–1921*. Manchester: Manchester University Press.

Rerup, L. 1992. "Folkestyre og danskhed: Massenationalisme og politik 1848–1866" [Democracy and Danishness: Mass nationalism and politics 1848–1866]. In *Dansk Identitetshistorie* [The history of Danish identity], vol. 3, ed. Ole Feldbæk. Copenhagen: C.A. Reitzel.

Smith, A.D. 1991. *National Identity*. London: Penguin.

Vind, O. 1999. *Grundtvigs historiefilosofi* [Grundtvig's philosophy of history]. Copenhagen: Gyldendal.

Wåhlin, V. 1994. "Grundtvig i politik op til 1830" [Grundtvig and politics until 1830]. *Grundtvig Studier* 45: 59–91.

– 1989–90. "Grundtvigs økonomiske tænkning" [Grundtvig's economic thinking]. *Grundtvig Studier*: 41: 246–302.

PART TWO

Enabling Conditions

4

Religious Revivalism in Sweden and Denmark

HANNE SANDERS

In modern research on society and history, it is quite common to focus on nationalism and ethnicity. For many this seems to be an important, even a natural, way to understand human life. But the question is: Has it always been as natural as it is for us? One way to discuss this is to analyze N.F.S. Grundtvig's nineteenth century, which is often seen as the formative century of nationalism. At the same time it is also a century of religious movements, or revivals, as they are often called in a Protestant context.

Grundtvig is known as one of the creators of Danish national identity, but, at the same time, he was a well-known member of the clergy and was highly active in religious life. In Grundtvig we meet religion as well as nationalism in their premodern forms. My intention is not to study Grundtvig himself but, rather, the revivalism that has been closely linked with him in the form of an idea of what is typically Danish, even though Grundtvig himself was critical of these revivals until the end of the 1830s. I studied these religious movements in my dissertation, "Bondevækkelse og sekularisering: En protestantisk folkelig kultur i Danmark og Sverige, 1820–1850," and, in order to discuss their national meaning, I compare them to Swedish revivals (Sanders 1995). In both countries, the period examined is the first half of the nineteenth century. In focusing on this specific period my intention is to analyze nationalism and religion as developing, rather than as essential, elements of culture and society. To do this I even make comparisons with the early modern (before 1800) as well as the modern (after 1850) periods.

For a long time the origin, or the essence, of nationalism has been an object of much discussion among historians the world over. Obviously, nationalism is of great importance today both in postcolonial conflicts and in European and American conflicts. Central parts of the world are comprised of national identities. Accordingly, it is natural to be curious about the history of these identities and to write about them. Commonly, people who research nationalism are divided into two groups (Kidd 1999, 1–6; Smith 1986, 7–13): (1) those who see nationalism as a modern phenomenon (dating from the nineteenth century) created in relation to such modern developments as industrialization and bourgeois culture (Anderson 1983; Gellner 1983; Hobsbawm 1990), and (2) those who see it as an older identity or as a part of human nature (Hastings 1997). Anthony D. Smith (1986) tries to make a compromise between these two viewpoints by arguing that nationalism is bound to modern time but that national culture, or ethnicity, as he calls it, is much older.

Common to these two groups is their focus on nationalism and their relative lack of interest in what appeared prior to it. If people were not "national" in the old societies, then what was the base of their identity? Looking at the beginning of the nineteenth century we can set aside this hegemonic interest in nationalism and, instead, search for alternatives (Korsgaard 2007).

TWO NATIONAL NARRATIVES OF REVIVALISM

Around 1800, both Denmark and Sweden had strong Lutheran state churches that had developed as a part of state building. Accordingly, revivals in the first half of the nineteenth century expressed a Lutheran culture. At the same time, they opposed the dominance of the State church in both countries. The nineteenth century was a period of increasing modernization, in economics as well as in politics, and the result was a liberal democracy and an expanding commerce based on agrarian and industrial products. Because of this development there are great differences between religious revivalism at the beginning of the century and that at the end. My focus is on the period before liberal constitutions appeared in Denmark and Sweden (1849 and 1866).

In Denmark, religious revivalism in the early nineteenth century occurs within a narrative of modernization (Bjørn 2003 [1990]; Lindhardt 1978). Around 1800 and following decades, Danish society developed radically from feudal and absolutistic to, with a new constitution in 1849, liberal and democratic. Religious revivalism among peasants is often analyzed as a way for them to take power from the state church and give it to ordinary people. It is a religious form of individualism and is parallel to the economic and political individualism of this time. The main form of Danish revivalism consists of religious meetings in ordinary person's houses, led by the laity and not by the clergy. These meetings are referred to as conventicles. Grundtvig opposed these, yet some of the revivalists joined the Grundtvigian movement (others, of course, made different choices). This popular revivalism, especially given its contact with Grundtvig, is seen as particular to Danish modernization. It developed within the church.

In Sweden, on the other hand, it is commonly stated that, before 1850, there were no such revivals (or at least they were not that important); they did not become common until the late nineteenth century (Hedenborg and Kvarnström 2006; Lundkvist 1977; Stråht 2012). When speaking of revivalism, Swedes often refer to free churches – that is, churches organized independently of the state church. In the Swedish context these religious organizations are compared to two other important organizations: the labour movement and the temperance movement. The descriptions are almost identical for all of them. Together they form a narrative of modernization, but quite a different one from what we see in Denmark. Sweden's is a social democratic narrative, with its main focus being on popular organizations that exist outside of the church and that organize modern groups of people (e.g., workers). In comparison with the Swedish narrative, the Danish narrative is more classically liberal, and it focuses on agrarian development and on a church and culture that are older than social democratic ideas (Sanders 2006).

REVIVALISM IN DENMARK AND SWEDEN BEFORE 1850

Obviously, with regard to revivalism, the two foregoing narratives of modernization do not refer to the same things. In my research I focus on the first half of the nineteenth century and ask whether or not we would find revivalism, in its Danish form, in Sweden before 1850? Is it possible that the contention that there were no revivals in Sweden before 1850 can be explained by the fact that we have been searching for other phenomena? And, indeed, I did find instances of revivalism. They were unknown because they did not match the needs of the social democratic narrative. At the same time, they were not identical to Danish revivals. Taken together, the revivals in Denmark and Sweden make it possible to present a picture of revivalism that is not national in its foundation but, rather, religious – or, perhaps more accurately, Protestant – and thus a part of a more traditional society.

First, it is important to underline that revivalism is about religion; second, that it creates conflicts; and third, that it is a social phenomenon created by a community of people, not by an individual or a theological phenomenon. It is possible to see a pattern in revivalism. It emanates from the official religious worldview, which was built on the conviction that there is only one correct understanding of the true word of God. It allows no possibility for personal interpretation. The clergy were the only ones who had the ability to understand and to present this word, and different members of the clergy could not have different ways of reading and interpreting the Bible: there was only one way. Religion was the basis of culture and knowledge, not a matter of individual belief. In order to better understand this I define secularization as religion's transition from being the basis of culture and knowledge to its being a matter of individual belief, which is our modern way of seeing it.

All types of revivals challenged the official religious worldview, but they did it to different degrees. In Sweden many revivals were led by members of the clergy whose only challenge to authority was to ask that they be able to offer different choices, while maintaining their status as the only ones who could interpret the word of God. The challenge to the clergy's monopoly on preaching came from the conventicle revivals, where people met in ordinary homes and had ordinary men as preachers. This type of revivalism can be found in both Denmark and Sweden, but it was stronger in Denmark and included a critique not only of clergy but also of teachers, who, it was held, did not properly teach children about religion. A still greater challenge was presented by those revivalists who tried to take over the role of administering the sacraments. The greatest challenge of all, however, was posed by those who tried to abandon the official church and to create free churches. This last challenge was not found before 1850. Most common were the first two challenges – revivals led by the clergy and conventicle revivals – and these are the topic of my investigation.

There are common elements in these revivals, and a very important one is a shared religious worldview. I have found that, in both Denmark and Sweden, revivalists used three types of argument. First, they all used the Bible to authorize their provocative activities. In describing their everyday life, they made liberal use of biblical quotations. They thought of the words of Jesus as words said to the revivalists and of the activities of the apostles as their own activities. According to the revivalists, the eternally true word of God was to be found in the Bible. This being the case, everybody should be able to read and use the Bible, and, therefore, there was no reason to maintain a clerical monopoly. This dependence on the Bible was fundamental to Protestant ideology. The supporters of revivalism built their arguments on a common and essentially Protestant basis. At the same time, the Bible gave them useful roles to follow with regard to their individual provocative behaviour.

The second argument used by revivalists in both Sweden and Denmark was that they did what they had to do to secure their salvation. Behind this argument lay a dualist worldview, with a clear conflict between God and the Devil. Revivalists fought for people's souls. Every person belonged to either God or the Devil, and everything could be explained as deriving either from God or from the Devil. Between these two powerful forces, there was little place for individual human influence. In order to avoid hell, all you could do was to give yourself to God and believe in "Him." Again, this is a very basic Protestant idea and again it is at the heart of the revivalists' argument. It could be claimed that this idea did not motivate the revivalists to act but just to believe. However, it did motivate them to act. Similar to Weber's idea of the importance of the Protestant ethic to capitalism, my research indicates that these people acted not in order to be saved but, rather, in order to show that they belonged to the people of God, to the Blessed.

The last argument used by revivalists in Sweden and Denmark is that they behaved in a manner only to be expected from Christian subjects of a Christian state. Again, in a very Protestant way and through the use of biblical quotations, they anxiously expressed their acceptance of the authorities appointed by God. They used an argument popular during the Reformation: one should render to God what is God's, and to the emperor what is the emperor's. In earlier times, the second phrase had been the important one; now they stressed the first. The secular authorities only had the right to demand what was theirs, and this did not include the relations between the revivalists and God.

The provocative nature of revivalism did not originate in its traditional elements but, rather, in its modern and secularized elements. Their fundamental belief was that the individual had the right to decide his or her own religious life. People were to read the Bible and then determine for themselves what was right and what was wrong. Revivalists asserted that individual salvation was a matter only for the individual. Although it is possible to contrast these beliefs with the traditional beliefs, it seems to me that they are bound up with each other. Revivalism got the strength to make a distinctive contribution to the modern, secularized concept of religion by stressing the traditional elements in the religious world picture. God's word was the best safety net that one could wish for. In this fundamentalist and dualist conception of the world, the revivalists were more traditional than were many of their opponents, but they used Protestantism in their own way, and this is what created conflict. I call this revivalist movement a form of popular Protestant culture typical of the first half of the nineteenth century, and its dynamic is the interplay between traditional and modern elements. Revivalists lived in a time full of change, and they cried, "Stop!" But this kind of modern individualism required the backing of a traditional power, and their combination was enough to give revivalists an important role in how modernization unfolded in Scandinavia.

It is not only when examining the purpose and the worldview of the revivalists that one finds this interplay between tradition and modernity. It is important to emphasize that these revivals were not organized in a modern way. There was no formal organization, or popular movement, that included all of the country: there was nothing of which to be a member. The revivalist movements centred on the relationship between a speaker and his or her listeners, and this relationship existed only during a religious ceremony. It could be the clergyman's service in the church or the lay preacher and his conventicle in an ordinary house. Relations between the revivalists were emotional. The arguments for fomenting a religious struggle involved individual needs and emotions. Viewed this way, we can see these revivals as part of a bourgeois political culture, stemming from the individual principle of one person, one voice.

In order to get closer to how revivalism was organized, I examine how it was spread. This is important because one does not find revivalist movements all over Denmark and Sweden. As mentioend, they do not involve a national or all-inclusive organization. In Sweden we find revivalists in the western part of the country; in Denmark, we find them on the islands. And religious ceremonies did not create conflicts in all of these areas.

Two elements of revivalism were important: speakers/preachers and peasants. Wherever the speaker or preacher went it was possible to see a revival because he brought it with him. Although it is possible to look at the speaker as a charismatic leader, this does not explain everything. If we examine the revivalist members of the clergy in Sweden, we see that they opposed other clergy's interpretations of the Bible and their propensity to decide when people should take the Sacrament. Revivalists believed that one should take it when one had a personal need for it, and this was not something that could be decided by the church. For the pre-secularized church, when to take the Sacrament was a matter of knowledge, not personal need. And it was thought that twice a year was enough. Even if these rebellious members of the clergy, for whom people walked long distances every Sunday, were unpopular among their colleagues, they had clerical authority and they used it. The problem was not the church but, rather, that the actions of its clergy were contrary to what the revivalists thought was right. A main feature of these revivalist movements was conflict over the election of local clergy. In other words, it was an old organization whose old authority gave power to this type of revivalism.

The other important part of the revivalist movements, concerns the network of involved peasants: neighbours, families, and agrarian households. Among Danish historians it has been important to decide whether the revivalists came from the freeholders or the poorest members of the agrarian population or whether there was a conflict between generations (Bjørn 2003 [1990]: 213–22; Clausen, 1965–68; Lindhardt 1978; Pontoppidan Thyssen 1967). I cannot find any conflict, whether having to do with freeholding or with age, in the material on the agrarian population. I suspect that this is a line of argument that would be relevant to a modern society. What I did find is that the agrarian household itself was important. If someone in a household became a revivalist, then everyone did: men and women, young and old, parents and children. Revivalism often spread through young people taking it from their own family to the household in which they served, or vice versa.

The household is important not only to explaining why people became a part of the revivalist movements but also to understanding how they were organized. It was in these agrarian households that the ceremonies were held. The conventicle was a type of *husandagt*, and, during the eighteenth century, these ceremonies were part of religious life in both Denmark and Sweden. Accordingly, the organization of the conventicle was taken from the old church, but it was taken from the agrarian economy and culture as well. Agrarian production was carried out in the household, and the household was the centre of local political culture. The leader of the household had a responsibility to everyone in this little community. In order to understand the specifics of these revivalist movements, I refer to them as "household revivalist movements." In doing so I underline once again the importance of old organizational structures to understanding the power of revivalism before 1850 – that is, before the birth of modern popular movements.

In order to be effective, it was crucial that these households be powerful, not small or poor. What was not crucial was whether or not the agrarian leader owned his land. The importance of being a freeholder may be relevant to a modern capitalist society; however, at the beginning of the nineteenth century it was local power and the size of production that mattered. Areas with revivalist movements showed a strong agrarian economy, with strong actors.

Even though there were national movements in urban areas as well as among a political elite in the nineteenth century (Bjørn 2003 [1990]; Feldbæk 1991; Stråht 2012; Vammen 1988), I conclude that, in the first half of the nineteenth century, nationalism was not relevant to the important revivalist movements among ordinary people. What *was* important was a religious identity – Protestantism. And it should be noted that differences between national types of Protestantism were not important. Revivalism was a part of Protestant culture, and national differences were not as important at the local level as has been claimed. If we examine the differences inside this Protestant culture, we find that they were regionally defined and dependent upon social differences and social structures, such as strong agrarian households. Revivalists were part of the development of modernization, but in a very particular way. According to them, they were against modernization, and they utilized a powerful traditional worldview as well as a traditional social structure. But it was their individual protest that expressed the modern, and this protest was made in a religious, Protestant way that had relevance for people who lived in a Protestant, not a nationalist, culture.

DIFFERENT DEVELOPMENTS AFTER 1850

With regard to revivalism, it is possible to see some differences between Denmark and Sweden, and these are of importance for the period after 1850. The conflicted nature of revivalism was more pronounced in Denmark than it was in Sweden. There were no revivals led by clergy, and the conventicle revivals were more aggressive, more widespread, and included criticism of the teacher. This is probably because, in the non-absolutist and much less feudal Swedish society, the peasants had the right to choose their clergy. They had a developed local political culture and they used it. In Denmark, revivalism was part of a great transition from an absolutist and feudal society into a modern bourgeois society, which was completed with the Constitution of 1849, which included a form of religious freedom. In Sweden, on the other hand, the democratic Constitution of 1866 did not include religious freedom. In fact, it was not until 1951 that religious freedom was formally implemented in Sweden.

Generally, Swedish society was more modern than Danish society during the first half of the nineteenth century (although not in religious matters). Because of this, revivalists in Sweden did not exacerbate the conflicts associated with revivalism or interact with other social movements. After 1849, Danish society was more tolerant, or modern, than Swedish society. In the field of religion the new Constitution created a *folkekirke* – that is, a church organization based on the interests of the people. It was still a state church, but it had various ways of accepting religious freedom. Therefore, most people stayed in the old church, which really did become the church of the Danish people. It was part of a general democratization of society that included, for example, a parliament of the people.

In Sweden, during the second half of the nineteenth century, the church was broken up and lots of free churches were created. There was no successful *folkekirke*, as in Denmark. It was not until the social democratic period that a *folkekirke* actually came into being, at which time it was a part of the creation of the so-called *folkhem* – the Swedish welfare state – and politicians saw the possibility of utilizing the power of the church to formulate and spread moral values. The dogmatic aspect of the church was therefore not as important as the moralistic aspect (Claesson 2004). Being a good human being was the focus, and it was easy to connect this idea with the ecumenical ideas already popular in Sweden. The purpose of the church was to teach people to be good human beings. In Denmark, on the other hand, it was, and is, of considerable importance that the Danish church is Protestant. This mattered greatly when these two *folkekirker* were created, in the middle of the nineteenth century and in the beginning of the twentieth century, respectively (Claesson 2004; Sanders 2006).

This explains the differences between the two narratives of revivalism. It is said that it is the winner who writes history, and in Sweden the concept of the social democrats won, whereas in Denmark the concept of nineteenth-century liberalism, with its focus on religion, bourgeois culture, and bourgeois democracy, won. The narratives of revivalism are the history of these two concepts (Bjørn 2003 [1990]; Hedenborg and Kvarnström 2006; Stråht 2012).

It is now possible to evaluate some ideas about the differences between being Danish and being Swedish today. In Denmark, the national identity is a creation of the nineteenth century, and the focus is on classical elements such as language, culture, traditions. In Sweden, the national identity is a creation of the twentieth century, and there is less focus on such classical elements and more on being good, on being moral. In a way this may be seen to be inspired by the Enlightenment, but, indeed, it is a product of modern social democratic ideas and, perhaps, of natural sciences as well (Sanders 2006).

The impact of nationalism today depends on when it was developed: in the nineteenth century or in the twentieth. Again, this shows the variation of the modern notion of nationalism and how it was dependent on the non-nationalist first part of the nineteenth century, the period of revivalism.

RELATIONS BETWEEN RELIGION AND NATIONALISM: N.F.S. GRUNDTVIG AND PEDER WINSTRUP

The revivalism of the first half of the nineteenth century is, as I have argued, not to be understood in nationalist but, rather, in religious terms. I want to trace the relation between nationalism and religion to two important churchmen: Bishop Peder Winstrup, who lived in the seventeenth century and was active in Denmark as well as in Sweden, and N.F.S. Grundtvig, the main focus of this book.

Peder Winstrup was bishop when Scania became Swedish in 1658. The history of this transition has often been written as nationalist history, involving conflicts between Danes and Swedes and resulting in a "swedification." If you really want to examine the relationship between religion and nationalism, it is interesting to see how Peder Winstrup explained this shift of state. He was not happy about it as he had been a keen civil servant of the Danish king. He explained the new condition as God's punishment for the sinful lives lived in Denmark and, especially, in Scania. It was simply a matter of accepting this punishment and making the best of it. He emphasized that it was a good thing that the Swedish king, like the Danish king, was Protestant. He wrote about the Danish people and the Swedish people, likening them to the people of Israel: they all acted in relation to God, as his tools. Peace as well as war came from God. This is not a narrative about two states or about two national cultures. What was most important to Winstrup – always – was the Protestant base and the relation to God (Sanders 2001, 2008).

It is also interesting to trace the ideas of nationalism and religion to N.F.S. Grundtvig's historical writings about the Danish people. Here we may be led by the ideas of Colin Kidd (1999; Vind 1999). For Kidd it is crucial to show that ideas about peoples are neither new nor fundamentally national. They existed within, and were born from, a religious, or biblical, worldview. It is crucial to realize that this religious notion of "people" is not the notion we have today. In the religious view, different peoples are not against each other; rather, they are integral parts of the same history, from Adam and Eve to the end of the world. They all correspond to God. This is exactly what we see in the historical narratives of Grundtvig. The Danes and the Swedes had different places in history. And that is why it was easy for Grundtvig to talk about the Nordic people long before the five Nordic countries were defined. They were a people among others, not against others. In Kidd's words, what we see is a differentiation among peoples, which is something very different from the modern, national notion of people, which underlines the differences between peoples, thus making it impossible to be members of more than one people at a time.

For both Peder Winstrup and N.F.S. Grundtvig, in the middle of the seventeenth century as well as at the beginning of the nineteenth century, the meaning of "people" was religious. It is possible to follow this religious meaning to a more nationalist meaning, and for Grundtvig this was a serious issue. I will not attempt to say when the religious worldview changed into a nationalist worldview, but I want to underline that the impact of this change, among others, included the church and religion being made secondary to the nation.

NATIONALISM AFTER 1850

When we follow Grundtvig until the end of his life, it is obvious that he developed nationalist ideas that remain an important part of the Danish identity today. But what happens if we try to follow ordinary people? When do they express nationalist ideas? Inspired by Peter Sahlins's (1989) work on the development of Spanish and French identity around the border in the Pyrenees, I look for the meaning of nationalism in the everyday life of people living near the border between Denmark and Sweden, around Øresund. I have examined a Swedish newspaper from four different years – 1895, 1935, 1965, and 2005 – analyzing what was considered Danish and what the newspaper felt was happening in the Danish capital over this period of time (Sanders 2007).

In 2005, nationalist descriptions and nationalist differences formed a main part of how Danish people were characterized. This is interesting, but it is even more interesting when compared to what one finds in the other years. In the newspapers from 1895 and 1935, there is no trace of this nationalism but, rather, a developed market for goods and labours (this is obvious from numerous advertisements). At the same time, such signs of a common market are not found in 1965 or, indeed, in 2005. In 1935, one even finds a common market for culture and sport, which are normally considered to be two main elements of modern nationalism. This was clearly not the case in 1935. One sees interests in Danish culture (e.g., literature, theatre), with no mention that it is Danish, as such, but only that it is culture. And you see many examples of cooperation and competition between different types of sports. It was not Danes against Swedes but, for example, someone from the town of Malmö against someone from the town of Helsingør. The 1930s is often viewed as a very nationalist decade, but in everyday life around Øresund it was not, especially when compared with 2005.

It is interesting that, even if people were conscious of being Danish (and they could well have been), this had little relevance when they tried to fulfill their everyday need for food, clothes, culture, work, and so on. After the Second World War it is quite different. The border is closed and one looks within the state to fulfill one's needs. And when one talks about the other side of the border, one is talking about something different, something Danish. This is typical for 1965 and 2005; however, in 1965 one also finds an idea that emphasizes common elements between Danish and Swedish – the idea of the Nordic. In 2005, even this has gone: only national stereotypes and differences remain when one tries to understand what one sees upon crossing the border. The time of globalization is perhaps the most nationalist time in history.

CONCLUSIONS

The purpose of this chapter is to discuss national identity and national historiography from the perspective of revivalism in the first half of the nineteenth century in Denmark and Sweden. I present an alternative to nationalism as the basis of society's worldview, and that alternative is religion. From my research on revivalism, it is obvious that the role of Protestantism was vital to understanding the strength of this popular movement. It was the interplay between traditional and modern religious elements that made the peasants important actors in the process of modernization in both Denmark and Sweden. It is not necessary to look for national differences between these revivals in order to explain them: they can be seen as variations of a Protestant commitment.

My wish to avoid the modern (mis)understanding of an older society is further developed in the examination of how revivalist movements were organized. They were popular *household* movements built on traditional structures; they were not *modern* popular movements. Furthermore, they were tied to an agrarian economy and culture.

I follow the relationship between religion and nationalism from the middle of the seventeenth century until modern times, from the clergy to ordinary people, all with the purpose of discussing the meaning and the extent of nationalism. In the religious worldview expressed by Winstrup and Grundtvig, the idea of a people has religious connotations, expressing differentiation within the same religious history. From a modern perspective, the differences between peoples are important, and church and religion are secondary to nationalism.

At the same time, it is important to show that it is not necessarily true that nationalism has meaning for ordinary people simply because the elite write about it. When, around Øresund, one follows the movements of ordinary people across the border between Denmark and Sweden, one does not find nationalism until after the Second World War. And it has never been as strong and hegemonic as during our era of globalization.

Last, I show the differences between these modern national identities by comparing those of Denmark and Sweden. In Denmark, nationalism dated from the nineteenth century and had a traditional, cultural form, whereas in Sweden it dated from the twentieth century and was more modern, moralistic, and social democratic. This becomes particularly obvious when studying the narratives of revivalism from the first half of the nineteenth century. In Denmark these revivalist movements are seen as part of modernization, in Sweden they are not.

Religious revivalism in the first half of the nineteenth century existed in both countries and was part of the modernization process, but in Denmark its development was most intense in the middle of the nineteenth century. For both countries it is important to realize that revivalist movements occurred during a time of history when religious cultures, and not national movements, were dominant and that even the former contributed to the building of modern society. This underlines the modernity of nationalism, and it gives us a reason to complement the history of identities with identities other than nationalism and to search for the different ways in which nationalism has developed.

REFERENCES

Anderson, B. 1983. *Imagined Communities*. London: Verso.

Bjørn, C. 2003 [1990]. *Gyldendal og Politikens Danmarkshistorie bd 10: Fra reaktion til grundlov, 1800–1850* [The history of Denmark. Vol 10: From reaction to constitution, 1800–1850]. Copenhagen: Gyldendal and Politiken.

Claesson, U. 2004. *Folkhemmets kyrka: Harald Hallén och folkkyrkans genombrott – En studie i Socialdemokrati, kyrka och nationsbygge med särskilt hänsyn till perioden, 1905–1933*, [The church of the people's society: Harald Hallén and the national church breakthrough – A study in social democracy, church and nation building with particular attention to the period 1905–1933]. Uppsala: Acta Universitatis Upsaliensis.

Clausen, H.P. 1965. "Den sociale problemstilling ved udforskningen af de gudelige vækkelser" [The social issue in the exploration of the spiritual revivals]. *Kirkehistoriske Samlinger* [Church history collections] 1965–68: 137–67.

Feldbæk, O., ed. 1991. *Dansk Identitetshistorie 2. Et yndigt land, 1789–1848* [The history of Danish identity II. A lovely country, 1789–1848]. Copenhagen: C.A. Reitzel.

Gellner, E. 1983. *Nations and Nationalism.* Oxford: Blackwell.

Hastings, A. 1997. *The Construction of Nationhood: Ethnicity, Religion and Nationalism*. Cambridge: Cambridge University Press.

Hedenborg S., and L. Kvarnström. 2006. *Det svenska samhället 1720–2000, böndernas och arbetarnas tid* 2 uppl [Swedish Society, 1720–2000, the era of peasants and workers]. Lund: Studentlitteratur.

Hobsbawm, E.J. 1990 *Nations and Nationalism since 1780*. Cambridge: Cambridge University Press.

Kidd, C. 1999. *British Identities before Nationalism. Ethnicity and Nationhood in the Atlantic World 1600–1800*. Cambridge: Cambridge University Press.

Korsgaard , O. 2007. "Hvad fortæller ordbøgerne?" [What do the dictionaries tell us?]. *Nord Nytt* [North news] 102: 17–29.

Lindhardt, P.G. 1978. *Vækkelse og kirkelige retninger* [Revival and church movements], 3rd ed. Aarhus: Hans Reitzel.

Lundkvist, S. 1977. *Folkrörelserna och det svenska samhället, 1850–1920* [Popular movements and Swedish society, 1850–1920]. Stockholm: Almqvist och Wiksell.

Pontoppidan Thyssen, A. 1967. "De religiösa folkrörelserna och samhället ca. 1750–1850, Danmark" [Religious social movements and society ca. 1750–1850m Denmark]. Nordiska Historikermötet, Bd. 1 [The Nordic historians' meeting, vol. 1], 7–38. Helsingfors: Suomen Historiallinen Seura-Finska Historiska Samfundet.

Sahlins, P. 1989. *Boundaries. The Making of France and Spain in the Pyrenees.* Berkeley: University of California Press.

Sanders, H. 1995. *Bondevækkelse og sekularisering: En protestantisk folkelig kultur i Danmark og Sverige, 1820–1850* [The peasant revival and secularization: A Protestant popular culture in Denmark and Sweden, 1820–1850]. Stockholm: Stads-och kommunhistoriska institutet [Institute of Urban History].

– 2001. "Religiøst eller nationalt verdensbillede? Skåne efter overgangen til Sverige i 1658" [Religious or national worldview? Skåne being part of Sweden in 1658]. In *Mellem Gud og Djævelen: Religiøse og magiske verdensbilleder i Norden, 1500–1800* [Between God and the Devil: Religious or magical worldviews in the Nordic countries, 1500–1800], 231–52. Copenhagen: Nordisk Råd.

– 2006. *Nyfiken på Danmark – klokare på Sverige* [Curious about Denmark – Wiser on Sweden]. Göteborg and Stockholm: Makadam.

– 2007. "Øresundsregionen i avisen: Danmark i Sydsvenska Dagbladet, 1895–2005" [The Sound region in the newspaper: Denmark in Sydsvenska, 1895–2005]. In *Öresundsgränser: Rörelser, möten och visioner i tid och rum* [The limits of the Sound: Movements, meetings and visions in time and space], ed. F. Nilsson, H. Sanders, and Y. Stubbergaard, 179–220. Göteborg and Stockholm: Makadam.

– 2008. *Efter Roskildefreden 1658: Skånelandskapen och Sverige i krig och fred* [After the peace of Roskilde in 1658: The Skåne provinces and Sweden in war and peace]. Göteborg: Makadam.

Smith, A. D. 1986. *The Ethnic Origins of Nations.* Oxford: Wiley Blackwell.

Stråht, B. 2012. *Sveriges historia, 1830–1920* [History of Sweden, 1830–1920]. Stockholm: Norstedts.

Vammen, H. 1988. "Casino 1848." *Historisk Tidsskrift* [Historic journal] 88: 253–81.

Vind, O. 1999. *Grundtvigs historiefilosofi* [Grundtvig's philosophy of history]. Copenhagen: Gyldendal.

5

The Nation as Event: The Dissolution of the Oldenburg Monarchy and Grundtvig's Nationalism

UFFE ØSTERGÅRD

The Danish theologian, poet, educational, and political thinker Nikolaj Frederik Severin Grundtvig lived a very long and productive life from 1783 to 1872. In this long life, he not only witnessed enormous changes in his own society and state but also lived through the intellectual periods of the Enlightenment and romanticism, both of which left a deep imprint on his thinking. He is the single person most responsible for the national culture and political thinking that came to characterize the Denmark of the late nineteenth and twentieth centuries. It may even be argued that he still plays a dominant role in the national and social thinking of the globalized inhabitants of Denmark today, even when they operate as relatively successful managers in transnational companies all over the world. He certainly was the most influential national thinker of his day and may even be considered the most prominent Danish nation builder, even though he never accepted the loosely organized movement, or, rather, intellectual hegemony, that came to bear his name: Grundtvigism (in Danish *Grundtvigianisme*).

When he was born in 1783, it was only a decade after a revolutionizing episode in the long life of the Oldenburg Monarchy. In 1772, the state experienced the end of Johan Friedrich Struensee's short-lived attempt to revolutionize the Danish-Norwegian monarchy from the top down, using his privileged position as physician for the weak and insane absolutist king Christian VII, and to introduce a whole series of radical reforms recommended by enlightened philosophers. His reforms quickly came into disrepute, and when he was exposed as the queen's secret lover he was arrested and subsequently executed in February 1772. Struensee's well-intended reform regimen was perceived as despotic by the majority of the population, and anti-German sentiments exploded. Struensee's sixteen months in power thus marked a turning point in the relations between Danish and German speakers in the multilingual state. Before Struensee, Germans had been criticized because they were foreigners who occupied positions that "rightfully" belonged to Danish-speaking inhabitants of the realm. After his aborted revolution, these people were criticized simply because they were Germans – that is, not Danish (Feldbæk 1992, 87). The feelings of the time may be summarized in the sentence "all our troubles are German," which the poet Johannes Ewald (1743–81) let one of his protagonists utter in a play written in 1772 (Christiansen 1988, 163).

Struensee's attempt at an enlightened revolution was followed by a "national" reaction under the rule of a commoner, a professor of history, Ove Høegh-Guldberg (1731–1808) from Sorø Academy. He initiated a different form of change in the absolutist monarchy with the introduction of a "patriotic" ideology for the whole of the far-stretched realm. When the new government took over in 1772 it immediately made it clear that it would tolerate no public debate that might lead to civil disturbances. In February, the government let the king ordain that, in the future, the government should be composed of men "who knew the laws and institutions of the country," that "the administration of Denmark and Norway should be conducted in Danish," and that "Danish should succeed German as the language of command in the army" (Feldbæk 1992, 87). For the first time since 1660 the council of the king was now composed of men born within the realm – four Danes and a Holsteinian born in the king's part of Holstein. An ordinance of 1775 decreed that "boys should be taught Danish in order to write it fluently and that they should be taught the history of their country and be imbued with love of the fatherland."

On top of this, in 1776 the government passed a law reserving government jobs for those born inside the realm, the so-called "Law of Indigenous Rights" (*Indfødsret*). Such a law was unique in *ancien régime* Europe, and it was backed by a whole series of well-meant – but, as it turned out, futile – attempts to build a common patriotic feeling for the realm in general and for the king in particular. Examples of this ideological enterprise are the publication in 1776 of Peter Suhm's "History of Denmark, Norway and Holstein" and Ove Malling's "Lives of Eminent Danes, Norwegians and Holsteinians" in 1777, written in the tradition of Plutarch and meant to be taught in the Grammar Schools (*Latinskoler*). However, whether this program was an expression of Danish nationalism, as claimed by Ole Feldbæk in a major investigation of Danish identity, is debatable (Feldbæk 1991–92). Upon a closer look, the program involved a deliberate attempt to install a kind of "patriotism from above" that was intended to unify the three peoples of the realm, as demonstrated by Tine Damsholt (2000) in a convincing analysis of "love of the fatherland" during this period.

This attempt to roll back enlightened reforms and replace them with a "patriotic" ideology for the whole of the composite state provoked, in its turn, a virtual revolution from above. This revolution was led by the young heir to the throne, the son of the insane king Christian VII, Crown Prince Frederik, who, only in 1808, on the death of his father, was crowned King Frederik VI. On 14 April 1784 he carried out a peaceful coup d'état in alliance with a group of primarily German-speaking aristocrats who had lost influence under the former "patriotic" regime from 1772 to 1784. At the very first meeting of the royal council, which Crown Prince Frederik attended after having reached the age of sixteen, he persuaded his father to dismiss the prior cabinet and to grant him the reins of government. The former ministers were caught completely off guard and put up no resistance. The young prince was not educationally well prepared for the task as absolutist ruler, but he had the good luck to have a gifted group of advisers. They were headed by the minister of foreign affairs, Count Andreas Peter Bernstorff (1735–97), and the minister of finance and trade, Count Ernst Schimmelmann (1747–1831). Both men followed illustrious German-born predecessors, bearing the same family names – an uncle and a father, respectively. They were joined by Count Christian Ditlev Reventlow (1748–1827), who had influential relatives in Holstein, and the Norwegian lawyer Christian Colbiørnsen (1749–1814).

With the exception of Colbiørnsen, these were all noble landowners, among the biggest in the country. Yet they immediately set off to follow up earlier endeavours to reform the agriculture that had been discussed in learned journals from 1757 onwards. Andreas Peter Bernstorff and Christian Ditlev Reventlow chaired the "Great Land Commission" with Colbiørnsen as secretary from 1786. The commission worked with unprecedented speed and immediately effected a series of measures that were eventually to grant the Danish peasants as much personal freedom as their English counterparts but that also offered better protection against economic exploitation and thus prepared the way for the rise of the peasant farmers in the nineteenth century. First, in 1786 and 1787, landlords were deprived of their right to impose degrading punishments on their tenants, such as riding the "wooden horse," and tenants were granted the right to economic compensation for improvements they had made should they be evicted from their plots (Bjørn 1977). In 1788, the Danish equivalent of serfdom, the so-called *Stavnsbånd*, was abolished. Literally, *Stavnsbånd* means "adscription."

It was a peculiar form of servitude enforced by the state on the tenant peasants that had come into existence as late as 1733 in order to secure soldiers for the army. Serfdom in the East-Elbian sense never made it further north than Holstein, but the *Stavnsbånd* came close. It was to be terminated in stages, which would leave all peasants completely free by 1800; however, from the beginning, 1788 was seen as the point of no return for the agrarian reforms in particular and for the whole complex of reforms in general. Lately, the degree of servitude under the *Stavnsbånd* has been questioned by Danish historians, and the intention of the legislation seems primarily to have been to secure peasant recruits to supplement the mercenary army mainly recruited in German states, with adscription of peasants from the Danish core lands (Holmgaard 1999). Yet, the abolition of the *Stavnsbånd* and the many other reforms then and later took on a symbolic importance that was to have a profound impact on the subsequent development of Danish society and the peculiar form of nation building, based on the peasant farmers, that characterized the rump state after 1864 (Østergård 2006).

The Agrarian reforms of 1784–88 and 1793–96, which also implied a break-up of the age-old communal villages, were followed by a thorough overhaul of the legal system in the spirit of the Italian legal theorist Cesare di Beccaria (1738–1794), bearing the unmistakable imprint of Christian Colbiørnsen. Legal processes were rationalized and prison conditions improved. A regular system of poor relief was instituted, financed by compulsory contributions from the peasants under the supervision of the priests in their capacity as local representatives of the state. The king was head of the church in this Lutheran country since the Reformation in 1536 (Østergård 2011b). The system worked relatively well until the middle of the nineteenth century, when the peasant farmers, as a result of democratization, took over local government and subsequently cut down on poor relief. A liberal tariff abolishing many import prohibitions was introduced in 1797, and the corn trade was liberalized. In 1792, Ernst Schimmelmann took steps to end the slave trade in the Danish West Indies, which Denmark finally abolished in 1803, the first country in the world to do so. However, because of intransigent resistance among the planters and fear of lost revenue, he failed to abolish slavery itself on the Danish West Indian islands. He also presided over a commission that, in 1789, proposed the introduction of universal free elementary schooling for all children between seven and fourteen, a measure to be enacted in the so-called Great School Law of 1814 in the midst of military defeat and economic catastrophe. Likewise, Jews were emancipated in 1798 with full rights to marry Christians and to enter secondary schools.

Most of the reforms were only implemented in the core lands of the Oldenburg Monarchy – Jutland and the Danish isles. Norway, for geological reasons, had never had many manors and was dominated by free peasants, while Holstein and southern Schleswig were dominated by large manors. On the other hand, agriculture in Holstein had introduced modern agrarian technologies long before the agrarian reforms in the Danish regions of the monarchy, which copied many of the advanced features of Holsteinian agriculture. The composite state not only comprised regions with very different political institutions but was also multilingual. Because of the long religious and administrative cohabitation, most Norwegians had come to speak a language fairly close to Danish, which was the language of the church, the schools, the administration, and the courts of justice. The Same nomads in the far north spoke Lappish, a language very different from Scandinavian. In the remote Faroe Islands the small population had kept its Old Norse language, but Danish was preached in the church and was used by the administration. The Icelanders used Old Icelandic in their daily life as well as in the church, the administration, and the courts. In Greenland, since 1721 Danish missionaries preached to the Inuit in their own language and translated the Gospel into Inuit, thus giving rise to the first written Inuit language, Greenlandic. In the two duchies High and Low German dominated, especially in the towns and among Holstein's German-speaking nobility, even though the majority of the peasant population in northern Schleswig spoke Danish (albeit a particular dialect – *sønderjysk* [Low Danish]), while Low and High German was used by the church, in the schools, by the administration, and by the courts. The population along the North Sea coast from the River Ejder to Niebüll, just south of the present border between Denmark and Germany, spoke Frisian, a language related to both German and English. As long as language was not considered a vital component of identity, this multilingual situation did not cause any problems. On his birthday the king would receive congratulatory poems not only in Latin and French but also in Danish, German, Icelandic, and Lappish (Feldbæk 1992, 81).

After having reconciled itself to the loss of the Scanian provinces in the seventeenth century, the Oldenburg Monarchy initiated an orientation towards the south aimed at incorporating the German-speaking duchies Schleswig and Holstein. This policy met with success in 1720 with the incorporation of the Gottorp parts of Schleswig, and in 1773 of the Gottorp parts of Holstein. As Holstein in particular was economically and culturally more advanced than the rest of the state, and both duchies held a much larger urban population, the reorientation of the state towards the south meant a growing influence of German speakers in the rest of the state, Norway included. Furthermore, the Crown encouraged the immigration of German artists, administrators, and skilled workers in order to revive the country after the intellectual and economic devastations caused by the wars and occupation of foreign troops in the seventeenth century. Thus, German speakers came to exercise considerable influence in the Oldenburg Monarchy. According to calculations by the British historian William Carr (1963, 27), there were some thirty-five hundred civil servants and nine thousand teachers and church officers in the two duchies of Schleswig and Holstein. Most teachers and lower officials in the county districts in Schleswig spoke Danish. But the highest-ranking officials, the prefects (*Amtmand*) and his assistants, pastors, and the intermediate authorities for Schleswig and Holstein, were invariably German speakers, even in such Danish-speaking counties as Aabenraa and Sønderborg in North Schleswig. In the capital of the monarchy, in 1800 about sixty Germans from the duchies occupied key positions in the administration, especially in the so-called *Deutsche Kanzlei*, which was responsible for the duchies and most of the foreign policy of the whole state. All in all between four hundred and 450 German officials were employed in Copenhagen (Paulsen 1936, 48).

Whether the multilingual state might have survived as long as the Hapsburg Empire or even longer it is impossible to say. Its demise has been taken for granted by all subsequent historians, be they Danish, German, Norwegian, Icelandic, or Faroese. Only in the last few years have some historians begun to deplore the vanishing of the relatively benevolent Northern Atlantic Empire, and an interest in the trade, urbanization, administration, and religion of the multinational composite state has surfaced. Examples of this are collective volumes such as *Urbanization in the Oldenburg Monarchy, 1500–1800* (Riis 2013) and a history of Iceland, the Faroe Islands, Western Norway and Greenland entitled

Naboer i Nordatlanten: Færøerne, Island og Grønland – Hovedlinjer i Vestnordens historie gennem 1000 år (Neighbours in the North Atlantic: The Faroe Islands, Iceland and Greenland – Major lines in West Scandinavian history over 1000 years) (Thór et al. 2012). Whatever the prospects of survival might have been, it is a fact that the Oldenburg Monarchy was the state hardest hit of all European states at the peace treaty in Vienna in 1815 as it lost a third of its territory and population and its strong position as a naval power. The Oldenburg state had sided with Napoleon after the pre-emptive British attack on Copenhagen in 1807, which resulted in the loss of the large Danish-Norwegian fleet (Munch-Petersen 2007). Frederik VI allied his state with Napoleon in order to persuade him not to occupy the peninsula of Jutland because the supply of grain from Jutland to Norway was the geopolitical raison d'être of the over-stretched monarchy. As the British fleet cut the supply line to Norway, the population suffered and influential circles began plotting against the king. Stubborn and true to his word, Frederik maintained the French alliance to the bitter end and, as a consequence, lost Norway to Sweden, which, in 1809, had elected a French general, Jean-Baptiste Bernadotte, as king under the name Carl XIV Johan. With the peace treaty signed in Kiel in 1814, Norway was signed over to Sweden. Before that, however, the Norwegians under the Danish viceroy, the later Christian VIII, had proclaimed their independence and, at Eidsvoll in spring 1814, produced one of the most liberal constitutions since that of the United States. Only an armed intervention by the battle hardened Swedish army forced the Norwegians to relinquish independence and to join a union with Sweden, which left the Oldenburg state dismembered and poor after having declared bankruptcy in 1813.

GRUNDTVIG AND THE CATASTROPHES OF 1807 AND 1814

The brutal British bombardment of Copenhagen in 1807 and the loss of the Danish-Norwegian fleet left a deep impression on the young Grundtvig. As a good patriot, he railed against the "perfidious Albion" and wrote patriotic hymns in praise of the courageous hero Peter Willemoes (1783–1808) who died in a naval battle against superior British naval forces near Sjællands Odde on 22 March 1808. Depressed by the defeat of Denmark by Great Britain in the war of 1807–14, Grundtvig took it upon himself to re-establish what he took to be the original "Nordic" mind, or "spirit," as he called it. He translated the

Icelandic Sagas, the twelfth-century historian Saxo Grammaticus, the Anglo Saxon poem *Beowulf*, and many other sources of what he considered the true but lost core of "the Nordic Spirit." His sermons attracted large crowds of enthusiastic students, and his address, *The Light of the Holy Trinity*, delivered in 1814 to a band of student volunteers willing to fight the English, inspired a whole generation of young followers, including the priest Jacob Christian Lindberg (1791–1857), who later organized the first Grundtvigian movement among young theologians (Baagø 1958). All Grundtvig's enthusiasm, though, could not prevent the Oldenburg state from dissolution. Grundtvig deeply deplored the loss of what he considered the monarchy's "true Norse" parts and feared for its future as a "Nordic" state. He even considered taking up a call from the new university in Christiania, our day's Oslo. But for various reasons the professorship never materialized and he stayed in Copenhagen where he would soon witness the next phase of the dissolution of the Oldenburg Monarchy.

The war with Great Britain between 1807 and 1814 caused an economic and political upheaval in the Oldenburg Monarchy that, among the urban elites, created an opening for the formulation of new national ideas imported from France and the German states. In Norway this development looked back at the proud history of the country in the High Middle Ages, when the Norwegian monarchy, before the Black Death and the agrarian crisis of the Late Middle Ages, was one the strongest and most centralized states in Medieval Europe. Language, culture, and history was studied in much detail in order to strengthen a national identification that could set Norway apart from Sweden (with whom it was joined in a personal union from 1814 to 1905) and from Denmark (with whom, since 1380, it had shared ruling the dynasty). Prior to 1814 Danish elites had tended to downplay differences between Danish and Norwegian nationality in favour of a common Danish-Nordic identity, which, on the other hand, was often contrasted with the concept of German culture – with or without Holstein and Schleswig. Some Norwegian patriots, however, had already (before 1807) come to believe that the close cultural community between Denmark and Norway would threaten a separate and "authentic" Norwegian identity. According to the recent research by Rasmus Glenthøj, some members of the Norwegian elite who were trained at the university in Copenhagen developed a complex double concept of fatherland, distinguishing between the fatherland as their state (i.e., the Oldenburg Empire) and their "natural" fatherland, or homeland (i.e., Norway). This led to a split in Norwegian nationalism between (1) the "Danish-minded," who constructed their reborn Norwegian culture in the image of the former Danish-Norwegian state, culture, and language and (2) the so-called "Swedish-minded," who tried to create a national culture in contrast to the former state, seeking their inspiration in a "true" and "independent" Norwegian past (Glenthøj 2008, 2012). The most striking example of this latter tendency may be found in the priest Henrik Wergeland (1808–45), who fought what he called "Danomania" among the educated classes.

The battle between Danish-oriented civil servants and self-proclaimed Norwegian nationalists dragged on throughout the nineteenth century and left a profound mark on the political culture in Norway, which is still noticeable today. The distinction between state and nation led to an understanding of nationalism as being political and belonging to the left, whereas nationalism in Denmark, partly because of Grundtvig's endeavours, was primarily defined in cultural terms. Danes, because of their age-old monopoly of the state in the Oldenburg Monarchy, did not seem to have the same need as Norwegians to distinguish between the concept of state and nation. Their fatherland (nation) and their state bore the same name: Denmark. However, in the later confrontations with the German speakers in Denmark and Schleswig and Holstein the situation was perceived in a different way because, in this case, Danes felt inferior, whereas in their dealings with Norwegians and the North Atlantic dependencies they had felt superior. This Danish double speak was brought out in the open in an interesting booklet by a young Danish linguist and ethnologist named Svend Grundtvig (1824–83), son of Nikolai Severin Grundtvig, in 1845. In *Dansken paa Færøerne: Sidestykke til Tysken i Slesvig* (Danish in the Faroe Islands: A parallel to German in Schleswig) Svend Grundtvig compares the oppressive role of the Danes with regard to the Faroese language (which was close to Old Norse) to the attitude of the Germans towards Danish in North Schleswig. He argues that it was untenable to deplore the German oppression of Danish in Schleswig and at the same time ignore the Danish oppression of Faroese in the Faroe Islands.

The treaty of Kiel of 1814 separated two peoples who had shared a history and a state for more than four hundred years. As a result the notion of a Danish national identity as something different from the common Nordic identity, which was propagated under the heading of "Scandinavianism," was strengthened at the expense of the former state-sponsored patriotism of the Oldenburg Monarchy (*Helstaten*). Both elites began to look back to different versions of the culture and history of the High Middle Ages. The elite in the young Norwegian nation-state displayed a strong need for national recognition on the part of other states and thus embarked on an extensive construction of national symbols. In Denmark, Frederik VI did his best to make Danes "forget" Norway. The reason for this was not only that the loss constituted a personal trauma for him but also that Norway, with the most liberal Constitution in Europe, represented a fundamental challenge to his own absolutist rule. Among Danish intellectuals the loss of Norway led to a growing interest in the duchy of Schleswig, which then became a battleground between Danish, German, and regional identifications (cf. Østergård 2011a). As a result, Holstein came to be seen by Danish intellectuals as a foreign element in the state rather than as the "Danish Holstein," which had been the dominant denomination for the two duchies in the eighteenth century, when German authors often depicted Holstein as a "Nordic" country, albeit German-speaking (Frandsen 2008).

One of the first protagonists of this perception of Holstein as German and thus "foreign" was Grundtvig, who, in 1831, wrote a pamphlet in response to the French Revolution – *Politiske betragtninger med Blik paa Danmark og Holsteen* (Political considerations on Denmark and Holstein). The pamphlet was primarily intended as a defence of the principle of absolutism as the best expression of the will of all the "people" as opposed to the liberal ideas in the French Revolution. The immediate occasion for the pamphlet was the 1830 announcement of the introduction of representative assemblies (*Stænderforsamlinger*) in the Oldenburg state. These consultative estates were introduced as an answer to an older obligation to introduce consultative political representation in Holstein, which belonged to the German Federation, where such institutions were called for. But the timing was obviously an attempt to forestall democratic demands triggered by the French Revolution in 1830. The king had chosen to install four estates in his multinational state – in Zealand, Jutland, Schleswig, and Holstein – in order to keep his state together and to treat it as one entity, even though, strictly speaking, he would only have had to introduce one representation. But this assembly would have had to include Schleswig as a concession to the demands of the Schleswig-Holstein movement for its own state in personal union with Denmark, and this threatened the coherence of the monarchy. As a reaction to the demands from the Schleswig-Holstein movement, Danish intellectuals began to call Schleswig by its old name *Sønderjylland* (South Jutland) in order to underline its Danish character (Østergård 2011a).

In this tense situation Grundtvig proposed to get rid of Holstein in order to keep Denmark Danish or Nordic. The proposal was based on his interpretation of world history, which he published the following year in the huge poem *Nordens Mythologi* (Norse mythology). In a combination of fundamentalist Christianity and optimistic belief in the progress of humanity he describes how the peoples of the world, according to the Bible, had separated from each other four thousand years ago, each with their own language, mythology, spirit (*ånd*), and destiny. Grundtvig attributed a driving role in world history to only four peoples: the Jews, the Greeks, the Romans, and the "Norse" (Vind 2003, 17). He proclaimed his vision of liberty for all who belonged to the real "people" in the famous sentence: "Freedom for Loke as well as for Thor." This ethnically based understanding of world history was the reason for his intervention in 1831. Because of his fundamentalist identification of language and people, he had no understanding of linguistically mixed areas such as Schleswig, where people might identify with the Danish king in German. To him, the mixing of peoples was against nature, and he referred to it as "bastardization" (Vind 2003, 20). Later, the same analysis, combined with his respect for the will of the people, led him to take a courageous stand when, on 14 March 1848, in the middle of the most heated turmoil at the outbreak of the civil war over Schleswig, he suggested a division of Schleswig according to the will of the people (Korsgaard 2012, 100–6). He detested multinationalism and envisaged an organization of the world based on the principle of people. In the 1830s and 1840s, he saw that this would be best secured when expressed by one voice in the form of a king with absolute power. As a consequence, he abstained from voting for the Danish Constitution in 1849, even though he had been elected to the Constituent Assembly. Later, though, in 1866, he changed his attitude and defended the very same Constitution against the attempts to restrict the influence of the democratically elected Lower House (*Folketing*). This, as it turned out, was in vain as, that same year, the Constitution was altered in a more conservative direction. This move towards popular representation is typical of Grundtvig's ability to learn from experiences – in this case, his pleasant surprise at the ability of the peasant representatives to participate in government. But it also points to a fundamental ambiguity in his concept of people, which could just as easily lead to liberal democracy as to authoritarianism. Mainly because of the defeat in 1864 and the subsequent cultural, economic, and, finally, political hegemony of the peasant farmers, the liberal understanding of "people" and "popular" came to dominate Danish political culture (and does so to this day) (Østergård 2012a). But we only have to look at Germany between 1870 and 1945 in order to see the opposite unfolding of the authoritarian potential of *Volk* and *völkisch* (see Østergård 2011c).

NATIONALISM IN THE OLDENBURG MONARCHY AFTER THE LOSS OF NORWAY, 1814–64

Around 1800, the Danish king, despite the losses in the seventeenth century, still ruled over a vast, though thinly populated, realm, stretching from Greenland, Iceland, and Norway to Altona just outside the suburbs of Hamburg, encompassing half of the total European coastline towards the Atlantic. According to a reliable 1801 census, the total population of the kingdom was 2.5 million. Denmark and Norway had 1.8 million inhabitants, 51 percent of whom lived in Denmark proper; Schleswig and Holstein had 600,000 inhabitants, of whom 54 percent lived in Holstein; other German possessions counted for some ninety thousand people and the North Atlantic islands some fifty thousand (Rasmussen 1995, 25). No reliable censuses for the colonies in India, Africa, and the West Indies exist as their status was different.

The loss of Norway in 1814 after Denmark was defeated by the United Kingdom and Sweden in the Napoleonic wars completely altered the balance between the German and Nordic elements in the composite state. The number of German speakers rose from less than 20 percent to 35 percent, and nationalist sentiments soon began to tear the state apart. In 1806, the duchy of Holstein was annexed to Denmark as a consequence of the disintegration of the Holy Roman Empire. However, with the establishment of the German Confederation in 1815, Holstein was reestablished as an independent duchy, which implied that the Danish king participated in the German Federal Assembly in his capacity as Duke of Holstein. As was the case with the Hapsburg Empire, the multinational state was soon to be torn apart by two antagonistic national programs, a "Danish" (either a Danish-Danish or a Scandinavianist – that is, Danish-Swedish – variant) and a "German" (either a Schleswig-Holsteinian or a pan-German variant). The main proponents of these two programs were the academic elites in the two cities with a university: Copenhagen and Kiel (Østergård 2011a).

Until 1814 the three major linguistic and national groups in the multinational state had balanced each other numerically. The economically more advanced German-speaking parts were balanced by the much larger number of Danish and Norwegian speakers. Whether these three groups and the other small peoples, such as the Icelanders and Faroese, perceived themselves as nationalities and not just as people with different languages under the same ruler is debated among contemporary historians. As the majority of intellectuals, primarily the priests, had been trained at the university in Copenhagen they shared language worldview. The university in Kiel, which was founded in 1665 by Christian Albrecht of Gottorp as a competitor to Copenhagen University, only had an impact from 1773, when it was reorganized and civil servants for Schleswig and Holstein were required to study there at least for two years – the so-called *biennium* (Frandsen 2008, 28). The University in Christiania, Norway, only came into being in 1811. National identifications and national programs only emerged in the nineteenth century, primarily due to the influence of rising German nationalism, which was channelled into the Oldenburg Empire through the reinvigorated university in Kiel.

In the process of Danish nation building, the "Schleswig-Holstein question" played an important and instrumental role. The university in Kiel soon came to be considered one of the best universities in German-speaking Europe, and it took the lead in the awakening of nationalism in Schleswig and Holstein. The emerging nationalism took two forms: (1) a pan-German demand for a united Germany and subsequent break-up of the Oldenburg Monarchy and (2) a Schleswig-Holsteinian movement that did not at first imply the dissolution of the Oldenburg state, at the time referred to as *Helstaten* (in German *Gesamtstaat*). Contrary to the Schleswig-Holstein movement, which was supported by the traditional noble rulers in the *Ritterschaft* and a rising group of liberal intellectuals, pan-German nationalism was not very strong in the beginning. The largest town in Schleswig was Flensburg, and it played an important economic role throughout the entire realm. Besides its economic importance in the multinational Danish monarchy, Flensburg also played an important role in the economic and cultural life of the Province of Schleswig. This may be difficult to understand today, now that Flensburg has become just another sleepy German provincial town, albeit with a Danish flavour. But it was not long ago that the town was an active metropolis (whose interests extended worldwide) and the economic centre of a province within the Oldenburg Monarchy. In order to avoid being influenced by the "unruly masses" of this large town, the Consultative Estates Assembly (*Stænderforsamling*) for the Province of Schleswig, which existed from 1834 to 1848, was convened in the much smaller and quieter town of Schleswig south of Flensburg. Schleswig was on par with Roskilde in Zealand, Viborg in Jutland, and Itzehoe in Holstein (Jensen 1931–34). Besides an upper class of big merchants and officials, the majority of whom spoke German, Flensburg comprised a large Danish-speaking class of workers and craftsmen. Danish and German, or, more accurately, the South Jutland dialect (*sønderjysk*), Low German (*Plattdeutsch*), and Frisian co-existed, occasionally supplemented by Standard Danish and High German as the languages of the church and the courts.

As mentioned, the university in Kiel was instrumental in the formulation of separatism in the duchies. The universities in Copenhagen and Kiel underwent quite different developments in the eighteenth century, even though both had as their primary task the training of civil servants. This task became more important after the introduction of the nationality law in 1776, whereby positions within the state administration were reserved for residents born within the borders of the realm. As a result of this law, the Crown could no longer import its officials from abroad, as had been the case in past centuries, but had to educate them itself. Copenhagen University received a new charter, hurriedly penned by a commission. The regeneration, though, merely amounted to a modest modernization, and the revolutionary years in the 1790s and the Napoleonic Wars were dull and unexciting in contrast to the lively Kiel University, which was marked by political tension and renewal. The number of students in Kiel had already begun to rise in 1768, and in the 1770s the number of recently matriculated students stabilized at between fifty and sixty, compared to eight in 1767, when the university hit a low point. In the 1780s, Kiel became a cultural centre, with the monarchy's first college of education for teachers (1781) and a Schleswig-Holstein "Patriotic Circle" (1786). The hiring of a range of highly qualified younger professors within a short time span had turned Kiel University into one of the most modern in the German-speaking area, a position it managed to keep until late in the nineteenth century. In the Department for German Affairs, which was responsible for foreign policy and Schleswig and Holstein, the young university was closely watched, and the authorities were wary of any signs of sympathy for the French Revolution. When a fervent admirer of the revolution, Professor C.F. Cramer, praised one of the Girondists, Jérome Pétion (who later voted for the death penalty for Louis XVI), he was not only fired but also exiled from Kiel. Following the death of the moderate president of the Chancellery, Andreas Peter Bernstorff, in 1797, control was tightened further

(Feldbæk 1998, 259). This control is a testimony to the almost complete integration of Schleswig and Holstein into the Oldenburg Monarchy. In 1806, after Napoleon's dissolution of the Holy Roman Empire, Holstein was incorporated in the Oldenburg Monarchy and serfdom was abolished (Hvidtfeldt 1963). These steps were opposed by nobles in Schleswig and Holstein, and, as a result of the organization of the German Federation (which saw the Danish king participating as the Duke of Holstein), the incorporation was reversed in 1815. Thus, the scene was set for the national confrontations of the nineteenth century.

The Schleswig-Holstein program advocated by German intellectuals and aristocrats in the 1830s did not build on the Schleswigian regional identity of old; rather, it was a modern national-political program for both of the duchies (seen as one state in competition with a Danish-national program) and it called for the incorporation of the whole of Schleswig, as far as the River Ejder, into a centralist Danish national state. In 1838, in the debates over a liberal constitution, the leading Danish nationalist and liberal ideologue Orla Lehmann (1810–70) claimed: "There are no regions in Denmark" (*i Danmark gives der ikke regioner*) (Frandsen 1996a, 1996b). But a region or province was exactly what Schleswig had become since the early Middle Ages. The Danish call for the incorporation of all of the province of Schleswig provoked a separatist reaction in Holstein in the 1830s and 1840s out of fear that the Danish state would "Danisize" the province. Because of that, the majority moved from loyalty to the Danish king to separatism for Schleswig-Holstein. This change is witnessed in *Itzehoer Wochenblatt* and the politics of the radical Kiel democrat Theodor Olshausen (1802–69) (Frandsen 2006, 2008). In the long run, the old Schleswigian identity almost disappeared as a result of the civil war of 1848–51 and Schleswig-Holstein's incorporation into Prussia in the united Germany after 1870 (Jahnke 2005). The principal losers were the concept of a tolerant multinational Danish state (*Helstaten*) and the idea of an independent Schleswig-Holstein. After 1864, the two duchies of Schleswig and Holstein in fact remained *ungedeelt* (undivided) but only as a rather neglected and militarized periphery within the new German Empire.

In Copenhagen a program for an ethnically and historically defined nation was formulated by the National Liberals in the 1830s under the leadership of a Danish politician – Orla Lehmann – who had spoken German in his home in Copenhagen in the 1820s (Degn 1936). The years between 1830 and 1848 saw the rise of modern political ideas in

Denmark. As a result, the peasant farmers began to organize in line with their own interests. According to the liberals, members of society ought to organize themselves on the basis of ideas and compete for political power in free elections. It should be noted, however, that the liberals believed that only those who "understood how to govern" should have the right to vote. Demands for a liberal constitution in the absolutist Danish monarchy were first formulated in minority circles of liberal academics in the first half of the nineteenth century, primarily among students and civil servants. In Denmark as well as in Holstein, the move away from international, or supranational, liberalism towards national liberalism occurred between 1836 and 1842. Until that point, the liberals in Copenhagen and Kiel had been allied in their resistance against the absolute monarchy, which continued to prevail even after the introduction of the consultative assemblies in 1834 (Jensen 1931–34). The bourgeoisie was so small that it was in no position to shake the absolutist regime. Had this not been apparent before, it became so after the accession of Christian VIII to the throne in 1839. The liberals had high hopes in Christian VIII, who had presided over the writing of the free Constitution in Norway in 1814 before its forced union with Sweden. Much to their disappointment, the liberals soon realized that the intelligent king had no desire to limit his own powers and to deliver himself into the hands of the increasingly nationalist liberals. His main intent was to preserve the composite *Helstat* and defend it against rising nationalist antagonisms.

Under these circumstances, around 1842 the two liberal reform groups in the capitals of Copenhagen and Kiel each established its own strategic alliances. In Denmark, the liberals allied themselves with the peasant farmers, an alliance that, in 1846, led to the establishment of a political party known as *Bondevennerne* (Friends of the peasants). In Holstein and parts of Schleswig, a more informal alliance was established with the landed aristocracy, and this later developed into the Schleswig-Holsteinian movement. The confrontation of 1848, though, was not the only possible result of the nationalist confrontations in Schleswig (despite its being depicted this way, by both sides, in nationalist historiography) (Frandsen 2008; Østergård 2011a). But neither of the two national liberal groups was able to gain power without fomenting a "nationalist" polarization over an abstract ideology – something that would allow it to mobilize allies among the other strata of the population. Thus, nationalism came to tear apart the relatively well-functioning composite state known as *Helstaten*, or the Oldenburg Monarchy.

The nationalist radicalization of the language eventually led to rebellion and subsequent civil war in 1848. In Danish historiography the revolution is normally presented as a peaceful and consensual change from absolutism to democracy. In fact, it was a bloody civil war over Schleswig, primarily fought in Jutland and at sea, where the Danish fleet blockaded German harbours. The proponents were two nationalist coalitions, both of whom appealed to "the people." In the first years of the conflict, Prussia and other German states supported the Schleswig-Holstein rebels militarily and politically. Eventually, though, the European powers, led by Russia and Great Britain, sided with the legitimate ruler, the king of Denmark, and restored the status quo. After the Prussian forces were forced to withdraw, the Danish army won a narrow victory over the Schleswig-Holstein army led by German voluntaries at Isted near Schleswig on 25 July 1850. Grundtvig wrote a moving poem in praise of the fallen "Danish" heroes entitled "Kærmindesong" (Song of loving remembrance). After the defeat of the rebels, and in order to secure the survival of the unstable bilingual *Helstat,* the Danish administration took revenge and tried to roll back German language and culture in the disputed territories. Neither this episode nor the Danish revenge against the Schleswig-Holstein liberals (who were driven into exile in United States) and the demise of the castle of Gottorp in Schleswig (which was stripped of its furniture and turned into barracks for the Danish troops) have been treated by Danish historians.

Neither the Danish nor the German side wanted to give in, and, after long and fruitless deliberations, in 1863 an intransigent Danish government proclaimed the annexation of the whole of Schleswig. The international political climate and international agreements notwithstanding, the ruling National Liberals demanded a Danish nation-state within the "historical" framework – that is, all of Schleswig to the River Ejder – regardless of the opinions of the inhabitants. This move would have resulted in a large German-speaking minority within Denmark. After the crushing defeat of the Danish army at Dybbøl on 18 April 1864, and the conquest of Als on 29 June 1864, Bismarck secured all of Jutland and provided Prussia and Austria with an opportunity to take all of Schleswig and Holstein. The defeat finally turned Denmark into a nationally homogeneous state; however, it was so small that many wondered whether it would be able to survive on its own. And the loss of both Schleswig and Holstein had left 200,000 Danish speakers outside the state under Prussian rule. This apparently unfortunate situation, though, was turned to Denmark's advantage primarily because, through protracted political fights, the peasant farmers were able to establish a cultural, economic, and, finally, political hegemony. The single most important element in this hegemony was the influence of Grundtvig's thoughts, loosely described as "Grundtvigism" (in Danish *Grundtvigianisme*).

GRUNDTVIGISM AND DANISH NATIONAL IDENTITY

When, in the 1820s, Grundtvig engaged in a heated polemical exchange with his superiors in the church on matters of theology, he was banned from all public appearances and his publications were censored. This drove him into what he called his "inner exile" in the 1820s and 1830s. This inner exile, however, gave him time for reflection, enabling him to formulate a program for the revival of the stagnant official religion. Long before the ban was lifted in 1839 he produced a massive number of sermons, psalms, and songs – a literary legacy that, until a generation ago, was the core of the socialization of most Danes. Also, in the 1832 *Nordens Mythologi*, he formulated an all-embracing view of nature, language, and history based on a fundamentalist Christian interpretation of world history. Here and in many other writings he formulated liberal and populist principles that gradually came to permeate Danish political culture. In 1848, after the outbreak of the civil war over Schleswig, Grundtvig produced a refined definition of national identity, which helped set the tone for a nationalism that was less chauvinistic than most in the nineteenth century. As is sometimes the case with prolific writers, his most precise theoretical expressions were to be found in the disciplined form of poetry: "People! What is a people? What does popular mean? Is it the nose or the mouth that gives it away? Is there a people hidden from the average eye in burial hills and behind bushes, in every body, big and boney? They belong to a people who think they do, those who can hear the Mother tongue, those who love the Fatherland. The rest are separated from the people, expel themselves, do not belong" (Grundtvig 1848, my translation).

This definition, though produced in the heat of the battle with the German-speaking rebels in the duchies of Schleswig and Holstein, most resembles the definition of national identity produced by the French thinker Ernest Renan (1882) in what has since become one of the standard texts on nationalism, *Qu'est-ce qu'une nation?*. Originally Renan's intention was to "scientifically" demonstrate the right of the German-speaking population in Alsace-Lorraine to preserve its French nationality, even after the provinces had been signed over to Germany by the peace treaty of 1871. After their defeat in the French-German war, the French changed their minds regarding whether a nation should be defined in cultural or political terms. The same happened in Denmark after the defeat in 1864, which, in 1867, was followed by Schleswig's incorporation into Prussia. But Grundtvig anticipated this change of thinking – at least in some of his writings. Through a long and complicated history Grundtvig's understanding of national identity became official Danish policy, and it was successfully applied in the border region between Denmark and Germany after 1920 and, particularly, after 1955 (Kühl and Weller 2005). But there is much more to Grundtvig and his influence on Danish political culture. The core of his thinking is the assumption that culture and identity are to be found in the unity of life and language. Although this kind of thinking may be labelled chauvinistic, Grundtvig himself, like his opposite Herder, did not assume a hierarchy of nationalities. Cultural diversity, yes; cultural dominance, no. Whether these assumptions are truly viable need not concern us here. What does concern us, though, is the fact that, in this small state, his thinking caught on among a class of people left over from the wars of the middle of the century.

As mentioned, Grundtvig's influence dated back to his nationalist sermons in 1814. But his breakthrough to a larger audience only occurred after 1839, when those involved in religious and political movements decided to transform his thinking into practice. First, his thinking influenced the revivalist religious movements; later, it influenced more explicitly political movements; and, eventually, it came to serve as the foundation for independent economic and educational institutions. Grundtvig himself did not seek such popular support. He delivered his message either in writing or orally and then stood aside when others decided what to make of it. This is why some of today's guardians of the thoughts of Grundtvig speak of him as having been "taken prisoner by the Grundtvigian movement," which transformed his message into an ideology known as "Grundtvigism" (Pontoppidan Thyssen 1991). Because of his distance from his followers, some do not think of him as a nation builder in the strict sense of the term. He was influential, but others had to do the organizational work. This is clearly demonstrated in his influence on the established church, which he ended up completely reforming. Originally, the revivalists in Denmark came to Grundtvig of their own initiative. This religious movement of the first half of the nineteenth century resembled many other Pietist movements throughout Europe. Because of the negative attitude of the official Lutheran state church, revivalists chose to meet outside the churches and referred to their movement as "the meeting movement" (*Forsamlingsbevægelsen*). They were attracted by Grundtvig's independent interpretation of the Lutheran heritage. Grundtvig, however, succeeded in giving an optimistic tone to the normally somewhat gloomy, Germanic Pietism. In their struggles with the officials of the absolutist state, these revivalists learned how to organize – something that they would soon put to political use (Wåhlin 1987). The leaders of the peasant movement of the 1840s were recruited from the ranks of the revivalists. Initially working under the tutelage of the liberal intellectuals, the peasant party in the 1850s broke with the National Liberals.

Soon, though, the various political factions of the peasant party began to establish independent institutions. They began with the church. With the transformation of the monarchy from an absolutist regime into a constitutional regime in 1849, the organization of the church had to be changed accordingly. The result of these endeavours differed in important ways from the otherwise comparable situation in the Lutheran monarchies of Sweden and Norway. A state church with a proper constitution never came into existence, though it had been envisaged in the Constitution of 1849. This was a result of the influence of Grundtvig and the revivalist movement. They wanted guarantees of religious freedom; this being the case, the church was to be the creature of the state, or its agent of socialization, as it had been under absolutism. They found that these guarantees were best preserved in an anarchic state of affairs. In this way, Denmark acquired a most peculiar mixture of freedom and state control in religious matters. Grundtvig also profoundly influenced educational institutions, but this is dealt with in other chapters of this book. His influence on the cooperative movement in the nineteenth century is also considerable, but it is difficult to demonstrate as it was more indirect (see the several investigations of the late Claus Bjørn). All in all, though, it is impossible to over-estimate the influence this single figure has exercised on Danish society, its understanding of nationalism, and its political culture and behaviour in today's globalized economy (Østergård 2012b). The main precondition of this influence was the dissolution of the multinational Oldenburg Monarchy and the rise of the national small state. In many ways this is a success story, although it is most certainly not the result anyone intended, least of all Grundtvig. Even so, he must be considered the ultimate nation builder. Whether the experiment can be repeated in other cases remains doubtful as the precondition is a devastating defeat that does not result in complete annihilation. And, as Norman Davies (2011) convincingly demonstrates in his *Vanished Kingdoms*, complete annihilation is the usual result. For its part, Denmark survived and even prospered because larger powers had an interest in having an independent but weak state located at the entrance to the Baltic Sea.

REFERENCES

Baagø, K. 1958. *Magister Jacob Christian Lindberg: Studier over den grundtvigske bevægelses første kampe* [Master Jacob Christian Lindberg: Studies of the Grundtvigian movement's first struggles]. Copenhagen: Gad.

Bjørn, C. 1977. "The Peasantry and Agrarian Reform in Denmark." *Scandinavian Economic History Review.* 25: 117–37.

Carr, W. 1963. *Schleswig-Holstein, 1815–48: A Study in National Conflict.* Manchester: Manchester University Press.

Christiansen, N.F. 1988. "Danmark og Tyskland i det 19. Århundrede" [Denmark and Germany in the 19th century]. In *Fjende bileder & fremmedhad* [Images of the enemy and xenophobia]. ed. K.K. Kristiansen and J.R. Rasmussen, 161–74. Copenhagen: FN-forbundet.

Damsholt, T. 2000. *Fædrelandskærlighed og borgerdyd* [Patriotism and civic virtue]. Copenhagen: Museum Tusculanum.

Davies, N. 2011. *Vanished Kingdoms: The History of Half-Forgotten Europe.* London: Penguin.

Degn, C. 1936. *Orla Lehmann und der nationale Gedanke* [Orla Lehmann and the national idea]. Neumünster: Wachholz.

Feldbæk, O., ed. 1991–92. *Dansk identitetshistorie* [The history of Danish identity]. Vols. 1–4. Copenhagen: C.A. Reitzels.

– 1992. "Clash of Culture in a Conglomerate State: Danes and Germans in 18th-Century Denmark." In *Clashes of Culture*, ed. N. Steensgaard, J. Christian, V. Johansen, E.L. Petersen. and H. Stevnsborg, 80–9. Odense: University Press of Southern Denmark.

– 1998. *Nærhed og adskillelse, 1720–1814: Danmark-Norge, 1380–1814* [Proximity and separation, 1720–1814: Denmark-Norway, 1380–1814]. Vol. 4. Oslo: Universitetsforlaget.

Frandsen, S. Bo. 1996a. *Opdagelsen af Jylland: Den regionale dimension i danmarkshistorien, 1814–64* [The discovery of Jutland: The regional dimension in the history of Denmark, 1814–64]. Århus: Aarhus University Press.

– 1996b. "Regions and Nationalism in the Danish Monarchy, 1814–1864." In *Regional and National Identities in Europe in the XIXth and XXth*

Centuries, ed. H-G. Haupt, M.G. Mülller, and S. Woolf. The Hague: Kluwer Law International

– 2006. "Helstatens første opinionsavis: Theodor Olshausens *Kieler Correspondenz-Blatt* som forum for en liberal holstensk regionalisme, 1830–1848" [The entire state's first opinion newspaper, Theodor Olshausen's *Kieler Correspondenz-Blatt* as a forum for liberal Holstein regionalism, 1830–1848]. *Historie* 2006 (2): 283–317.

– 2008. *Holsten i Helstaten: Hertugdømmet inden for og uden for det danske monarki i første halvdel af 1800-tallet* [Holstein in the united monarchy: The duchy within and outside the Danish monarchy in the first half of 1800]. Copenhagen: Museum Tusculanum.

Glenthøj, R. 2008. *En moderne nations fødsel: Norsk national identifikation hos embedsmænd og borgere, 1807–1820* [The inception of a modern state: Norwegian national identification of assets and citizens, 1807–1820]. Odense: University Press of Southern Denmark.

– 2012. *Skilsmissen: Dansk og norsk identitet før og efter 1814* [Danish and Norweigian identity before and after 1814]. Odense: University Press of Southern Denmark.

Grundtvig, N.F.S. 1848. "Folkeligt skal alt nu være" [Of the people is our watchword]. In *Danskeren* [The Dane], vol. 1. Copehagen: F.H. Eibe

Holmgaard, J. 1999. *... uden at landet besværes: Studier over Frederik IV's landmilits med henblik på spørgsmålet om bøndernes vilkår i øvrigt* [...without troubling the country: Studies of Frederik IV's rural militia and what it tells us about the general conditions of farmers]. Viborg: Udgiverselskabet for Landsarkivet for Nørrejylland.

Hvidtfeldt, J. 1963. *Kampen om ophævelsen af livegenskabet i Slesvig og Holsten, 1795–1805* [The struggle for the abolition of serfdom in Schleswig and Holstein, 1795–1805]. Aabenraa: Historisk Samfund for Sønderjylland.

Jahnke, C. 2005. "Die Borussifizierung des schleswig-holsteinischen Geschichtsbewusstseins, 1866–1889" [The Borussifizierung of the Schleswig-Holstein historical consciousness, 1866–1889]. *Zeitschrift für die Geschichte Schleswig Holsteins* [Journal of the history of Schleswig-Holstein] 130: 161–90.

Jensen, H. 1931–34. *De danske Stænderforsamlingers Historie, 1830–1848* [The history of the Danish state councils, 1830–1848]. Vols. 1–2. Copenhagen: J.H. Schultz.

Korsgaard, O. 2012. *N.F.S. Grundtvig*. Copenhagen: Jurist- og Økonomforbundet.

Kühl, J., and M. Weller, eds. 2005. *Minority Policy in Action: The Bonn-Copenhagen Declarations in a European Context, 1955–2005*. Flensburg and Aabenraa: European Centre for Minority Issues and Department of Border Region Research, University of Southern Denmark.

Munch-Petersen, T. 2007. *Defying Napoleon: How Britain Bombarded Copenhagen and Seized the Danish Fleet in 1807*. Gloucestershire: Sutton.

Østergård, U. 2006. "Denmark: A Big Small State – The Peasant Roots of Danish Modernity." In *National Identity and the Varieties of Capitalism: The Danish Experience*, ed. J.L. Campbell, J.A. Hall, and O.K. Pedersen, 51–98. Montreal and Kingston: McGill-Queen's University Press.

– 2011a. "Schleswig and Holstein in Danish and German Historiography." In *Disputed Territories and Shared Pasts: Overlapping National Histories in Modern Europe*, ed. T. Frank and F. Hadler, 200–23. Houndsmill: Palgrave Macmillan.

– 2011b. "Lutheranism, Nationalism and the Universal Welfare State: National Churches and National Identity after the Reformation and the Development of the Welfare State in the Nordic Nation States." In *Europäisches und Globales Christentum: Herausforderungen und Transformationen im 20. Jahrhundert* [European and global Christianity: Challenges and transformations in the 20th century], ed. K. Kunter and J.H. Schiørring, 54:78–101. Göttingen: Vandenhoeck and Ruprecht.

– 2011c. "Dänemark und Deutschland als europäische Nachbarn: Geschichte und Erinnerung" [Denmark and Germany as European neighbours: History and memory]. In *50 Jahre Goethe-Institut Dänemark* [In 50 years Goethe-Institute Denmark], ed. S. Fabrin and M. Müller-Wieferig, 219–24. Copenhagen: Goethe-Institut.

– 2012a. "The Danish Path to Modernity." In *Nordic Paths to Modernity*, ed. J.P. Árnason and B. Wittrock, 49–68. New York: Berghahn Books.

– 2012b. "Danish National Identity: A Historical Account." In *Global Collaboration: Intercultural Experiences and Learning,* ed. M.C. Gertsen, A-M. Søderberg and M. Zølner, 37–55. Houndsmill: Palgrave Macmillan.

Paulsen, J. 1936. "Tyske embedsmænd i København i Tiden 1800–1840. En Oversigt over deres Indflydelse paa Udviklingen af den nationale Modsætning indenfor den danske Helstat" [German officials in Copenhagen in the time from 1800 to 1840: An overview of their influence on the development of the opposition in the Danish United Monarchy]. *Sønderjyske Aarbøger* [Yearbook of Southern Jutland]: 43–84.

Pontoppidan Thyssen, A. 1991. *Grundtvig og den grundtvigske arv* [Grundtvig and the Grundtvigian legacy]. Copenhagen: Anis.

Rasmussen, J.R. 1995. "The Danish Monarchy as a Composite State." In *European Identities, Cultural Diversity and Integration in Europe since 1700*, ed. N.A. Sørensen, 23–36. Odense: University Press of Southern Denmark.

Renan, E. 1882. *Qu'est-ce qu'une nation?* Paris: Sorbonne.
Riis, T., ed. 2013. *Urbanization in the Oldenburg Monarchy, 1500–1800*. Kiel: Verlag Ludwig.
Thór, J.T., D. Thorleifsen, A. Mortensen, and O. Marquardt, eds. 2012. *Naboer i Nordatlanten: Færøerne, Island og Grønland – Hovedlinjer i Vestnordens historie gennem 1000 år* [Neighbours in the North Atlantic: The Faroe Islands, Iceland and Greenland: Major lines in west Scandinavian history over 1000 years]. Tórshavn: Faroe University Press.
Vind, O. 2003. "Grundtvig og det danske: Med sideblik til Sverige" [Grundtvig and the Danish: With a look at Sweden]. In *Grundtvig – nyckeln til det danska?* [Grundtvig – The key to the Danish?], ed. H. Sanders and O. Vind, 38–59. Göteborg: Makadam Förlag.
Wåhlin, V. 1987. "Popular Revivalism in Denmark." *Scandinavian Journal of History* 11: 363–87.

6

Why Denmark Did Not Become Switzerland

JASON O. JENSEN AND JOHN A. HALL

In the middle of civil war Meïr Goldschmidt (1894), editor of the cosmopolitan periodical *North and South,* made a strong plea for a federal solution to Denmark's problems. Our concern here is with a particular element of his case – namely, his insistence that much could be learned from Switzerland, whose short civil war in 1847 had been settled through the creation of a new federal constitution. It takes but a moment's thought to realize that much more is involved here than constitutional details of the mid-nineteenth century. The fundamental moral consideration raised by Goldschmidt is obvious – namely, the desirability of different peoples living together under a single political roof. Contemporary India shows that this is just about possible. But the key question for comparative historical sociology concerns the politics of transition. Can traditional regimes decompress so as to remain multinational in character? More precisely, was the move from empire to nation-state inevitable?

Comparisons can enlighten through difference as much as through similarity. Switzerland had never had an empire. Further, superb recent scholarship has distinguished myths about that mountainous country from the realities of its social formation. The civil war did not concern the struggles between different nationalisms, and such conflicts have not been much present in Swiss history. Nor is Switzerland a multinational country today; rather, it is a multi-ethnic nation-state. So the argument here is that Denmark could not become Switzerland because its social formation was utterly different, closer in kind to Austro-Hungary than to the Helvetic Republic. In other words, Goldschmidt was asking a question that was largely misplaced, admirable though it was to ask it. Understanding why this was so can still illuminate, adding a little to the excellent analyses of Uffe Østergård (chap. 5, this volume) and Korsgaard (chap. 9, this volume).

REPUBLICANISM AND PATRIOTISM IN SWITZERLAND

Switzerland's long and complex history of confederal arrangements came to an end with Napoleonic invasion and the creation of the unitary state of the Helvetic Republic. Though that was followed by a (slightly changed) restoration of cantonal powers, revolutionary ideals remained. Reforming republican cantons, all dominated by Protestants but by no means uniformly German-speaking, undermined the powers of patrician elites in the thirty years after Waterloo. There was a reaction. Catholic cantons, especially those in the High Alps, formed the *Sonderbund*, which refused an order to disband, thereby leading to the short-lived civil war in which fewer than one hundred died. The Constitution of 1848 stressed federalism, although it had strictly limited powers. Switzerland was dominated by Protestants until Catholics gained their place in the 1870s, with workers joining an idiosyncratically coordinated elite in the years after the end of the First World War.

There are two crucial points to be made about the settlement of 1848. Negatively, the settlement should not be seen in any way as a "deal" designed to integrate separate linguistically based nationalisms. To the contrary, language was rarely mentioned in the new Constitution for the simple reason that politicization of linguistic groups had not taken place (Dardanelli and Stojanovic 2011; Stojanovic 2003). In other words, modern Switzerland was formed before this sort of national consciousness. A crucial condition that must exist in order for a multi-ethnic nation-state to develop is this: "the networks of civil society organizations [must have] emerged *before* the modern nation-state was formed and *before* the question of 'who is the people' arose for the first time" (Wimmer 2002, 247). Of particular importance is the presence of elite unity across differences, of trans-ethnic identity capable of creating solidarity able to manage and diffuse moments of great conflict. Cleavages were cross-cutting in Switzerland: cantons contained both religious groups, while many Catholic bourgeois had liberal inclinations. From the mid-eighteenth century civil society groups, celebrating Switzerland, rifles, and gymnastics, had been present throughout the territory, often meeting in different locations every year, and these typically involved members from all linguistic groups (with French-speakers playing an especially active role after the fall of the *ancien regime*). The presence of this sort of civil society grouping depended upon high levels of literacy (partly created by religious competition between Catholics and Protestants) and upon significant economic development throughout the territory (Wimmer 2011).

The struggle in Switzerland had been between progressives and conservatives, between, if you like, new and traditional class elements. A key analytic point can be made here: class dominates nation when a political system is open enough to accommodate political change. Liberal regimes allow this; empires prevent it. A negative case proving the point is that of the late Hapsburg Empire. The blocked, stalemated polity in Vienna prevented reform, thereafter encouraging nationalist mobilization (Bugge 1994, 316). All of this can be highlighted in the simplest of ways. The Swiss "came together" in 1848 because they were already together.

ABSOLUTISM AND NATIONALISMS IN THE OLDENBURG MONARCHY

The history of Denmark's homogenization culminated in a national-liberal coup in 1848, which spurred a civil war between the Kingdom of Denmark and the duchies of Schleswig and Holstein, and the misguided war with Prussia that followed sixteen years later and resulted in the loss of both duchies. The causes behind the composite monarchy's disintegration highlight the crucial differences between Switzerland and Denmark in the early and mid-1800s.

Denmark was not absolutely unlike Switzerland. For one thing, its absolutism had, as Tine Damsholt argues (chap. 7, this volume), a contractual element between king and people within it. For another, brilliant work by Juliane Engelhardt (2010) covering the years from 1769 to 1814 shows that bourgeois reform societies, patriotic to the core, were spread throughout the kingdom seeking enlightenment reforms such as an increase in the general education of the population, the alleviation of social ills, and the expansion of liberal political freedoms. No obvious signs were apparent of linguistic conflict; the early patriotic societies even praised the idea of establishing strong connections across the country, but there is no evidence that any were pursued (81). Of course, there were significant differences from Switzerland despite this particular commonality: this was not a world of proto-industrialism, nor was there a general history of civil society groups across the monarchy that encouraged trans-ethnic identification. The Schleswig-Holstein elite, for example, seems to have been both integrated and circumscribed:

"There was everywhere [in Schleswig-Holstein] a German estate class and a wealthy German bourgeoisie; there was a German judicial- and civil-service class; there was a plethora of German lawyers and a clergy, which like the others had received their education at the University in Kiel. Within these groups, a true fellowship reigned, founded in common language, a certain level of German culture, and scientific literacy. They had similar occupational interests and had common associations. It was of course here, that Schleswig-Holteinism took hold" (Møller 1958, 23).

There were few linkages between the elite in Copenhagen and the elite in Holstein, not surprisingly, perhaps, as Holstein was an especially distinctive possession within the Oldenburg realm after 1815, given its status as an independent duchy in the German Confederation. A lack of references to connections between Copenhagen and Holstein in the Copenhagen press of 1848, notably in *Kjøbenhavnspasten* and *Fædrelandet*, certainly suggests that civil society connections were not extensive, although this is very sparse evidence.

Still, one may consider a counterfactual: had the empire turned itself into a constitutional monarchy before, say, 1830, it might have been possible to maintain the monarchy. Such a total change in the monarchy's identity did not take place, indeed, could not take place, given that its raison d'être was wholly different. The result is absolutely clear. In a very short period, from something like 1830, politicization by linguistic groups took place, thereby creating the social dynamite that led to the ending of the composite monarchy. Nationalism in Holstein appears to have been negligible up until the 1830s, and it remained marginal among the elites of both the kingdom and the duchies up until the 1840s. The first call for a Schleswig-Holstein separatism came in the form of a pamphlet in 1830 by Uve Lornsen calling for a constitution for the duchies giving them autonomy in all but military affairs (Neergaard 1892, 52). While the pamphlet did not gain much support, it spurred Frederik VI to increase regional autonomy by creating assemblies, serving in an advisory capacity in the duchies as well as in the rest of the country (Møller 1958, 37). By 1842, the German-dominated assembly in Schleswig had taken to passing many separatist motions. Examples include a motion to unite the assemblies of Schleswig and Holstein, a motion to separate the finances of the kingdom and the duchies, a motion for making an official flag for Schleswig-Holstein, and a motion to replace the plates on ships currently labelled "Property of Denmark" with "Property of Schleswig-Holstein" (Neergaard 1892, 66). Frustrated with this supposedly anti-Danish sentiment, the member P.H. Lorenzen began speaking Danish in the assembly, an act that was met with much antagonism and that eventually resulted in his physical removal from the assembly. This event spurred nationalist rage in the rest of Denmark.

Prior to 1842, liberals in both Holstein and the kingdom were primarily concerned with obtaining a constitution to ensure political freedoms as well as greater bourgeoisie control of the state. By the mid-1840s, both had shifted their focus to the national cause. This shift was marked when the *Fatherland* (*Fædrelandet*), the mouthpiece of the National Liberals, proclaimed: "We seek *first* Slesvig and *then* a constitution" (Neergaard 1892, 14). In Holstein, constitutional concerns were also favoured prior to the mid-1840s. In 1842, the Holstein assembly deliberated constitutional and national motions in about equal amounts (66). More tellingly, a central liberal party in Holstein, the New Holstein Party, was, up until the mid-1840s, ready to separate from Schleswig if it would mean a liberal constitution for Holstein (54). To summarize, despite clearly separate elite networks, until only a few years prior to the civil war of 1848 bourgeois elites in both Holstein and the kingdom were mainly concerned with liberal constitutionalism rather than with a nationalist agenda. Before 1842, the two university cities, Copenhagen and Kiel, had been powerhouses in the liberal opposition to absolutism, and the two groups worked closely together. But in 1842 the liberals became national, thereby fragmenting the liberal front against absolutism. The initiative for this politicization was taken by such leading Copenhagen liberals as Orla Lehmann, D.G. Monrad, and Carl Ploug, all closely linked to the *Fatherland*. Naturally enough, a counter-movement developed rapidly among the intellectuals in Kiel's liberal environment. So, in a very short time, close allies became implacable enemies. Given the apparent severity of the shift, one might question the sincerity of actions around the Lorenzen affair. It is possible that liberal leaders realized that they might be able to obtain their constitutional goals by using the more populist nationalist ideals to gain power. Such a strategy would be all the more appealing given that, from 1839 onwards, Christian VIII was responsive to liberal requests but always watered them down to the extent that they lost their potency in terms of both the extension of freedom they enabled and the popular support that could be rallied behind them (10).

This is not to deny that attempts were made to put the genie back into the bottle – that is, to contain nationalisms once they gained political consciousness. Goldschmidt's position has already been noted.[1] The monarchy itself sought ways in which to manage nationalism. As an example, Frederik VII proposed a new, essentially federal, constitution in January 1848 that would give equal representation to the kingdom and to Schleswig-Holstein. J.P.M. Grüne (1848a), editor of the liberal newspaper the *Copenhagen Post* (*Kjøbenhavnpasten*), argued in support of the proposal. But there was never any large crowd supporting *Kjøbenhavnposten* (Neergaard 1892, 27). Then there were members of an imperial ethnicity within the state. As the civil war was ending, the lawyer and civil servant A.S. Ørsted argued against nationalism in *For the Sake of the Danish State's Preservation in Its Entirety* (1850). Still more important was the officer and politician A.F. Tscherning, who sought to hold the state together through federal means (Glædemark 1939, 614; Vammen 2011, 90, 211). Despite being central in Danish politics in the years following 1848, his federalist views were marginalized when, in 1842, his fellow leaders of the agricultural party Friends of the Farmers (*Bondevennerne*) entered a coalition with the National Liberals in order to oust the incumbent loyalists (*Helstatsfolk*). As the National Liberals were advocating a division of Denmark, Tscherning declined to partake in the new coalition.

But all such attempts were too late. Two major areas of contention eventually proved irreconcilable. The first involved disagreements and concerns over the distribution of power between the kingdom and the duchies. This point concerns exclusion, the raising of political consciousness by fear – or, differently put, by the absence of voice (Hirschman 1970). And beyond this generality often stands (and particularly so in this case) what can best be termed the vicious game of mirrors: the fear of one side leads to actions that reinforce the fears of the other, with the continual interaction leading to a dreadful downward spiral that takes on increasingly nationalist framings. The second major area of contention involved disputes over the linguistic and national fate of Schleswig.

Elites in Schleswig and Holstein had good reason to be wary of closer integration with Denmark as such integration could potentially lead to their eventual irrelevance. Copenhagen's 120,000 inhabitants (around 1843) was an order of magnitude above the size of other cities, the only exception being Altona in Holstein, with almost thirty thousand inhabitants (Frandsen 2008, 55). The economic geography surrounding Holstein in 1848 may have had further lasting impacts on the eventual outcome of the Danish-German border. While Danish societies before the war, and the Crown's administration after the war, pursued active policies in support of the Danish language in Schleswig, the steady spread of German up through Schleswig in the first half of the nineteenth century cannot be attributed to similar actions on the German side. Rather, in a

Gellnerian fashion, the spread of German can be attributed to the overwhelming economic pull of Hamburg on a region that itself possessed little economic gravity (Gellner 1983). While Hamburg's population of around 130,000 was of a comparable size to Copenhagen in the 1840s, Hamburg's integration into a European rail network increased its economic pull. In 1851, Holstein's trade with the kingdom amounted to about 190,000 Rdlr., while trade with Hamburg amounted to almost 6 million Rdlr. (Møller 1958, 12). While these numbers are, unfortunately, from the end of the first civil war, Møller notes that they are in accordance with what we know in general about Holstein's trade at the time. It is not much of a stretch to assume that Hamburg's economic pull on Schleswig would be of a comparable size to that of Copenhagen. The consequent spread of the German language in Schleswig in the 1800s suggests that nineteenth-century industrial centres may have had a significant effect on the eventual demographic and political map of Europe where these lines had not already been drawn by powerful states.

Nationalist sentiments began taking over economic projects and processes. In the 1830s, plans to increase integration between the kingdom and the duchies through the extension of roads and railways fell apart: "Once the national ideology became popular, integrating traffic projects became unwanted as they threatened exposing the populace to influences which could endanger the construction of a closed nation-state" (Frandsen 2008, 163). The loss of interest in integrating projects appears to have been mutual in Denmark and Holstein. As the monarchy showed only limited interest in these projects they would have had to be initiated and mostly funded by the private sector. As such, nationalist currents on both sides of the divide had a larger influence than would have been the case had there been a state-led integration initiative. These early disagreements eventually became increasingly enforced by economic gatekeepers: landed proprietors were in general in need of loans from German banks, which could only be obtained with the assent of a lawyer from Schleswig-Holstein. By controlling the lawyers, the Schleswig-Holsteiners ensured that they had the support of the landed proprietors (Neergaard 1892, 71). In addition, Danish-minded merchants would systematically be cut off from credit and Danish-minded intellectuals were increasingly shunned. In effect, the mid- to late 1840s saw a closing off of what few linkages remained between Holstein and the kingdom.

This is the material background to the spread of nationalist ideas amongst German-speakers. Kiel University had survived as part of a traditional exchange of territories between the Romanovs and Oldenburgs in 1773, and it now began to gain enormous intellectual power and prominence. Østergård (forthcoming) offers a brilliant account of a cadre – whose core included F.C. Dahlmann, J.C. Droysen, B.G. Niebuhr, and T. Mommsen – who saw the Danes as an autocratic and backward peasant state and who therefore wished to align themselves with liberal developments to the south. Here, too, there was a myriad of approaches, from demands for special status for Schleswig and Holstein within the monarchy, to calls for secession for Holstein alone or Holstein with Schleswig, either as a separate realm within the German Confederation or as part of the unified nation-state that had been glorified by Fichte.

From the Danish side there was long-standing tension towards the German-speaking community, not least as German-speaking aristocrats in the court – first Struensee and Colbiørnsen – had sought to push through Enlightenment reforms from above. Naturally such tensions increased as the level of education among Danes slowly increased, thereby creating feelings of blocked social mobility, particularly in Copenhagen – sentiments that were exacerbated by the increasing role of German-speakers in the state once Norway was lost. But what mattered most was the fear that Denmark might cease to exist, that German-speakers, blessed with an external homeland, might expand and eventually call in a nascent external power. This is the background that led to the desire to strengthen the Danish core through policies of homogenization. In these circumstances varied approaches were possible, from Scandinavianism to the full incorporation of Schleswig and Holstein, and from the incorporation of all or merely the northern parts of Schleswig – both policies designed to homogenize Denmark and to exclude German-speakers, either by allowing the secession of Holstein or by diminishing its place within the monarchy.

Disagreements over these distributional concerns were made crystal clear when, in January 1848, Frederik VII proposed a new constitution that would give equal representation on joint affairs to the kingdom and to Schleswig-Holstein. Opponents on the Danish side objected that the German-speaking population would be overrepresented not only because the duchies contained fewer people than the kingdom but also because the elite in Schleswig was overwhelmingly German-speaking and would thus accentuate the imbalance (Giødwad and Ploug 1848). Opponents on the Schleswig-Holstein side, on the other hand, were worried that the Schleswig-Holstein seats would nevertheless contain a few

Danish nationals and that, this being the case, German nationals would constitute a minority and, therefore, German nationalist interest could be consistently outvoted (Frandsen 2008, 313).

The distribution of power between the increasingly antagonistic parts of the composite monarchy was thus of central importance in lining up the conflict, but it was control over the national fate of Schleswig that brought it to civil war. Michael Mann's (2005) splendid analysis of the "dark side" of democracy makes much of the game of mirrors that has just been described. But he adds to it a final consideration: murderous conflict is most likely when two sides stake claims to the same piece of territory. Schleswig illustrates his point perfectly, not least as it had a predominantly German-speaking population with a large Danish-speaking minority that, in the north of Schleswig, constituted a local majority. But irony is called for here. Judson's (2006) marvelous account of the borderlands of the Hapsburg realm makes much of regional identities and of the way in which people could align themselves with different ethnicities in different censuses – very much to the irritation of nationalizing intellectuals. While elites in both the kingdom and Holstein chose to fight a war over the fate of Schleswig, many in Schleswig were mainly concerned with maintaining their own autonomy (Madvig 1883, 323). Much like Holstein, Schleswig's primary objective was autonomy, but, unlike Holstein, part of this goal included a marked opposition to entering the German Federation until very late in the developments. It was similarly unenthusiastic about the prospect of being lobbed in with Denmark. The ambiguous national composition of its people made Schleswig an aggravating factor in the Danish case. This was all the more complicated by the lopsided language preferences of the local elite and the impression, in the kingdom, that, during the 1800s, the German language had steadily been encroaching upon larger sections of Schleswig; even as late as 1850, Danish-speaking elders could supposedly be found in the southern parts of Schleswig (Møller 1958, 18). Erik Møller is convinced that, at the dawn of the nineteenth century, the language line was at Schleswig-Husum, far south of the current Danish-German border, which is generally considered the language-line that existed at the time of the civil war. The first response to this supposed encroachment of the German language came in 1832, when a bourgeois society was formed for the purpose of securing the position of the Danish nationality in Schleswig. This organization founded and maintained a high school in the duchy. A later organization of a similar nature devoted its resources to providing Danish-language books to local libraries and to supporting a few Danish-language publications (Neergaard 1892, 16).

When the National Liberals seized power in Copenhagen in March of 1848, they did so on the basis of a rumour that the duchies had revolted (Vammen 1988) and in response to demands that the ties between Denmark and Schleswig (but not Holstein) be secured (Danmarkshistorien.dk 2013). When news of the coup returned to the duchies, the rumoured revolt turned into an actual revolt.

By 1848, federalism was an extremely unlikely outcome for Denmark and Schleswig-Holstein. Nationalist sentiments had become suffused in politics in both the kingdom and Holstein, with both sides preferring to be rid of the other but not at the expense of forsaking nationalist claims on Schleswig. The thirteen years that followed the end of the civil war were characterized by a remarkably consistent policy in Holstein, despite shifting governments in Copenhagen, aimed at suppressing the German language and culture in Schleswig, due largely to the fact that a single loyalist nationalist, J. Th. A. Regenburg, managed to maintain control over church and school policy in Schleswig throughout the years between the wars (Vammen 2011, 38). Such repressive cultural policies likely made a federal solution an increasingly impossible option. The civil war in 1864 was, however, not spurred by an uprising in the duchies but, rather, by nationalist fantasies that ignored basic European geopolitical realities (Vammen 2011). The desire to unite all of Denmark, so to speak, got in the way of rational geopolitics. Ultimately, attempts to determine the national character of Schleswig led to two civil wars and to the eventual splitting of Schleswig in 1920.

DENMARK: THE EARLY AUSTRO-HUNGARY?

As can be seen above, the conflicts in the Oldenburg composite monarchy shared more traits with the Hapsburg Empire than with nineteenth-century Switzerland. This conclusion raises further questions of comparison, which I can only briefly touch upon. The nationalities question was fully evident in the Hapsburg Empire by the mid-nineteenth century, yet a state of "bearable dissatisfaction," to use the formulation of Count Taaffe, staved off collapse until 1918. The uniqueness of Denmark in the nineteenth century is that its empire collapsed so early on. Beyond the factors listed above, the area of geopolitics requires further highlighting.

One important factor not covered above is that of geopolitics. There is something to the view that Austro-Hungary lasted for such a long time because it was in the interests of the great powers to maintain it (Hiers and Wimmer 2013). The great powers acted in a similar way towards the Oldenburgs in 1851. In contrast, the great powers did not much care about Denmark's loss of Schleswig and Holstein in 1864, though Great Britain did act so as to make sure that the rump state survived. Further, Vienna had considerable powers, and it was only defeat in war that so weakened the state that it could no longer corral its nationalities. The Danish state was, of course, bankrupted by war and so, after 1814, was fundamentally weak. But in most other ways the Danish situation differed from that of Switzerland. The very character of the population changed as the result of the loss of Norway, which totally unbalanced the state – a situation, it is worth noting, wholly different from that in Switzerland, where territorial integrity was maintained at all times. In one sense, this resembles the situation of the Hapsburgs once the Magyars gained great autonomy in 1867. But the differences between the two cases are very great. German-speakers in Cisleithenia were a dominant and cultured minority, whereas the Danes were the less socially advanced majority within the country. Crucially, the German-speaking population of the Oldenburg monarchy had an external homeland wholly lacking for Magyars and Czechs – albeit not for the German-speakers of Vienna, who came to rely increasingly on Berlin.

CONCLUSION

The Oldenburg case does cast some light on one of the claims with which we began. The Oldenburgs were unable or unwilling to liberalize in time, making the transition from empire to nation-state all but inevitable. Here is evidence that nationalism, in part created by imperial actions, dooms empires to destruction.

But the larger point, and the one with which we must conclude, is that of the similarity between contemporary Denmark and contemporary Switzerland. Campbell and Hall (2010; chap. 21, this volume) suggest that the vulnerability of Denmark, a small nation in danger of absorption, was the background to its ability to create certain advantages – notably, a determination to work together, at least when faced with disaster, so that survival would be possible. They claim that this sort of social portfolio was likely to characterize other small, nationally homogeneous entities. What, then, of Switzerland? What can be said about it from, so to speak, a Danish perspective? The key descriptive point is simple: to take Switzerland as an exception, as a multinational society, is a terrible mistake – as has been suggested here. The two countries share much in common, above all a powerful sense of national identity.

Denmark went through several stages, culminating in increased homogeneity through welfare provision. So did Switzerland. The period from 1848 to the mid-1870s is best seen in terms of republican patriotism, loyalty to a set of ideas. But in the years that followed a rich cultural texture was created (mountains, Rousseau on shepherds, William Tell) that made Switzerland a multi-ethnic nation – that is, an entity in which there is a sense of national identity (Zimmer 2003). So Switzerland is not an exception to the claims of Campbell and Hall, merely another exemplar. One can note in this regard the Swiss debate on immigration, led by a party in which Pia Kjærsgaard would feel at home. But that is not to say that Switzerland is similar to Denmark in many other ways. Nation building from below lent Danish culture an occasional touch of populism wholly absent from the world of the Swiss burghers. Then there are the multiple identities and institutions below that of the nation within Switzerland, from commune to canton, which are wholly lacking in Denmark.

NOTES

1 Grundtvig engaged with Goldschmidt in interestingly inconsistent ways (Bredsdorff 1974). Before the war he cautioned, in agreement with Goldschmidt, that it would be foolish to assume that the Schleswigians were naturally part of Denmark; it would be better to ask them what they wanted (Grundtvig 1848a; Grüne 1848b). But, by mid-1849, he wanted to devote all of Denmark's resources to conquering all of Schleswig (Neergaard 1892, 398). Finally, in November 1849, he attacked Goldschmidt for being a Jew in Denmark and, therefore, a foreigner who should not meddle in affairs concerning the Danish nation. He noted that Goldschmidt was a guest, even though he acted as though he was at home (Grundtvig 1848b). It appears that the war put a lot of strain on Grundtvig's nationalist heart, making him lash out more than he normally would. Had Denmark lost the first war, or had Denmark settled on a multinational solution, it is possible that Grundtvig would have alienated his followers and not have passed into history as the Danish icon we know today. Although his thoughts on educating the populace as a precondition for democratic rule can be seen as quite

independent of nationalism, for him these two were tied together: educating the populace was a means of creating the (nation's) people (Korsgaard 2004, 265–7). In a divided Denmark, with no singular and unified people, the ideological foundations for Grundtvig's legacy would likely have been absent.

REFERENCES

Bredsdorff, A. 1974. "(1) Denmark." *International Library Review* 6 (3): 257–61.

Bugge, P. 1994. *Czech Nation-Building, National Self-Perception, and Politics*. Aarhus: Aarhus University Press.

Campbell, J., and J.A. Hall. 2010. "Defending the Gellnerian Premise: Denmark in Historical and Comparative Perspective." *Nations and Nationalism* 16: 89–107.

Danmarkshistorien.dk. 2013. *Resolutionerne Vedtaged på Casinomødet 20. Marts 1848* [The resolutions agreed on at the Casino meeting, 20 1848]. Available at http://danmarkshistorien.dk/leksikon-og-kilder/vis/materiale/reso lutionerne-vedtaget-paa-casinomoedet-20-marts-1848/.

Dardanelli, P., and N. Stojanovic. 2011. "The Acid Test? Competing Theses of the Nationality-Democracy Nexus and the Case of Switzerland." *Nations and Nationalism* 17: 357–76.

Engelhardt, J. 2010. *Borgerskab og Fællesskab: De patriotiske selskaber i den danske helstat, 1769–1814* [Citizenry and community: The patriotic societies in the Danish Helstat, 1769–1814]. Copenhagen: Museum Tusculanum Press.

Frandsen, S. B. 2008. *Holsten i Helstaten: Hertugdømmet inden for og uden for de danske monarki i første halvdel af 1800–tallet* [Holsten in the Helstat. The duchy within and outside the Danish monarchy in the first half of the 1800s]. Copenhagen: Museum Tusculanum Press.

Gellner, E. 1983. *Nations and Nationalism*. Oxford: Blackwell.

Giødwad, J.F., C. Ploug. 1848. "Om Forfatningsrescriptet, Foreløbige Bemærkninger" [Concerning the constitution-announcement, initial remarks]. *Fædrelandet* [Fatherland], 29 January.

Glædemark, H.J.H. 1939. "A.F. Tscherning: Nogle Betragtninger" [A.F. Tscherning: Some considerations]. *Historisk Tidsskrift* [Historic journal] 10: 607–24.

Goldschmidt, M. 1849. "Foderayivstaten" [The federal state]. *Nord og Synd, et Ugeblad* [North and south, weekly], 2 December.

Grundtvig, N.F.S. 1848a. "Tale I den Slesvigske Hjælpeforening" [Speech in the Schleswigian aid-society]. *Dankeren, et Ugeblad* [The Dane, weekly], 26 April.

– 1848b. “Svar paa hr. Goldschmidts Udfordring til Danskheden” [Reply to Mr. Goldschmidt’s challenge to Danishness]. *Danskeren, et Ugeblad* [The Dane, weekly], 10 November.

Grüne, J.P.M. 1848a. “Den nye Constitution” [The new Constitution]. *Kjøbenhavnsposten* [The Copenhagen Post], 2 February.

– 1848b. *Kjøbenhanvsposten* [The Copenhagen post], 13 March.

Hiers, W., and A. Wimmer. 2013. “Is Nationalism the Cause or Consequence of the End of Empire?” In *Nationalism and War*, ed. J.A. Hall and S. Malesevic. Cambridge: Cambridge University Press.

Hirschman, A.O. 1970. *Exit, Voice, and Loyalty: Responses to Decline in Forms, Organizations, and States*. Cambridge, MA: Harvard University Press.

Judson, P. 2006. *Guardians of the Nation: Activists on the Language Frontiers of Imperial Austria*. Cambridge, MA: Harvard University Press.

Korsgaard, O. 2004. *Kampen om folket* [The battle for the people]. Copenhagen: Glydendal.

Madvig, J.N. 1883. “Et Bidrag til historisk Belysning af Tanken om Slesvigs Deling som Løsning af den danske-slesvigholstenske Strid” [A contribution to shed light on the idea of the splitting of Schleswig as a solution to the Danish-Schleswigian strife]. *Historisk Tidsskrift* [Historic journal] 5: 316–74.

Mann, M. 2005. *The Dark Side of Democracy: Explaining Ethnic Cleansing*. Cambridge:: Cambridge University Press.

Møller, E. 1958. *Helstatens Fald, 1855–63* [The fall of the Hellstat. Copenhagen: Gads.

Neergaard, N. 1892. *Under Junigrundloven: En fremstilling af et danske folks politiske historie fra 1848 til 1866* [During the June constitution: A telling of the Danish people’s political history from 1848 to 1866]. Copenhagen: P.G. Philipsen Press.

Østergård, U. Forthcoming. “Nation-Building and Nationalism in the Oldenburg Empire.” In *Nation-Building in the Core of Empires: A Comparative Perspective*, ed. S. Berger and A. Miller. Manchester: Manchester University Press.

Stojanovic, N. 2003. “Swiss Nation-State and Its Patriotism: A Critique of Will Kymlicka’s Account of Multinational States.” *Polis* 11: 45–94.

Vammen. H. 1988. ”Casino 1848.” *Historisk Tidsskrift* [Historic journal] 15 (3): 253–81.

– 2011. *Den tomme stat: Angst og ansvar i dansk politik, 1848–1864* [The empty state: Angst and responsibility in Danish politics, 1848–1864]. Copenhagen: Museum Tusculanum Press.

Wimmer, A. 2002. *Nationalist Exclusion and Ethnic Conflicts: Shadows of Modernity*. Cambridge: Cambridge University Press.
– 2011. "A Swiss Anomaly? A Relational Account of National Boundary Making." *Nations and Nationalism* 17: 718–37.
Zimmer, O. 2003. *A Contested Nation. History, Memory and Nationalism in Switzerland, 1761–1891*. Cambridge: Cambridge University Press.

PART THREE

Grundtvig and the People

7

"Hand of King and Voice of People": Grundtvig on Democracy and the Responsibility of the Self

TINE DAMSHOLT

A review of Grundtvig's political theories – especially his negative view of democracy and positive view of absolute monarchy – raises a problem in the contemporary estimation of Grundtvig since he and the Folk High School movement have traditionally been considered part of the foundation of Danish democracy. This chapter takes a closer look at Grundtvig's political ideas, especially his negative estimate of democracy, his idealization of "opinion-guided monarchy," and his idea of a utopian people constituted by a common aspiration for the general good. I look at this political ideal within the context of its legacy from late eighteenth-century patriotic discourse in Denmark and according to its interpretation and translation of the political theories of the French Enlightenment.

There has been relatively little research conducted on Grundtvig's political activity. This is interesting as he was, after all, a political writer, member of the Constituent Assembly, and, for almost nine years, a member of the Danish Parliament. Considering the vast number of books, dissertations, and articles written on his theology, poetry, and the Danish Folk High School it is striking how few who have dealt solely with Grundtvig as a politician (exceptions are Bjørn 2007; Dam 1983; and Korsgaard 2012). This lack of research is not due to missing material. Grundtvig wrote numerous political pamphlets and articles, and, from 1848 to 1851, he published, almost single-handedly, the weekly periodical *Danskeren*. Furthermore, Grundtvig's speeches in Parliament were published in *Rigsdags-tidende*, and many of his sermons and songs may be read as comments on contemporary political questions (Dam 1983, 15).

We also know how Grundtvig reacted in March 1848, when war against the rebellious German-speaking and German-oriented population in the southern part of the Danish realm was declared (what many historians now interpret as the breakout of civil war). Political meetings in Copenhagen culminated in a mass procession addressing the newly proclaimed king, and the new absolute monarch promised a democratic constitution. According to a contemporary friend, reverend Birkedal, during these events Grundtvig was like "a lion fuming in his cave and impossible to please" (Dam 1983, 22). Quite a few have tried to excuse this apparently "undemocratic" attitude and to explain Grundtvig's irritation as due to the fact that he felt left out. In the light of his engagement with the making of the Danish Constitution and, later, in the Danish Parliament, it is said that, in 1848, Grundtvig turned a political somersault, suddenly becoming a democrat after having been a fervent adherent of absolutism. However, this is hardly the best way to understand Grundtvig's politics. Instead, I argue that, if one examines Grundtvig's basic political opinions, one finds a striking continuity and coherence in his political visions and actions.[1] Thus, it is possible to interpret what appears to be a change of attitude as the inevitable consequence of what Grundtvig saw as the effect of a changing political situation, of what he believed to be central democratic elements, and of what he regarded as the "true Danish" Constitution.

GRUNDTVIG AND EIGHTEENTH-CENTURY PATRIOTIC DISCOURSE

The analysis of Grundtvig's view of democracy and representative government must start with the political tradition of Danish eighteenth-century society, with which Grundtvig grew up. The Danish-Norwegian double monarchy of the eighteenth century was a "multicultural state." The different parts of this state were tied together in a dynasty personified by the king. This person was king of Denmark and Norway and was also duke of Schleswig and Holstein.[2] Absolutism was rooted in the continental tradition of natural law, and Danish absolutism was further interpreted as a "second" social contract between the king and his people,[3] in which the ruler pledged to bear the responsibility for the common good and the people pledged to obey him. It was thought that the differences among the multicultural population could be overcome by the idea of the state as a fatherland.

However, a contemporary philosophical controversy haunted the Danish monarchy, calling into question whether absolutism could, in fact, be reconciled with the idea of the social contract. In his *De L'Ésprit des Lois* (1748), the prominent French philosopher C.L. Montesquieu questions this and describes the Danish-Norwegian form of government as despotism. Furthermore, he links different forms of government with specific forms of attachments or ruling principles: the ruling principle of despotism is fear; the principle of monarchy is honour; and only in republics are citizen virtue and love of government the ruling principles. Thus fear rather than civic virtue was to be expected among the Danish-Norwegian people.

In spite of the fact that the Danish-Norwegian state, together with Prussia and Sweden, was one of the most militarized (Lind 1987) and centralized states in Europe, a counter-discourse argues not only was Denmark-Norway under monarchic rule but also that virtue and love of the fatherland were the ruling principles of this monarchy. An important concept in this late eighteenth-century political discourse is what the Norwegian historian J.A. Seip (1958) coins "opinion-guided absolutism," according to which the autocrat is expected to work for the general good as formulated in free public debate. This idea differs from so-called enlightened absolutism, which was celebrated in contemporary Prussia and Russia and by Goethe (see Øhrgaard, chap. 10, this volume), according to which an enlightened ruler defined the general will or good, which the people were considered incapable of formulating by themselves. However, in the Danish-Norwegian context the crowned king, Christian VII (1766–1808), was considered too unbalanced to rule unguided, and public debate and opinions were, if not welcomed, at least relatively uncensored. Thus the ideal interpretation of absolutism as opinion guided became pivotal, and it grew in importance as the political debates moved from the "trauma of Montesquieu" to the concerns of his more radical colleagues, such as J.J. Rousseau, and the question of civic rights became unavoidable.

In Danish, the concept of the people, or the "folk," implies the Greek concepts of *demos* and of *ethnos*. It is a crucial concept in Grundtvig's ideology and it was born out of the contractual theory of the state which holds that the people, as citizens, enter into a social contract with the king. Although the contractual theory of the state provided a new ideological framework for the notion of absolutism, it simultaneously involved recognizing the idea of the people as the true sovereigns. Thus, in deciding the common good, free public debate came to be considered the fundamental element, and it was only in so far as the king allowed and listened to the free public debate that he was considered a legitimate ruler. This idea was actually considered closer to pure democracy than were systems of representation since, in principle, the entire people had a chance to speak. It is thus possible to argue that, in the late eighteenth century, Danish-Norwegian absolutism was interpreted within a "republican" framework, with the people as the true sovereign and the people's morality and responsibility as the pivotal issue, transcending questions of nationality.

Eighteenth-century social contract theory thus implied a particular perception of the state and of the citizen. Civic freedom, which emerged from the discourse as the crucial human right, meant that the citizen complied with what had been decided by the general will (Boll Johansen 1989, 228). The citizen's ethical imperative consisted of putting aside his or her own interests in favour of the general will and for the sake of the general good, which, ultimately, meant that he or she would be willing to give his or her life for the fatherland. This utopian citizen-subjectivity – in eighteenth-century parlance articulated as "the love of the fatherland" – was primarily a question of sense of duty and responsibility, and it was supposed to elevate the individual above his or her specific interests.

The political discourse was based on the fiction that individuals were capable of subjecting passion and interest to the rule of reason (Landes 1998, 132). This civic subjectivity was a utopian ideal, but, in relation to Grundtvig's ideas, it is interesting that morality and responsibility is expressed as the feeling of love (of the fatherland), which became the central virtue in his complex of political ideas. However, the patriotic concept of love of the fatherland differed from the national-romantic concept. A central message in patriotic rhetoric was that all the nations that lived side by side in the Danish-Norwegian state could be good citizens of the same fatherland. Patriotism was thus a feeling that, in principle, could be shared by all citizens because their origin, language, and culture were expected to be subordinated to their patriotism. Thus, in late eighteenth-century Denmark-Norway, political tradition was patriotic rather than nationalistic, and it had several republican dimensions: emotions and morality became entangled, and love (of the fatherland) should ensure a loyal and responsible population.

The idea of love as a token of responsibility and the idea of the people as constituted by the desire to achieve the general good are essential to Grundtvig's ideology, as is the idea of the absolute monarch as the interpreter of the people's voice. This background is essential to understanding Grundtvig's praise of Danish absolute monarchy both before and after the Danish Constitution came into effect. Grundtvig's political ideology can be epitomized as the uniting of two concepts: "the hand of the king and the voice of the people." In other words, what is desirable is an absolute king who listens to the voice of the people (i.e., an enlightened and responsible population), which is expressed in free debate, writing, and speech.

Grundtvig expressed this idea in many poems and songs. In *Kærlighed til Fædrelandet* (Love for the fatherland) (1853), for example, he states that love of the fatherland is the virtue that enables civic rights and that love in general is the virtue that guarantees the future happiness of Denmark (in spite of current wars).[4] Grundtvig's politics are also articulated in the 1839 poem *Kongehånd og Folkestemme* (Hand of king and voice of people). The first verse reads:

Hand of King and Voice of People:
both are strong and both are free.
They have found their home in Denmark
many hundred years ere we.
Flaws, fears, dangers all defied,
may they triumph and abide,
and create, in age of gold,
for old Denmark wealth untold.[5]

The following verses inscribe the events of 1660, when absolute rule was imposed almost by a coupe d'état in Denmark (Lind 1994), as the formation of a social contract and peaceful agreement between a ruler and the people. Grundtvig emphasizes that the king was entirely free to make his decisions as long as he listened seriously to the arguments of the people as expressed in a free public debate. This was, to Grundtvig, the ideal of the (strong and free) hand of the king ruling in accordance with the voice of the people.

This ideal was already displayed in Grundtvig's first political publication in 1831, in which he argues against the idea of a parliament as something that is necessary for the improvement of a country. Grundtvig praises what would later be referred to as an opinion-guided absolutism, claiming it to be more likely to find good will in one person – the king – than in a crowd of people forming a parliament. A king had the advantage of being above selfishness, while everybody else is part of, and therefore beholden to, an estate or a party. In Grundtvig's view, an absolute king guaranteed that the general good, rather than special interests, would be primary.

In 1831, Grundtvig believed that "the voice of the people" could only be found if it was expressed in a free written debate. Interestingly, the voice of the people was to be expressed in writing. Grundtvig argued that a free debate would involve a larger number of people than could be found in the confined group of a parliament. The question of freedom of the press was crucial since, in those days, written debate was inhibited by the restrictions on the press that banned statements that were critical of the state and the government. In fact, beginning in 1825, Grundtvig himself was subjected to censorship.

Grundtvig proposed that a number of enlightened men of letters, who were over forty, be selected and invited to express their opinions. For one of the first times he mentioned the idea of a high school for "popular knowledge and citizen education," whose purpose would be to increase the number of men able to express their opinions within the framework of the general good.

Later, in 1836, after having experienced public debates due to the introduction of advisory assemblies of the Estates, he became an admirer of the "oral" voice of the people, which he considered to be a miracle, a sort of political analogue to the "living word" (Grundtvig 1836). This also led him to emphasize the need to educate more men who could perform this task. Grundtvig went so far as to raise the question of gender, stating that he preferred male citizens as matters of state were not issues for "women and children." Whether he considered women and children to form one category or two, I leave to the reader to decide. However, it is clear that Grundtvig's utopian people did not include the entire population. The purpose of the suggested high school was to produce an ideal citizen subjectivity, to create in youth an inclination towards the general good rather than self-interest. This was to be accomplished through gaining enlightenment stemming from one's own life, by awakening the love of the fatherland, and by strengthening one's knowledge and experience of Danish history and the mother tongue (see Korsgaard, chap. 16, this volume).

Grundtvig's utopian citizen subjectivity presupposed heart-felt moral imperatives, not just a superficial performance in the public sphere. In fact, as early as 1815 Grundtvig contrasted the French and the Danish people, describing the former as superficial, external, and impious, and the latter as heart-felt, internal, and Christian. To Grundtvig, the Danes were the "people of the heart," and thus Denmark had the potential to become a nation of responsible citizens (Damsholt 2007; Grundtvig 1815).

GRUNDTVIG AND THE FRENCH REVOLUTION

In his *Du contrat social* (1762) J.J. Rousseau defined *la volonté générale* as something different than the sum of individual wills (*la volonté des tous*) as the general will was determined by the interest of the general good. In this sense, the people came into existence in their aspiration for the general good, with the individual subordinating his or her own interests out of concern for the collective. Grundtvig's concept of the voice, or the will, of the people has many parallels with Rousseau's concept of *volonté générale*. Only power exercised in agreement with the will of the people was considered legitimate. The problem, however, was (and is) how to determine the will of the people, both in political philosophy and in practice: Must the will be expressed in public debate, interpreted by an absolute ruler, decided in a vote or by a representative assembly? Grundtvig had a very strong sense of these problems, and, therefore, he preferred "opinion-guided absolutism" to the French Revolution, just as he translated and transformed Rousseau's ideology into a national-romantic context.

His reflections evolved in his so-called *Mands Minde forelæsninger* – that is, lectures on what lay "within Grundtvig's living memory" – given in the summer of 1838 and, by many, considered the first "talks," or lectures, in the People's High School tradition. This is because they treated historical topics in a subjective manner in taking their point of departure in Grundtvig's own experiences. Also, the lectures involved community singing and, as such, inaugurated a set combination of songs and lecture, later to be taken for granted in Folk High Schools and other Grundtvigian communities.

The main subject of the lectures was the political history of Grundtvig's lifetime, including a discussion of the French Revolution. To Grundtvig, French history was an instructive warning that showed that neither a monarch nor a people could be spared. According to Grundtvig, the French Revolution was doomed to failure for two reasons:

1 The abolition of the monarchy in France created a political vacuum, and, after listening to the voice of the people, no new political centre

gained the authority to decide the common good. On the contrary, everybody claimed to speak on behalf of the people but nobody turned out to speak above self- or sectional interests.

2 In the revolution an unenlightened mob, not a "people," assumed power. To Grundtvig, the enlightenment of the people and, more specifically, the forming of civic responsibility towards the general good was essential. It was for this reason that a People's High School education was deemed a necessary precondition for people's involvement in political decisions. Without enlightenment the crucial citizen subjectivity could not be formed. In this critique Grundtvig echoes Rousseau's idea of the general will as constitutive of the people. Without the ability to put the general good above self-interest, the will of the people could be neither formed nor formulated. Without responsible citizens only populism would rule.

To Grundtvig, his comparison between French and Danish history provided proof that the appointment of a responsible and fatherly absolute ruler was the best way to ensure the general will. Not only the ideal but also the touchstone of the kings responsibility was to be guided by the people's opinion: "Yes, gentlemen, I am an old Royalist. That you doubtless know. But if you did not know it previously, I hope that my historical lecture has taught you this: that even so, in no way do I belong with those extremists who want to turn kings into false gods, upon whose altars the people are to be sacrificed. But him alone I call a real King who – like all Denmark's Scyldings[6] with few exceptions – will sacrifice himself for the people and will listen to its voice as his best counsel" (Grundtvig 1877, 564).[7]

Grundtvig only acknowledges the king when the latter regards himself as the interpreter of the voice of the people, and he only acknowledges the population as a people once they acknowledge their responsibility towards the common good (which, in practice, can only occur after they have attended a People's High School).

I find the *Mands Minde* lectures central to an understanding of Grundtvig's political worldview since it is here that he, in an exemplary way, interprets eighteenth-century ideas about the general good (i.e., as the purpose of constitution and society) within the framework of national-romanticism. According to national-romantic logic every people has something distinctive – a *volksgeist* or national culture – and therefore a distinctive way of governing. Within this discursive framework Danish eighteenth-century ideas about opinion-guided absolutism were interpreted as original and, hence, as truly and specifically Danish. Thus, being a true national-romanticist, Grundtvig argued that the Danish people should not imitate the political constitutions of other people: to do so would be to misunderstand Rousseau's ideas as being universal. Instead, Grundtvig pointed to Nordic mythology as the source of a truly Danish constitution. He regarded Odin as a "god-king," a sort of opinion-guided but absolute king, and his assembly of advisory gods beneath the ash *Ygdrasil* as emblematic of the core of Danishness – that is, the hand of the king and the voice of the people, both of which are necessary.

Grundtvig's idea of history – namely, that history, especially Nordic antiquity, was the principal source of true Danishness and of the core of nationhood – was shared by many contemporary historians. At the same time, history was regarded as the prime educational tool for conveying responsibility for the general good. Grundtvig's interpretation of Nordic antiquity as opinion-guided absolutism was opposed by those who interpreted the Nordic past as a golden age of "popular freedom" and democracy. Whatever the ideal, history served as source and proof for whatever form of constitution one preferred (Damsholt 1995b).

GRUNDTVIG AND THE DANISH CONSTITUTION

As mentioned earlier, Grundtvig was a member of the Constituent Assembly that formed and passed the new Constitution. Grundtvig wanted to create a constitution that was in accordance with his ideals. And, in his attempts to influence the design and in the views he expressed in the periodical *The Dane*, one finds that his ideas are the same as they were earlier. His idea that opinion-guided monarchy was the original and true Danish form of constitution was still alive in 1848, although it was opposed by the majority of the assembly.

However, what the majority favoured made no impression on Grundtvig, who strongly advocated that the Danish Constitution had to be Danish – that is, it had to be in harmony with what he considered to be truly Danish. In the article entitled "Om Constitution og Statsforfatning" (Concerning the constitution), written in August 1848, Grundtvig criticizes the very concept of democracy not only because it was Greek but also because it expressed the idea of a people who guided and ruled themselves according to their own interests. To Grundtvig (1848a) this was incompatible with a civil society whose concern was to enact the general will, which required a political centre to be put into effect.

In *The Dane* the aforementioned article is followed by the song "Folkeligheden" (The people's character), which can be seen as a poetical expression of Grundtvig's political visions. According to the poem everything has to be Danish, or *folkeligt*, – that is, like the people (Grundtvig 1848b). Grundtvig did not like foreign words, and "Danish" and *folkeligt*/folkish can in fact be seen as his translation of "national" (Lundgreen-Nielsen 1992). In the poem the words *folkeligt* and "Danish" signify the same thing: the political system must correspond with the national culture of the Danish people, which, to Grundtvig, meant an opinion-guided monarchy.

"If the estates should break away from the common and national spirit, then society will fall apart" (Grundtvig 1848b, verse 5). Here Grundtvig displays his strong reservations about the parliamentary system of political parties, which he saw as an institutionalization of sectional interests and, thus, as a threat to true democracy since it undermined the ideal of the people as constituted by the common pursuit of the public good. Responsibility for the general good should guide everybody, and, this, in short, is what Grundtvig's concept of *folkelighed* is all about – at least in this context. The lines "To a people everybody belongs, who reckons him- or herself part of that people" sound inclusive, as though Grundtvig defines nationality as a matter of subjective choice. These two lines are often quoted out of context. Grundtvig, however, continues: "who has an ear for the mother tongue and who has 'fire' for the fatherland" – that is who is eager to defend the fatherland. Grundtvig's (1848b) definition of a people is subjective (as loyalty and the "heart" are decisive), but it presupposes not only the will but also the skills to be part of Danish culture and to speak the Danish language – otherwise one excludes oneself from the people. Grundtvig was aware of these principles as he was chair of the parliamentary group, which, in 1850, dealt with applications for obtaining Danish citizenship. His main criterion was that the applicants for citizenship be able to speak and understand Danish and that, by birth or through family, be connected with the Danish people and, thus, with the common good (Lundgreen-Nielsen 1992, 145).

Grundtvig wished for "Danish laws" – that is, he wanted a constitution that was in keeping with the Danish political culture. The Danish Constitution (*Grundloven*) was modelled on the Belgian Constitution of 1830, but, according to Grundtvig, it was inspired by French and German models and was, accordingly, designed for a "suspicious, quarrelsome and restless people." The Danish king and his advisors did not need "a safeguard against the ravishing voice of the people." On the contrary, according to Grundtvig, the Constitution should institutionalize "the hand of the king and the voice of the people, both strong and free." In other words, it should institutionalize some version of an opinion-guided monarchy that involves itself in free and open public debate with as many citizens as possible (always assuming such citizens are permeated by a desire for the general good).

The Constitution never lived up to Grundtvig's expectations, not even in its wording, in spite of his attempts to provide what he considered to be good Danish words as substitutes for foreign words. Of his innumerable proposed amendments only one succeeded, and it concerned oral proceedings and openness in the public administration (Dam 1983).

According to Grundtvig, the Danish Constitution expressed mistrust of the will and the voice of the people; therefore, he could not vote in favour of it. But he would not vote against it either since that would have placed him with those who wanted less freedom and fewer civil rights than he wanted. Grundtvig stuck to his political ideas even after the implementation of the Danish Constitution in 1849. For example, in 1850 he "confessed" to still believing in opinion-guided absolutism. His behaviour as a member of Parliament also confirmed this: he did not participate in regular parliamentary conventions and never joined a political party; rather, he turned Parliament into a platform from which he could address the public and the government.

Grundtvig advocated the idea that the Constitution should conform not only to the national culture but also to the historical situation. In 1866, when he was eighty-three years old, he was elected to Parliament, where he protested against the planned introduction of a privileged vote. Once "universal suffrage" was introduced,[8] Grundtvig believed that it should not be withdrawn, even though he was critical of the idea of representative democracy. Nevertheless, according to him, development could not go "backwards."

GRUNDTVIG AND LIBERAL GOVERNMENTALITY

Grundtvig believed in a degree of liberty that seemed unrealistic to his contemporaries (and probably to us as well). Not only did he advocate freedom of speech, press, religion, education, trade, assembly, and other traditional civic rights, but he also believed in an open and public discussion of military strategy during war, in voluntary participation in the defence of the country, voluntary contributions to poor relief, and even voluntary paying of taxes (Dam 1983).

This may sound like liberalism, but Grundtvig did not believe in Adam Smith's "hidden hand" – that is, that the individual pursuit of wealth is the best way to secure a happy society. On the contrary, extensive freedom presupposed citizens with a strong sense of responsibility towards the common good and the survival of the nation. In Grundtvig's (1848c) view, if young men were not ready to volunteer for the military defence of the country this would be a sign that the spirit of the people was already dead and, thus, there would be no reason to defend the country.

In this way Grundtvig was a radical spokesman for the eighteenth-century political logic of Rousseau, according to whom the Constitution should be inscribed in the hearts of the citizens rather than in the laws. Civic ethics, rather than laws and regulations, were to govern. In the perspective of the French philosopher Michel Foucault, this could be seen as a governmental practice that governs through "freedom itself and the 'soul of the citizens,' the life and life-conduct of the ethically free subjects" (Gordon 1991, 5). In his later lectures, Foucault defined and explored what he called "governmental rationality," or "governmentality" (1).

In this chapter I am concerned with such an emerging governmentality based on the government of the self (Rose 1999). The subjectivity of the people (i.e., morality or sense of responsibility) was the key problem for this form of government, which differed from earlier forms based on physical coercion. The governmentality of the emerging democratic nation-states presupposed that moral imperatives were heart-felt (e.g., inward urges or emotions). Thus, the ideas of the general good, of civic morality, and of the voice or the spirit of the people can be interpreted as part of the gradual development of a modern Western form of governmentality involving new technologies or "didactics of citizenship."

This is in keeping with the logic developed by J.J. Rousseau in his *Du Contrat Social* (1762), in which he argues that, because political and social unity are necessary, they must be supported by what he calls a civil religion. A civil religion works by making the fatherland the object of the citizens' worship and by teaching them to serve the state. It thereby secures a feeling of unity within, and the morality of, each citizen. Traditional religion might work in the same way, but it has certain dangers: for example, Christianity detaches the citizens' hearts from all earthly things. And, as Rousseau states: "I know of nothing more contrary to the social spirit" (1997 [1762], 147). Furthermore, Christianity preaches servitude and dependence, which is extremely favourable for tyranny.

However, as Rousseau points out, since it certainly matters to the state that each citizen has a religion that makes him/her love his/her duties, it is up to the sovereign to fix the articles of a purely civil profession of faith. The dogmas of this religion are only of concern to the state insofar as they "bear on morality and on the duties which everyone is bound to fulfil toward others" (Rousseau 1997 [1762]: 150). The articles of civil faith should be formulated as "sentiments of sociability, without which it is impossible to be either a good citizen or a loyal subject." "Beyond this everyone may hold whatever opinion he pleases," Rousseau argues, confirming the eighteenth-century idea of religion as something private. Indeed, religion was configured as an inner non-political zone in opposition to a secular political space (McCutcheon 2003).

The ideas that faith, emotion, and morality were inextricable and that they were the agents that could secure a heart-felt subjectivity called for new technologies related to the utopian civic self. Rousseau developed his reflections further in his exemplary *Considerations sur le gouvernement de Pologne et sur ca réformation projecté* (1772). Here he pondered the need for the Constitution to be inscribed in the hearts of the citizens, which, in his philosophy, was one of the central locations of the interior, moral topography of the self:

> There will never be a good and solid constitution unless the law reigns over the hearts of the citizens; as long as the power of legislation is sufficient to accomplish this, laws will always be evaded. But how can hearts be reached? That is a question to which our law-reformers, who never look beyond coercion and punishment, pay hardly any attention; and it is a question to the solving of which material rewards would perhaps be equally ineffective … How then is it possible to move the hearts of men, and to make them love the fatherland and its laws? Dare I say it? Through children's games; through institutions which seem idle and frivolous to superficial men, but which form cherished habits and invincible attachments. (Rousseau 1986 [1772], 162)

With reference to antiquity, Rousseau (1986 [1772], 165) argues that public ceremonies are perfect for increasing citizens' love for the fatherland: national religious ceremonies, games, exercises, and spectacles "touched their hearts, inflamed them with a lively spirit of emulation, and attached them strongly to that fatherland with which they were meant to be incessantly preoccupied." This, according to Rousseau, is "the art of ennobling souls" (170). In keeping with Foucault's characterization of the emerging governmentality of nation-states, Rousseau finds that education and the setting of a good example are more successful than are prohibition and the enforcement of strict rules. Education has the ability to give souls a "national formation" and make them "patriotic by inclination, by passion, by necessity" (171). According to Rousseau, civic subjectivity had to become an inward urge rather than an outer claim. And festivals and rituals were perceived as technologies by which the civic self could be transformed and generated.

These ideas pertain to several of the key figures in Grundtvig's Utopia of responsible citizens. As mentioned, the idea of the heart and "love" as a central moral topography is also important in understanding Grundtvig's political reasoning (see Jonas, chap. 8, this volume). The idea of "internal and heart-felt" morality was also crucial in eighteenth-century pietism, and, as with the leaders of contemporary popular religious movements, Grundtvig saw no contradiction between Christianity and civic virtue. On the contrary, though he seldom referred to religious life when discussing his political visions, Grundtvig believed that the reason the French people were superficial and their morality merely external had to do with their neglect of religion. It was precisely because of their Christianity that the Danish people's love was stronger, and their responsibility towards the common good superior, than that of the French. The Danes were, indeed, "the people of the heart" (Damsholt 2007, 137–8).

Love and the heart, however, should not be subject to external rules. An example of the causal relationships between freedom and responsibility may be seen in how Grundtvig and his fellows argued against the introduction of poverty laws. They completely opposed instituting a law stipulating that people not able to provide for themselves should be "entitled" to receive public support (Stendal Pedersen 1999).

Grundtvig did not believe that what he referred to as the "bonds of love" between rich and poor should be institutionalized as an article of right. If the "natural and voluntary help" from the wealthy became an obligation, it would ruin the reciprocal responsibility that "naturally permeated" the population. Instead of being a matter of rights and obligations (which, to Grundtvig, meant a matter of coercion), helping should be voluntary, something that one chooses to do. In Foucault's words, it should be a result of the government of the self. Grundtvig seems to have held the classic liberalist idea that "governing was always governing too much" (Foucault 1997, 76). Governing (too much) risked destroying the utopian subjectivity of reciprocal responsibility, which is what Grundtvig expected from the Danish population. In this sense,

Grundtvig had a strong sense of the inner logic of the Western governmentality that Foucault characterizes as the "government of the self."

CONCLUSION

The core of Grundtvig's political ideology is freedom – freedom of the voice of the people, and freedom of the king (or the government) to consider the common good and the will of the people. To Grundtvig, the central democratic element is free public debate and, especially, a general responsibility towards the common good. However, to ensure that all potential members of the public participate in the debate and display their responsibility as citizens, they must be enlightened. In other words, enlightenment was needed to inscribe civic virtue in their hearts.

This being the case, Grundtvig's view of democracy and representative government is indebted to eighteenth-century political (and even republican) philosophy, with its central concepts of the people, of the general will of the people, and of absolutism as a mutually binding contract between a king and his people. A people might consist of several nations as long as patriotism permeated their actions. However, in Grundtvig's hands, eighteenth-century ideology is interpreted within the framework of national-romanticism and, thus, is translated and transformed. Grundtvig articulated the reciprocal relationship between freedom and responsibility and "opinion-guided government" not as a universal political vision but, rather, as a specific political culture developed in Denmark and specific to the Danish people.

Are Grundtvig's ideas of democracy of interest today? With his nationalism, his advocacy of absolutism, and his insistence on the principle that the performance of all civic duties must be voluntary, many would consider his political program a threat to multicultural and democratic welfare societies and, therefore, as unrealistic today as they were when he first voiced them. However, Grundtvig's political visions go beyond nationalism as they are inscribed in a broad Danish tradition of the interpretation of democracy, which focuses more on the debate, the responsibility, and the spirit of the people than on democracy as a formal system of voting and representation. This idea of democracy is older than that of the democratic nation-state as its legacy is the eighteenth-century republican ideology of the people as constituted by the general will and by the pursuit of the general good. It presupposes a willingness to take the people as a whole into consideration instead of focusing only on separate interests. This is the reason Grundtvig insisted on a monarch rather than on what would amount to special interests as the best interpreter and guarantor of the general good, as well as of the enlightenment and education of the people. The king's hand and the people's voice – both strong and free.

The republican tradition also presupposes that civic virtues and responsibilities are emotional and heart-felt. Though Grundtvig was a national-romanticist he never believed that the Danes were responsible and democratic by nature alone. Grundtvig would only consider a given population as "a people" if it had achieved the necessary sense of responsibility towards the common good. It was for this reason that the People's High School or some other means of citizen education was always necessary. Thus, one can see that the Danish People's High School movement is deeply entangled with ideas about the utopian subjectivity of responsible citizens and the governmentality of the self.

NOTES

1 See Damsholt (1995a). The argument is also partly in line with (Dam 1983; and Thanning 1949).

2 He also ruled over Iceland and the Faroe Islands, asserted his rights to Greenland, was duke of Stormarn and Ditmarchen, and was count of Oldenburg-Delmenhorst.

3 The Pufendorf tradition of interpreting absolutism as a second social contract between a ruler and his people was introduced in Denmark-Norway by Ludvig Holberg (1716).

4 The song is the last part of the poem *Den Danske Nødvendighed* (1853)

5 Translated by Sid Bradley.

6 According to translator Sid Bradley, this English form of the word occurs in *Beowulf*.

7 Translated by Sid Bradley.

8 According to the Danish Constitution, only males of a certain age and heading their own household could vote. Approximately 15 percent of the population.

REFERENCES

Bjørn, C. 2007. *Grundtvig som politiker* [Grundtvig as a politician]. Copenhagen: Anis.

Boll-Johansen, H. 1989. "Romantik og nationalisme: Relationer mellem individ og stat i det 18. og 19. Århundrede" [Romanticism and nationalism:

The relationship between the individual and the state in the 18th and 19th centuries]. In *Kaos og kosmos* [Chaos and cosmos], ed. H. Boll-Johansen and F. Lundgreen-Nielsen. Copenhagen: Museum Tusculanum.

Dam, P. 1983. *Politikeren Grundtvig* [Grundtvig the politician]. Copenhagen: Aros.

Damsholt, T. 1995a. "Jeg er en gammel royalist, det ved de nok: Elementer i Grundtvigs politiske tænkning" [I'm an old royalist, you know: Elements of Grundtvig's political thinking]. *Grundtvig Studier* 46: 140–62.

– 1995b. "On the Concept of the 'Folk.'" *Ethnologia Scandinavica* 25: 5–24.

– 2007. "Udvorteshedens triumph: Fransk og dansk politisk kultur" [The triumph of the exterior: French and Danish political culture]. In *Danmark og Napoleon* [Denmark and Napoleon], ed. E. Lerdrup Bourgois and N. Høffding. Gjern: Hovedland.

Foucault, M. 1997. "The Birth of Biopolitics." In *Ethics: Subjectivity and Truth*. Vol. 1: *Essential Works of Foucault, 1954–1984*., ed. Paul Rabinow, 73–80. London: Penguin.

Gordon, C. 1991. "Governmental Rationality: An Introduction." In *The Foucault Effect: Studies in Governmentality*, ed. G. Burchell, C. Gordon, and P. Miller. Chicago: University of Chicago Press.

Grundtvig, N.F.S. 1815. *Europa, Frankrig og Napoleon, en dansk historisk Betragtning* [Europe, France, and Napoleon: A Danish historical view]. Copenhagen: Andreas Seidelin.

– 1836. *Det Danske Fiir-kløver eller Danskheden partisk betragtet* [The Danish four-leaf clover or a partiality for Danishness]. Copenhagen: Wahlske Boghandel. Reprinted in *The School for Life: N.F.S. Grundtvig on Education for the People*, trans. and ed. E. Broadbridge, co-ed C. Warren and U. Jonas, 126–65. Aarhus: Aarhus University Press.

– 1848a. "Om Constitution og statsforfatning i Danmark" [Concerning the constitution in Denmark]. *Danskeren* [The Dane] 24 (August): 369–80.

– 1848b. "Folkeligheden" [The people's character]. *Danskeren* [The Dane] 24 (August): 381–4.

– 1848c. "Dansk Rigsdag-Tale imod den saakaldte 'almindelige Værnepligt'" [Danish parliament-speech against the so-called "ordinary conscription"]. *Danskeren* [The Dane] 41 (December): 641–55.

– 1877. *Mands Minde, 1788–1838: Foredrag over det sidste halve Aarhundredes Historie holdte 1838 af Nik. Fred. Sev. Grundtvig* [Within living Memory, 1788–1838. Lectures on the History of the last half century given in 1838 by Nik. Fred. Sev. Grundtvig]. Copenhagen: Karl Schønbergs Forlag.

Holberg, L. 1715. *Moralske Kierne eller Introduction til Naturens og Folkerettens Kundskab* [Moral Care, or introduction to natural and international law]. Copenhagen: Johan Kruse.

Korsgaard, O. 2012. *N.F.S. Grundtvig*. Copenhagen: Djøf.

Landes, J.B. 1998. "Bodies in Democratic Public Space: An Eighteenth-Century Perspective." In *Making Worlds: Gender, Metaphor, Materiality*, ed. S.H. Aiken, A.E. Brigham, S.A. Marston, and P.M. Waterstone. Tucson: University of Arizona Press.

Lind, G. 1987. "Military and Absolutism: The Army Officers of Denmark-Norway as a Social Group and Political Factor, 1660–1848." *Scandinavian Journal of History* 12: 221–43.

Lind, G. 1994. *Hæren og magten i Danmark, 1614–1662* [The army and power in Denmark, 1614–1662]. Odense: Odense Universitetsforlag.

Lundgreen-Nielsen, F. 1992. "Danskhed i krige og kriser 1800–1864" [Danishness in wars and crises, 1800–1864]. In *På sporet af dansk identitet* [On the trail of Danish identity]. Copenhagen: Spektrum.

McCutcheon, R. 2003. *The Discipline of Religion: Structure, Meaning, Rhetoric*. London: Taylor and Francis.

Rose, N. 1999. *Governing the Soul: The Shaping of the Private Self*. 2nd ed. London: Routledge.

Rousseau, J.J. 1997 [1762]. *The Social Contract and other Later Political Writings*, ed. V. Gourevitch. Cambridge: Cambridge University Press.

Seip, J.A. 1958. "Teorien om det opinionsstyrte enevælde" [The theory of opinion-guided absolutism]. *Norsk Historisk Tidsskrift* [Nordic journal of history] 38: 397–463.

Stendal Pedersen, F. 1999. "N.F.S. Grundtvig og socialpolitikken i Den grundlovgivende Rigsforsamling i foråret 1849" [N.F.S. Grundtvig and the social policy of the Constitutional Assembly in the spring of 1849]. *Historie* 1999 (1): 32–58.

Thanning, K. 1949. "Grundtvig og den grundlovgivende rigsforsamling" [Grundtvig and the Constitutional Assembly]. *Grundtvig Studier* 2 (1): 35–73.

8

On the Church, the State, and the School: Grundtvig as Enlightenment Philosopher and Social Thinker

UFFE JONAS

> Is spelling right or wrong a light
> alone to scholars given?
> Oh no, God grants this good to most,
> his light a gift of heaven.
>
> Grundtvig 2011 [1839a], 255

VARIOUS KINDS OF ENLIGHTENMENT

Grundtvig's song "Enlightenment" (1839), so beloved of the People's High Schools, has achieved such widespread popularity due to its emphasis on educating the people rather than just the scholars. Yet it should not be read as an anti-intellectual proclamation. What Grundtvig is rejecting is a particular rationalist view of education – one that leads to self-centredness and that excludes the broader public from enjoying its fruits.

He prefers to speak of "various kinds of enlightenment" – in the plural (Grundtvig 2011 [1834], 111). There are Jewish, Greek, Latin, French, German, British, and Nordic enlightenments since each of these peoples may claim to have developed its own specific traditions. Indeed, in principle, every living creature undergoes its own "enlightenment." That is how Grundtvig can say: "There are as many enlightenments given as there are days in the year, in fact there are as many kinds of enlightenments as there are heads with eyes in them." And this is how he can go on to emphasize: "When I speak of people's enlightenment ... it is above all their own enlightenment I mean" (ibid.).

The human world, too, contains "various kinds of enlightenment." Grundtvig defines the "individual's enlightenment," the "people's enlightenment," "life enlightenment," and "Christian enlightenment" as four different modes, or concentric spheres, of enlightenment. Each of them surrounds and forms human life in various ways, and each includes experiences from the previous spheres, moving them into a broader dimension and each time adding some crucial new element. According to Grundtvig's vision, during our lifetime we do not live in one society only but, rather, undergo the expansive experience of a variety of "societies." And, when seen together as a historical unfolding, each of these societies will be in a particular relation, either harmonic or dissonant, with the others.

In the innermost circle lies the first, and most elementary, of societies – that between a child and her/his family. At the age of discretion this dissolves into the society of citizens and the state, which, for Grundtvig, is a natural extension of the "heart-tie" that links the family. Premodern society was also pre-individualized, a social order based on principles of heredity and kin-relations. On the other hand, modern society presupposes a weakening if not a severing of the blood-tie that links parents and children. And it is precisely at this point in the transition from the old, hierarchical society of kin and stations into the shared civil society of the new nation-state that Grundtvig proposes the establishment of the People's High Schools. A popular boarding school system designed to procure a rite of passage from the old, more literal, sense of kinship and into the new civic awareness.

In the next sphere, beyond the single nation-state, lies human society in general, with the university as the outpost of all state-supported institutions, building on humanism as its ideal and the pursuit of science and learning as its method. The outer sphere, corresponding to the idea of "one humanity," is a global civil society with a new cosmopolitical social awareness and new globalized social forms. It was for the fulfilment of such humane and neoclassical ideals that Grundtvig proposed the establishment of a new internordic university in Gothenburg (Grundtvig 2011 [1839c]).

Beyond these three inner spheres lies, according to Grundtvig, the classical Christian image of "God's State" (St Augustine's *Civitate Dei*), an imagined spiritual society realized only in glimpses. The revelatory State of Jerusalem suggests a future society in which wisdom is linked with reason, the gods with humans, and the heavens with the earth. For Grundtvig, the conscious fulfillment of this spiritual community of love – reaching from the individual family through the national and into the international community – represents the final harmony of the spheres, the ultimate spiritual archetype, and the cosmic destination of all human social development. For the sake of furthering such divine-human interaction Grundtvig even suggested the future possibility of a church-school, signifying not only a Sunday school for children but also a sort of divinity school for spiritual grown-ups. And he named it a "School for Song" because there you would learn how to join in the celestial harmonies; how to listen, sing, and walk with the gods; and how to make the love, wisdom, and welfare of the heavens become manifest on earth. His great poetical achievement, "Collection of Songs to the Danish Church," with its body of more than fifteen hundred sacred hymns, was meant exactly for such divine song practice.

ENLIGHTENMENT CRITICISM

Grundtvig was both a champion and a critic of enlightenment. The battle against "false enlightenment" is one of his most distinctive hallmarks for he regarded the prevailing Latin, German, and French concepts of enlightenment as being far too slanted towards individualism and rationalism. The latter is a dangerous form of superstition for it not only terrorizes our emotions and actions but also instills in us the illusion of knowledge, even though, in reality, this is only a much restricted and fragmented form of expertise: "For sense and reason clearly have just as much superstition, infatuation, and fanaticism as imagination and feeling. Indeed sense and reason are even more dangerous now: not only are they far too dominant in human life, but their aberrations have the appearance of enlightenment" (Grundtvig 2011 [1834], 84).

Grundtvig did not oppose enlightenment as such, he simply pleaded for a more universal and down-to-earth approach to it as it should encompass the entire human experience and not be confined merely to one side of the brain. The imagination, the emotions, and also the hands make as strong a demand for enlightenment as does the brain. With history as our guide and all our cognitive faculties activated, we should gradually learn to see reality through the lens of wisdom; that is, from many experience-based angles and dimensions at the same time: "Superficial enlightenment must be fought with a more comprehensive enlightenment if it is to be defeated" (Grundtvig 2011, [1834], 82).

The abstract concept of enlightenment that was issuing from the universities and pervading the entire educational system in Grundtvig's time – and that to some extent continues to do so today – should be neither ignored nor eradicated; rather, it should be supplemented and balanced by a more expansive and pervasive concept based on history and human experience. It is no use

> either ignoring the superficial enlightenment that has taken place of its own accord or attempting to eradicate it. We must simply try to procure a competent counterweight to it in a deeper enlightenment – not just one on paper but one that actually influences life and thereby demonstrates its legitimacy. Already in this latter regard such a deeper enlightenment constitutes a counterweight to university education and cannot therefore thrive in connection with it, so that if the People's High School and the university are bound together, one of them must change its nature. This means that either civil education will lose its character at the university or that the university academics will acquire the desire actually to influence life. (Grundtvig 2011 [1834], 97)

Enlightenment is not a human invention but an inherent characteristic of the universe. It is the actual light breaking through the spheres of the world that brings about a life-awakening enlightenment as an inner growth process in living organisms.

Against this light-and-growth image Grundtvig sets "the black school," the school for rationalist reduction and spiritual torpor, for it functions as a systematic restraint and a denial of the possibility of human growth. Through the fearful examination system of his day the idea of universal light and growth is reduced to a petit bourgeois dream of a life of economic security under social control. In place of human growth in an ever-expanding universe it offers an "assured livelihood" and causes us "to sacrifice our lads with cheeks a-glowing / to Latin Grammar and a certain death" (Grundtvig 2011 [1839b], 261).

Enlightenment is pictured here as a rebellious offspring of the monastic church and the Latin school. Here, the human body is disowned and all its natural instincts are driven into the brain. In Grundtvig's (2011 [1847], 334) view, the prevailing Franco-German rationalism is still the product of such forced enlightenment as it abolishes "all laws of human nature" to introduce a new religion instead – that is, "a new faith in reason and knowledge, in grammar and mathematics, in short:

in the omnipotence of theory, which is regarded as the only means to salvation."

However, Grundtvig argues, it is not the scholars' task to raise everyone up to their own abstract sphere of existence. Instead of wishing "to drag the people up to our airy emptiness" – an idealistic, abstract level of understanding leading to egocentricity and self-alienation – the academics (and Grundtvig includes himself here) ought to try "lowering ourselves into the people's vitality" in order to enlighten them "from the inside" (Grundtvig 2011 [1847], 325–6). Grundtvig imagined that the meeting between the people and the scholars at the People's High School would give rise to a new learning based on conversation and life-wisdom, on the one hand, and a flourishing civil society, on the other.

Here we see the immanent feature of Grundtvig's own concept of enlightenment – namely, his particular Christian insistence on the principle of incarnation. It is not we human beings who are to be pulled up from below or who rise to the skies above in order to become purely abstract, bodiless spirit; rather, it is the spirit that comes to meet us, tangibly and cordially, in order to enlighten and inspire us and to help us improve our actual life conditions.

In Grundtvig's chronology, since the Renaissance we have lived in "the Age of Reason" – that is, in the rising era of reflection, learning, and rationalism. And "the enlightenment of reason" is first and foremost "the enlightenment of the individual" because it yields only an ever-increasing individualization. He also refers to this as "the Era of the School." Since this is the era in which he lives, Grundtvig fully recognizes that enlightenment must begin with the freedom, the development potential, and the educational needs of the individual. Simultaneously, he contests the validity of individualism, of unbridled criticism and the cultivation of the intellect, as being a kind of modern pseudo-religion that raises narrow-minded academic standards into the highest law of enlightenment. If the intellect is not managed properly it is likely to turn us away from our emotional commitment to the group (or the social class) in the direction of egocentric careerism with no sense of the needs of nature, of the whole individual, or of the whole of society. From being our best helpers, reason and learning become an impending danger for society and its ability to cohere. For in the nature of things experience confirms "that the superficial enlightenment which self-conceit and self-will naturally develop and propagate perpetually turns bad into worse. It suppresses and as far as possible kills off imagination and feeling, which have created our social relations and are therefore their born guardians and internal spokesmen" (Grundtvig 2011 [1834], 83).

IMAGINED COMMUNITIES

If, as Grundtvig claims, our social relations rest largely on the imagination and the emotions, this means that society is bound together by something other than laws and institutions, bricks and mortar. A society is primarily a community of feeling that lives in the imagination of its citizens. It is what Benedict Anderson (1983, 6) calls an "imagined community," which brings and holds together people who neither know nor associate with one another, yet who share the experience of a common interest and destiny.

We are "Danes" or "Canadians" simply because we think, feel, and regard ourselves as Danes or Canadians. We are "Europeans" and "world citizens" only insofar as we experience ourselves as citizens of a world endowed with the same dignity and value as ourselves. And we are citizens of the cosmos only to the extent that we are able to think, feel, and act as citizens within a spiritual world order. Enlightenment must therefore promote not mere individualism, learning, and rationality because when cultivated one-sidedly these are counter-productive to the state's interest and cohesion, which rest on our human sense of fellowship and powers of imagination. In principle, enlightenment should be able to penetrate all areas of consciousness and thus open the senses of each individual to life in all its depth and variety.

It is such an enlightenment that Grundtvig refers to as "Education for the State." As the chief guardian of this fellowship, the state should see its own interest in supporting a civil education that encompasses the whole of human life and not merely the life of the intellect. And this should occur at every level of the educational system, from the village school to the university. To protect itself against the many and serious social sicknesses that ensue from a one-sided educational focus on the intellect, the state should take pains to "vaccinate" its citizens against this at as early an age as possible – before the decay of our innate spiritual abilities becomes irreversible:

> This spiritual vaccination will probably not safeguard us entirely, any more than the physical kind does against natural smallpox, but many will thereby escape it, and if the vaccine is genuine, even the most malignant smallpox will be appreciably allayed by those who

> are prepared. For self-conceit, self-will, and the whole greed for self-dependence is like the path of small-pox, in that once they have broken out, inoculation is of no use. It must therefore be undertaken the sooner the better, while imagination and feeling are still the strongest powers and form a natural counterweight to the aberrations of reason.
>
> However, a genuine enlightenment extends itself to the whole of human life; it shows the deep coinherence between the life of the individual, the nation, and the whole human race, and it develops a way of thinking that is desirable for all social relations. Such an enlightenment the State must by no means leave to its own devices, i.e. leave it to the individual, scattered householders and to teachers who will always do their best to disseminate it in their local circles. This genuine enlightenment the authorities must take a fatherly responsibility for at all levels of education, from the common people to the erudite scholars, if the State is to be rescued and to blossom instead of perishing from "enlightenment." (Grundtvig 2011 [1834], 83)

Grundtvig thinks of the state as an imagined community, as an emotional bond, and as a concrete working society. All three dimensions – the head, the heart, and the hand – belong to a valid concept of "the State." The social, emotional, creative, and spiritual abilities are at least as important as are the purely intellectual – what he imagines is a kind of enlightenment "in depth," whereby everyone gradually becomes involved in wider and wider spheres of life. They will then experience an increasing degree of spiritual intensity and creative freedom, while at the same time confronting the collective and personal shadows that resist such integration.

Grundtvig's belief that the cohesion of the state rests primarily on imagination and feeling requires that citizens be able to form an image of the state in their hearts. "A State," he says, "is a real life expression of the heart-relation." As educated citizens we should be able to conceive an image of the state and to love this image. In Grundtvig's early and little-known work, "On the Church, the State, and the School" (1819), which is his major work on social philosophy, he puts it thus: "If we are to conceive of the State from its foundations, we must see it in our hearts! … [B]eyond question, in our hearts, for you can easily convince yourself that only those who agree in their hearts make common cause, and can you imagine a truly powerful, living State where that is not the case?" (Grundtvig 1819, 47f).

In this early article no clear distinction is made between state and nation. However, such a distinction is evidently latent in the imagery that Grundtvig employs. The heart-state relation does not mean that the state can take all its members to heart but, rather, that all its members should take the state to heart for, as Grundtvig (1819, 50) says: "What was to be shown was not that the State embraced the heart-relation but the exact opposite, that the heart-relation embraced the State!" In other words, the state is an organization within civil society, not the other way round. It is the physical heart-muscle that distributes and guides the spiritual streams that emanate from the larger heart of civil society. The state guards society and administers its infrastructure, while society embraces the state as its inner life, foundation, and reason for being. Thus, built into the image of the state as a heart-relation is the idea of a "civil society" as the spiritual and reflexive dimension of the state.

In 1820, with the publication of his Philosophy of Right, Hegel completely changed the meaning of civil society, giving rise to a modern liberal understanding of it as a form of market society, which leads through Marx into modern economics. Grundtvig's 1819 concept is less reductive and more in line with the older distinctions, for example, those of Hobbes and Locke, who did not hold civil society to be a separate realm from the state. However, Grundtvig's peculiar image of the state as a heart leans towards a clearer distinction between "state" and "nation." And it is this distinction that Grundtvig develops in his educational writings from the 1820s and 1830s. Without ever cutting the heart-tie between state and society, he gradually transfers his social emphasis from the state to the people and thus takes a somewhat more distanced stance towards the state as such.

In a material sense the state is held together only by power relations – that is, political and economic interests – but Grundtvig argues strongly against this being its true foundation. And he warns against the cynicism that politicians and the civil service are tempted to cultivate. The education of the state, on the other hand, rests mainly on the quality of its heart-relations – that is, on the level of its social integration and the enlightenment of the people. Likewise, a healthy political system is based on the strength of civil society – that is, on the well-developed public spirit of its civil servants, on its politicians' ability to formulate a collective community vision, and on the citizens' shared love of an imagined community. A love centred on the so-called "four-leaf clover" – that is, the national symbols of God, king, fatherland, and mother-tongue. Grundtvig's original idea for the People's High School was therefore to establish a higher educational institution in the civil and national public spirit for future civil servants. This would replace the current practice, whereby civil servants learned Latin, spoke German, and saw themselves as a special breed above the common people (Jonas 2011a, 126f). It could well be argued that from such a non-elitist philosophy, and only secondarily from the influence of socialism as such, stems the typical Scandinavian emphasis on relative equality in social, political, and economic relations.

CHURCH, STATE, AND SCHOOL

The main concern of Grundtvig's article is to establish the proper distinctions and relations between the three principal domains of society. In his classic concept of concentric spheres, the "school" (i.e., education) is enclosed by the state. The state, in turn, is enclosed by the church. The successful training of children in their family feeling of kinship may dissolve into the more abstract kinship that links the citizens of a "nation," which, in turn, leads to the idea of a kinship of all humanity beyond nations and to the even more fantastic concept of a "holy community," the true church that unites and unties all who, in their hearts, seek union with God: "For just as the true Church on earth must be a community of faith in a Word that reveals man's eternal destination and the path to it, so must the true State be a united endeavor to fulfill man's temporal destination. And since this cannot be other than steady steps on the road to his eternal destination, it is clear that the true State is a creation of the true Church" (Grundtvig 1819, 47f).

In Grundtvig's model society, love of self is expanded into love of one's neighbour, of one's community, and then of one's country. Conversely, the belligerent, self-serving tendencies of the state can be restricted by its regard for the citizens' welfare, community, and love of God, which is the goal of all education and enlightenment in humanity and the church.

At the deepest level, Grundtvig's organic mode of thought links the social body with the human body, which, in turn, is "created in the image of God." The essential qualities of the soul, which are united in humanity, are found again apportioned in the most important institutions of society for "the Church signifies the imagination, the State signifies feeling, and the School signifies the intellect" (Grundtvig 1819, 21). Society's three main organs, the church, the state, and the school, are thus an expression of the three fundamental dimensions in which the human heart-relation unfolds itself.

The first dimension of our heart-relation is "to the invisible outside us," which is primarily imaginary and which Grundtvig therefore calls the spiritual relation, or, in more religious terms, the God-relation. The second is our kinship and neighbour-relation. This constitutes the bonds of society, which have deep roots in the marital and family-relation, and it is largely defined by feeling. It is from these, says Grundtvig, that social feeling – the feeling for one's community – springs, through a gradual extension (or dilution) of the family-feeling, which "diffuses its branches in every possible direction such as family, and family through marriage."

Third, and last, is the relation to oneself, which is the personal, psychical, and educational self-relation. This has its roots quite naturally in the personal life in that each is closest to him- or herself. The self-relation is administered by the guardian-state through its educational institutions until this cultural training is assumed either fully or partially by each individual – in the same way that the state-relation was administered under the church's guardianship until it felt mature enough to declare its independence. According to Grundtvig, this spiritual tripartition of humanity and its social relations arises quite naturally from the Christian revelation, for

> just as the Christian revelation teaches us that spiritual love has three branches: to God, to our neighbor, and to ourselves and that in the last two cases ought to keep its pace and equilibrium, so we also discover in human life the tangible effects of love in all three directions:
>
> 1 Love of God, which clearly must be sought in the church, itself an effect of the Word of power, and which unites its actions and effects in glorifying that Word.
> 2 Love of one's neighbor, which has its roots in the marriage-relation, from which it shoots into a twin branch in the mutual relationship between parents and children, the stem of which in turn extends its branches in every possible direction such as family, and family through marriage.
> 3 Love of self, which has its roots in personal existence, and since each is closest to himself, it cannot fail to involve itself in all our heart-relations. But it is no less true that love of God, by seizing all manner of love unconditionally, demands its integration into itself, and that love of one's neighbor presupposes its limitation.
>
> From this we can conclude that the philosophers who held that all human life springs from love of self have thought and said something very sensible, in that our common sense cannot be other than

> an intelligent perception of our personal existence and the relations that stem from that. But we must also admit that the philosophers have thereby denounced the entire human race, which was undoubtedly bound to an unrestricted, exclusive love of truth, and to a love of kin, that in its temporal relations was a match for love of self. (Grundtvig 1819, 306ff)

Thus, it is to safeguard these three fundamental dimensions of human experience that the three main institutions of society are organized. In Grundtvig's words: "The Church expresses man's relation to God, the State his relation to the human race, and the School his relation to himself" (20).

THE CHURCH AS A SCHOOL OF THE IMAGINATION

When Grundtvig writes that the church "denotes the power of the imagination" he is thinking of the church as an imagined community built by "the living word." The church is neither a building nor a book but, rather, a community of words. It constitutes a comprehensive symbolic corpus, a specific logo-poetical language, whose grammar is dogmatics and whose structure (linguistics) is manifested in the historical community of conversation and understanding of the church. Over the course of time this language has been further formed through the development of a particular hermeneutic, or art of interpretation (see, for example, Frye 1982).

As with other languages, the language of the church has users who are more or less skilled. The most skilled, the nestors, are also called the church fathers, the church teachers, or the church doctors; while the innovators, the spiritual seers and social pioneers of the language, are called Apostles, Prophets, Mystics, and Reformers. The distinctiveness of this corpus of symbols lies neither in the language itself nor in the difficulty that may accompany its appropriation. It lies in the exceptional surroundings to which the language refers and from which it acquires its validity. For it is not a normal world of visible objects, events, and phenomena; rather, it is an invisible world, a prismatic spiritual corpus that entrenches itself in wisdom and lucidity around the material world. This imaginary corpus is also called "the body of Christ."

When the name "Jesus" is uttered or called upon as though the person to whom it refers were spiritually and physically present, he appears to the inner ear, the inner eye, and the inner sensitivity. Thus, an invisible heart-tie is formed to an invisible world. In principle, this is like any other highly specialized language: only those whose inner senses, sensitivity, and sensibleness have been awakened through the training of their spiritual imagination can begin to perceive the reality to which the words refer. This is why people go to church: to hear the Word, to learn the language, to enter into the fellowship of enlightenment, and to come closer to the mysterious world that it reveals. This is why, in this language, Christ is called "the living word" (Logos).

The church is the spiritual and social instance that obliges the imagination to transform from a daydreamer into an exact instrument of cognition. Ideally, the church constitutes the spiritual fellowship, or cultural community, whose purpose is to rouse the human imagination and to bring human creativity into harmony with divine inspiration. This, says Grundtvig, is the greatest "Human Path" imaginable for it embraces our idea of the whole universe, its origin, its coherence, and its ultimate purpose, along with our personal and social relation to it.

The idea of a loving God is essential not for the state, as such, but for the development of the human imagination and the altruism upon which the state and its citizens' welfare builds. It is the human ability to imagine, the ability to conceive metaphorically and conceptually what cannot yet be seen or touched, that is the spiritual force that builds a society. Similarly, altruism is the creative social force that stems from the ability to imagine the advantage of actions that are not performed for one's own immediate gain.

Grundtvig was a strong supporter of mythology, poetry, and stories as symbolic forms of cultural education. The mythical, mystical world of symbols and the narrative universes of literature are not mere fictions, or dead traditions, or ancient superstitions that need to be eradicated. On the contrary, myths are forms of advanced cognition born by images and holistically oriented. They must be transmitted, taught, and trained from generation to generation in order to stimulate and discipline the spiritual imagination, thus pointing it in the right direction. They strengthen our ability to build a community that is permeated by living visions and not just mechanical and economic calculations.

It was therefore crucial for Grundtvig to create an educational system in which the school's natural focus on developing the intellect was balanced by a corresponding focus on pupils' artistic, musical, creative, historical, and social skills. If an increasing individualization and rationalization were not balanced by a deeper and more creative sense of "community," then society would gradually fall apart in a tangle of insentient egoism and materialism, offset only by strict laws, state provisions, and naked economic necessity.

For Grundtvig, the church's body of stories, myths, and symbols constitutes the grand narrative of the spiritual fellowship of humankind, of the supremacy of the invisible world over the visible, and the victory of life over death. Just so, in its long labyrinthine cellars the church contains all the spiritual incentives and practices that are required to awaken and sanctify not just the spiritual imagination of the individual but also the spiritual human being as such, the being who, as the image and embryo of God, lies hidden in all of us.

THE STATE AS THE CHILD OF THE CHURCH

The relation between state and church may be conceived in both an ideal and a historical perspective. According to Grundtvig, the state has its spiritual source in the true and invisible church, while historically it springs from the dominant and visible church – that is, it emanates from the idea of an ideal community of love of God and neighbour, and from the revelation that pictures the genesis of such a fellowship. Even though he allows the state relative autonomy in relation to the church, it cannot exclude this ideal image without falling into a jumble of conflicting selfish interests.

From a spiritual viewpoint it is the love of God that creates a society because it is a belief in, and a love of, the highest Good that enables us to imagine, feel, and manifest what we cannot yet see. A purely materialist concept of society characterized by the logic of "guns, germs, and steel" will miss that mark. To Grundtvig, nation building is just as much a spiritual and symbolic endeavour within the hearts and minds of the people as it is a material and practical realization of the hands of the people. The truly creative actions are those that are performed as a result of the spiritual attraction to an inspiring ideal, the attraction to something intangible that needs to be pictured and manifested, not to those ideals that are practised for the sake of personal or collective gain alone. Society will always develop in that space of tension between spiritual and practical incentives.

One question that was fought over in the discussion of the philosophy of the "state" in the eighteenth century was whether the idea of "God" could be separated from the idea of the "church" as the formal head of the state. Grundtvig rebukes the secularist arguments of the "so-called enlightenment," here represented in hypothetical form by Voltaire:

> Seen in this way, can the State itself stand on its own two feet; can it live without a ruling Church; can it be indifferent to whether the Church is true or false?
>
> If in answering these questions we also allow it to remain undecided whether God exists, then we must begin by examining whether or not the preservation of the State is founded on the will of those who constitute it. And the undeniability of that fact would then prove how the overriding self-interest of the individual of necessity undermines and gradually dissolves the State. From this again we might conclude, as Voltaire said, that if God did not exist, the State would have to create such an entity. It would be equally easy to demonstrate that if the god or the revelation was to be of any benefit to the State, it would – even if it was a god and revelation of its own making – have to profess it to be something higher and place it above itself. For otherwise it would at most be a theatrical entertainment for the people which could distract their thoughts for a moment but could never unite their wills or bend their hearts to obedience and sacrifice for the State. (Grundtvig 1819, 131)

As we have seen, Grundtvig does allow the state a certain autonomy. Indeed, he was even a secularist to the extent that he learned – at least over time – to recognize the state's right to independence from the rule of the historical church. But he remained convinced that the state could only function as a temporal reproduction of the ideal spiritual image of a society based on love. Even if, in order to preserve itself, the state can manage very well without succumbing to the will of the historical church, it cannot survive without the idea of "the true church" as this depicts the supremacy of the invisible world over the visible and our relation to this supremacy.

Like the church, the state is itself an invisible community that only lives and breathes because we believe, or have confidence, in it. A breach in the confidence between a state and its people amounts to a weakening or severing of the heart-tie. And this again manifests itself as a weakening of the state's cohesion, a lack of communal visions and values, and a corresponding increase in all sorts of egotism. As with the church, the welfare and prosperity of the state build on the notion that, although we cannot see it, we can nevertheless visualize it. And in order to visualize an invisible society, and thus also a better future for the present society, the imagination must be formed by an image of the ideal society. According to Grundtvig (1819, 134), in this ideal society exists the link between state and church, as invisible as it is necessary: "If the Church expresses man's relation to the supremacy of the invisible, it follows that even if solely for its own preservation, the State must turn to the Church, indeed it must be very concerned to find the true Church, since it is obvious that only the Church can protect it, only the true revelation of the invisible and human relation to it can teach and seek supremacy where it is, and seek its attention in the proper way."

However, the state does not need any specific image of God in order to fulfill its purpose, only a common concept of a society with God. In time – from around 1830 onwards – Grundtvig found his own solution to the philosophical problem of state-church relations by separating the universal idea of a loving, creative God shared by the Abrahamic religions, and thus by all Western and Middle Eastern societies, from the more specific portrayals of God in the individual faith communities (Jonas 2011b, 42f). It was based on this distinction that, in 1839, he proposed the erection of a new Nordic university in Gothenburg. The plan was for an institution with history (or humanities) in one wing and science in the other, but without a theological faculty proper (Grundtvig 2011 [1839c], 224f). "This may indicate that theoretical learning in classical languages, church history etc. is to be carried out within the new faculty of universal-historical learning. Meanwhile the actual mystical, liturgical and ortho-practical elements of spiritual instruction are referred upwards to his likewise unrealised idea of a future 'Church School' (The School for Song), which was to crown his educational vision" (Jonas 2011c, 224f).

It is the same tendency towards a toning down of the image of God and a secularizing of the state that we find in the modern concept of the "state" (in Voltaire, among others), although Grundtvig insisted on maintaining the symbolic link between the state as a heart-relation and the Church as its archetype. Just as in his vision for a secular school system, he maintained the symbolic image of Christ or, less specifically, the living word as the embodiment of Truth.

Grundtvig therefore supported a formal separation of state and church, a separation that, in practice, has never taken place in Denmark, where the state is the official guardian of the church – although, in the wake of Grundtvig's influence, it allows room for the formation of free churches at the periphery of the Danish Lutheran Church. On this point, his ideas are closer to the liberal American model, whereby every congregation can freely form its own church and call its own pastor. Consequently, there is no longer a single, relatively homogeneous church but, rather, a multiplicity of churches that together constitute almost the entire prism of forms of human consciousness. These range from fundamentalist, traditionalist, modernist, and postmodernist churches to genuinely mystic communities of experience (Smith 2011). In Protestantism, therefore, the Catholic idea of a single indivisible church with its many inherent facets, tensions, and opportunities for cultural enlightenment has diversified into a wide variety of specialized and mutually competitive communities.

At the core of every social community that is more than a robbers' den of greed and selfish interests lies the idea of the invisible heart-tie that binds it together in a common vision of the spiritual superiority of, if not love, then at least humanity. In Grundtvig's thought, disasters caused by misplaced national sentiment are not due to a lack of common sense but, rather, to an eclipse of feeling and imagination – that is, to an inability to sense and imagine the "other person." If our school systems do not support the education of feeling and imagination with sufficient fervour and insight, these spacious and impressionable faculties may easily fall prey to heartless and headstrong leaders and preachers who harbour authoritarian images of God and cynical notions of the state. The holocausts and gulags of modern dictatorship were not perpetrated due to a lack of sagacity or raison d'état but, rather, due to a lack of common humanity and compassion – that is, due to eclipsed emotions and a warped Eros in combination with an insipid, or even satanic, imagination.

As Grundtvig (1819, 124) says, with a reference to Rousseau's concept of "natural man":

> If we regard man as a sensible beast, a conscious animal who by nature sees only his own advantage, it follows that the "natural state" is one that leads to all individuals becoming mutually hostile and envious when they reach the age of discretion. Only mutual fear can make the one allow the other undisputed possession of something that pleases a sensible beast. Only the conversational and sexual instinct account for his need of company. Only fear and rapacity explain why he joins forces in a State gang under a kind of chief. If this is truly the case, then Rousseau was undoubtedly right to claim that the State is an unnatural hospital and prison in which the medicine is worse than the illness, as well as being a teachers' college for rogues, a greenhouse for unnatural vices, and a graveyard for the freedom of man.

It is precisely this determination to develop the state through civil self-enlightenment within the domains of feeling, imagination, and Eros that seems to have vaccinated Grundtvig's concept of the nation against the darker tendencies of romanticism and nationalism. What makes us human is the vision of a united humanity of truth and love, coupled with the will to sacrifice ourselves for the imagined community, sensed and wished for even if not yet tangible or fully realized:

> In addition to the curious ability to hold powerful ideas about what is invisible above us – an ability for which I know no other name than "spiritual imagination," even though I know it is common to rank the imagination (which has given rise to the highest and greatest ideas) among the lower faculties of the soul [i.e., imagination, feeling, and sense] – in addition to this, I hold that man has had, and to some extent still has, what we call a "heart." And this heart has the peculiar ability to bring together what seems farthest apart: namely, living and apparently independent persons, and unite them even with what is hostile to their personality. (Grundtvig 1819, 304)

In the same way as the church forms the framework around our higher imagination in order to strengthen our spiritual interaction with the divine, so the state and social life form the framework around our emotional life through our daily contact with other people. The state challenges us as "feeling-creatures" and forms us into heart-creatures as we gradually learn the difficult art of associating with our fellow-creatures in an unforced and mutually enriching interaction. The state, says Grundtvig, constitutes our relation to our neighbour, which, fundamentally, is a heart-relation. For the heart possesses the almost magical ability to join together what seems at first glance to be well and truly separated and in a natural state of conflict – namely, living independent people. And it even joins them in such a manner and to such a degree that they are willing to act in ways that, at first glance, are in total conflict with their own personal leanings and interests.

If the heart beats strongly enough for an idea, it can even make people do things that are directly inimical to their own personal being – for example in the sacrificing of oneself to God or to another person, or in going to war for one's country. This willingness to sacrifice body and soul for a higher cause, be it national or spiritual, comes from the imagination of the heart:

> That which can love the higher, spiritual imagination more than its own personality (i.e., oneself) is what we call the heart in the highest sense. And this ability to love, to cherish, and to be affected is – again in the highest sense – what we call love. And just as spiritual power is the highest that we can imagine, under the image of the Word of power, so must love be both the strongest and the most beautiful thing that we can feel, the love, that is, that causes the personality within to sacrifice itself – what Christianity calls the love of God and our corresponding love for Him. (Grundtvig 1819, 305)

THE STATE AS AN EXTENSION OF THE FAMILY

The sense of belonging to society comes not just from the idea of an ideal, invisible community based on loving God. It is also closely linked to a sense of kinship or family. The love in both marriage and family life is the first heart-relation we experience, and it is upon this that the ongoing social sense is modelled. According to Grundtvig, in the intersection between love of self and love of family lies a spiritual image of humanity as one connected body, "a spiritual body of the limbs of the human race." The image of the national state is one of a natural balancing point midway between a tribal society and a global society. Grundtvig's nationalism is clearly inscribed within an overall spiritualizing perspective, while still being anchored in a pragmatic perception of self-love and family love and, thus, in the natural and historical preference for a love of one's country rather than of an abstract humanism:

> For it is my opinion that just as the human body shows us a structure that constitutes a living unity through a balance in the limbs between their urge to sustain themselves and their urge to support each other, so must a balance between love of self and love of family generate a spiritual body of the limbs of the human race. Since on everyone's admission a State is more or less perfect according to the degree that it constitutes such a body, I consider it proved that the family is destined to constitute a State. (1819, 309)

Fifteen years later, Grundtvig might very well have used the word "people" or "nation" instead of "state" here. The distinction between the state and the nation becomes ever clearer to him, and his emphasis changes, while his former idealization of the state tends to wane somewhat. Yet we find that quite a similar equivocal use of heart imagery in 1819 is still applied in "Education for the State" in 1834 (Grundtvig 2011 [1834], 76ff). And the meaning, after all, is clear enough: a state is only perfect to the degree that it constitutes a spiritual body – that is, a natural, voluntary, and imaginary bonding of people, which is to say a nation. The nation is the heart, or raison d'être, of the state. And the state, in turn, is the executive organ of the people's common spirit, or will. Where this reciprocal tie is weakened or severed by a breach in confidence both the people and the state will suffer from a lack of cohesion, or community.

The concept of "a people" develops over the course of time. In premodernity it was closely linked to the household, and only in modern times has it become abstracted from ties of kinship and station (see Korsgaard, chap. 9, this volume). Thus love of family naturally and historically precedes love of country, just as love of country is a natural and historical precondition for imagining the whole of humanity as a spiritual, social body. The very ability to imagine a trusting society that far exceeds the borders of who we know, what we can sense, or where our immediate personal interest lies can only come from our own original experience of trust in family life. The deeper – that is, the more naturally unspoiled or culturally illuminated – this heart-tie may be, the more supple, flexible, and spiritualized it may in time become. Therefore the quality of the heart-relations within family life and its cultural means of upbringing are crucial to the quality of society at large. We can only organize and regulate society on the basis of, and to the extent that, our heart, our imagination, and our common sense tell us. An education in our kinship and family relations is therefore part of the "education in depth" that Grundtvig sees as necessary not only for the individual but also for the whole nation, even though he believed that, in his time, these attachments were still too strong and too unconscious to be touched without endangering the security and cohesion of the state.

Grundtvig's entire line of thought is based on one of the most radical statements in the New Testament. In order to enter the kingdom of God and win community with Christ we must first break away not only from our family and kin but also from our own earthbound and emotionally attached self: "If anyone comes to me and does not hate father and mother, wife and children, brothers and sisters – yes, even their own life – such a person cannot be my disciple" (Luke 14:26). In every breakaway of this kind we must give up certain things. All families have their secrets and lies that cannot bear the light of day. But if the exposure of these most intimate relations comes too early, it will only further our individualization and alienation. If the elementary cohesion in our blood-relation is not replaced with a freer heart-tie, globalization will amount to an evasion of any true human community. For a breakaway to become not just a rebellion or a flight but a true reconciliation with the past, it requires an in-depth enlightenment that touches the soul.

However, according to Grundtvig, the more spiritualized and abstract the notion of a social tie becomes, the more difficult it is to connect the fulfillment of our humane ideals and purposes to the concrete "dealings and links that outwardly denote the State" (Grundtvig 1819, 310). To imagine a community and to feel a natural kinship with other people simply becomes more difficult the more culturally diverse and alien to each other we become. The aim in forming any supranational community must therefore be to find the balancing point between the higher aspirations for the unity of the human heart on which it rests and the lower feelings that it arouses. This point can only be sought and found in the higher feeling that allows for these contradictory incentives of light and dark to be purified and united over time. Moreover, the only higher feeling that is strong enough and pure enough to link love of self, love of society, love of country, and love of humanity is love itself: that is, the spiritual love of truth that Grundtvig equates with loving God. Whatever the differences in our perception of truth or God may be, it is the shared love of truth in its highest conceivable form that is the only force in society capable of ultimately uniting all people:

> Love wants love, and can have no other goal without abolishing itself. I believe this is understandable. Any link that comes from love must have as its definite goal to be united in love. Consequently, the true link to the State that comes from spiritual love can never find its goal – but possibly its conditions, never find the fulfillment of its purpose, but possibly its necessary means – in the visible intercourse and practical dealings that outwardly denote the State. The purpose, the aim, and the goal must be a heart-transfiguration of the dark, contradictory feelings, and this transfiguration can only be found in a higher feeling whereby they are both united, i.e., in the love of truth, or what amounts to the same thing for human beings: love of God. (Grundtvig 1819, 310)

What prevents this inter-socializing between peoples is first and foremost the emotional rifts that divide us according to religion, culture, and upbringing. That is why the potential of the church for the enlightenment and education of our imaginative and emotional life is so crucial to the state and its well-being, even if the word "church" must carry a much more enlivening and universal and practical meaning than is normally perceived in our modern societies in order to be able to fulfill such a task.

According to Grundtvig, at first glance "the multiplicity of peoples and individuals" appears to be "a hitherto unsolved but not unsolvable problem." But what has been tied into cultural and emotional knots in the course of history by nations and individuals can also be loosened in the course of time. Grundtvig sees very well where this knot can come undone – namely, "in the dissolving of the ties that link parents and children." He realizes the gravity and explosiveness of the issue but makes haste to add that he is not going to stick his neck out to solve these troubled relations "for they are the tenderest spot in the family and would probably not survive examination." For that would mean the dissolution of kinship ties into a society of nothing but separate individuals; it is better not to force the matter but, rather, wait until the civil societies and family individuals are matured and ready for such a break:

> In fact I accept the multiplicity of peoples and individuals for what they are: a hitherto unsolved yet by no means unsolvable problem, and just as I never doubt for a moment that all races of man on earth are of one blood, so can I see very well where this knot will come undone through history, namely in the dissolving of the ties that link parents and children. The ties are visible, but I cannot loosen them, and would not attempt to do so even if I could. For they are the tenderest spot in the family, which would probably not survive their examination. And even if the society of kin and station is more or less obsolete, it has not yet died out. (Grundtvig 1997 [1817], 186)

As the world expands, the heart must follow – and the concept of a cosmopolitical world is beyond the spiritual imagination of a tribal warrior. So until Grundtvig's designated point of maturity is reached by the individual peoples – and preferably on their own natural and historically consistent terms and paths – it would be preferable by far to strengthen our national symbolic communities and civil societies rather than to follow an abstract, forced humanism into a soulless globalized world society.

Today our modern individualized consumer society stands face to face with just such a crisis of vision sprung from forced ideals of freedom:

(1) a one-sided, enlightenment ideology dominated by intellect and (2) an unbridled amoral liberalism. The rational Western concept of education and enlightenment often fails to take cognizance of the vital importance of the imagination, the emotions, and the language of mythology for the formation of human society. Managing the language and emotion of conflict arising from cultural clashes at the individual, national, and international levels is a colossal psychological task that Western ideas of enlightenment and the state are simply not geared to tackle. New and more genuinely creative forms of globalized education are required, supported by nations united but driven by the people themselves.

REFERENCES

Anderson, B. 1983. *Imagined Communities: Reflections on the Origin and Spread of Nationalism*. London: Verso.

Frye, N. 1982. *The Great Code: The Bible and Literature*. Fort Washington, PA: Harvest Books.

Grundtvig, N.F.S. 1819. "Om Kirke, Stat og Skole" [On the church, the state, and the school]. *Danne-Virke* [The Dane-work] 4: 1–65; 97–154, 295–396.

– 1997 [1817]. "Om Mennesket I Verden" [On man in the world]. In *En Orm – En Gud* [A worm, a god], ed. O. Korsgaard, 153–205. Odense: Odense University Press.

– 2011 [1834]. "Education for the State." In *The School for Life: N.F.S. Grundtvig on Education for the People*, trans. and ed. E. Broadbridge, co-ed C. Warren and U. Jonas, 76–120. Aarhus: Aarhus University Press.

– 2011 [1839a]. "Enlightenment." In *The School for Life: N.F.S. Grundtvig on Education for the People*, trans and ed. E. Broadbridge, co-ed C. Warren and U. Jonas, 252–56. Aarhus: Aarhus University Press.

– 2011 [1839b]. "Open Letter to My Children." In *The School for Life: N.F.S. Grundtvig on Education for the People*, trans. and ed. E. Broadbridge, co-ed C. Warren and U. Jonas, 257–65. Aarhus: Aarhus University Press.

– 2011 [1839c]. "On the Union of Learning in the North." In *The School for Life: N.F.S. Grundtvig on Education for the People*, trans. and ed. E. Broadbridge, co-ed C. Warren and U. Jonas, 224–51. Aarhus: Aarhus University Press.

– 2011 [1847]. "A Congratulation to Denmark on the Danish Dimwit and the Danish High School." In *The School for Life: N.F.S. Grundtvig on Education for the People*, trans. and ed. E. Broadbridge, co-ed C. Warren and U. Jonas, 300–44. Aarhus: Aarhus University Press.

Jonas, U. 2011a. "Introduction to 'The Danish Four-leaf Clover or a Partiality for Danishness.'" In *The School for Life: N.F.S. Grundtvig on Education for the People*, trans. And ed. E. Broadbridge, co-ed C. Warren and U. Jonas, 300–3. Aarhus: Aarhus University Press.

– 2011b. "Introduction to 'Nordic Mythology (1832).'" In *The School for Life: N.F.S. Grundtvig on Education for the People*, trans. and ed. E. Broadbridge, co-ed C. Warren and U. Jonas, 42–3. Aarhus: Aarhus University Press.

– 2011c. "Introduction to 'On the Union of Learning in the North.'" In The School for Life: N.F.S. Grundtvig on Education for the People, trans. and ed. E. Broadbridge, co-ed. C. Warren and U. Jonas, 224–5. Aarhus: Aarhus University Press.

Smith, P.R. 2011. *Integral Christianity: The Spirit's Call to Evolve*. London: Continuum.

9

How Grundtvig Became a Nation Builder

OVE KORSGAARD

FROM HOUSEHOLD BODY TO NATIONAL BODY

Nikolai Frederik Severin Grundtvig is rightly regarded as the single individual who has had the greatest importance in the formation of the Danish nation. In arguing this I make two claims that run as red threads through what follows. First, the building of a nation is a process of both creation and formation; second, the building of the Danish nation takes place in Grundtvig's lifetime, with he himself laying the foundation.

In his younger days Grundtvig had no ambition to be a nation builder. He was convinced that it was only a matter of time before the society into which he was born would outlive itself (Grundtvig 1817, 179). However, he would not contribute to this for – to use Hegel's expression – Minerva's owl had not yet flown. In any event, Grundtvig failed to keep his promise not to intervene. Indeed, he became a kind of spiritual guide for many of those who were leaving the old "household body" in order to join the "national body."

Grundtvig was born into a society in which the concepts of "nation" and "people" were not yet linked. This happened only after the French Revolution (Greenfeld 1992, 6). In the *Dictionary of Old Danish, 1300–1700*, "people" is defined as a family concept: "my people and my father's house with fathers, family, and mothers, my first kin, my great-grandfather, my family founder." For its part, the *Dictionary of Old Nordic* defines "people" as "kindred, persons belonging to one's family or lineage" as well as the "household, persons belonging to one's house and its housekeeping". Thus the term "people" has roots that go much deeper than is implied in Herder's and Rousseau's concepts. The difference is an important one for it is the change from people as kin or household to people as a political and culturally sovereign body that constitutes the great watershed in the history of Europe.

Grundtvig's political interest was aroused in earnest in the latter half of the 1820s due to three main factors. First, he was convicted of libel in 1826 and sentenced to life-long censorship, meaning that all his publications had to first be screened by the police. Second, he felt provoked by, and therefore protested against, the tough line that the authorities took with the new religious movements of the time, the so-called "godly assemblies." And third, he was much inspired by his reading of the British periodicals the *Westminster Review* (1824–27) and the *Edinburgh Review* (1820–27). In these periodicals Grundtvig came into contact with the British liberalist ideas on church and school, ideas that he pursued with three trips to England – in 1829, 1830, and 1831, respectively – that introduced him to modern society. His horror at the shady side of industrialization was offset by his enthusiasm for the power and energy that confronted him in England, and which he expressed in his masterpiece *Nordic Mythology* (1832) in his references to "boxing and steaming." Whether Grundtvig ever witnessed a boxing match we do not know, but he wrote enthusiastically about the power of the steam engines that he saw on the factory floor and that he personally experienced on the railways of England. This meeting with modern society sharpened his understanding of the importance of the liberal view of freedom for economics, politics, education, the church, and spiritual life.

Grundtvig is difficult to place within the history of ideas. He was deeply inspired by both British liberalism and German idealism. He was influenced by German philosophers such as Herder, Fichte, and Hegel, but it is equally clear that John Locke, Adam Smith, John Stuart Mill, and the freedom ideals of British liberalism also made an impact. With regard to his *political* ideas, however, England was his greatest inspiration. In 1839 he wrote: "In all parliamentary matters [I] think of the English" (Grundtvig 1839, 7). He went on to make this abundantly clear from the rostrum of the Danish Parliament in 1855, six years after democracy was introduced into Denmark through the Constitution of 1849: "In answer to the question of my love for England I say that the greater part of my disagreement with the other gentlemen in the house is because I have most certainly not gained my political upbringing in or from France, but in and from *England*" (quoted in Korsgaard 2014).

Grundtvig differs in two ways from classic political thinkers such as John Rawls, Jürgen Habermas, and Hannah Arendt. In the first place he did not produce any systematic presentation of his political theory but, rather, developed it in a number of writings (on both education and social philosophy) and, not least, in his songs, where we find a number of his most characteristic political statements. Take, for example, "Far Greater Mountains," a song in which he formulates the much-quoted lines: "In this lies our wealth, on this tenet we draw: / that few are too rich, and still fewer too poor." In the second place, Grundtvig was not merely a theorist. He was also politically active, formulating his political ideas to a great degree from the rostrum of the upper and lower houses of Parliament. On the other hand, there is a kinship between Grundtvig and the aforementioned classic philosophers in their joint interest in normative political problem areas, including ethical questions and their causes.

FROM THE AGE OF THE ESTATES TO THE AGE OF THE PEOPLE

For Grundtvig, it was not the conflict between absolute monarchy and representative democracy that formed the poles of his political philosophy but, rather, that between the *estates* of the realm against the *people* of the realm. To understand Grundtvig's contribution to the formation of the Danish nation it is therefore necessary to outline its conceptual basis and composition. Society in Grundtvig's time was hierarchically structured, with the king at the top of the pyramid. Below him came the four estates, each with its own function, special rights, and specific duties. Society still followed what was regarded in the late Middle Ages as a divinely ordained order of rank and division. In Roman Catholic times the first "estate" was the *clergy* since the church was regarded as the essential intermediary in the salvation of souls. The second estate was the *nobility*, or *landed proprietary*, whose purpose was to defend the realm. These two estates enjoyed a privileged position and regarded themselves as free. In contrast, the third and fourth estates, the *citizenry* and the *peasantry*, respectively, were deemed "unfree and of humble birth." The task of the citizenry was to trade and that of the peasantry was to till the soil. At the Reformation in 1536, the clergy lost its privileged position, leaving the nobility as the sole "free" estate. As a result, over the next one hundred years the nobility's position in society was so dominant that some historians speak of "the age of absolute nobility." Their privileges were laid down in coronation charters: only the nobility could sit on the Royal State Council (*rigsraad*), a gathering of twenty or so nobles who supposedly acted as representatives of the entire people, supervised the king's power, and gave their consent to important decisions such as the imposition of taxes and the declaration of war. Finally, the nobility held a monopoly over the appointment of the country's lord lieutenants, whose task it was to oversee the Crown estates and act as the highest authority in both civil and military matters. The landed proprietor was the police authority on his own estate and could arrest people and then punish them once a judgment had been passed. In the peasant's eyes, therefore, the proprietor was not only a man of noble rank but also the public authority.

In the "estates society" the household was a central institution, in fact society was *constructed* on households. Each of these contained a head of the house and a number of staff. The "father" and the "people" were twin concepts: no father without a people, and no people without a father. In the society into which Grundtvig was born, the word "people" was primarily used with reference to the fourth estate – that is, the peasants, villagers, and servants. It was not commonly used to cover all four estates. At the same time, the Danish word "folk" was applied to all manner of people. There were seafolk and firefolk, harvestfolk and courtfolk – but only seldom were their *Danish* folk. The division into estates was so extensive that, when Danish replaced Latin in the Late Middle Ages, no designation existed for the population as a whole. When the Danish kings addressed all their subjects, they referred to them not as "the Danish people" but as the estates. For instance, in a North Jutland decree from 1466 the following formula is used with regard to the estates: "bishops, abbots and ordinary clergy, knights, journeymen, merchants, peasants and common people of Jutland" (Christensen 1976, 265). Not until the patriotism of the eighteenth century was the concept of the estates seriously threatened by the concept of "the nation." In his major work from 1808, *Thoughts on a Patriotic Education*, the historian Laurids Engelstoft, a later exponent of this patriotism and a source of inspiration for Grundtvig, pointed out that a new understanding of the concept of "nation" was under way: "To some degree England was the first and for a long time the only nation that with unprejudiced impartiality opened the temple of honor for all classes" (Engelstoft 1808, 266). Gradually this inclusive concept of nation gained ground in other countries, including Denmark, where, according to Engelstoft, it served to strengthen social cohesion in the country as the more the estates' privileges were eroded, "the more society's inner strength increase[d]" (182). With the arrival of national romanticism in the early nineteenth century came the idea of the people as an *organism* – bound together by a common language, a common history, and a common culture. The estates lost ground to the concept of a people in this transition, with Grundtvig becoming a major leader. In the Parliament that voted the Danish Constitution into being in 1849, Grundtvig (1949, 81) proclaimed: "The age of the estates is over, now it is time for the age of the people," and the age of the people required the education of the people in order for the nation building to begin.

GRUNDTVIG'S CONTRACT THEORY

Although formally Denmark remained an estates society until the democratic Constitution of 1849, the old order was partially breaking down some time before then. An important step in this process was the introduction of absolute monarchy in 1660, which marked the change from an elected monarchy to a hereditary monarchy and the ending of the requirement that the elected monarch should sign a coronation charter. When Frederik III's charter of 1648 was discarded, the foundation of his rule was thereby invalidated. In response to the estates' promise to grant him the rights of both succession and autocracy, he agreed to promulgate a new inheritance act. This was drawn up by Frederik himself and his lord chamberlain, Peder Schumacher (later Griffenfeld). The result was the Royal Danish Constitution of 1665 – the only Constitution in Europe that ever enshrined the principle of absolute monarchy.

The theoretical basis for absolutism as a form of government was formulated by the English political philosopher Thomas Hobbes (2008) in his famous work *Leviathan* (1651). Autocracy, he writes, rests on a contract between the king and the people. It is important to note that Hobbes's use of the word "people" differs fundamentally from the concept of the "multitude," which he makes clear in *On the Citizen* (1642): "In the last place, it's a great hindrance to Civil Government, especially Monarchical, that men distinguish not enough between a People and a Multitude. The People is somewhat that is one, having one will, and to whom one action may be attributed; none of these can properly be said of a Multitude" (Hobbes 1949, 135). On this point Grundtvig was in full agreement with Hobbes – as indeed he was with the Danish-Norwegian Ludvig Holberg (1716), who argues in *The Core of Morality or Introduction to Natures and Knowledge for the Common Man* that the introduction of absolutism should be seen as an *agreement* between a ruler and his people. The king undertook to care for "the public weal," while the people promised to obey him. Hereafter it was the task of the king to ensure the common good and thus a just and civil society. Holberg believed that it was this move that marked the end of the estates society – and, in particular, the privileged position of the nobility. In his view the weakening of the power of the nobility had freed all the Norwegian, Danish, and German members of the Danish monarchy in the sense that they were now placed on an equal footing under one master.

Grundtvig applied the same contract theory to the introduction of absolute monarchy into Denmark. The king did not seize power in 1660; power was "handed over" to him by the people, a circumstance to which Grundtvig often returned in his writings. To understand Grundtvig's view of autocracy it is important to note that, in the Royal Danish Constitution of 1665, there are two figures that legitimize autocracy: (1) the king's sovereign power is mediated directly by God and (2) the people transfer "absolute power" to the king. In arguing for his contract theory, Grundtvig distanced himself from the theocratic idea that the king had his power "by the grace of God." In his view it was "a gift from the people" and obliged the king to do everything in his power to promote "the common good." Grundtvig's scepticism towards democracy was linked to this idea of "the common good." If society is to hold together, it requires an authority charged with promoting the common good. Grundtvig believed that the king was best able to do this. He was not blind to the possibility that – like everyone else – the king could be egoistic, ambitious, and self-serving. But this would not have a destructive effect on society for, unlike everyone else, the king was not open to the temptation to separate his own interests from those of his country since "power, reputation, and welfare" were closely connected with how his kingdom proceeded (Grundtvig 1994 [1831], 31). Grundtvig championed what the Norwegian historian Jens Arup Seip calls a "popular monarchy," the core of which Grundtvig himself summarized in the watchword: "king's hand and people's voice – both strong, both free" (Damsholt, chap. 7, this volume).

Grundtvig's recurrent examples of how the Danish autocracy worked better than other forms of government included the king's abolition of adscription in 1788 and the ban on the slave trade in 1792. The former, he argued, had secured a much freer position for the common people than was the case in England and France, for instance. Already in his early work, *World Chronicle* (1812), Grundtvig writes: "The lord can no longer pull the peasant out of his manor, like a horse out of the stable every morning only to let him stand idle, pull the cart, or be put to the trot at his discretion." Now it was the lord himself who had to "ride the wooden horse at his pleasure, or use it for the young master's gymnastics" (Grundtvig 1905 [1812], 377).

"FROM A CASTE SYSTEM TO EQUALITY IN ALL CIVIL AFFAIRS"

In article after article Grundtvig (1849, 85) is ruthless in his criticism of the estates' treatment of the common people, who seem "to exist like domestic animals for the sake of the other estates." What he wants, in essence, is to turn the estates on their head and install the peasantry as the core of the nation. As he writes: "By raising the lowest of our estates to a preeminence we are literally setting the peasant above the lord of the manor" (91). Though this formulation might seem distasteful, for Grundtvig it expresses an irreversible and welcome trend of the times. In his view the transition marks the change from "slavery to freedom, from a caste system to equality in all civil affairs, and from secrecy to openness in everything that has to do with the needs and the common good of the whole!" (59). Openness and freedom of speech and the press thus became cardinal points in Grundtvig's political philosophy.

The transformation from the age of the estates to the age of the people meant that education would now have to play a far greater role in the relation between the individual and society. Whereas before it was the church that was closely related to the state, now it was the school that moved into the centre of society. The promotion of schooling, says Grundtvig (2011 [1834], 85), is for every government "the most important task of the state, since its well-being depends on this both now and in the future." Grundtvig uses the concept of "school" in its extended sense and goes so far as to call his own times "the age of the school." From this follows "the age of the individual." Compared with Classical times and the Middle Ages, the age of the school sees the individual moving further towards centre-stage. And with this change come both joyous possibilities and dangerous consequences. In 1789, the French Revolution showed just how dangerous these could be as the individual desire for freedom clashed fatally with the state's guardianship of the common good. The desire for freedom can lead the individual to cut him- or herself off from social life and become his or her own master, thereby breaking the underlying structure that links the individual to the people and to the whole of humankind (Grundtvig 2011 [1834]).

Despite the experiences of the French Revolution, and the danger that individual freedom may undermine society's essential sense of the common good, Grundtvig does not argue for less freedom than before but for *more*. To be a member of society involves shouldering a responsibility for the common weal, and this is best ensured if society grants freedom to the individual to take on that responsibility. Grundtvig's social philosophy builds on the liberal idea that only through freedom can the individual *voluntarily* impose restraints upon him- or herself. He is not advocating a total individual freedom for, in the long run, this would lead to the dissolution of society. For the public-minded citizen unlimited freedom has no place. Absolute individualism is incompatible with the idea of a society since every society depends on the ties between itself, the collective, and the individual. Society always rests on a certain basic agreement regarding the common good: "For where such a basic agreement cannot be traced, no civil society has ever existed, only a master-race and a slave-race in a sharp opposition that together may be *called* a state but is in no way what we are talking about here, since in such circles 'the right of the strongest' is without doubt the basic law" (Grundtvig 2011 [1834], 104).

How, then, does one go about establishing this essential "basic agreement"? The French political philosopher Montesquieu had faced the same fundamental question before Grundtvig. In his major work, *The Spirit of the Laws* (1748), he introduces love as an essential power. He speaks of social spirit as a political virtue that can be defined as a "love of the laws and the fatherland" (Montesquieu 2001). Similarly, Grundtvig regards love as a driving force for reform that contributes to the building of the nation. In this context, neither Montesquieu nor Grundtvig use "love" in the sense of "love for each other" (e.g., for one's neighbour), but, rather, in the sense of "love for what one has in common." What Montesquieu emphasizes is *the laws and the fatherland*; what Grundtvig emphasizes is the "four-leaf clover" of the people, the king, the mother-tongue, and the fatherland.

THE NATION AND THE PEOPLE: AN IMAGINED COMMUNITY

The invisibility of the nation is a central idea in modern theories of nationalism. The Irish-American anthropologist Benedict Anderson (1983) summarizes the idea elegantly and effectively when he calls the nation an "imagined community." Nations are not like elephants or volcanoes. They cannot be seen or described objectively through empirical surveys. They are subjective or, more precisely, intersubjective phenomena since they are a product of their members' idea of holding something in common. More generally, we can say that it is the sharing of common ideas that constitutes the fuel that drives a society forward. Such ideas should not be interpreted in a narrow, intellectual way; they are broad and inclusive, and comprise common knowledge and experience, common intelligence and feelings, common symbols and a common imagination. Yet these ideas alone are not enough to make a society cohesive; they must be symbolized in order to be maintained, and they must be institutionalized in order to provide stability. For example, if belief in Christ had not been anchored in the Bible as a text and in the church as an institution, Christianity would surely never have gained its universal significance. In Denmark, the nation became rooted in institutions such as the people's church, the people's school, the People's High School, the people's libraries, the people's parliament, and the people's political parties.

Of course, Grundtvig (1834, 557) does not call nations and peoples "imagined communities," but he comes close to doing so when he argues that "nationality and the mother-tongue … belong to the poetic realities on earth." His understanding of "the people" did not grow out of his association with empirical individuals but out of his study of history. This can be seen in his monumental work *New Year's Morning* (1824), which consists of 312 stanzas divided into eight songs. The crucial breakthrough in the text occurs at the beginning of the seventh song: "Now sounded in meddow to people its voice / in songs and in legends its children for joy" (Grundtvig 2009, 93). The voice to be awakened is that of the people, but they were not to be identified with the present age, in which the people's voice was silent. The people's voice that Grundtvig hears comes from history, and he saw it as his task to unite "the people with the people" (Auken 2005, 424). In other words, on the basis of his studies of history Grundtvig constructed "a Danish people," whom he then made into his model – that is, a cultural category. He did so primarily for the *common* people, who should no longer regard themselves as the fourth estate but, rather, as a full and valid part of the people in Denmark.

Grundtvig encouraged the underclass to reflect on and recognize itself as more than just "the humble folk" for they, too, were part of the Danish "people." Grundtvig had no faith in either the scholars or the peasants as rulers of the land for ruling required persons who were self-aware. In his article "On Civil Education" (1834) he writes: "The common people can just as little represent themselves as govern themselves, even if we filled the state council with them. In order to do so, they need a higher education to leave their station behind spiritually and no longer *be* common people" (Grundtvig 1968, 259). They would then be a people with a new form of consciousness. They must stop thinking of themselves as an "estate" and start thinking of themselves as a "people." For Grundtvig there was a qualitative difference between the "common people" and the "general public," primarily one of consciousness and education. When the common people think of themselves as the general public, they are no longer an estate. Grundtvig also employs the terms "people" and "multitude," or "people" and "masses," to clarify this qualitative difference between the two consciousness. The transition from a society in which the multitude/peasantry and the people are synonymous concepts to a society in which they are more or less antonymous requires an enormous mental adjustment. The transformation can be compared to that of paganism into Christianity in Denmark one thousand years ago, and of Roman Catholicism to Protestantism five hundred years later.

DEMOCRACY AS A TERM OF ABUSE

To understand Grundtvig's view of democracy, it is important to remind ourselves that, for over two thousand years, the word "democracy" was used almost exclusively either as a neutral or as a negative designation for a specific form of government. In *The Republic*, for example, Plato quotes Socrates as saying that democracy arises "when the propertyless class defeats the opposing party and kills all those who do not save themselves by fleeing their country" (Nevers 2011, 29). Plato's criticism of Athenian democracy remains the mother of all criticism of democracy. In his *Theory of the State* Aristotle defines democracy as an illegitimate form of government on a par with tyranny and oligarchy. Nor do the Roman writers, Polybius and Cicero, have much to say in its favour.

Right up to the Enlightenment and the American and French revolutions democracy remained unpopular. It was regarded as an extreme form of government, unsuited for implementation. Even a political thinker like Rousseau, later to be feted as the great philosopher of democracy, regarded the idea as impracticable. In *The Social Contract* he writes that "[t]aking the term in its strict sense, there never has existed, and never will exist, any true democracy" (Rousseau 2002 [1762], 201). According to Rousseau, democracy requires a small state, great simplicity in habits and customs, and great equality of wealth. And he came to the famous conclusion that, "if there were a nation of gods, it would be governed democratically." "So perfect a government is unsuited to men" (202). Rousseau's central position in the history of ideas is due, rather, to his emphasis on the people as a community in possession of sovereignty.

More than any other event, the French Revolution marks the transition from the aristocratic to the democratic epoch, meaning the transition from guardian rule to self-rule as a political and educational ideal. The democrats in France were in agreement first and foremost in their opposition to the aristocrats. Yet the French Revolution itself helped to push the concept of democracy into the background of political rhetoric and theory, due not least to the Reign of Terror in 1793–94, which reinforced the old association of democracy with disorder, anarchy, and mob rule. For Grundtvig, the French Revolution had close to a determining importance. When he gave his series of lectures published under the title *Within Living Memory* in 1838, it was the French Revolution that was his central point of reference. His manuscripts show that he had great insight into the course of events during the revolution as well as a thorough knowledge of the persons and various factions in the dispute. Grundtvig saw the French Revolution as a disaster because it ended in the Reign of Terror (Grundtvig 1877, 577).

THE "PEOPLE" AS A CATCHWORD

Grundtvig was far from alone in his criticism of democracy – on the contrary. Even when Denmark acquired its democratic Constitution in 1849 the term "democracy" did not appear in its wording, and it was seldom used by the liberal bourgeoisie who led the revolution in 1848–49. For the national liberals it was not a question of introducing a "democratic" constitution. That is how the Danes – with some degree of justification – have chosen to regard the move, but for the key players, such as D.G. Monrad and Orla Lehmann, it was more a matter of reining in autocracy through a new constitution. In other words, it was a matter of creating a constitutional monarchy. Yet even though they did not fight for a democratic constitution, Monrad and Lehmann had a strong faith in the people as the only legitimate foundation for the power of the state. The famous Danish critic and scholar Georg Brandes was later to employ the same argument as Grundtvig, Monrad, and Lehmann. In 1884, he gave a speech on the Constitution in which he clearly distinguished between the people and democracy: "While I wish with all of my heart to serve the people, I cannot say that I will serve *democracy*" (emphasis in original).

He makes a point of stating: "I am not a *democrat*; in other words I do not believe in the value of majority voting. But of course I admit the necessity of allowing the majority to decide the issue where it is a question of the people's right to self-determination" (Brandes 1987, 7, emphasis in original). It was the concept of a "people" and not of "democracy" that was the sticking point in Danish political discourse in the nineteenth century. This is bound up with the fact that in its early days the concept of a "people" developed in the struggle not *for* democracy but in the struggle *against* the estates as a fundamental principle.

In the nineteenth century this concept of a "people" became electric, moving from being a fairly new political catchword to being a firm political principle to an extent that is hard to understand today. We take the link between people and democracy for granted, but it was only at the start of the twentieth century that "democracy" made serious inroads into the language of politics. If we tighten the screw, we might even say that it was during and after the Second World War that the concept of democracy became electric in the same way as did the concept of a people in the nineteenth century.

Even though Grundtvig dismissed democracy, in *Within Living Memory* he predicts that sooner or later the people could themselves choose their government. In his view, the French Revolution and "Napoleon's tyranny" had enabled people and princes to experience how interdependent they were. That is why, at the beginning of the nineteenth century, the princes had made every effort "to arouse and encourage the spirit of the people, educate their subjects as to their common good, and improve their circumstances." Grundtvig was never in any doubt that such efforts to educate the people would have historical and universal consequences. "To reorganize bourgeois societies in the people's spirit" demanded "an awareness of history" that was not yet present (Grundtvig 1877, 355ff). When, in his earliest political work, *Political Considerations with a Glance at Denmark and Holstein* (1831), Grundtvig warns against democracy as a form of government he argues for the first time for a high school for *all* the people. Despite his strong royalist views he clearly sought a model that would enable the common people to join the political process. The king may have been in a position to find good and able people who could run the country better than an uneducated peasantry, but the latter needed to be educated in order to actively participate in political life. Once they had been through this process, they could at some future point establish an effective rule of the people. Rome was not built in a day, Grundtvig said again and again. Democracy could not be introduced from one day to the next: it required patience, which, in Grundtvig's view, was the greatest form of courage.

GERMANY: A THREAT

In spring 1848, when the second democratic revolution rolled from Paris across Europe, discussions blazed through Copenhagen and meetings were held to debate the future. On 11 March the first of these was held in the Casino Theatre, with the main subject being the incorporation of Schleswig into the Kingdom of Denmark. Three days later, at the Society for the Support of Schleswig, Grundtvig made a speech in which he professed his political credo. Not only was he a firm advocate of the monarchy, but he had also noticed of late that it was not enough for him to have a king: "I would like to be a *little* king myself and see nothing but small kings around me, provided we have learned the noblest of all arts: the royal art of controlling *oneself*" (Korsgaard 2014, 114 (emphasis in original). He proceeded to his view of Europe and emphasized that the events of recent weeks had brought the question of Denmark's borders to the fore. Some would draw these along the River Elbe, others along the River Eider, and yet others along the River Kongeaa. And certain German nationalists, he added, would draw them at Skaggerak or the Sound. On the basis of his linguistic studies the German folklorist Jacob Grimm claimed in *Geschichte der deutschen Sprache* (1848) that "the unruly Jutland peninsula" was German and only temporarily under Danish administration. This would be soon corrected: "Once Germany is reorganized, Denmark cannot possibly exist as before" (Adriansen 1990, 52). The possible destruction of Denmark as a sovereign state was a reality of the time, and this is something that is often overlooked these days. The bone of contention was Schleswig. Should both Schleswig and Holstein be incorporated into the German Federation or should Schleswig become part of Denmark? The National Liberals in Copenhagen wished to separate Schleswig from Holstein and make it Danish: the National Liberals in Kiel wished to incorporate it into the German Federation of which Holstein was already a member. Both solutions would cause major problems for the resulting minorities. Either there would be many Germans in Denmark or there would be many Danes in Germany.

Grundtvig offered a third, liberal, solution – that borders should be determined by national sentiment: "For facts are stubborn things, as the English say, and it is a stubborn fact ... that the kingdom of Denmark – whatever the case in days of yore – does not stretch a foot longer than to the border with the duchy of Schleswig. The land of Denmark stretches only so far as the language is spoken, and certainly no further than people *wish* to speak Danish, in other words, somewhere that no one knows in the middle of the duchy of Schleswig" (Korsgaard 2014, 116–17). Grundtvig thereby rejected the demands made at the Casino Theatre that Schleswig should be incorporated into Denmark as he predicted that this would only lead to war. In the end, his views on Schleswig made no impact on the National Liberal assembly.

On the question of Holstein, however, Grundtvig did agree with the National Liberals. It would be to the detriment of Denmark if the German-speaking duchy was not handed over since, in the long run, its presence in the Kingdom of Denmark could only undermine the possibility of the country's remaining an independent state. In his *Within Living Memory* lectures in 1838, Grundtvig expresses his content with Germany's being divided into small states from time immemorial and hopes that it will remain a divided country (a view that government leaders Thatcher [United Kingdom], Mitterand [France], and Schlüter [Denmark] repeated in 1989). For, as he said, if everyone who spoke German was gathered "under one hat, under a German Emperor Napoleon, it would become a far more frightening power to human eyes than France at its most dangerous" (Grundtvig 1877, 368ff). Grundtvig was convinced that the unification of Germany would lead to the emergence of a "monstrous German war machine" and result in a highly aggressive major power in Europe (377). It would, therefore, be a threat to the future of Denmark if Holstein were to remain in the kingdom.

THE ELITE: A THREAT

When the Royal Danish Constitution of 1665 was replaced by the Democratic Constitution of 1849, it was far from clear what form of democracy would be the result. The National Liberals were strongly influenced by Hegel's state nationalism and its associated idea that the will of the people was best governed by the educated. What the National Liberals actually advocated was a form of "elite democracy," with themselves as the elite governing the state. The idea was formulated in its clearest form by Orla Lehmann, who, in a speech in Vejle in 1860, directed a powerful attack on the Friends of the Peasants, an association founded in 1846 to emancipate the peasantry. Lehmann accused them of abusing the general franchise in order to promote their own interests: "When Denmark carried out the brave venture of transferring power to the entire people in 1848, it was not in order to place the government of the state in the hands of an unenlightened peasantry." They might have gained the right to vote, but governmental *power* belonged to "the educated, the men of property, and the intelligent" (Lehmann (2006 [1860]). After the military disaster of 1864, the idea that the people constituted a *threat* to democracy gained considerable credence. Despite his eighty-two years, Grundtvig was again roused to action, throwing himself into the struggle to prevent the privileged classes from appropriating power in the upper house of parliament, the *Landsting*.

The fact of the matter is that after the loss of Schleswig and Holstein in 1864 Denmark was left with the sticky problem of having two constitutions: the Constitution of 5 June 1849 and the Constitution of 18 November 1863. Efforts at revision were hampered by the need to apportion blame for the catastrophic defeat: Was it the fault of the National Liberals or of "absolutism dressed in a peasant's coat" (a phrase used by a number of speakers in Parliament about the common people who had abused their power)? Grundtvig resumed his political activity by allowing himself to be elected to the *Landsting* as the left-wing spokesman opposing a revision of the Constitution and, in passing, the senior member of the House. Even though the Constitution of 5 June contained limitations on the franchise, it rested on a general franchise for the *Landsting*. Any constraint on this would leave the propertied landowners in control of the *Landsting*. Grundtvig's view was that the general franchise was so valuable for society "that once a people had legally acquired it, they should not let go of it at any price." With the proposed revision would come "a *Landsting* that at least in the view of the people was so far from being rooted in the general franchise as to have its actual taproot in privilege, the private purse, and the ability to calculate: three things that at all events will never be part of 'the people' in Denmark" (Korsgaard 2014, 131).

In one of his last speeches Grundtvig came close to urging a popular rebellion. He predicted that, despite the wish for "everyday peace and quiet," an undemocratic *Landsting* might make the people realize that they would rather, "if it had to be so, fight hard for their lives for a while than only have the choice between dying in their beds and committing suicide" (Rigsdagstidende [Landstinget] 1866). Despite Grundtvig's opposition to the proposal, also known as "Estrup's Constitution," it was passed in both the upper and the lower houses (*Landsting* and Folketing). As senior member of the lower house, A.F. Tscherning also opposed the new Constitution, and the two senior members now joined forces to make a last-ditch attempt to stop its implementation. On 26 July they sought an audience with the king to ask him not to sign it into law. No audience was granted. Instead, at the end of the parliamentary session, both Grundtvig and Tscherning received a vote of thanks from their supporters in both houses, with the "warmest recognition of your entire contribution to public life and particularly of your work on the matter of the constitution" (Dam 1983, 92).

In this, his last political speech, given in the *Landsting* on 16 July 1866, Grundtvig took the representatives of the upper class to task. During the debate on the revised Constitution a number of them had asked: "Who are the people?" To this Grundtvig replied: "My simple point is this. Since we are all elected *by* the people, we all have the right to speak responsibly in the name *of* the people" (Korsgaard 2014, 64 {emphasis in original). The upper class, however, found it difficult to swallow the idea of speaking in the people's name since they did not consider themselves part of "the people" of Denmark. In contrast, Grundtvig had a clear understanding that, in a democracy, political legitimacy is only achieved in reference to the people and the nation. On this foundation the Danish nation state was built.

REFERENCES

Anderson, B. 1983. *Imagined Communities: Reflections on the Origin and Spread of Nationalism*. London: Verso.

Adriansen, I. 1990. *Fædrelandet, folkeminderne og modersmålet* [Fatherland, folklore and the mother-tongue]. Sønderborg: Museumsrådet for Sønderjyllands Amt.

Auken, S. 2005. *Sagas spejl* [Saga's mirror]. Copenhagen: Gyldendal.

Brandes, G. 1987. "Tale paa Grundlovsdagen (Sommerlyst ved Frederiksberg, 5. juni 1884)" [Speaking on Constitution Day (Sommerlyst at Frederiksberg, 5 June 1884]. In *Udvalgte skrifter*. Bd. 9: *Politiske artikler og taler* [Selected writings, vol. 9: Political articles and speeches], ed. S.M. Kristensen, 7–13. Copenhagen: Tidende Skifter.

Christiansen, A.E. 1976. *Danmark, Norden og Østersøen: Udvalgte Afhandlinger* [Denmark, the north, and the Baltic Sea]. Copenhagen: Den danske historieforening.

Dam, P. 1983. *Politikeren Grundtvig* [Grundtvig the politician]. Copenhagen: Aros.

Engelstoft, L. 1808. *Tanker om Nationalopdragelsen* [Thoughts on a patriotic education]. Copenhagen: Gyldendal.

Greenfeld, L. 1992. *Nationalism: Five Roads to Modernity.* Cambridge, MA: Harvard University Press.

Grundtvig, N.F.S. 1817. *Danne-Virke* II [The Dane-work II]. Copenhagen: Schmidt's Forlag.

– 1834. "Den danske Rim-Krønike" [The Danish rim-chronicle]. In *Den Nordiske Kirke-Tidende* nr. 33. Copenhagen: Paa Udgiverens Forlag.

– 1839. *Tale til Folkeraadet om Dansk Kirkefrihed* [Speaking to people on Danish church freedom]. Copenhagen: Wahlske Boghandels Forlag.

– 1849. *Danskeren* II [The Dane 2]. Copenhagen: F.H. Eibe.

– 1877. *Mands Minde: 1788–1838: Foredrag over det sidste halve Aarhundredes Historie, holdte 1838* [Within living memory: 1788–1838. Lectures on the history of the last half century given in 1838 by nik. Sev. Fred. Grundtvig]. Copenhagen: Karl Schønberg.

– 1905 [1812]. *Verdens Krønike* [World chronicle]. *Udvalgte Skrifter,* bd. 2. Copenhagen: Nordisk.

– 1968 [1834]. "Om borgerlig Dannelse" [On civil education]. In *N.F.S. Grundtvigs Skoleverden* [Grundtvig's educational world], 256–67 . Copenhagen: Gads Forlag.

– 1994 [1831]. "Politiske Betragtninger med Blik paa Danmark og Holsteen" [Political considerations, with a look at Denmark and Holstein]. *Grundtvig Studier* 45: 16–58.

– 2009. *New Year's Morning.* Translated by Kristian Schultz Petersen. Copenhagen: Forlaget Vartov.

– 2011 [1834]. "Education for the State." In *The School for Life: N.F.S. Grundtvig on Education for the People,* trans. and ed. E. Broadbridge, co-ed. C. Warren and U. Jonas, 76–120. Aarhus: Aarhus University Press.

Hobbes, Thomas. 1949 [1642]. *De Cive* [On the citizen]. New York: Appleton Cetury-Crofts.

– 2008 [1651]. *Leviathan.* Oxford: Oxford University Press.

Holberg, L. 1716. *Introduction til Naturens- og Folke-Rettens Kundskab* [The Core of Morality or Introduction to Natures and Knowledge for the Common Man]. Copenhagen: Johan Kruse. New Digital Version of Holberg: http://holbergsskrifter.dk/holberg-public/view?docId=NF/NF.page;toc.depth=1;brand=&chunk.id=start.

Korsgaard, O. 2014. *Grundtvig – As a Political Thinker.* Copenhagen: DJØF's Publishing.

Lehmann, O. 2006 [1860]. "De begavede, de dannede og de formuende" [The educated, the wealthy, and the intelligent]. http://*danmarkshistoriskoversigt.*systime.dk/1849-junigrundloven/25-orla-lehmann-de-begavede-de-dannede-og-de-formuende.html.

Montesquieu, C. de. 2001 [1748]. *On the Spirit of Laws*. Maryland: Rowman and Littlefield.

Nevers, J. 2011. *Fra skældsord til slagord: Demokratibegrebet i dansk politisk historie* [From swear-word to catchword: The concept of democracy in Danish political history]. Odense: University of Southern Denmark Press.

Rigsdagstidende (Landstinget). 1866: col. 20–21. Copenhagen.

Rousseau, J-J. 2002 [1762]. *The Social Contract*. New Haven, CT: Yale University Press.

PART FOUR

Comparison

10

Fichte and Grundtvig as Educators of the People

PER ØHRGAARD

Johann Gottlieb Fichte (1762–1814) and Nikolai Frederik Severin Grundtvig (1783–1872) may seem unlikely bedfellows, yet both saw it as their task to educate their nations, and Fichte was one of several German influences on Grundtvig.

Especially among non-philosophers Fichte is known for his thesis of the "pure I," which creates its own world for itself: "The I posits the non-I." In other words, consciousness defines reality. This represents the ultimate point of German idealism. The consciousness of which Fichte speaks is not the empirical everyday consciousness: it is pure consciousness in principle, not unlike a platonic "idea." This puts it on par with God, or, as Fichte's critics (including Grundtvig) said, actually *replaces* faith in God. Charged with "atheism" Fichte lost his professorship at the University of Jena in 1799, but owing to the lack of a central German state, he survived the scandal and became the first elected principal of the University of Berlin in 1811–12. This was formally founded by Wilhelm von Humboldt, but ideally it was also the foundation of both Fichte and the theologian Friedrich Schleiermacher.

On one side of this chapter lie various writings by Grundtvig, on the other lie Fichte's *Reden an die deutsche Nation* (Addresses to the German Nation) (1919 [1808]).[1] In these he argues for the special qualities of the Germans – to such a degree that he was later considered by some to be an early herald of fascism and Nazism. However, the fact that the Nazis occasionally claimed Fichte for their own does not validate their view: it is a long way from Fichte's idealism to their racial theories.

In contrast to Fichte, not only is Grundtvig's piety plain to see, but he also occupies both a central and a many-branched position in Danish history. Grundtvig was theologian, poet, politician, and educator of the people. His hymns make up the core of *The Danish Hymnbook* and fill the pages of every anthology of nineteenth-century poetry. They represent a unique renewal of poetic hymn-writing at a time when hymns in most other Western European countries were succumbing to a strain of sentimentality. Grundtvig's ideas for a "People's Academy" or "High School" (taken from the German *Hochschule* and close to "university" in meaning) were realized in practice by an increasingly strong movement named after him – the Grundtvigian movement. With their residential six-month general courses the Danish People's High Schools became crucial to Danish social and political history. The Grundtvigian independent churches within the Danish Lutheran Church (*valgmenigheder*) challenged its orthodoxy to such a degree that their spirit was at work throughout the twentieth century. Last but not least, Grundtvig was active in the debate surrounding the first democratic Constitution in Denmark, passed by Parliament in 1849.

Fichte gave his speeches in Berlin around the time Napoleon defeated Prussia at Jena and Auerstedt in October 1806 and made it a client state following the Treaties of Tilsit in 1807. Prussian morale had collapsed, and Fichte's attempts to revive it were made at personal risk: in 1806 a Nuremberg bookseller named Palm was executed by the French for publishing an anti-French pamphlet.

It was also around the Napoleonic wars that Grundtvig's ideas began to take form. Denmark lost its fleet to the English in 1807 and then had to cede Norway to Sweden in 1814. As the conflict over the Schleswig-Holstein duchies developed later in the century, so did Grundtvig's anti-German tone, not least in his self-published periodical *Danskeren* (The Dane) from 1848 to 1851. However, unlike many others in his day, he had no wish to annex a large German minority by claiming both duchies for Denmark.

LOST IN TRANSLATION

Before defining Fichte's and Grundtvig's views of "the people" we need to distinguish between the German word *Volk* (Danish *folk*) and the English word "people." In the American Declaration of Independence the words "We, the people" have ethnic, social, and political overtones and correspond to *Volk/folk* in Fichte and Grundtvig. To this day, Denmark has several *folkepartier* (lit. people's parties). This association with the people has no such equivalent in the Anglo-Saxon world; although "popular" is the adjectival form of "people," its English meaning is now closer to "loved by the people" than to the Danish/German "*of* the people." By contrast "national" in Denmark and Germany has a more restricted use than it does in the Anglo-Saxon world.

The German-Danish concept of *Volk/folk* can be traced back to the German philosopher Johann Gottfried Herder (1744–1803), to whom both Fichte and Grundtvig are indebted. Herder defined "the people" as a community that has developed a common culture based on a common language. He juxtaposed the many "peoples" and refused to define them as above, below, or against one another. Herder was particularly interested in "the people's poetry" (Danish *Folkedigtning*). The English language has retained this definition of "people" in phrases such as "folk music" or "folk song," but its usage is far more restricted than in Danish, where we speak of *folkedrab* (genocide), *Folkeforbund* (the League of Nations), or *folkesundhed* (national health). To this day the Danish Lutheran Church is called the *folkekirke*. But even for Herder, the people were not yet the unit that later crystallized into what became known as the "nation-state." For Grundtvig, "people" becomes a predominantly national concept with political ramifications. In later German history, the word *völkisch* appears as an equivalent to the Danish *folkelig*, but its adoption by the Nazis prevents it from being used today.

FICHTE'S VIEW OF "THE NATION"

Fichte's aim is best expressed in his fourteenth and final speech. It is centuries since the Germans were together in the present way, he says, placing himself in direct line to Martin Luther. His audience must commit themselves to "undo what has happened and delete the less than honorable interlude in the Germans' history book" (Fichte 1919 [1808], 232) – that is, the decline of morals that has led to Germany's being defeated. While accepting that natural forces exist, Fichte argues that "mankind's particular idea of time and mankind's organizations, these are made solely by people themselves and not in any way by some power outside them ... If you just acquire spirit and do not remain stuck in simple plant life, the unity and harmony of the spirit will follow of its own accord. And once you have come so far, everything else that we need will inevitably follow" (234). It is the youth who must put their minds to it for they are still relatively unspoiled. Fichte argues that his speeches are meant to be a help but that, if people can find better help, that is fine with him: "But ... [my] conviction [is] that something must be done, and be done here and now, and be drastic and decisive, and that the time for half-measures and delaying tactics is over" (242). Above all, according to Fichte, it is only Germans who can bring into being the true humanity – and even spread it to others, who often long for it without realizing it: "If you succumb now, then the whole of humanity will succumb together with you, with no hope of being regenerated. Here at the end of my speeches that is what I wanted, and felt obliged, to say to the whole nation" (246).

Here Fichte is summarizing what he argued in detail in the previous thirteen speeches: that we human beings are capable of perfection but that the Germans alone are destined to achieve it first. Or at least they have a greater chance (and need!) of doing so than other nations. They may then spread their perfection to others – with the ultimate goal of the common liberation of humankind.

LANGUAGE AS AN EXISTENTIAL MARKER

What, then, in Fichte's view constitutes a "nation"? An indispensable element is language – the "one thing that is absolutely necessary" (Fichte 1919 [1808], 63). People and language are and will remain one and the same thing, even in their transformations. Of course the German language looks different in 1800 than it did in 800, but at no point did those who used the language fail to understand one another: there is no gap or leap, only a continuum. Because language is original, wrong usage creates not just a cursory confusion; rather, it leads to a deep deviation from the people's very destination. Fichte's favourite examples – used already in both the first and the fourth speeches – are the words "humanity," "popularity," and "liberality." These are foreign words that mean nothing to Germans, he argues, and therefore those foreigners who use them (and also those Germans who take them over) are foreign to the people, who ought instead to use *Menschenfreundlichkeit*, *Leutseligkeit*, and *Edelmut* (71). But even then the German words would mean something else: there is no one-to-one translation for language that is more than superficial communication. The use of foreign words makes Germans foreign to *themselves*. The German words represent a different world of ideas than that represented by the foreign words. There is only one advantage in using the latter, and that is to make the acquaintance of the foreigner.

But Fichte is no modern racist. He clearly sets aside the claim that racial mixing is negative:

> Nobody should] place any emphasis on the fact that the German extraction in the conquered lands has mixed with its former inhabitants; for the victors and rulers and creators of the new people that arose from the mix, were nevertheless exclusively German. Moreover, the same mixing followed in just the same way as took place abroad with the Gauls, the Calabrians and so on when they presumably mixed with their slaves. So it would not be easy for any people of German descent to demonstrate a greater racial purity than any other. (Fichte 1919 [1808], 61)

For Fichte the central point is to preserve what has *formed* us, whoever we may be, "since human beings are formed far more by language than language is formed by human beings" (ibid.). German forms the Germans, and if they embrace what is foreign, they are no longer Germans in thought. Conversely, "whoever believes in spirituality and its freedom – wherever he is born and whatever language he speaks – is of our kin, belonging to us and joining us" (122).

Unfortunately, the Germans do not realize that the watering-down of the language has already occurred. During the eighteenth century they had indeed imported words such as "humanity," "popularity," and "liberality" – and with them came an idea of the state as something that was dead and mechanical. The French ascendancy may well be sensible and orderly, but the Germans will always fight against "the merely mechanical organization and computation of the state" (Fichte 1919 [1808], 141), just as the German tribes of antiquity must have readily realized that the Romans had organized everything in an ingenious way but that nonetheless they wished to be themselves: "Freedom for them meant remaining German" (136).

Here the question of who is German and who is foreign is determined by spiritual attitude. Fichte (1919 [1808], 146) speaks of a "foreign or domestic outsider," the latter being the person who lives in Germany but whose head has been turned by a foreign way of thinking. But this person has no right to speak, says Fichte, who is generally so convinced of the rightness of his argument that he does not care a jot for any analysis of it. Even if millions of Germans denied that there existed a special *German* love of the fatherland, he is prepared to wave them aside, for he himself has experienced it (146).

FICHTE AND "THE PEOPLE"

In Fichte's view there exists only one form of genuinely patriotic people – namely, the Germans, for they are an *ur*-people. He goes into more detail in the seventh and eighth speeches regarding the Germans as an *original* people and regarding "the people" in a higher sense of the word – as a collective culture with a long history that wishes to prolong itself even after its empirical demise. Yet here again Fichte (1919 [1808], 109) tends towards the abstract idea of "the one, pure divine life – in itself," which, being eternal, is detached from all empirical life. Everything begins with this pure, divine life, which is to be followed by life's practical consequences, such as the possibility of a state constitution. If this is regarded merely as a machine, then the prince may be regarded as its chief engineer. Against this Fichte sets the German "art of governing" (*Staatskunst*), which "from the very beginning and as the very first and only link is a firm and decisive *spirit*" (113, emphasis added). While other nations look backward and try to recapture their golden ages, the Germans look forward: "the true and proper person *himself* creates history, not by simply repeating what has already been, but by creating something completely new in his time" (115, emphasis added).

Fichte's thought is at heart revolutionary, but truly it can lead in a multitude of directions, and although most later political movements have at some point referenced him, it is, in particular, the chauvinistic application of his thought that has left its mark. To Fichte, the "state" is merely a technical arrangement, whereas the "fatherland" is quite different. Love of the fatherland is therefore "the flourishing of eternity and divinity ... in this world" (Fichte 1919 [1808], 131). The state is "not the first thing to come into being, existing in itself" (139); rather, it is solely a vehicle for the creation of a humane nation. The lack of a central state in Germany was therefore not a problem for Fichte as the definition of "German" had never been a prince's prerogative: Germans had found "the highest freedom in exploration and information" (140), the latter being what nowadays we would call "communication."

Freedom is more important than the state. It is the earth in which higher culture grows, however difficult it might be to administer. A free people will comply with the state if it has grown out of the *people*. Neither constitution nor law can create "the consuming flame of the higher form of patriotism which cloaks the nation like a cape of eternity; for this the noble-at-heart gladly sacrifice themselves, while the ignoble, who exist solely for the noble, must simply sacrifice themselves" (Fichte 1919

[1808], 134). This is the democratic impulse behind Fichte's speeches. The last quotation, however, is also an example of his uncompromising absolutism (elsewhere he writes that he will "force" his readers to understand him). The "ignoble" are allowed no voice, they must simply do as they are told.

Fichte gives full rein to his concept of "the people" in his thirteenth speech. Although he previously took a relatively liberal attitude towards racial mixing, he now stands firmly against it: "Such a people cannot be willing to incorporate a people of another origin and language and mix with them without becoming confused over such a severe disturbance in the steady development of their culture" (Fichte 1919 [1808], 207). A people are not a people because they live in a particular place; rather, they live in a particular place because they are a people. Europe will do well as long as the Germans are the peaceful influence at its heart and stop the others from fighting one another. But this does not seem to suit "the calculated self-interest of foreign countries," and "foreign cunning easily overcomes German integrity and naivety" (210). The way the world is developing there is only one solution: in order to be themselves and to feed themselves, the Germans must *rely* on themselves. In other words: "Immediately after the Germans' inner unity [comes] their domestic trading independence as the other means to their own salvation and thus to Europe's salvation" (213ff). The Germans must realize that they have been defeated in weaponry: "The battle with weapons is over; now begins the new battle of principles, mores, and character, if we so wish" (217). In Fichte's words: "Only a total transformation, only the charge of a brand-new spirit can help us" (223). Fichte's speeches expressly urge rebellion – but a spiritual rebellion.

GRUNDTVIG'S ATTITUDE TOWARDS FICHTE

Grundtvig's scepticism towards speculative German philosophy is well known. Yet he was also fascinated by Fichte, particularly in his youth and particularly by his radicalism. Looking back over the past year Grundtvig (1904, 112) writes on 31 December 1806: "I read Fichte's fine book on the destination of man." In *World Chronicle*, Grundtvig (1905a [1812], 350ff) writes that Fichte *approached* Christianity but never *embraced* it:

> At the start of the French Revolution an excellent new thinker appeared: Gottlieb Fichte from Lusatia, who for a brief moment

> turned heads towards a new movement. He regarded the existence of the "I" as being the only certainty, and thereby in a way made man the creator of the world and allowed man at least to speak of his "I" as he otherwise only did of God ... But whatever maze he has entered on his loose rambling, we must admit that he came close to Christianity, that is, the truth. Few others have so clearly seen through the degeneracy of the times, and he was indignant at seeing Kant's stringent teaching on virtue distorted ... Fichte too lost his way through pride, but either he says what he does not mean, or after a humiliation he must end up becoming fully Christian and realize that death is a real occurrence.

In *World Chronicle* (1817), Grundtvig (1905b [1817], 708) writes:

> We know that Fichte himself divided his works into scholarly and popular, or into the words of his head and the words of his heart, and we must in no way lose sight of this; for his head was warped, but his heart was in the right place, and even though it could not heal his brain, because that had got stuck, it nevertheless relieved his sickness and gave light and strength to come closer to the truth and life than any other famous German philosopher.

In the same breath, Grundtvig calls Fichte "a lost son of Martin Luther" (Grundtvig 1905b [1817], 708). In *Danne-Virke* (The Dane-work) from 1816,[2] he attacks Fichte for failing to properly understand the importance of history, and that, indeed, is one of the areas that divides them (Grundtvig 1905b, 335). But on Fichte's death in 1814 Grundtvig (1941, 211) wrote a memorial poem in which, as a Christian, he clearly shows his respect for the pagan Fichte:

> Fichte! Yes, as long as I may live,
> you I neither can nor must forget,
> nor yet deny that I have held you dear,
> and to your mighty voice was once in debt.
> That aroused me from my peace of mind
> to doubt, and yet have faith in God above,
> awakened me to evermore recall
> the light of truth and flower of His love.[3]

Grundtvig calls Fichte a "lightning-flash." But what the lightning revealed to Fichte was the aberration of thought and its self-satisfaction – witness the German idealism that imagined the world from the Creator's viewpoint and therefore failed to give either Him or the Saviour their rightful place.

THE LANGUAGE CRITERION

For Grundtvig, as for Fichte, language is absolutely central to the definition of a people. He is forever talking about the mother-tongue as the root of all good – for example, in the 1848 poem "Of the people" the watchword is (*Folkelighed*):

> Kin and blood make up a people,
> not mere air or steely blade;
> From the common speech of people
> is the mother-tongue so made.
>
> Ringing out and glowing brightly
> in the mouth of Dane and Jew,
> so with hidden bonds in union
> mother's tongue holds spirit true.[4]

Although Grundtvig's "kin and blood" are almost the same as the later German ideology of "Blood and Soil" (*Blut und Boden*), his words are immediately modified in the same stanza, and even more so in the next. "Dane and Jew" might sound disconcerting to our modern way of thinking, but for Grundtvig they are *inclusive*. All "who regard themselves as such" belong to the people, the criteria being a common *language* and a common *history* in the fatherland. In practice, therefore, there are not so many foreigners who can seriously belong to "the people": so even if "those whose mother-tongue sounds sweetest" and those who "their fatherland love much" are not in principle excluded, they may have some difficulties in joining the Danish "folk."

Grundtvig's defence of the language criterion becomes steadily more energetic as, in the 1840s, the conflict with Germany over the Duchy of Schleswig comes closer. But still a few years before the outbreak of war, Grundtvig (1909 [1847], 32) credits language with the ability to solve this national problem: "The time is over, God be praised, when fists and fingernails, either with or without pens in them, determined 'the conflict between languages.' Now the conflict must be set right by the tongues in the mouths of the people." In *The Dane* (1848–51) Grundtvig's tone verges on the zealous, but at this point war with Germany is imminent.

Denmark must turn away from Germany and towards England.[5] The Danes should learn the English language better for, as Grundtvig argues: "[English] could never be dangerous for our mother-tongue, whereas bitter experience has taught us that only by a great miracle has our mother-tongue avoided being forced out of the Church, the School, and the educated circles of the people by High German" (181) – and this despite there being a strong argument for a living connection between the Danes and the Germans. Grundtvig agrees with Fichte that language creates what it names, and that it does not create the same in every language: "So Danish words in parliament that could make the war against Germany follow the Danish head and heart would be worth their weight in gold – even for the Germans. For it would not only give them the opportunity to write new books, they would also be forced to think new thoughts!" (158).

Time and again Grundtvig derides the Germans for their abstract deductive thinking: they have always "begun from the top, way up in the air, with what they call 'the idea' – what we in Danish call *hjernespind* ('figment of the brain')" (1909 [1847], 147). In Grundtvig's view the rejection of Germany in favour of England is not only a political goal but also "a necessary step in the transition of the Danish people from death to life" (179).

> If we compare England and Germany with regard to civil society, to their laws and organizational forms, we find exactly the same relation [i.e., between common sense and figments of the brain], then the High Germans have this cast-iron notion that Our Lord has created the world the wrong way, so they must make sure it is created according to their own brains and pure reason. The English on the other hand take the world as it comes and aim to make it as useful to themselves as possible. It may be true that the English find it easy to be clumsy, and are somewhat boorish on many delicate questions, but it is nevertheless a fact that they always gets something for their trouble, whereas the Germans basically can only whistle for it. (182)

Grundtvig's complaint that the Germans want to change the Creator's plan is a dig at Fichte's idealism, but the distinction holds good. Before we can understand national differences, says Fichte (1919 [1808], 61), "I must invite you to a consideration of the nature of language in general." Such a "consideration" is foreign, or at the least irrelevant, to Grundtvig's thought. To him, a relationship to a linguistic community is defined by actual experience of the mother-tongue. Grundtvig's starting point is the family, the nucleus of the world: "Mother's voice is the baby's joy," he writes in the song "Mother's Name Is a Heav'nly Sound" (Broadbridge, Warren, and Jonas 2011, 189). The language is imbibed with mother's milk in an organic process that cannot be otherwise.

FICHTE'S VIEW OF "UPBRINGING"

When dealing with the question of upbringing Fichte is more loyal to the state than he is when dealing with the question of theory. Although he argues that only patriotism will rouse the state into being, once that state is a reality, it will clearly take over many duties. It must realize that these are only temporal duties, however, and "if anyone wishes to be saved, they must work that out for themselves" (Fichte 1919 [1808], 176). Among other duties, the new state must educate its *people*, those who are "the true soil of the human race" (177) and who have previously been neglected since higher education, rather than general education, has been the priority.

According to Fichte (1919 [1808], 180), the state has one task only: the rearing of coming generations, with the present generation being the "seed for worthy successors." The state cannot wait for people to come up with good ideas such as those that Fichte has nurtured; it must actively call up those statesmen who have studied and raised themselves up, and it must then, "as the highest overseer of human affairs, and in the sight of God and its own conscience the only guardian of all minors, have the absolute right to force them to their salvation" (183). Here again Fichte the authoritarian raises his head, although he avows that the use of force will lead to a free personality – and this despite his argument that knowledge cannot be divorced from love: "The pupil's cognitive ability must never be stimulated unless love of the object is also urged. And vice versa, love must never be urged unless the cognitive ability is present, for otherwise love will be blind" (160).

The "state" in the singular is no more than an idea at this point in German history, but Fichte believes that there will be a healthy competition between the various territories and that one of them will realize his thoughts. Then, little by little, the whole nation will follow (just as the world may follow Germany). And if none of them does, then there are private patrons. They, however, must be on their guard against using their privilege as Fichte (1919 [1808], 189) is thinking of "the poor orphans, and those who lie in misery on our highways and byways, and everything that adult humanity has expelled and cast away." They need bread *and* education.

Fichte's idealism – in the philosophical definition – is apparent in the sense that he is only interested in getting *started*. Once the German people "acquire a character," simple logic will ensure that everything develops from there: "Everything from above will intervene in the immediate present in its own way, and whoever truly lives in the above also lives in this age" (Fichte 1919 [1808], 194). The transformation must not be violent but, rather, must come about only through higher moral conduct: in short, the human race must develop from "earthly, physical creatures into pure, noble spirits" (204). Fichte is adamant in not limiting education to the higher estates. Educating the people has a virtuous ring to it, and Fichte's project is precisely to create a new German nation in which all the people feel at home. As a true idealist he envisages "this unity as [already] having arisen, been perfected, and being totally present" in *spirit*. At this point all his words merely fill in the space between the anticipation and the realization. But what is needed is "a complete transformation of the present education system as the only way to preserve the existence of the German nation" (21).

Nonetheless, one must begin somewhere, and so Fichte (1919 [1808], 103) turns to the members of the educated class, who have come to the fore through their city culture and who possess "the spirit of piety, honesty, modesty and community feeling." German history should be written as "a chap-book." but it should also be philosophical. And its content will be so full of philosophical theory that it is without doubt the educated who will be the first to see the light. However, the educated will then become "the people," while "from the previous people another, better-educated, class will see the light of day" (26). What is needed is for the students to be imbued with the *ideal*. Left to their own free will they may well choose the bad rather than the good, so their free will must be eradicated in order to ensure "the creation of a firm, determined, steadfast being" (28) – absolute and unchangeable, one who "is no longer becoming but who *is*" (emphasis added). This is the only serious goal of education, and the students' free will must be turned towards gaining an insight into this necessity, which must, for its part, be understood as the absolute and fundamental *meaning* of things. The students must not settle for learning about things that have come into being and exist; they must acquire the philosophical insight into *why* they are so (33). Fichte seeks to combine learning with self-activity since it is the latter that promotes learning. Once the student's activity is aroused – we might call it "curiosity" – the rest will follow, provided the flame is kept alight.

"Education towards pure will" is the ultimate goal. If this is to be reached, students must remain "totally and perpetually under the influence of this upbringing" (Fichte 1919 [1808], 38) and be shielded as far as possible from other stimuli that could turn them in the wrong direction. To this end, the education of the first generation of educators must take place far away from the disturbance of biological families. If all goes well, students will come to see that they are partners not only in their own society but also in "the great chain of being." They must therefore become aware of, and form an image of, "the transcendental world order," which is eternal and unchanging, beyond history and the individual. There is no other truth but "the life of the spirit" (44), and only in "the immediate contact with God" can we be satisfied (45). Thus education also includes an upbringing in religion, but the spiritual life and the divine life are now one and the same – in contrast to what is taught in the "ancient" religions: "For in the new time eternity breaks through not just on the other side of the grave but comes on the contrary into the midst of the present life" (ibid.). Previous education has regarded us as sinful by nature, but Fichte regards this as an insult. Although it has been corrupted, "at the root of humanity there is a pure enjoyment [*Wohlgefallen*] of what is good" (54).

NO CHRISTIANITY WITHOUT A PEOPLE

On one common ground Grundtvig and Fichte can meet – namely, in the idea that knowledge and love belong together. Among the most commonplace Grundtvig quotes are the lines from the song "Here Is a Revelation": "It has been well contended / We never comprehended / what first we did not love." The same insight lies behind the lines in "New Year's Morning": "that light without heat / is a torment of hell." The link between knowledge and love is a fundamental idea in all of Grundtvig's educational works: "Enlightenment must be our joy," he writes in the poem "Enlightenment." But despite every enlightenment, the human eye nevertheless "alone by God's great light shall be completed" (from "A Plain and Cheerful, Active Life on Earth"). Not for a moment does Grundtvig doubt that God stands behind everything, nor that Christianity must be the foundation on which everything else must build, including the education of the people. He wishes "to remind you that when I speak of the capability of the peoples and the individual for true spiritual achievement, I presuppose Christianity, without which they are completely incapable of wishing for or perfecting anything in the world of the spirit that can stand the test of truth" (Grundtvig 1905b [1817], 350).[6]

This might seem to conflict with what is perhaps the most famous of Grundtvig's words: "Human comes first, and Christian next / for that is life's true order." However, the order here is not to be understood as relegating Christianity to second place. Christianity comes first and last for Grundtvig, but for it to become manifest there must be *people*, indeed there must be *a* people among whom it can grow. And there is only a people where there is a history, hence Grundtvig's intense occupation with both world history (e.g., *World Chronicle*, Grundtvig 1905a [1812], 1905b [1817]) and with Nordic mythology. He interpreted the latter as a kind of precursor of Christianity, as the richly ploughed field into which its seeds were cast. In *The Sound of the Hunting-Horn* (1844) he writes: "Thus, only where human life, both the natural and the Christian, comes into its true form and is neither seen as an angel-life nor treated like a dog's life – only there can the light arise and spread over it, until, penetrated by it human life is thereby transfigured" (Grundtvig 1909 [1847], 61). History is to the people what the Old Testament prophets were to the evangelists.

In *The People's Culture and Christianity* (1847) Grundtvig makes his position even clearer when he and his supporters, already known as "the Grundtvigians," are accused of confusing nation and church. He responds by defining

> the proper relationship between the people's life and culture (*folkelighed*) and Christianity. To take the original relationship first: we all know that Christianity – even in Israel where it arose, not to mention the heathen countries to which it was propagated – was related to the people's life and culture as a heavenly guest to an earthly home. The guest came not to be served but himself to serve, and although all traces of this have been obliterated as far as possible in the days of the priestly hierocracy, the original relationship continues to be the only proper, natural one. (Grundtvig 1909 [1847], 81)

If the culture of the people dies, this is tantamount to their spiritual death; they must then "be healed through the restitution of their culture before one can talk meaningfully to and with the people about living

Christianity" (Grundtvig 1909 [1847], 87). This must of course be done in the mother-tongue:

> Just as it is only in the mother-tongue that the Word of the invisible acquires life and power for us, so does our living relation to the past and the present in general depend on the feeling of our heartfelt link to our parents and our progeny. It is therefore essential for Denmark and everywhere else, just as in Israel, that if the Word of God is to find a well-prepared people, then words of the people in the mother-tongue must first have turned the children's hearts to their parents and the parents' hearts to their children, so that they feel that death in every form is the arch-enemy of both themselves and all humankind, and that He is the only true Savior who can and will grant us eternal life. (88)

A heavenly guest in an earthly home – the image is recurrent in Grundtvig, not least in his hymns. It is consistent with his insistence on the family and, more broadly, on the people as the units on which to build. In the 1840s he sets this up against the German idea of the state and argues that the Danes have "stumbled across the right idea of the common good, which is far from being the secret of the German concept of a state but will always be the core of the people's idea of a civil society" (*The Sound of the Hunting-Horn*, Grundtvig 1909 [1847], 239). Even if this is directed more at Hegel's idea of a state than at Fichte's concept of a nation, Grundtvig's imagery keeps a noticeable distance from Fichte, not least in its origins of "family" and "gender." Already in *Danne-Virke* [The Dane-work](1816) Grundtvig declares that "the Danish people is very much a woman" (Grundtvig 1905b [1817], 322); he refers constantly to "the mother-tongue" and draws happily on the family for his metaphors (e.g., "the little ones in their mother's lap and on their father's arm"). In *The School for Life and The Academy in Sorø* he refers to "the Danish woman" and "Mother Denmark" as his audience. His educational ideas encompass the early years of schooling, shunning mathematics and grammar in favour of a balance between brain and body – namely, "the love of bodily activity, a grasp of civic pursuits, and a thirst for an independent position from childhood" (Grundtvig 1950, 201). Most of all Grundtvig addresses the mothers of Denmark, and, in contrast to Fichte, he never advocates removing children from their homes in order to board them elsewhere, as happened to himself at the age of nine. For Grundtvig, the family is not a crippling restriction but, rather, the prerequisite for happy growth, for education, and for cultural awareness.

THE NATION AS "ANCHOR"

There is much that links Fichte and Grundtvig, most notably their anchoring of the idea of education and culture in the concept of a "nation" that both extols language as a "nation builder" and breaks up a society based on rank in a move towards forms of democracy. In Fichte this becomes "republicanism," whereas Grundtvig wishes to retain the monarchy even after the introduction of a democratic constitution in Denmark in 1849. This difference has much to do with the history of the two nations. Germany was divided into constituent states with an emperor who was not anchored in the nation. Denmark, on the other hand, had enjoyed almost a thousand years of monarchy, the last regicide having occurred in 1286. Fichte and Grundtvig agree that the vision of their peoples' future must be "home-grown." Even though "far higher mountains" exist elsewhere, Grundtvig insists that the Danes must stick to their hills. Similarly, Fichte admits that the organization in some foreign countries might be more practical – but then it is not German! And Grundtvig (1909 [1847], 88) writes in The People's Spirit and Christianity (*Folkelighed og Christendom*): "The reason why I want the elementary school to be exclusively *Danish*, is in no way because Danishness can make us either omniscient or overjoyed; it is simply that we must be *Danish* first, just as everybody first has to be *alive* before it makes sense to tell them about temporal or eternal life."

However, there is also much that divides Fichte and Grundtvig. For the most part Fichte thinks and writes in the abstract and his style is argumentative. Even for Germans his style and language are rugged – to the extent that we can wonder how his supporters were able to follow his speeches. However difficult Grundtvig's style he is always more direct in his appeal to the reader than is Fichte. The difference lies not least in their point of observation. Fichte thinks of society and education from above, Grundtvig from below. For Fichte it is a matter of course that to achieve a *national* education those who *are* educated should take the lead in educating those who are not. Grundtvig's revolution lies in his advocacy of freedom from conventional learning in favour of a foundation in language and history.

Grundtvig was no enemy of learning, but some of his supporters turned his attacks on the Latin- and German-oriented education of his day into a kind of anti-intellectualism. Grundtvig himself was forever on guard against freedom turning into populism. In *Danskeren II*, 1849 (the year democracy came to Denmark), he writes that, because the peasant farmers had been oppressed for so long, "[they come into government] with both an ignorance that leaves them open to all manner of error and a rancour against their previous masters that tempts them to all kinds of violence and injustice. Here it is important that the Danish farmers find good friends among their more educated, cultured compatriots, and possess both the humility and the magnanimity to follow in general their wise and well-intentioned counsel" (Grundtvig 1909 [1847], 191ff).

However, the crucial difference between Fichte and Grundtvig is in their perception of temporal and eternal life. Fichte may *speak* about God and religion, but his perspective is always earthly and temporal. His idea of eternity reaches no further than the ongoing preservation of kindred generations. The idea of original sin is anathema to him, and he believes in human perfectibility through human means. Grundtvig, by contrast, states: "My conflict is called Life and Death." His perception of death is thus particularly concrete and insistent: "Recall, I pray, / the dark grave grants no pardon" and that death comes with "his ice-cold gust" (*At sige Verden ret Farvel* [To bid this life a true goodbye]). There is no perfectibility this side of the grave, but our whole life is illuminated by God with a view to eternity, as Grundtvig writes in "Open Letter to my Children" (in Broadbridge, Warren, and Jonas 2011, 263–4):

> Our eye, as it was made, to heaven turned
> alert to beauty, and by greatness greeted,
> yet knowing where the deepest longings burned
> alone by God's great light shall be completed.

In *Noten und Abhandlungen* (Notes and Queries) in his *West-östlicher Divan* (West-eastern Divan) Goethe (1819, 280ff) writes about the difference between poets and prophets:

> Both are held fast and stirred by a god, but in his joy at conveying pleasure, winning honor with his product, and perhaps also a pleasant life, the poet is extravagant with the gift granted him. He neglects all other purposes and tries to be manifold, to show that he is limitless in sentiment and representation. The prophet on the other hand sees only a single, specific goal, and to achieve it, he uses the simplest means. He wishes to preach one or other particular message,

> and through this and around this he wishes to gather the nations as round a banner. To this end all he requires is that the world believes; he himself must be, and remain, unwavering; he cannot believe in a plurality, that is only something he can acknowledge.

In this light we might venture to say that Fichte was a prophet but that Grundtvig was both a prophet and a poet. And, after all, the true legacy of Grundtvig is his poetry. His articles and essays – let alone his sermons – are today read only by scholars. But many quotations from his poems remain part of the common Danish cultural heritage.

NOTES

1 Translation of this chapter, and all prose and verse translations from both German and Danish are by Edward Broadbridge.
2 Grundtvig's journal *Danne-Virke* [The Dane-work](1816–19) took its title from the ancient earthworks stretching along the southern border of Jutland and Germany. Symbolically it represented Danish autonomy.
3 This poem was not published until 1880.
4 Grundtvig 2015 (translated by Edward Broadbridge).
5 On his combined trips in 1829, 1830, 1831, and 1843, Grundtvig, all told, spent over a year in England, the only foreign country he ever visited.
6 In *Danne-Virke I* (Grundtvig 1816).

REFERENCES

Broadbridge, E., trans. and ed. C. Warren, and U. Jonas, co-eds. 2011. *The School for Life. N.F.S. Grundtvig on Education for the People*. Aarhus: Aarhus University Press.
Fichte, J.G. 1919 [1808]. *Reden an die deutsche Nation* [Addresses to the German nation]. Edited by F. Medicus. Leipzig: Felix Meiner.
von Goethe, J.W. 1819. *West-östlicher Divan* [West-eastern divan]. Stuttgart: Cotta.
Grundtvig, N.F.S. 1816. *Danne-Virke I* [The Dane-work I]. Copenhagen: Schiøtz and Mandra.
– 1904. *Udvalgte Skrifter, Bind 1* [Selected writings, vol. 1]. Edited by H. Begtrup. Copenhagen: Gyldendal.
– 1905a [1812]. *Udvalgte Skrifter, Bind 2* [Selected writings, vol. 2]. Edited by H. Begtrup. Copenhagen: Gyldendal.

– 1905b [1817]. *Udvalgte Skrifter, Bind 3* [Selected writings, vol. 3]. Edited by H. Begtrup. Copenhagen: Gyldendal.
– 1909 [1847]. *Udvalgte Skrifter, Bind 9* [Selected writings, vol. 9]. Edited by H. Begtrup. Copenhagen: Gyldendal.
– 1941. *Værker i Udvalg, Bind 7* [Selected works, vol. 7]. Edited by H. Koch and G. Christensen. Copenhagen: Gyldendal.
– 1950. *Grundtvig i Udtog ved og med indledning af Hal Koch* [Grundtvig in excerpts. Assembled by and with introduction by Hal Koch]. Copenhagen: Martin.
– 2015. *Living Wellsprings: The Hymns, Songs, and Poems of N.F.S. Grundtvig*. Translated and edited by Edward Broadbridge. Aarhus: Aarhus University Press.

11

Come Together: Thoughts and Theories on Social Cohesion in the Work of Nikolai Grundtvig and Émile Durkheim

KATRINE BAUNVIG

The long nineteenth century was a troubled period in European history, violently initiated by the French Revolution and devastatingly ended by the First World War. During this time, Europe and North America underwent remarkable demographic, economic, and social changes. In more than one sense this was the century of revolutions. The political revolutions and wars of independence in France, Serbia, Poland, Belgium, Italy, Switzerland, Greece, and so on, all motivated by a new-found sense of national self – and typically rooted in or connected to liberal and democratic ambitions – are obvious examples of the trend. Naturally, the years 1830, 1848, and 1870 are particularly exemplary. Also, revolutions of a different kind swept through city and countryside; technological innovations – such as metallurgy, steam power, and a number of chemical discoveries – increased efficiency in, for example, textile manufacture and agricultural production. Infrastructural and demographic changes were an integral part of, or spin of, this development. Trains pierced the land on newly established railways, rapidly changing possibilities in transportation; farm workers entered the urban factories and left their rural existences behind (Ayres 1989; Berlanstein 1992). Furthermore, the political-democratic and industrial-demographic revolutions were in a sense backed by yet another ground-breaking change: a revolutionary decoupling of nature from the divine became indisputably evident in the Enlightenment period and climaxed in Charles Darwin's 1859 publication *On the Origin of Species* and the theory of natural selection. As is well known, this had vital consequences in academia and in popular opinion regarding the status of humankind in the world (Randall 1929). It was no longer possible to maintain a view of humans as creatures of a different ontological category than the rest of the species inhabiting the earth. God withdrew from the Universe with the deists, and now He had left humankind entirely – dead, as it was proclaimed. Thus, these revolutions destabilized the hitherto dominant political institutions, social structures (between occupational groups and in family arrangements), and (Christian) worldview. Moreover, these developments were perceived as particularly destabilizing to the relation between the individual and society – weakening the social cohesion, as it were. And this experience expressed itself in two general concerns or "fears." One accentuated what could be conceived as elements in a process of individualization *avant la lettre*.[1] The liberal torrent pushing forward the rights of the individual was seen as running towards social isolation and concerns were raised over this overly centrifugal development. Contrarily, another fear was rooted in and highlighted the horrors of "crowd events":[2] terrifying outbursts of violence in the collective setting of a riot.[3] This phenomenon was portrayed as transforming normally rational individuals into raging brutes who – in their overly centripetal activities – represented a very destructive, although social, power in terms of upholding stability and community over time.[4]

So how was the balance between individual and society to be reestablished? How to reinstate social cohesion?[5] How to turn this crisis, this degenerate state, around? Answers were needed; ideologies and theories were articulated. Fears ran across or beneath the political spectrum. The job was to restore the balance while steering free of the equally destructive centrifugal and centripetal powers. Liberalism and socialism presented themselves as competing solutions on a macro level. For their part, at the close of the century, psychiatrists and psychologists such as Wilhelm Wundt and Sigmund Freud keenly analyzed the consequences of the unstable situation on a micro level. But the issue was of general concern and was central to countless thinkers of the day. Among them were the French fin de siècle sociologist of religion Émile Durkheim and the Danish pastor and polyglot Nikolai Grundtvig. Between them they roughly cover the long century: Grundtvig was born in 1783 and Durkheim died in 1917. It may seem surprising, but, despite obvious differences in geography, generation, and occupation, a number of significant structural similarities in the way they approached the crisis of social cohesion is contained in their work and writings. This, I hope, will become apparent in the following comparative sketches of Grundtvig's and Durkheim's respective diagnoses of and cure for the fundamental social problems surrounding them. Remarkably, their diagnoses can be applied to the general experience of crisis in Europe and North America today, where national cohesion is under pressure from the multitude of phenomena often characterized as "globalization" and "individualism," – phenomena that are challenging, among other things, our economies and sense of social unity. Put another way, today we detect an awareness of the fact that our societies and cultures are only one generation away from extinction – an awareness that was similarly acute in the nineteenth century. This awareness not only leaves its mark on public and political discussion but also motivates work in academia.

GRUNDTVIG AND BIEDERMEIER BLUES

To some extent it is possible to regard Grundtvig as a representative of the Biedermeier trend that dominated central and northern European art and literature from 1815 to 1848. The harmony of domestic (bourgeois) existence was the focus of architecture, interior decorating, art, and literature – though typically with a melancholic tang (Murray 2004, 89; Rolleston 1990). Grundtvig detects this tang: the future conditions of the family as a social institution are uncertain, he declared uneasily in 1817. Times were changing, and though one might have some idea of the direction, it was impossible to predict the development in detail: "I see how the knot will unravel through history – by loosening the bonds that binds parents and children; this is so because it is possible to see the bonds but not to untie them. And I probably wouldn't untie them if I could, since this is the sore point of the family, the examination of which it presumably wouldn't survive. And though it is obsolete before long, it is, nevertheless, not yet superseded" (Grundtvig 1817, 179).[6]

In a certain sense, this anxiety is one of the key motivations behind Grundtvig's prose writings. Accordingly, his interest in and concern for the upholding of social units – communities of different types (religious as well as secular) and of different sizes (small congregations with identifiable members as well as large imaginary abstractions such as "the people" [Anderson 1991] and the Christian church as such) – is a recurrent theme in his texts.

TOO CLOSE BUT TOO FAR APART

Grundtvig's uneasiness was boosted by the Trois Glorieuses of the twenty-seventh, twenty-eighth, and twenty-ninth of 1830 Paris and the following revolutionary attempts in the Netherlands, Brussels, the southern parts of the United Kingdom, Italy, and Poland (Church 1983; Tardy 2012). The turmoil of the mobs and its representation in the public sphere is in the back of his mind when, in 1834, Grundtvig (1983 [1834], 23) states: "'These are troubled times,' it is repeated so often nowadays that the mouth almost says it on its own hand ... The bodies in our days are restless." In fact, the violent behaviour so connected with "the crowd" has been offered as one of the key explanations for Grundtvig's sceptical attitude towards democracy – an attitude shared by the majority of the cultural elite in Denmark in the first half of the nineteenth century (Nevers 2011, 119–44). He was, however, at the same time concerned by a development running counter to the politically motivated physical, collective, and violent outbursts: the gradual social fragmentation that was sneaking up on communities – religious as well as secular. Thus, he follows up his anxiety regarding revolutionary crowds with this fretted analysis: "World history teaches us that all peoples, when they reach a certain age, by and large will arrive at an enlightenment by which the individual, young or old, ... separates himself and all he calls his from everything else in the sky as well as on Earth and demands, at any cost, what he, a being of reason, claims to be his right" (Grundtvig 1983 [1834], 27). And it was understood that the age in which Grundtvig lived had reached precisely this developmental stage.

These trepidations are equally evident in the two focal domains of Grundtvig's oeuvre – in his writings on the community of the Danish people, on the one side, and in his writings on community within the Danish Church, on the other.[7] Consequently, he used a scale of social equilibrium as an analytic tool in both areas of his work: on the too-dense/too-close/too-centripetal end of the scale he thus places the politically enraged crowds *and* religious revivalist movements, such as the "godly gatherings" (*gudelige forsamlinger*) that flourished among the common people on the Danish islands and parts of Jutland from 1790 to 1840, threatening to tear to pieces the bonds of the state church (Koch 1954, 97–122).[8] The challenges raised by the complex socially fragmenting developments of individualization inhabit the too-loose/too-far-apart/too-centrifugal end of the scale. These are expressed in the condition of the churchly communities, which are in need of regeneration, and the secular community (i.e., the Danish people), which is in need of awakening.

AWAKENING THE DANISH PEOPLE

As has often been pointed out, Grundtvig's vision of the secular community of Denmark increases in degree of articulation and gains in precision from the early 1830s onward (Korsgaard 2012; Thaning 1963). At this point Grundtvig arrives at the conclusion that the transition he intuitively sensed in the above quote was the shift in the fundamental base of social organization from the estates to the people (*Folket*). In a series of publications, Grundtvig thus calls for enlightenment of the public as well as education in and enthusiasm for the Nordic heritage. This is a project aimed at awakening the slumbering spirit of the people. And what is unlikely to escape even those only vaguely familiar with Grundtvig and his work is that his strategy was pedagogical. Grundtvig's ambition was to found an academy in the Zealandic village Sorø – a privileged location representing historical continuity, in his view, because it had been an educational centre since medieval times. The idea was to teach people (national) history, Nordic mythology, relevant scientific matters, and so on. But the main purpose was to inspire the students to seek this knowledge for themselves: to nurture a natural curiosity that had suffered heavily from wounds inflicted in the Danish school system of the nineteenth century (Grundtvig 1832, 1834, 1836, 1877). This system, Grundtvig insisted, was based on a destructive focus on examinations, leaving pupils passive and apathetic when confronted with the content of the curricula. Furthermore, there was a problem with the curricula as such: disciplines such as the (much loathed) study of the Latin language and Roman history was antiquated and irrelevant to most Danes. Instead, Grundtvig opted for useful or at least pertinent teaching in the vernacular. Likewise, he encouraged a casual and lively learning environment in which the relationship between student and teacher would revolve less around the strict accordance to behavioural expectations and the memorization of a corpus of facts and more around facilitating the understanding of how the subject in question could be made relevant to the lives of the pupils (Bugge 1965). And this was primarily the lives of young men, which accounts for Grundtvig's focus on andragogy – teaching strategies developed for adult learners (Warren 1989).

It is necessary to add that, among Grundtvig's numerable catchphrases, the one associated with this particular niche of his work is, of course, "the living word" (*det levende ord*). Among other things, this concept covers (or, more accurately, has in the Grundtvigian tradition and popular use been treated as an epitome of)[9] Grundtvig's opinions regarding the ideal form of educational communication: free and "relaxed" oral dialogue between teacher and pupils in an atmosphere of honest interest not only in the subject matter but also in the personal education of the agents involved in the discussion (Lyby 2001; Nielsen 1983). With regard to this Grundtvig also used the word *Vexel-Virkning*, which designates a reciprocal, intensifying communicative action whereby what is stressed are the social and situational aspects of the learning process.

Although the vision of the academy in Sorø was never realized, Grundtvig's influence on the Danish educational system is undeniable. This influence is naturally detectable in the milieu of the Folk High Schools. A great many factors have to be accounted for in their historical development and a great many have been (Engberg 1988; Hjermitslev 2007; Korsgaard 2006; Nissen 1994; Simon 1967; Skovmand 1944; Thyssen 1958). But, unquestionably, a decisive event was Grundtvig's lectures in the fall of 1838 for an audience at the collegé de Borch. These were eventually published in *Mands Minde* (1877). The lectures were evidently a great inspiration to the young men in attendance: by the mid-1840s Grundtvig's first public addresses on his visions of the reformation of the school system[10] – in his mind a necessary first step towards freeing Denmark of its cultural crisis – had led to the first Folk High School being set up in Rødding in North Schleswig. First and foremost, Grundtvig's ideas were animated by establishing these Folk High Schools around the country. But his ambition to enlighten the people also found an outlet in *folkelige fordrag*, informal ad hoc lectures on subjects of national history, Nordic mythology, and so on that were inspired by Grundtvig's lectures. This ambition was institutionalized in societies and associations such as *Danske Samfund* (Danish Society), which were dedicated to hosting events that promoted this type of communication (Baunvig forthcoming). Interestingly, an integral part of this genre – which, by the way, remains a flourishing aspect of Danish cultural flora – involves the joint singing of a song from the Folk High School songbook (*Højskolesangbogen*). And this tradition originated on an October evening in 1838 when the audience applauded Grundtvig for a lecture on the war against England at the beginning of the century by spontaneously singing "Kommer hid, I Piger smaae" (Come here, little girls), one of his many patriotic songs (Lundgren-Nielsen 1998).

In sum, I argue that Grundtvig's ambition to awaken the slumbering Danish spirit was brought to life by his setting up the infrastructure to deal with the education and enlightenment of the people. This was done by his recognizing the fact that education was a process rooted in concrete social events typically involving musical and other "invigorating" elements.[11] A parallel line of thought runs through Grundtvig's writings on the religious and churchly communities.

POWER TO THE CONGREGATION

If the Danish people needed to wake up and smell the national and historical identity, the Danish congregations quite literally needed to wake up. This was the refrain of a choir of churchmen who regretted that people were disengaged from, slept through, or simply did not attend service. The choir counted Grundtvig among its members (Grundtvig 1828).[12] As pointed out time and again, Grundtvig reached a sort of theological maturity around 1825. This peak is typically referred to in revelatory terms as the "exceptional discovery" (*den mageløse opdagelse*). From this time on, it is self-evident to Grundtvig that the congregational communities and liturgical praxis are the fundament of the Christian church. In this he opposed the ecclesiological definitions then in vogue, which proclaimed that the Bible and its exegesis were just as central. The Christian church is not based on the theological elite's analyses of the biblical texts. According to Grundtvig (1826, IV, 416) "the Christian church is a fact," and this fact is observable in the history of the congregations and in the main components of their ritual tradition – that is, the creed: "Which is the only thing common to all Christians in every positions, in all congregations, to all times; the one thing marking the church making it recognizable for friends and foes and the one thing that has united the congregation. It has, thus, been both trademark and bond of unity. This is the bank [to] carry his church in all days to come!" (417). In Grundtvig's opinion, when the church is anchored to actual ritual events and to the participation of its members it is important, first, that members actually show up and, second, that they engage in the appropriate procedures.

But how was this task to be undertaken? How were the churchgoers to be revived? According to Grundtvig, through collective singing. As early as 1807 in the dissertation entitled *Religion og Liturgie* (Religion and Liturgy), Grundtvig (1807, 190–1) reveals a special sensibility with regard to the importance of hymns in the liturgical framework:

> The song [is] the center of the liturgical poetry. This is the place for the union of all that man is able to create splendid and noble. Poetry presents itself clothed in harmonic verses, resting on melodic rhyme, and elevated by growing music. High above the earth we will be raised and a glimpse of the eternal life will float before our eyes fixed at the sky. Alas! Only seldom this befalls, and what is the cause for this? ... As long as the majority of the choirmasters have a lot to learn from bleaters and Peer Degn[,][13] even the most magnificent of hymns would lose their allure and be a source from which sluggishness and not deep emotion emanate.

Grundtvig was to eventually abandon this strictly aesthetic assessment[14] – evident in his description of the melodic and poetic aspects of the hymn and in his attention to the beauty of the performance as being vital to the effect of the song. At the end of the 1820s, after some clerical experience, his judgment is quite different. From that point on his main criterion for evaluation was whether or not the hymn was suited to "unison singing in a village church" (Grundtvig 1828, 15). The hymn was "no cantata to be applauded" (ibid.); similarly, the churchgoers were not members of an audience but, rather, participating agents. Pragmatic concerns thus led Grundtvig to conclude that hymns had to be ortographically and melodically accessible to the uneducated public majority. Following that line of reasoning, many of his hymns from the late 1830s onward were composed on the metric-melodic basis of popular contemporary songs. The aim was to get the congregations to sing; therefore, traditional measures of beauty had to be surrendered. According to Grundtvig, though: "This apparent sacrifice really isn't one at all. Because the thing that builds and moves us in the church song is far less the hymn as such than the congregation's devoted participation. All this we have forgotten in the cities under the influence of the theater and its habits of searching the text and listening to the music" (31–2).

These considerations appear in the wording at the heart of Grundtvig's own hymn production to such a degree that he was prompted to coin a new term for his manuals for collective singing: *Fest-Psalmer* (feast hymns). This was also the name of his popular 1850 hymnal, which was published for use in the Vartov congregation. This hymnal ran to ten editions in twenty years, while gradually expanding from an original thirty hymns to a final 330 (Auken 2008, 229). These were not intended for private prayers, one of the unavoidable features of the texts being the prevalent use of the first-person plural. In this way, Grundtvig stressed the congregational "we" as subject.

MANUALS FOR SOCIAL COHESION

Grundtvig, like his contemporaries, feared the forceful and violent phenomena associated with groups whose exhilaration threatened social stability. However, at the same time, he appreciated their regenerative and stabilizing potential. This is to some extent indicated by his pedagogical focus on the learning environment as something that should be both intense and socially relevant. Also, in addition to his thoughts on the role of the hymn, which directly reflect this positive emphasis, the quantitative and semantic aspects of hymnal production are implicit confirmations of the same. I tentatively extend this argument to include the patriotic songs and the community of the Danish people. On this basis, I suggest that Grundtvig intuitively treated the aforementioned collective and musical activities as a way of infecting communities with the type of herd behaviour that creates and/or regenerates social bonds – but in a controlled environment. Such experiences were increasingly important in a society that was gradually being colonized by the individual. In this sense, Grundtvig's songs, both religious and secular, might be seen as manuals for establishing social cohesion. Likewise, he might have seen them as vehicles for indicating social equilibrium, pointing out whether there was too much community or too little. In any case, the songs and social events stood the test of cultural selection, and the Folk High Schools and the *folkekirke* are now an integral part of Danish mainstream culture. This is indicated by the impressive number of Grundtvig's songs and hymns that are represented in the latest editions of the Folk High School songbook and hymnbook.

DURKHEIM AND MELANCHOLIA FIN-DE-SIÈCLE

In the words of Émile Durkheim (1973, 39), social and individual life is a "complex equilibrium whose various elements limit one another; this balance cannot be disrupted without producing unhappiness or illness." But disruption was the reality in fin-de-siècle France, which had been left decimated after the French-Prussian War of 1870–71. The defeat was conceived as part of a larger cultural degeneration that, among other things, could be detected in the apparently epidemic spread of mental, or "nervous," conditions such as the new diagnosis of neurasthenia. It was common practice in scientific journals, as well as in popular literature, to express concerns about the physical and mental exhaustion, devitalization, and degeneration that characterized the French population across social and economic boundaries (Fournier 2007, 295–6; Fournier 2005, 57–60; Goldstein 1987). This Durkheim (1995, 429) explained as transitional pains: "We are going through a period of transition and moral mediocrity. The great things of the past that excited our fathers no longer arouse the same zeal among us, either because they have passed so completely into common custom that we lose awareness of them or because they no longer suit our aspirations. Meanwhile, no replacement for them has yet been created ... In short, the former gods are growing old or dying, and others have not yet been born."

The epidemic of mental exhaustion was accompanied by the cultural and political exhaustion evident in the defeat and loss of Alsace and parts of Lorraine. These circumstances were associated with the state of the educational system: it was conceived as outdated and deficient, in acute need of reform. "To remake it (*La France*), it must first be educated" (Durkheim 1918 [1975], 452) was the credo (Lukes 1972, 42).[15] Against this background, in 1885–86 Durkheim was sent on an expedition to investigate German universities and the dominant scientific method and culture in Germany (Fournier 2008, 89–102). He visited the experimental psychologist Wilhelm Wundt at the University of Leipzig and was struck by the collaborative environment among the scholars working in close-knit teams. Likewise, he was impressed by the integration of empirical approaches into the study of things moral (in the sense of "cultural" or "social") undertaken by the researchers. On his return to France he was appointed professor of pedagogics at the University of Bordeaux. In the course of his academic career the inspiration he received in Germany stayed with him: he would insist on basing his work on empirical material (statistics, ethnographic reports, etc.) as well as on working in (or heading) a unit, an *équipe*. An example of the latter may be found in the editorial responsibilities that fell upon the group around the journal *L'Année Sociologique*, which was founded by Durkheim in 1898. It ran until 1925 and counted among its members Henri Hubert, Marcel Mauss, Célestin Bouglé, Robert Hertz, François Simiand, and Maurice Halbwachs.

A typical specimen of his generation, Durkheim was convinced that France had to work itself through the crisis by formulating an adequate moral ideology for the Third Republic (1870–1940). Durkheim's ambition was therefore to help in the construction of a secular, national worship – a midwife assisting at the birth of the gods appropriate for modern France. This was not to be a creation ex nihilo; nor would a simple cleansing of traditional supernatural elements be enough. Instead, to create a successful secular morality, a hermeneutical procedure was needed: a translation of elementary mechanisms evident in empirical material such as the ethnographic studies that formed the basis for Durkheim's (1973, 11) last and greatest work, *Les forms élémentaires de la vie religieuse: Le systeme totemique en Australie* (1912): "We must discover those moral forces that men, down to the present time, have conceived of only under the form of religious allegories. We must disengage them from their symbols, present them in their rational nakedness, so to speak, and find a way to make the child feel their reality without recourse to any mythological intermediary." The creative platform, Durkheim held, would be the newly established discipline of sociology, to which he is usually ascribed a certain amount of parental responsibility. Through a thorough sociological study of the French condition evident in porous social structures and an unstable economy, he wished to reveal the morality integral to the French people in crisis. But, anticlimactically, he died having only finished the introduction of *La Morale* (1917). Still, there are other sources to consult, although none of them offers the clear-cut entry into the French moral climate of 1900 that he had promised.

SOLIDARITY AMONG HOMO DUPLEX

To Durkheim, the human being is a mix of centrifugal and centripetal forces. The individual is a homo duplex: "each individual has a dual nature: Two beings exist in him" (Durkheim 1995, 134). On the one hand, he is a physical being attending to his daily business, driven by acute biological and private needs; on the other, he feels a social or moral force presenting itself as an inner voice of conscience and having imperative authority (Durkheim 1973, 31, 42). This is inculcated during childhood through the disciplining influence of family members as well as, in developed (complex) societies, by instructions received at school. The disciplining of biological nature is in fact what defines humans: "man's nature cannot be itself except as it is disciplined" (51). But it is also a matter of balance. Full and happy lives can be found neither among individuals who surrender completely to their desires (40) nor among those who suppress them in the form of extreme ascetic behaviour (51). Likewise, Durkheim indicates, societies as wholes must find equilibrium. In his opinion the task of modernity is thus to find the centre of social gravity, avoiding the extremes of liberalism and collectivism that easily plot onto opposing ends of the axis of too little community and too much. "Solidarity" is a keyword in Durkheim's early descriptions of social cohesion. It is well known that, in *De La Division Du Travail Social* (1893), he differentiates between the "mechanical" solidarity of primitive (simple) societies based on likeness in occupation and behaviour, on the one side, and the "organic" solidarity characteristic of developed (complex) societies, in which labour and routines are specialized and divided, on the other. Here theory and praxis meet: in a sense, the collaborative aspects of labour division are reflected in the work of the Durkheimian *équipe*. Furthermore, Canadian Durkheim scholar Marcel Fournier (2005, 52) suggests that the importance Durkheim attaches to immediate emotional phenomena, such as solidarity and "the associative dimension" of social life, in his early work is meant to suggest "a third way" between the equally unattractive socially atomized and socially condensed alternatives (see also Fournier 2008; Collins 2005, 107). In his later work Durkheim develops this emphasis in his theory of religion.[16] He points out the locus of human communities as such[17] – crowds.

TIME AND AGAIN: EFFERVESCENCE

In a well-known passage from *Les forms élémentaires de la vie religieuse* Durkheim (1995, 216–17) observes that human existence is split in two:

> Life in Australian society alternates between two different phases. In one phase, the population is scattered in small groups that attend to their occupations independently. Each family lives to itself, hunting, fishing – in short, striving by all possible means to get the food it requires. In the other phase, by contrast, the population comes together, concentrating itself at specified places for a period that varies from several days to several months. This concentration takes place when a clan or a portion of the tribe … conducts a religious ceremony or holds what in the usual ethnographic terminology is called a corroboree.
>
> These two phases stand in the sharpest contrast. The first phase, in which economic activity predominates, is generally of rather low intensity. Gathering seeds or plants necessary for food, hunting, and fishing are not occupations that can stir truly strong passions. The

> dispersed state in which the society finds itself makes life monotonous, slack, and humdrum. Everything changes when a corroboree takes place.

These phases – the humdrum life of individuals tending to their respective biological and private needs, on the one hand, and the intense atmosphere in which individuals tune in socially at a collective event, such as a religious ritual, on the other – may be mapped onto the creatures that make up homo duplex..

One of Durkheim's main claims is that, in both simple and complex societies, the fabric of social infrastructure is woven in a pattern of collective events that societal members perceive as recurrent. A regular ritual rhythm is the heart of a healthy community. This is the setting for emotional bonding between individuals and for the strengthening of the esteem for shared symbols (e.g., ideas and pictograms; beliefs, flags, and totemic animals). Physical density and synchronized movement seems to be the key:

> The very act of congregating is an exceptionally powerful stimulant. Once the individuals are gathered together, a sort of electricity is generated from their closeness and quickly launches them to an extraordinary height of exaltation. Every emotion expressed resonates without interference in consciousnesses that are wide open to external impressions, each echoing the others. The initial impulse is thereby amplified each time it is echoed, like an avalanche that grows as it goes along ... Probably because a collective emotion cannot be expressed collectively without some order that permits harmony and unison of movement, these gestures and cries tend to fall into rhythm and regularity, and from there into songs and dances. (Durkheim 1995, 218)

The emotional surplus is transferred to the normative domain – the "representations" (normative ideas and ideals) marking collective identity. Therefore, in Durkheim's mind, fixed social structures – institutions and society as such – must be regarded as "crystallized emotions" (Alexander 2005, 151): "What we have said of crowds, of ephemeral gatherings, applies *a fortiori* to societies, which are only permanent and organized crowds" (Durkheim 1973, 62).

Thus, in Durkheim's analysis, indigenous central Australian clans boost social bonds and clan society in the totemic ritual context of the corroborees. And the French nation was in need of precisely such ritual regeneration. Furthermore, France, in fact, had unique experiences of the strategic facilitation of effervescent states. The French Revolutionary Calendar of 1793–1805 was meant to institute "a whole cycle of celebrations in order to keep the principles that inspired it [i.e., the revolution] eternally young" (Durkheim 1995, 430). However, the collective representations – the "revolutionary faith [–] lasted only briefly," and therefore the "institution quickly perished." This process was accelerated by "disappointments and discouragements" that "quickly replaced the first moment of enthusiasm" (ibid.). It is telling that Durkheim's evaluation of the cultic initiatives is positive: his central hypothesis is that socially coherent and vigorous societies (religious as well as secular) are based on a ritual praxis. The problem was setting up this praxis in turn-of-the-century France. The problem was unravelling the adequate norms and collective representations (or "faith") suited for ritual celebration. While Grundtvig, still a child of the eighteenth century and romanticism, turned to Norse eddas and sagas, Durkheim did not, in age-old mythologies of the Franks, the Gauls, the Bretons, and the Normans, find a common denominator for the modern construction of *toute la France*. One finds no positive celebration of things French but, rather, a universal reflection on the condition of humankind as such.[18] This perspective is, however, naturally very much in line with the French philosophical tradition. Durkheim suggested that a "cult of the individual" would reveal itself as the institution that, paradoxically, inculcates social cohesion into modernity (Marske 1987). But he did not produce any effervescence manuals and he did not become the icon of a national movement to the degree that Grundtvig did in Denmark. He did, however, articulate a theory of the mechanisms of social cohesion that recent research seems to provide with a more explicit formulation (see Konvalinka 2010; 2011, Rappaport 1999).

COME TOGETHER

Groups of people become sui generis entities through regular physical gatherings – that is, in a ritual praxis that includes musical elements – that nurture social bonds and collective ideas and that strengthens social cohesion. This goes for secular as well as religious groups. Such is the logic behind Grundtvig's intuitive and pragmatically implemented thoughts on the community of the Danish people and the Danish church. Such is the logic explicit in Durkheim's speculative sociological theory.

The question of social cohesion and equilibrium is at least as old as Aristotle. It is perhaps even of paleolithic origin and connected to population size. The subject, not surprisingly, draws much attention in communities struggling in some way to uphold themselves. The conflict between centrifugal and centripetal forces is emblematic of modernity and is a condition that confronts us as much today as it ever did.

Additionally, the question of social cohesion is related to pedagogics. From the rough sketches of Grundtvig's and Durkheim's different approaches to pedagogical work and systematic thought, there emerges a topic for further consideration. Would it be possible to detect different types of pedagogical strategies piggy-backing on different types of governmental organizations? Does national homogeneity and a strong emphasis on the cultural and historical particularity of the people that make up a given country entail ambitions of nurturing "natural" characteristics of the individual as integral to pedagogical logic? This was the case with Denmark and Grundtvig. And, conversely, does national heterogeneity and a strong emphasis on a country's republican construction (as in the French and Durkheimian case) demand a pedagogical praxis based on discipline and the construction of the citizen? In any case, these are questions of identity making on both group and individual levels. What we are looking at is a social phenomenon dependent upon social events involving "devoted participation," or "effervescence."

NOTES

1 I am referring to that highly complex process of the ever-increasing specialization and fragmentation of social groups and the promotion of individual rights in most spheres of human existence – a process that claims hallmarks such as the Protestant Reformation, the Enlightenment, British Liberalism, and French Republicanism. In the twentieth century it has been described as a development transforming former community-anchored people with relatively stable identities into agents of eclectic cultural and religious consumption (Bellah 2006, 340; Wuthnow 1998). Furthermore, some are of the opinion that it is a process eroding human communities as such: obviously the analyses and arguments on the challenges faced by institutions and communities in modernity posed, respectively, by Ulrich Beck and Anthony Giddens would be such examples (Beck 1987; Giddens 1991).

2 By "crowd" I mean a group of people gathered spontaneously or as a result of preceding arrangements while collectively aligning their attention fields. It is often used as a synonym for "mob" and as a semantic relative of "mass psychosis" and "flock behavior."

3 Such events were often politically motivated, as in the revolutionary cases. However, instances of what George Rudé (1964, 19–77) calls "crowd action" was highly recurrent in the eighteenth and nineteenty centuries and was also spurred on for a number of other reasons. In rural districts lack of food was typically the decisive factor; in urban environments labour conditions were often the cause.

4 This emphasis on the destructive potential of "socially dense" situations was, however, an old one. Thus, the horrors of the English Civil War (1642–51) were in the back of Thomas Hobbes's mind when he proclaimed that humans are cruel creatures only able to live together peacefully by entering a contractual arrangement. Nonetheless, the position was ideologically nurtured by the brutalities of crowds during the French Revolution (1789–99) and by the obvious fact that the increase in population density as a result of growth in birthrates and urbanization simply made such events more frequent. It was considered a very real and dangerous phenomenon in need of scientific study and political precaution. Such a study was delivered by the French social psychologist Gustave Le Bon in his 1895 *La psychologie des foules*, which systematically describes the socially undermining powers of collective gatherings. Otto Stohl's *Suggesion und Hypnotismus in der Völkerpsykologie* [Suggestion and hypnosis in folk psychology] (1904) is another example. Additional representatives of this line of thought are turn-of-the-century sociologists Gaetano Mosca, Vilfredo Paredo, and Robert Michels. German scholar of Scandinavian literature Joachim Schiedermair includes mid-century authors such as Danish Johan Ludvig Heiberg and Norwegian Henrik Wergeland in this group.

5 I agree with Danish historian Kasper Støvring's (2011, 134) definition of social cohesion as an emotional and cultural phenomenon that does not depend on legal, economical, and political constructs alone: "cohesion cannot be and has not been the result of mere institution building: it is also a matter of culture." Likewise, I agree that there is more to the concept of social cohesion than can be monitored in census studies on national levels of trust, prosperity, mobility, and so on. Furthermore, I find it natural to inform the concept with results from the cognitive field pertaining to the physiological and psychological mechanism behind experiences of social connection and bonding. This is what I do in the following.

6 This and the following quotes are my translations.

7 Grundtvig was a keen advocate of a state church that allowed for different confessional groupings within the overarching churchly community as well as the right of members to choose or found a congregation (Lyby 1993, 217).

8 This does not, however, mean that Grundtvig worked against the lay-driven movement. In fact, on numerous occasions, he defended its position under the canopy of the state church. Furthermore, a number of young priests in Grundtvig's circle were involved in the movement. Even so, Grundtvig remained a steadfast critic of the pietistic theological premises that drove its leaders.

9 A quick search on the webpage korpus.dk – a resource that offers a representative selection of texts written in the period between 1990 and 2000 that facilite investigations of the use of Danish words and phrases – tentatively indicates that *det levende ord* is often associated with, or simply used as a synonym for, "oral" and "cheerful."

10 Though the thematic setup was Grundtvig's memory of and reflections on world events in the period between 1788 and 1838, a recurrent topic in the published notes is the condition of the Danish school system.

11 Here it is necessary to consider the question about humanity and movement (and reception). Obviously, I am not claiming that Grundtvig ingeniously and single-handedly generated, let alone carried out, the above-mentioned process. Rather, I side with Hegel and Marx in regarding him as an agent of history. Or, to put it another way, the process can be construed as a result of a complex cultural evolution in which phenomena and traditions associated with Grundtvig were selected and proven adaptive.

12 In Denmark, the concern about "empty churches," which was connected to a weakening of clerical authority as such, had been a recurring issue since the last decades of eighteenth century. Naturally, such concerns have been a reality for the church for millennia. But a qualitative break in the extent of the problem seems to have occurred when service attendance was no longer considered a civic duty but, rather, a matter of conscience (Koch 1954, 92).

13 A pitiful, grotesque parish clerk and character in the Danish Enlightenment thinker Ludvig Holberg's satirical play *Erasmus Montanus* (1722).

14 In the aesthetic approach Grundtvig is unmistakably influenced by the German Idealists in fashion (Lundgren-Nielsen 1983; Thaulov 2012).

15 However, the driving argument in Romanian-American historian Eugen Weber's 1976 classic *Peasants into Frenchmen: The Modernization of Rural France, 1870–1914* is that what Durkheim (representing a socio-

economic elite seated in government and at the universities) calls a "remake" was in fact more of a construction from scratch. The idea of *toute la France* was an urban, educated, and bourgeois idea that did not translate into rural and peasant reality. Nevertheless, the homogenizing transformation of the population was, in fact and in Weber's mind, characteristic of the forty to fifty years leading up to the First World War, giving an ideological ring to the word "urbanization."

16 The distinction between early and later work touches upon the issue of reception. In the first half of the twentieth century Durkheim was the author of *De La Division Du Travail Social* (1893), *Les Règles de la Méthode Sociologique* (1895), and *Le Suicide* (1897), in which he flirts "with materialist forms of structural theory" (Alexander 2005, 136). Gradually, however, there was a shift of emphasis. His later writings, such as "Représentations individuelles et représentations collectives" (1898) and *Les formes élémentaires de la vie religieuse* (1912), draw attention to "the spiritual program of Durkheim's later cultural sociology" (151). Here the religion-cum-society/culture interest and the emphasis on immediate emotional mechanisms come to the fore. The development in Durkheim's work is, by the way, often told as the story of his reaching scholarly maturity. Indeed, Durkheim himself deemed his early structural-material work thematically and methodologically insufficient.

17 In the preceding I use the terms "culture," "society," "nation," "church," and "congregation" somewhat interchangeably, my main focus being Grundtvig's and Durkheim's interest in the actual situated experience of "community," or "social connection," as the common denominator of these concepts.

18 In a sense Durkheim thought of his scientific task as a deciphering of hidden truths or basic mechanisms in an empirically gathered body of material. In this sense, his strategy is akin to Protestant theologian Rudolf Bultmann's demythologization. In any case, Durkheim's hermeneutical approach to the study of religion very much opposed the hitherto dominant strategies of scholars such as Victor Turner and James Frazer, whose ambition was, in some sense, to display the bizarre aspects and fundamental cognitive lapses at the root of religious behaviour and thought. Contrary to this, Durkheim wished to show what constituted religion as a social fact apparent in every part of the world in in every historical period. His overall sympathetic approach is unavoidably evident in the palindromic text "L'avenir de la religion" (Durkheim 1914), in which he considers the future of religion from the point of view of both believers and non-believers.

REFERENCES

Alexander, J.C. 2005. "The Inner Development of Durkheim's Sociological Theory: From Early Writings to Maturity." In *The Cambridge Companion to Durkheim*, ed. J.C. Alexander and P. Smith, 136–59. Cambridge University Press.

Anderson, B. 1991. *Imagined Communities*. London: Verso.

Auken, S. 2008. "Nordisk mytologi og salmedigtning – N.F.S. Grundtvig" [Norse mythology and hymns – N.F.S. Grundtvig].In *Dansk litteraturs historie bind 2: 1800–1870* [The history of Danish literature], ed. S, Schou, 199–237. Copenhagen: Gyldendal.

Ayres, R. 1989. *Technological Transformations and Long Waves*. Austria: Lachbruch.

Beck, U. 1987. *Risikogesellschaft: Auf dem Weg in eine andere Moderne* [Risk society: Toward a new modernity]. Frankfurt am Main: Suhrkamp.

Bellah, R. 2006. *The Robert Bellah Reader*. Durham, NC: Duke University Press.

Berlanstein R.L. 1992. *The Industrial Revolution and Work in Nineteenth-Century Europe*. London: Routledge.

Bugge, K.E. 1965. *Skolen forlivet: Studier over N.F.S.* Grundtvigs pædagogiske *tanker* [The school for life: Studies in N.F.S. Grundtvig's educational ideas]. Copenhagen: Gad.

Church, C.H. 1983. *Europe in 1830: Revolution and Political Change*. London: Allen and Unwin.

Collins, R. 2005. "The Durkheimian Movement in France and in World Sociology." In *The Cambridge Companion to Durkheim*, ed. J.C. Alexander and P. Smith, 101–35. Cambridge: Cambridge University Press.

Durkheim, Émile. 1912 [2008]. *Les forms élémentaires de la vie religieuse: Le système totemique en Australie*. Paris: Presses Universitaires de France.

– 1914. "L'avenir de la religion." http://classiques.uqac.ca/classiques/Durkheim_emile/sc_soc_et_action/texte_4_14/avenir_religion.html.

– 1918 [1975]. "La vie universitaire à Paris." In *Textes*, 1:453–83. Paris: Editions de Minuit.

– 1973. *Moral Education: Study in the Theory and Application of the Sociology of Education*. New York: Free Press.

– 1995. *Elementary Forms of Religious Life*. New York: Free Press.

Engberg, P. 1988. *Halvgudelivet i dødningesal: Træk af folkehøjskolens indre historie* [Demi-God life in the halls of the dead: Characteristics of the inner history of the people's high school]. Aarhus: Anis.

Fournier, M. 2005 "Durkheim's Life and Context." In *The Cambridge Companion to Durkheim*, ed. J.C. Alexander and P. Smith, 41–69. Cambridge University Press.

– 2007. *Émile Durkheim, 1858–1917*. Fayard: Paris.

Giddens, A. 1991. *Modernity and Self-identity: Self and Society in the Late Modern Age*. Cambridge: Polity Press.

Goldstein, J. 1987. *Console and Classify: The French Psychiatric Profession in the Nineteenth Century*. Cambridge: Cambridge University Press.

Grundtvig, N.F.S. 1807. "Om Religion og Liturgie" [About religion and liturgy]. http://www.grundtvigsværker.dk/tekstvisning/650/0#{"0":0,"k":1}

– 1817. "Om Mennesket i Verden" [On man in the world]. *Danne-Virke II* [The Dane-work II].

– 1828. P.A. Fenger. In *Theologisk Maanedsskrift* (April) [Theological monthly], 1–36. Copenhagen: Tengnagel.

– 1832 [1870]. *Nordens Mythologi – eller Sindbilled-Sprog* [Norse mythology]. Copenhagen: Samleren.

– 1983 [1834]. *Statsmæssig Oplysning: Et udkast om samfund og skole* [Education for the state: A draft on society and school]. Copenhagen: Nyt Nordisk Forlag. http://www.grundtvigbyen.dk/gr/3445.pdf.

– 1836. *Det danske Fiir-Kløver eller Danskheden partisk betragtet* [The Danish four-leaf clover or a partiality for Danishness] Copenhagen: Wahlske Boghandel. In *The School for Life: N.F.S. Grundtvig on Education for the People*, trans. and ed. E. Broadbridge, co-ed. C. Warren and U. Jonas, 126–65. Aarhus: Aarhus University Press.

– 1877. *Mands Minde: 1788–1838: Foredrag over det sidste halve Aarhundredes Historie, holdte 1838* [Within living memory: 1788–1838: Lectures on the history of the last half century given in 1838 by Nik. Sev. Fred. Grundtvig]. København: Schønberg.

Hjermitslev, H-H. 2007. "Brødrene la Cours kamp for naturvidenskab på de danske højskoler, 1867–1908" [The brothers la cour struggle for science at Danish schools, 1867–1908]. *Slagmark* [Battlefield] 50: 30–48.

Koch, H. 1954. *Den Danske Kirkes Historie VI* [Danish church history VI]. Edited by Hal Koch and Bjørn Kornerup. Copenhagen: Gyldendal.

Konvalinka, I. 2010. "Follow You, Follow Me: Continuous Mutual Prediction and Adaptation in Joint Tapping." *Quarterly Journal of Experimental Psychology* 63 (11): 2220–30.

– 2011. "Synchronized Arousal between Performers and Related Spectators in a Fire-Walking Ritual." *National Academy of Sciences* 108 (20): 8514–19.

Korsgaard, O. 2006. "Hvordan erindres folkehøjskolens historie?" [How to recall the history of the Danish people's high school?]. *Grundtvig Studier* 57 (1): 188–209.

– 2012. *N.F.S. Grundtvig*. København: Jurist- og Økonomforbundets Forlag.

Lundgren-Nielsen, F. 1983. "Grundtvig og Romanbikken" (Grundtvig and romanticism]. *Grundtvig og Grundtvigianisman i nyt lys* [Grundtvig and Grundtvigianism in a new light]. Ed. C. Thadberg and A.P. Thyssen. Aarhus: Anis.

Lyby, T.C. 1993. "Grundtvigs tanker om præstefrihed – og grundtvigianernes" [Grundtvig's thoughts on the priests' freedom – and the Grundtvigians]. In *Ordet, kirken og kulturen* [The world, the church, and culture], ed. by Per Ingesman, Carsten Bach-Nielsen, Susanne Gregersen og Ninna Jørgensen, 129–48. Aarhus: Aarhus University Press.

– 2001. "Skolen for livet' Grundtvigs tanker om folkeoplysning" [The school for life: Grundtvig's thoughts on public education]. In *Dannelse, Uddannelse, Universiteter – Festskrift for Henning Lehmann den 31. januar 2002* [Formation, education, universities – Festschrift for Henning Lehmann January 2002], ed. C. Bach-Nielsen. Aarhus: Aarhus University Press.

Lukes, S. 1972. *Émile Durkheim: His Life and Work*. New York: Harper and Row.

Marske, C.E. 1987. "Durkheim's 'Cult of the Individual' and the Moral Reconstitution of Society." *Sociological Theory* 5: 1–14.

Murray, C.J. 2004. *Encyclopedia of the Romantic Era 1760–1850*, vol. 1, 89. London: Routledge.

Nevers, J. 2011. *Fra skældsord til slagord: Demokratibegrebet i dansk historie* [From swear-word to catchword: The concept of democracy in Danish political history]. Odense: University Press of Southern Denmark.

Nielsen, V. 1983. "Grundtvigs brug af Det levende Ord – i skolen" [Grundtvig's use of the living word – at school]. In *Modersmål-Selskabets årbog* [Yearbook for the Mother Tongue Association] 4: 48–58.

Nissen. 1994. *Udfordringer til Højskolen: Danske Folkehøjskoler, 1844–1994* [Challenges to the people's high school: Danish people's high schools, 1844–1994]. Odense: Foreningen for Folkehøjskolers Forlag.

Randall, H.J. 1929. "The Intellectual Revolution in Nineteenth Century England." *Edinburgh Review* 249 : 41–62.

Rappaport, R. 1999. *Ritual and Religion in the Making of Humanity*. Cambridge: Cambridge University Press.

Rolleston, J. 1990. "The Legacy of Idealism: Schiller, Morike and Biedermeier Culture." *Modern Language Quarterly* 51 (4): 491–512.

Rudé, G. 1964. *The Crowd in History, 1730–1848*. New York: John Wiley and Sons.

Simon, E. 1967. *Réveil national et culture populaire en Scandinavie: la genèse de la højskole nordique, 1844–1878* [National Awakening and popular culture in Scandinavia: the genesis of the Nordic Peoples Highschool, 1844–1878]. Thesis. Paris: Presses Universitaires de France.

Skovmand, R. 1944. *Folkehøjskolen i Danmark 1841–1892: Studier over en Oplysningsbevægelse i det 19. Aarhundrede*, People Highschool in Denmark 1841–1892: Studies of an enlightenment movement in the 19th century. Copenhagen: The Danish Press.

Støvring, K. 2011. "The Cultural prerequisites social cohesion. With special attention to the nation of Denmark." *International Journal of Sociology and Social Policy* 32(3/4), 134–52.

Tardy, J-N. 2012. "Tuer le tyran ou la tyrannie? Attentat et conspiration politique: distinctions et affinités en France de 1830 à 1870" [Kill the tyrant or kill tyranny? Political attacks and conspiracy in France from 1830 to 1870]. In *La Révolution Française: Cahiers de l'Institut d'Histoire de la Révolution Française* [The French revolution: Papers of the Institute of History of the French Revolution], vol. 1. Paris: Institut d'Histoire de la Révolution Française.

Thaning, K. 1963. *Menneske først: Grundtvigs opgør med sig selv* [Human first: Grundtvig's showdown with himself]. Odense: Gyldendal.

Thaulov, V. 2012. Indledning til "Om Religion og Liturgie" og "Suar paa Resenjonen over min Afhandling om Religion og Liturgie" [Introduction to "On religion and liturgy" and "Response to the debate over my dissertation on religion and liturgy]. www.grundtvigsværketdk/tekstvisning/650/3.

Thyssen, A.P. 1958. *Den nygrundtvigske Bevægelse I, 1870–1887* [The new Grundtvigian movement I, 1870–1887]. Copenhagen: Det Danske Forlag.

Warren, C. 1989. "Andragogy and N.F.S. Grundtvig: A Critical Link." *Adult Education Quarterly* 39: 211–23.

Wuthnow, R. 1998. *Loose Connections: Joining Together in America's Fragmented Communities*. Cambridge, MA: Harvard University Press.

12

"The Gordian Knot": Grundtvig and British Liberalism

OLE VIND

For over three months each summer in 1829, 1830, and 1831, respectively, Grundtvig received royal grants to visit England for the purpose of studying the Old English manuscripts in London, Exeter, and Cambridge. Already in 1820 he had published the first modern (Danish) translation of the Old English heroic poem *Beowulf*, and he was now looking for further ties of kinship between Old English and Old Norse poetry and mythology – a kinship that plays a key role in his philosophy of history.

The meeting with modern England turned out to be of crucial importance for his political ideas as well. As he later phrased it, he learned in England "with regard to freedom as to all other human matters to set great store by *reality*" (Grundtvig 1909 [1871], 356, emphasis in original). London was then the greatest city in the world and Britain the world leader in technology, industry, and trade. In London, Grundtvig gained a first-hand impression of the spectacular but frightening consequences of industrialization and commercialization.

In 1838, in a much-quoted comment on his visits to England, Grundtvig (1877, 446) spoke of:

> a certain horror of machinery on a large scale that not only makes a racket so that no one can hear anyone else and it blackens and fries whatever comes close, but turns people by the thousand, large and small, into a sideshow, simply appendices to the machinery as the main purpose and the basic power. So even the Englishmen who give themselves time to think of anything else than turning everything they have into money, look in secret horror at each new invention

> and colossal application of basic mechanical power which is gradually driving out all the old craftsmen and making them mere tools in the machine-master's hand, unthinking slaves in the manufacturer's yard.

In England Grundtvig met a high degree of personal freedom in all life's circumstances, which, in his philosophy, signified progress towards a better, more perfect society. But he also remarked that the individualization of the time and the efforts towards personal liberation threatened to undermine and loosen all the ties between the people and, thus, the cohesion essential to the survival of every society. In 1834, Grundtvig (1983 [1834], 31) called this inequity "the Gordian knot in human development, which, when all is said and done, has up to now been cut by the sword of Alexander, but which must be untied with caution and with patience wherever the state is to be rescued and 'genuine' human enlightenment is to progress to the end of days" (see also Broadbridge, Warren, and Jonas 2011, 84).

Grundtvig was not the first to feel "a certain horror" as he watched the consequences of the Industrial Revolution and the rapid urbanization of England. Adam Smith himself notes, in *The Wealth of Nations* (1776), that the division of labour into specialized segments together with the new machines and increased competition are the prerequisites for growth in production and prosperity. However, all these innovations have a dehumanizing effect on the worker, who "generally becomes as stupid and ignorant as it is possible for a human creature to be" (Smith 1952 [1776], 340). An earlier but similar description of the "commercial society," though with more social detail, is to be found in *An Essay on the History of Civil Society* (1767) by Adam Ferguson, another Scottish philosopher. In comparing "the inferior branches of manufacture" with "the higher branches of policy and war" he notes how their members "are made, like the parts of an engine, to concur to a purpose, without any concert of their own" (Ferguson 2007 [1767], 138).

In the following I link Grundtvig's meeting with the "commercial society" in England and his view of British liberalism to Smith and Ferguson's observations – not because they are of special significance for Grundtvig but because the comparison sheds light on the similarities and differences between British liberalism and Grundtvig's particular Nordic conception of freedom. What links them is not direct inspiration but a common affiliation with the Enlightenment, for all three share its optimistic belief in the future through education and learning. This was particularly strong in the second half of the eighteenth century in French, English, and Scottish philosophy with names such as Montesquieu, Voltaire, Diderot, Condorcet, Hume, Burke, Ferguson, Smith, and many others as well as Lessing, Kant, and Herder in Germany. All agreed that world history moves in a steady progress from the earliest days of rough, wild tribes through the more civilized societies of Hellas and Rome to its present-day apex in modern Europe – more specifically in the enlightened Protestant countries of Northern Europe. Discoveries and inventions, science, technology, and trade had brought humankind to this point, not least through the many accounts in the seventeenth century of global discoverers finding coloured peoples who still appeared to be living in the childhood of human development.

In Denmark the most important Enlightenment philosopher was Grundtvig. He was first inspired by German philosophers such as Herder, Fichte, Schiller, and Schelling, believing that, in the course of world history, certain peoples had borne civilization along: the Hebrews, the Greeks, the Romans, and, in his own time, the Nordic nations, to whom he also assigned the Anglos and, thus, the English. Although sharing a kinship with both Hegel and Marx, Grundtvig's philosophy of history was original in its emphasis on the influence of the Nordic peoples and the Christian church. The same inspiration from German idealism underpinned his view of "the people" and "the people's spirit," until his meeting with England forced him to incorporate the Anglo-Saxon tradition. Like the French tradition, it was rooted in Calvinist Protestantism, but on one point only – its sense of civil freedom – it differed from both the French and the German traditions. England not only influenced Grundtvig's political ideas but also created a lasting tension with the German-Lutheran foundation of his thinking.

London in 1830 stood at the forefront of world history. For Grundtvig this meant that Denmark and the whole of the North stood alongside – pointing to an even more perfect future. The ethnic kinship between England and the Nordic countries enabled him to find living proof of the Anglo-Nordic spirit of antiquity in the huge factories and in the massive power of the new steam engines. Here were the modern parallels to Beowulf's sword and Thor's hammer. And from the external effects, Grundtvig deduced the inner cause: the spirit of the Nordic peoples, still alive and still forceful. Equally convincing evidence of this dynamic kinship with Britain was their shared view of political freedom and free competition between the powers. Central to Grundtvig's thought was the idea that, from the outset, the Nordic spirit had been characterized by a sense of both spiritual and civil freedom, to which, not least, the saga histories of Iceland testified. His experience of the more alarming side of industrialization was thus counterbalanced by his confidence that the Anglo-Nordic people's spirit that appeared to have invented these machines would also be able to "place them in a serviceable and serving relation to human activity and human fortune" (Grundtvig 1877, 447). His optimism and faith in the benefits of free, living activity was at its highest in 1838.

Since the 1820s Grundtvig had followed the social debates in Britain from the sidelines. Although as a Lutheran theologian he was sceptical of the rationalism of the Calvinist tradition that marked French and British philosophy, the Britain that shared ethnic roots with the Nordic peoples occupied a special position in his heart, which only increased after his visits in 1829–31. This was apparent not least in his interest in British social conditions. Grundtvig actually owned a copy of *The Wealth of Nations* and followed the debate on politics and economics that it generated,[1] not least by subscribing to two liberal journals of the 1820s (Baagø 1955, 22ff), the *Westminster Review* and the *Edinburgh Review*, which carried articles by Jeremy Bentham, James Mill, John Stuart Mill, and others calling for more freedom. The spiritual environment of these journals and the circles with which Grundtvig came into personal contact were mainly liberal; they included church dissidents, utilitarian philosophy, and "philosophical-radical" ideas. He in no way sympathized with such political thinkers but was interested in the ongoing British debate on greater spiritual freedom in church life, and in the schools and universities,[2] that these circles were conducting. It was a debate that he himself inspired when he returned to Denmark, and it was based on his experience of the crucial importance of spiritual freedom: "What is normally called freedom of speech and freedom of the press is really only freedom of religion by other words, since there is no freedom of speech about spiritual and eternal matters without freedom of religion" (Grundtvig 1908 [1843], 686).

And this debate concerned not just spiritual freedom but also personal and civil freedom. The word "freedom" carried its own ambiguities and presented a Gordian knot regarding the human consequences of endless "development." For, since the excesses of the French Revolution, the sound of "freedom" had had a disquieting effect throughout Europe. Grundtvig, for his part, linked it most often to spiritual freedom, to "freedom for Loki as well as for Thor" (Grundtvig 1907 [1832], 384; Broadbridge, Warren, and Jonas 2011, 49), where Thor represents the true Nordic spirit and Loki the ambiguous, often false, spirit. Having himself once suffered censorship, Grundtvig demanded *full* freedom of speech, print, and religion; only bestiality and violence were to be curtailed. Grundtvig believed that freedom was not just a matter of tolerance but something that should be actively extended to the "enemy" with whom one must openly do battle. Grundtvig refused to *tolerate* Loki, but he had to allow him the same freedom as he allowed himself. Behind this lies Grundtvig's philosophy of life as a battle and a competition,[3] a view he found illustrated in the images of Nordic mythology.

Adam Smith (1952 [1776], 300) gave the classic formulation of the first principle of liberalism: "Every man, as long as he does not violate the laws of justice, is left perfectly free to pursue his own interest his own way, and to bring both his industry and capital into competition with those of any other man, or order of men." Not only was this Grundtvig's own view, but he would also have added that Smith is expressing here the true Anglo-Nordic, competitive "spirit of the people," the same spirit that he recognized and admired in the force behind the steam engine. Freedom for the people's spirit and freedom for the individual's spirit means, for Grundtvig, freedom to do battle and to create competition – also in words. Words, unfortunately could take the form of empty or hopeless noise, as in the British Parliament's hefty debates that nevertheless could not "dissolve the dominance of money, which has made itself the soul of Parliament, the legislature, and the entire public life" (Grundtvig 1877, 436). As Grundtvig (1842, 255) later notes, "Freedom is a word as slippery as an eel." This was true not least for the political and economic liberalism that he encountered and that also left its mark on developments in his own country. When Denmark acquired its first democratic Constitution in 1849, Grundtvig gained a seat in the Lower House and was a sedulous participant in the political debate, primarily as a champion of greater freedom in all spiritual affairs but also as an active supporter of the liberalization of production and trade in the tradition of Adam Smith. It was his belief in the benefits of freedom in civil as well as in political society that led him to advocate such liberalizations. Arguing for free competition and rejecting all state regulation and welfare measures, he may be considered a staunch economic liberal (Møller 1950, 59–73; Baagø 1955; Wåhlin 1990), and he followed Adam Smith's line on the balance between individual self-interest and the common good – the Gordian knot of development. Neither of them wrote about economics as an independent discipline, preferring to regard the subject in a broader historical and philosophical perspective.

In Smith's (1952 [1776], 300) major work there are numerous examples from world history that illustrate how every attempt to regulate economic development artificially "retards, instead of accelerating, the progress of the society towards real wealth and greatness," whereas the removal of such regulations ensures that "the obvious and simple system of natural liberty establishes itself of its own accord."

In Grundtvig's works on world history he often discusses the beneficial effects of the sense of freedom on "civil society" and traces its development back to the Greeks, to medieval Iceland, to the Reformation, and, most recently, to modern France, Britain, and the Nordic countries. Like Smith he applauds this progress and sees it as part of the divine plan. In Smith's deistic view of Christianity, the word "natural" means in accord with the divinely created nature of humankind. God has created us with an instinct for sympathy so that, through religion and enlightenment, we can be motivated to work for the common good. Smith (1952 [1776], 331–56) strongly emphasizes the continued need for, and the state's commitment to, support for enlightenment and learning, and he solves the fundamental problem of finding the balance between private and public utility precisely by preaching enlightenment and moral education and by "erecting and maintaining certain public works and certain public institutions which can never be for the interest of any individual, or small number of individuals" (300).

This view also finds resonance with Grundtvig, as does Smith's (1952 [1776], 194) application of his economic philosophy to the optimistic pursuit of greater prosperity and happiness on earth – guided by the famous "invisible hand," which belongs to a God-created order. Grundtvig prefers a "historical" rather than a "natural" development and the guidance of Providence rather than an invisible hand, but the fundamental philosophy is the same, and Grundtvig comes to the same solution as does Smith: enlightenment and moral education.

The similarities between Smith's and Grundtvig's optimistic liberalism must not be allowed to overshadow the marked differences, however. Like Ferguson, Smith is a rationalist thinker and moral philosopher who puts his trust in reason as his guide and educator, and, in the face of egoistic self-interest, he cultivates the inborn instinct for altruism that is essential to society. For both men religion means enlightened deism. The natural order is the same as the divine order, so they have no need of any "superstition," but Ferguson has a sharper eye for the negative consequences of development. He regards contemporary Europe – and especially Britain – as the most developed society in history, under the guidance of Providence, and he draws on world history to support his moral philosophy.

Ferguson offers many examples of how attained progress can be lost again due to recession, weariness, and lack of alertness to new threats. He is particularly known for his description of the alienating effect of the division of labour and specialization, which are very much the mainspring of development and increased prosperity. The division of labour threatens "to break the bands of society, to substitute mere forms and rules of art in place of ingenuity, and to withdraw individuals from the common scene of occupation, on which the sentiments of the heart, and the mind, are most happily employed" (Ferguson 2007 [1767], 164). Ferguson illustrates this with the demise of classical Athens, where "men ceased to be citizens, even to be poets and good orators, in proportion as they came to be distinguished by the profession of these, and other separate crafts" (165). The good citizen is the one who, in the words of Pericles, gives "equal attention to private and public affairs; and in men who have turned to separate professions, a competent knowledge of what relates to the community" (164).

Grundtvig probably did not read Ferguson, but he would have shared the criticism. In his own portrayal of classical Athens, he also takes sharp issue with the democracy of the Greek popular assemblies. Nor did he himself vote for the Danish Constitution of 1849. Indeed, he was never a democrat in the modern sense of supporting the general franchise and majority decision making;[4] he preferred enlightened monarchy with advisory popular representation.[5] His enthusiasm for the expansion of freedom in Britain did not stretch to its parliamentary practices, which seemed incapable of stemming the "dominance of money" and other tendencies "to break the bands of society."

As pre-Herder Enlightenment philosophers, both Smith and Ferguson are without a deeper sense of history. Ferguson's *Essay on the History of Civil Society* is not so much a historical exposition as an accumulation of historical examples of the virtues and vices involved in the survival of society. There is no sense of chronology, and when Ferguson speaks of "national spirit," it is not only without any national characteristics but is also measured in relation to the same universal virtues and vices, be they in ancient Sparta and Athens or contemporary Paris and London. In similar fashion Adam Smith's examples from world history serve only as an illustration of general economic legalities, which are assumed to be globally valid and raised above local, national, and historical distinctions.

It is quite different with Grundtvig. For him, "national spirit" is historically rooted and conditional. Where the loftiest virtue in Ferguson (2007 [1767], 167) is "zeal for the good of mankind," Grundtvig prefers "a love of the fatherland," and nowhere does he share the enlightened faith of the French, the English, and the Scots in "reason" as the supreme human faculty that separates humankind from the animals. With Grundtvig – as with Herder and Fichte – it is the "spirit," with language and history, that separates human beings from "the dumb creatures." And with this follows the struggle for life and truth, including the historically transmitted faith of the church. In Smith and Ferguson's historical examples, Christianity and the church play no part since "the true religion" is the deism of rationalism with "the wise Providence" as its guarantor, whereas in England Grundtvig's scepticism was only strengthened by his meeting with the Anglican Church, which he considered to be spiritually dead.

What Smith called "natural liberty" was for Grundtvig a hard-won freedom in Protestant Northern Europe, achieved through spiritual struggle in the light of the Renaissance and the Reformation. Civil freedom was admittedly furthest advanced in Britain, but then so were its socially undermining dangers – despite the fine traditions of the British schools and universities for learning and moral education. What Grundtvig missed in Calvinist-marked Britain was a living Christian spirit that could bind freedom to the people – without external tyranny and compulsion. For Grundtvig the differences between the traditions of Luther and Calvin had *national* consequences. Where the Calvinist tradition held sway – in France, Holland, England, and Scotland – he found an understanding of freedom that was guided by reason and linked to individualism and self-interest. In the legacy of Luther, however, lay the belief that freedom cannot be steered solely by reason; only deeper bonds of the spirit and the heart can set limits to freedom.

Although it was therefore no surprise for Grundtvig that both the French Revolution and economic liberalism had come on Calvinist ground,[6] it *was* a surprise for him to find, in England of all places, the living, powerful spirit of the Nordic peoples! He regarded freedom in civil affairs as one of the major advances of his time, but it was an advance that only the Nordic – or Anglo-Nordic – people would be able to manage properly by allowing it to be counterbalanced by a genuine, heart-felt spiritual enlightenment. For in the history of the world it now fell to the Nordic people to loosen the Gordian knot – and to do so "cautiously." Enlightenment and learning were not enough in themselves for learning was being increasingly influenced by rationalism's fallacy that reason, self-interest, and naturalist materialism were pre-eminent – all of them the result of what Grundtvig called "false enlightenment." So it was the advances not only in civil freedom but also in academic learning that were damaging the bonds of the heart and spirit among people and threatening "to break the bands of society." For Ferguson, Smith, and Grundtvig, the Gordian knot of economic liberalism had been tied as a historical necessity and could be loosened by enlightenment and moral education. They differ in that Ferguson and Smith believed in the efficacy of science and knowledge, whereas Grundtvig believed both of these to be marked by a materialist, spiritless rationalism, turning everything into figures and then describing these with a lifeless Latin-based literalism.

Grundtvig's original contribution to the debate – many would call it an unrealistic one – was to loosen the Gordian knot through applying the Nordic spirit to: first, a new form of moral education; second, a popular education for all; and third, an alternative approach to learning. He proposed the introduction of People's High Schools as a kind of alternative to the universities, aiming to educate a wide range of young adults to a sense of the common good and the limits of freedom – also with a view to their recruitment in the governance of the new democratic society. Grundtvig's enlightenment would offset the individualization that – with each man's "independence of his people, his kin, and the God to whom he belongs, as well as chancing his arm to the utmost limit" (Grundtvig 1908 [1843], 514) – could only undermine any sense of community.

The new enlightenment was to be "historical and poetic" in order to illuminate "the deep coinherence between the life of the individual, the nation, and the whole human race" (Grundtvig 1983 [1834], 31; Broadbridge, Warren, and Jonas 2011, 77). It would thereby allow the individual to see himself as duty-bound not only to his fellow-citizens but also, and not least, to both his forefathers and his unborn successors – a truly Nordic way of thinking, according to Grundtvig. He further proposed an alternative joint-Nordic university in Gothenburg (Grundtvig 1968 [1839], 126–64) to replace the old "Latin" universities. The best brains in Denmark, Norway, and Sweden would meet and, in spiritual competition, explore the mysteries of nature and history. As a genuine Enlightenment philosopher Grundtvig was convinced that the highest and truest learning would show humanity the path to a more complete future. As a more atypical Enlightenment philosopher, he was also sure that genuine learning would turn out to confirm the teachings and absolute importance of Christianity and the church.

Grundtvig's plan to educate the Danish people received its first concrete realization with the establishment of Rødding People's High School in 1844 – to be followed by many more. However, it was never the alternative that Grundtvig had envisaged; rather, it became a support for a party interest – that of the peasant farmers. The People's High Schools helped to empower the peasant class, which gradually gained in political influence. Grundtvig was thereby given credit for the economic liberalism that served the peasant farmers' cause. His concept of "the people," inspired by Herder, embraced all those with a common language and history, independent of age, gender, or class,[7] but his ideas acquired particular significance for this one class. The farmers had been largely without education or political influence, but Grundtvig drew attention to them as being *true* Danes since, unlike the educated elite, they had not been weakened by any German or other foreign influence.

In particular, Grundtvig's ideas struck a spark with the broad middle class of freeholder farmers, whereas the considerable and growing number of Danish people living as a poor underclass, either landless in the country or among the poor urban proletariat, lay outside his idealistic horizon. His lack of a sense for political reality was also seen when, in 1848, he imagined that Denmark – on the brink of industrialization and urbanization – would be able to continue as an agrarian society dominated by the freehold farmers and organized on the sole basis of economic liberalism without any help for the weakest from the state: "In Denmark, where the number of freeholders is growing fast and where large factories are few, thank God, it will not be difficult to rescue the self-owners, abolish all rights to maintenance grants except between parents and children, and introduce such a freedom of trade that it can match the song where 'few are too rich, and still fewer too poor'" (Grundtvig 1848, 239).[8] So when the liberals invoked Grundtvig, it was not without cause, though it did require that his historical and philosophical contexts and his idealist demands were set aside. In the course of time it turned out that all the political parties – from the liberals to the socialists – could invoke Grundtvig by focusing on specific areas of his comprehensive authorship.

Unlike the People's High Schools, Grundtvig's audacious plan for an alternative Nordic university in Gothenburg was never realized but, instead, was passed over in silence as a utopian project. And with it went any understanding of Grundtvig's attempt to answer the core problem of liberalism – the Gordian knot of development. Ferguson, for his part, described it in the division of labour and in specialization, with its dehumanizing consequences, as both the cause and result of technological and economic development. To prevent the impending decay of true civic virtues, Ferguson could not put his trust in anything other than continued enlightenment and moral education, just as with Adam Smith and all Enlightenment thinking. This was where Grundtvig found the Calvinist tradition superficial: in putting its faith in reason and the power of rational thought to penetrate the human heart and spirit – "the sentiments of the heart, and the mind," in Ferguson's words.

The tension between the traditions of Calvin and Luther – in Grundtvig's philosophy between *freedom* and *spirit* (Vind 1999, 380ff) – did not decrease as the century progressed. His idealistic concept of freedom was confronted by both the growing individualism and the realities of economic liberalism, which actually meant that the Gordian knot was tightened. His relation to British liberalism remained at heart ambiguous. He was moved by the power of the machines and the real competition of free forces but not by the political debate or any socio-economic theories, and he continued to be repelled by the rationalist emphasis on individual freedom at the cost of the ties of heart and spirit. It is these that make for the cohesion of the state, and it is these that he found in their most developed form on Nordic soil.

NOTES

1 We do not know whether Grundtvig actually read Smith's book, to which he never referred, but, given current debates, he undoubtedly knew the ideology of liberalism.

2 The most detailed account of this is in Grell (1992).

3 According to Korsgaard (2012, 41): "Grundtvig's demand for freedom did not stem from the liberal conception of freedom, but built on the perception that struggle is the manifestation of spirit."

4 "Even if all our people put their ignorance together, no wisdom would come of it" (Grundtvig 1877, 72).

5 He nevertheless became reconciled to Danish democracy and took part eagerly in the Lower House debates while still retaining his principled opposition to majority-vote decisions, which he called "number majesty" (Vind 1999, 441ff).

6 Today we could add capitalism (Weber 2001 [1905]).

7 Such an ethnic concept of the people can be used to legitimize both nationalism and racism. This is also true to some degree of Grundtvig's philosophy (Vind 1999, 461ff).

8 Grundtvig quotes from his own poem, "Far Higher Are Mountains."

REFERENCES

Baagø, K. 1955. "Grundtvig og den engelske liberalisme" [Grundtvig and English liberalism]. *Grundtvig Studier* 8 (1): 7–37.

Broadbridge, E., trans. and ed., C. Warren, and U. Jonas, co-eds. 2011. *The School for Life: N.F.S. Grundtvig on Education for the People*. Aarhus: Aarhus University Press.

Ferguson, A. 2007 [1767]. *An Essay on the History of Civil Society*, 8th ed. Fairford, UK: Echo Library.

Grell, H. 1992. *England og Grundtvig* [England and Grundtvig]. Aarhus: Aarhus University Press.

Grundtvig, N.F.S. 1842. *Krønike-Riim* [The rhymed chronicle]. Copenhagen: Wahl.

– 1848. *Danskeren, et Ugeblad* [The Dane I]. Copenhagen: F.H. Eibe.

– 1877. *Mands Minde: 1788–1838: Foredrag over det sidste halve Aarhundredes Historie, holdte 1838* [Within living memory: 1788–1838: Lectures on the history of the last half century given in 1838 by Nik. Sev. Fred. Grundtvig]. Copenhagen: Karl Schønberg.

– 1907 [1832]. "Nordens Mythologi" [Norse mythology]. In *Udvalgte Skrifter, bd. 5* [Selected writings, vol. 5], ed. H. Begtrup, 378–767. Copenhagen: Nordisk.

– 1908 [1843]. "Haandbog i Verdens-Historien III" [Handbook of world history III]. In *Udvalgte Skrifter, bd. 7* [Selected writings, vol. 7], ed. H. Begtrup, 378–694. Copenhagen: Nordisk.

– 1909 [1871]. "Kirke-Speil, eller, Udsigt over den Christne Menigheds Levnetsløb" [Church-Mirror, or, overview of the Christian congregation's history]. In *Udvalgte Skrifter, bd. 10* [Selected writings, vol. 10], ed. H. Begtrup, 80–362. Copenhagen: Nordisk.

– 1968 [1839]. "Om Nordens videnskabelige Forening" [On the union of learning in the north]. In *Grundtvigs Skole Verden i tekster og udkast* [*The school for life: N.F.S. Grundtvig on education for the people*], trans. and ed. E. Broadbridge, co-ed. C. Warren and U. Jonas, 224–51. Aarhus: Aarhus University Press.

– 1983 [1834]. *Statsmæssig Oplysning: Et udkast om samfund og skole* [Education for the state: A draft on society and school]. Edited by Knud Eyvin Bugge and Vilhelm Nielsen. Copenhagen: Nyt Nordisk Forlag.

Korsgaard, O. 2012. *N.F.S. Grundtvig*. Copenhagen: Djøf.

Møller, E. 1950. *Grundtvig som Samtidshistoriker* [Grundtvig as contemporary historian]. Copenhagen: Gyldendal.

Smith, A. 1952 [1776]. *The Wealth of Nations*. Chicago, IL: Encyclopædia Britannica.

Vind, O. 1999. *Grundtvigs Historiefilosofi* [Grundtvig's philosophy of history]. Copenhagen: Gyldendal.

Wåhlin, V. 1990. "Grundtvigs økonomiske tænkning" [Grundtvig's economic thinking]. *Grundtvig Studier* 41 (1): 246–303.

Weber, M. 2001 [1905]. *The Protestant Ethic and the Spirit of Capitalism*. London: Routledge Classics.

13

Grundtvig and the Slavic Awakening in East Central Europe: (Con)textual Parallels, Mutual Perceptions

PETER BUGGE

Intuitively, writing on Grundtvig and the Western Slavs may seem a non-starter or an exercise in far-fetched analogies. As we shall see, Grundtvig showed only marginal interest in, and even less sympathy with, Czechs and Poles, or Slavs in general, while, conversely, his historical and theological writings remained unknown to the national "awakeners" of East Central Europe in the first half of the nineteenth century. However, as I show in the first part of this chapter, Grundtvig's thoughts on history, nationality, and popular enlightenment (or education) have a lot in common with the views and aspirations of contemporary Polish, Czech, and Slovak scholars/awakeners. Such commonalities, I argue, were not mere circumstance; rather, they reflect how these intellectuals shared not just key intellectual points of reference but also a national-political setting that brought them to understand the tasks and challenges facing the nations with which they identified in very similar ways. Against this background, I proceed by taking a closer look at Grundtvig's views of the Slavs and the peoples of East Central Europe in particular, before reversing the perspective by looking at the reception of Grundtvig among the Czechs of Bohemia and Moravia from the mid-nineteenth century until the First World War. Neither Grundtvig's aversions nor his disinterest were reciprocated as Czech intellectuals showed genuine interest in his pedagogical thinking and in the Folk High School in particular.

Despite the geographical proximity of Denmark to Poland and Bohemia, and their shared neighbouring of Germany, studies of nationalism have generally been prone to study the national movements of East

Central Europe separately from those of Western or Northern Europe. This disinclination to compare is, I believe, to some extent a product of the analytically untenable, mostly highly normative, yet very tenacious, distinction in nationalism theory between a benign Western "civic" and a malign Eastern "cultural" nationalism – a dichotomy placing Danish nationalism firmly in the former camp and Czech, Slovak, and Polish nationalism in the latter. A noble exception to this trend can be found in Miroslav Hroch's (1985, 2007) pioneering comparative studies of the social composition of patriotic groups among the "small nations" (or, as Hroch has now begun to refer to them, "non-dominant ethnic groups") of Europe. However, Hroch's distinction between "great nations" (i.e., those whose national mobilization had the support of a state in which the national activists formed the dominant ethnic group, such as the Danes) and the "small" nations of Czechs, Slovaks, and so on, who lived in states with a "foreign" dominant ethnic group, seems too rigid, and it also seems to suffer from the same weakness as the civic-cultural model.[1] Both overlook how all national movements in early nineteenth-century Europe made extensive use of cultural, ethnic, and historical markers to constitute a national self and its Other, while, conversely, none of these movements was stateless. In the Hapsburg Empire, no less than elsewhere, national awakeners interacted closely with regional and central elites without necessarily perceiving each other as "foreign."

As to the Danish case, the Oldenbourg Empire of the first half of the nineteenth century was, as Uffe Østergård argues elsewhere in this volume, almost as politically and ethnically heterogeneous as was the Hapsburg Empire. Nor did Grundtvig spend the first many decades of his life in an assertive, consolidated nation-state. The national bankruptcy of 1813 and the loss of Norway in 1814 testified to the profound vulnerability of the kingdom, and whether in Copenhagen or Schleswig, Grundtvig was confronted with a bilingual population, with German seemingly in the ascendancy in the larger context of things. Danishness and the Danish language could look just as threatened and in need of protection as Polishness or Czechness.

The very establishing of language and people as the inseparable nexus of both the Nordic and the Slavic projects of national "revival" owed much to the writings of Johann Gottfried Herder, a Protestant German who lived in Königsberg and Riga. Ole Vind accounts in detail for the impact of his philosophy of history on Grundtvig's thinking, while Herder's importance for the Slavic revivals is well documented. Inevitably, Slavic scholars/awakeners attribute great significance to Herder's short chapter in his *Ideas for the Philosophy of History of Humanity* (1784–91) on the pre-Christian Slavic world, in which he portrays the ancient Slavs as a united, peace-loving, virtuous community. However, if Grundtvig ever read this chapter, it left no trace on his perception of the Slavs (Drews 1990; Vind 1999, 65–81). Eventually, Herder's understanding of the habits of the old Slavs was strongly inspired by the historiographical writings of Gelasius Dobner (1719–90) and other Bohemian scholars of the eighteenth century, which testifies to the significance of transnational circulation in the formation of national ideas (Drews 1990, 45–57). Monika Baár's (2010, 112) conclusion with regard to Herder's legacy in the works of five East-Central European historians – "it is impossible to distinguish between stimulus, exhortation, direct and indirect influence, the intensification of an already existing autochthonous or borrowed idea and a combination of multifarious influences, when assessing Herder's impact" – thus seems both highly convincing and relevant beyond her specific cases.

One of the things Grundtvig must have appreciated in Herder's writings is his favourable view of the historical significance of the non-Roman north. Grundtvig, as has often been noted, wrote several attempts at world history but no history of Denmark or the Danes. Nevertheless, his aim with these attempts was not merely to demonstrate how Danish and Nordic history formed part of Providence's great plans for the evolution of humankind but also to take the argument further by suggesting that the Danish and Nordic cause was essentially the cause of all humanity: the High North, Grundtvig argued in 1855, was the seat of a unique world-historical enlightenment that was of value to everyone. Moreover, Denmark had also developed a pioneering method for bringing this enlightenment to the common people (this method was, of course, indebted to Grundtvig himself, a fact he modestly abstained from pointing out).

Vind (1999, 462–3) calls this idea of Danish historical exceptionalism "audacious" and implies that it was also unique. This latter observation, however, is rather problematic since Polish, Czech, and other national historians/mythologists were equally capable of identifying unique missions for their nations within the greater scheme of Providence. To give just one example, Hans Kohn sums up the significance of the historical writings of František Palacký (1798–1876) as follows: "Through [Palacký] Czech history became of importance for the history of Europe, the Czech question a universal question ... The Czechs found their place in modern Europe on the side of the great and progressive democratic currents and peoples" (cited in Zacek 1970, 92; see also Kořalka 2007).

A common trope in nineteenth-century historiography from East Central Europe is that the nation under discussion has served as the *antemurale Christianiatis*, that is, that it has defended European and Christian civilization against barbarian (i.e., Ottoman, Mongolian, Russian, etc.) onslaught, a sacrifice largely unrecognized by ungrateful Western Europe. Palacký and the Polish historian Joachim Lelewel (1786–1861) insisted that the Slavs (e.g., Poles and Czechs) were not mere latecomers to history; in certain ways they were paragons or avant-garde, be it through the legacy of the republican virtues of Polish gentry democracy or through the ideals of the Hussite Revolution, which resurfaced in the French Revolution and the nineteenth century. For Palacký, the Czechs had a special mission as transmitters of Romance, Germanic, and Slav influences in the heart of Europe, while Polish Messianism was present as a strong undercurrent in the Manifesto of the Polish Diet of 1831, largely drafted by Lelewel: "Yet, if Providence has appointed this land for eternal subjugation ... the true Pole will perish with joy in his heart that, if Heaven has not permitted him to save his own freedom and his Fatherland, he has at least in mortal combat protected the liberties of the peoples in Europe" (Baár 2010, 284; see also Jedlicki 1999, 3–50).

Herder's Protestantism and favour with the peoples of the North resonated well with several Slavic national awakeners. Palacký was a Protestant, and two Lutherans of Slovak origin, the clergyman and poet Jan Kollár (1793–1852) and the librarian and scholar Pavel Josef Šafařík (1795–1861), were prominent participants in the Czech national movement. Both ardently strove to establish the Slavs as good and worthy members of the European family of nations, and when Kollár defined "piety, diligence, innocent merriness, love of their language and tolerance towards other nations" as core characteristics of the Slavs, Protestant motifs are evident in several of these points. He and Šafařík also insisted that the Slavs were northern Europeans, a quality Kollár linked explicitly with piety (Pynsent 1994, 75–6). The Northern theme was even more pronounced in Lelewel's works and thinking about the place of Polish history in the larger European framework. Lelewel, who in 1807 anonymously published a book in Polish, *Edda: Or the Book of Religion of the Ancient Inhabitants of Scandinavia*, designated the Nordic people as the leading representatives of freedom and linked the Poles closely to the Scandinavians, arguing that the early Poles had lived in an egalitarian community of self-government – a theme also found with reference to Slavs and Czechs in the works of Palacký (Baár 2010, 174–7).[2]

If Grundtvig and his Slavic counterparts both found philosophical and practical inspiration in German sources, they also shared a programmatic striving to create models of their reawakened nations that set these as much apart from everything German as possible. In that respect, they all expressed what the Czech semiotician Vladimír Macura (1995, 39) calls a "negative and analogue tie" to the German cultural sphere. In the Czech case, the influential awakener Josef Jungmann (1773–1847) found much inspiration in the writings of Johann Gottlieb Fichte (1762–1814) and, especially, Friedrich L. Jahn (1778–1852), parts of whose *Deutsches Volkstum* (1810) he translated into Czech. Like Jahn, Jungmann was a strong advocate of national purity, and in an 1814 essay he condemned mulattoes and other "miserable bastards – refuse in the midst of the peoples, without character, without virtue, without a common spirit, without nationality" (Jungmann in Vodička 1948, 57).[3] As Grundtvig, too, praised the purity of the Danes and their old language, and condemned racial mixing and bastard nations, I find it natural to conclude that his and Jungmann's ideas had not only their philosophical roots in common but also the urgency with which this craving for national purity was articulated. It stemmed in both cases from the perceived need – be it in Schleswig or in Bohemia – to segregate as strongly as possible Danish/Czech from German (Vind 1999, 466–9).[4]

A further common feature among all these awakeners was the pronounced syncretism of their efforts. To call Palacký or Šafařík scholars, and Grundtvig a poet and clergyman, does little justice to the multifaceted nature of their endeavours, which, at the core, represented a deliberate strategy to mobilize all genres in a concerted effort to awaken and express national life. The young Palacký wrote poems and a work on Czech prosody, while Grundtvig wrote world histories, and while the differentiation of genres and the professionalization of scholarly disciplines increased with the advance of the century, early nineteenth-century "awakening gestures" are best understood as attempts at a total embrace of the national spirit – as the construction of a national foundation myth. Grundtvig's plans for a new kind of Nordic university in Gothenburg thus have a lot in common with Karel Slavoj Amerling's (1807–84) contemporaneous and equally unsuccessful project of an all-encompassing Slavic university, Budeč, in Prague (Macura 1995, 94–101; Vind 1999, 16–200).[5]

There is, however, a major difference between Grundtvig and the East Central European scholars-awakeners in their communicative strategies as the latter, far more systematically than Grundtvig, address different sets of audiences. Of course, they all wrote in the national vernacular, thereby contributing to its consolidation and refinement while also, in a sense, talking a national general public into being. But Lelewel, Palacký, Šafařík, and so on also wrote in German or French to address a European public in perceived need of information about the mythology, antiquity, and history of the Slavs and/or the individual Slavic nations. They corresponded eagerly with each other and with German, French, British and other colleagues; they travelled and studied and became members of learned societies. In short, they were ardent and accepted members of a transnational republic of letters, or, perhaps more accurately, an informal "International" of propagators of national ideas.[6]

Grundtvig stands out here. With the partial exception of his travels to England between 1829 and 1831, and his studies of Old English literature, he showed little interest in joining any transnational (or extra-Nordic) networks of kindred spirits. After very favourably reviewing Grundtvig's *Nordic Mythology* (1808), Friedrich Schlegel (1772–1829) vainly contacted Grundtvig in 1812 to ask for contributions to his journal *Deutsches Museum* (Vind 1999, 94–5, 201–2). Grundtvig readily studied foreign scholars, but he seems to have wished to address only a Danish or Nordic public. An answer to why this was the case can only be tentative. The Slavic peoples (along with Lithuanians, Hungarians, Romanians, etc.) were largely unknown to the "learned European public" and carried with them the stigma of primitivism, backwardness, and peripherality. Despite reservations about ignorant Western Europe, all East Central European awakeners thus strove to have their nations recognized as worthy members of the European family of civilized peoples. In the Polish case, foreign support was deemed crucial to any hope of regaining national sovereignty after the three partitions of the country and the failed uprising of 1830 (Jedlicki 1999; Walicki 1994).

The Kingdom of Denmark was better off in this respect, although Grundtvig, as argued above, had good reason to feel that his country was in peril. But no matter how wounded and politically and economically marginal it was, Denmark – and the Nordic peoples in general – enjoyed the advantage of belonging to a larger Germanic realm whose myths and prehistory had become the object of increasing adoration since the late eighteenth century. However much Grundtvig sought dissociation from Germany, being Germanic – or Gothic, in his attempt at relabelling – had its advantages, even in the eyes of others. Nordic exclusivity could thus be proclaimed and practised at a much lesser cost than could, for example, Pan-Slavism. So, in his philosophy of history, Grundtvig had no need for Romance or Slavic partners.

Nor did he have any room for them. Throughout his life, Grundtvig had only poor opinions of Slavs. Russia, he wrote in 1812, "has since times immemorial been inhabited by raw, Slavic races" whose history could only begin through the initiatives of the Nordic chieftain Rurik and his entourage. "The Poles," he continues, "are also a Slavic, unpoetic people," and although they had Christianity given to them at an early stage from Germans and Northerners, and later experienced a significant exposure to Lutheranism, it could not bring about any "spiritual fermentation" in the people (Grundtvig 1905, 310–12). The verdict remained unchanged in the second volume of *Handbook in World History*, written in 1836. Here, Grundtvig compares the Danish and German missionary expeditions in the Baltic areas and Eastern Europe to the Crusades. However, the Slavs were totally devoid of the spirit and higher life force that create strong societies, therefore they were able to pick up only the vices when learning from more civilized (*dannede*) people. As Grundtvig (1862, 617–18) sums it up: "Under these circumstances Christendom is shown only ingratitude for its mild attempts to spread a higher view; for the barbarians are blind to this" (see also Vind 1999, 358–9). Evidently, in his view, the power of the Gospel was not sufficient to overcome the negative force of Slavic racial inferiority.

A similar hostility permeates a manuscript written in 1855 during the Crimean War. The Slavic circle of peoples, we hear, inhabits "the East ... from the sea of Azov all up to the Baltic sea," an area that has remained marked by immobility and stagnation except for the Medieval German expansion and subjugation of the Slavic tribes of Prussia, Brandenburg, Pomerania, and Mecklenburg, and, later – since Peter the Great – by Russia's attempt to "oppress human life" in both Europe and Asia. Grundtvig was now deeply worried about the growing power of Russia, which he (with a trope common also in German Russophobe writings) explains as due to the continued impact of the blood of the Goths who had once settled there. Despite the "unnaturalness" of such an alliance of Gothic and Romance, Grundtvig wished England and France all the best in their efforts to "smash the head of the Slavic circle of peoples [*Folke-Kreds*]."[7]

Unlike the Russians, the Czechs (or, as Grundtvig and his contemporaries called them, the Bohemians) were neither Orthodox nor a political threat to Denmark, and in Jan Hus (c. 1371–1415), one of the main precursors of Luther in the struggle for ecclesiastical freedom and sermons in the vernacular, they had a historical figure with the potential to be recognized by Grundtvig. In his Preface to the second volume of his *Handbook of World History*, Grundtvig confesses to his doubts about how and where to treat Hus. He acknowledges his importance but places him outside of chronological context as a portent of the religious struggles of the "new era" (*Nyaarstiden*). He gives this as his reason for abstaining from discussing Hus and the Bohemian attempt at church reformation in his current volume (Grundtvig 1862, iv, vi).

This happened instead in the third volume of the *World History,* entitled *Handbook of the History of the New Era*, which Grundtvig began publishing in 1843. Now, Hus was no longer a harbinger: he and his close ally, Jerome of Prague (ca. 1379–1416), were "the last and probably the greatest martyrs for fatherland and mother tongue of the Middle Ages," without any connection to what was to come with Luther. Grundtvig's Hus was a largely positive figure, a "solid, pious and eloquent man" who became the natural leader of the Bohemian popular rising against the Germans (*Tydskheden*) and the ruling theology, and against the Pope and the Roman ecclesiastical system. It was therefore villainy (*Nidingsværk*) to burn two "innocent people and great men" at the stake in Constance; however, with an almost dialectical subtlety, Grundtvig combines his condemnation of the behaviour of the council with the assurance that, in a larger historical perspective, the destruction of this "Slavic national leader [*Folke-Leder*]" and his followers was an expression of the higher will of Providence. The triumph of the aspirations of the Czechs, along with the Poles and Hungarians, would only have threatened the role that Germany and the Nordic peoples were destined to play: "The Slavs do after all lack the German and Nordic profundity, so their education and thinking [*Dannelse og Vidskab*] will always be French-like, and the error of the fifteenth century was by no means to combat Hus and his followers, but that they were in all ways opposed with the worst possible means (Grundtvig 1908, 413 [quotes pp. 411–12]; see also Vind 1999, 358). In the end, Grundtvig's racial philosophy of world history thus forced him to ignore the evident historical and theological impact of Hus on the German Reformation.

Grundtvig's dismissal of the Slavic Bohemians and Poles included the Hungarians, but he bestowed on the latter a special mission in the larger frame of European – that is, universal – history: the introduction of Christianity and German migration, we hear, had mellowed the features of Hungarian barbarism and allowed them to play a glorious role as an *antemurale Christianitatis* in the struggle against the Turks in 1456 (Vind 1999, 359). There are strong similarities here to the double standards applied by another Lutheran, Leopold von Ranke, in his assessment of the Slavs. In 1824, Ranke excluded the Slavs wholesale from the community of Occidental, Christian, and European peoples due to their "strange and peculiar nature"; but, whereas Ranke remained dismissive of Czech and/or Polish attempts at national development (as these inevitably would come into conflict with German aspirations in the region), he praised the Serbian struggle against Ottoman rule as a vindication of old European principles (Bugge 2002, 408–9; see also Vind 1999, 481–2). Such views seem to confirm Larry Wolff's (1994) argument that, in a "semi-orientalist" Western European discourse, the Slavs of Eastern Europe were adjudged to belong to a halfway house between civilization and barbarism, real Europe and the Orient.

In evaluating Grundtvig's views on the Slavic peoples we must take into account how far his position was in conformity with the general attitudes and levels of knowledge among his contemporaries. That Grundtvig, in his text of 1843, noticed the Bohemians only as a medieval tribe, as a phenomenon of the past, was not uncommon in a non-German pre-1848 Western European context, although contemporary British views of Hus were uniformly positive (Bugge 2009).[8] Curiously, when travelling in England between 1829 and 1831, Grundtvig met John Bowring, a liberal political economist, writer, and traveller. Grundtvig was invited to Bowring's family estate and spent considerable time with him, and Bowring deeply influenced Grundtvig's understanding of liberty. There were, however, limits to his impact. Bowring was a polyglot with a keen interest in the nations of Eastern Europe, but his sympathy for their national aspirations obviously found no resonance with Grundtvig (Abrahamowitz 2010, 195, 199).[9]

The 1848 "springtime of nations" brought the national aspirations of the peoples of Central and Eastern Europe to the attention of a larger European public, and when Grundtvig, in an 1848 article, strongly attacked German political and spiritual expansiveness, he was referring specifically to the German claims to Schleswig, Bohemia, and Posen (Grundtvig in Jørgensen 1993, 92). Grundtvig thus had some awareness of the national conflicts brewing in the latter regions, and it would not have been unnatural to see the Poles and Czechs as potential allies of Denmark in the struggle against German – and in the Polish case also Russian – expansionism. We may therefore surmise that Grundtvig's life-long, racially motivated dismissal of everything Slav (a view well in line with dominant trends in contemporary German thinking) was key in preventing him from seeing these possibilities.[10] Neither political expediency nor the presence of strong Lutheran voices among Czech and Slovak patriots sufficed to bring about a change in perception.

Thirty years after Grundtvig's death in 1872, Arnošt Kraus (1859–1943),[11] an ardent admirer of everything Danish and propagator of Grundtvig's pedagogical ideas, lamented this lack of mutual comprehension and collaboration in a report on an excursion of Czech farmers to Denmark. After visiting Askov and Skibelund with its newly erected memorial to King Magnus, victor and conqueror in battles against the Vends, Kraus (1902, 9–10) wrote: "We are leaving Skibelund, thinking about how it can be that Slavic guests now with sympathy are studying a monument of a warrior against the Slavs, and how it could happen that Slavs and Danes fought each other so fiercely, all to the benefit of a third party who rules today both on Slavic Rügen and in Danish Schleswig: history is a great teacher and we all walk sturdily – behind the school."

Whatever the reasons for it, Grundtvig's disinterest in the Czech cause thus did not prevent Czech intellectuals from following events in Denmark or from appreciating his importance for the Danish national awakening. Nor was Kraus the first Czech to notice Grundtvig. In 1859, Palacký's son-in-law František Ladislav Rieger (1818–1903) initiated the publishing of an encyclopaedia in Czech (eleven volumes, 1859–74). Its third volume contains an entry on Grundtvig, which, in over three hundred words and with rich references in Danish to his major works, describes him as an "outstanding Danish writer in the fields of history, theology, and poetry" (Rieger 1863, 509–10). The text highlights his studies in Nordic mythology and world history, while also noticing his fervent national patriotism and political work. The entry is signed "Mü," in all likelihood the signature of Jan Bohuslav Müller (1823–1885), an art historian, journalist, and translator with a doctoral degree from the University of Jena for a dissertation (1857) on Jan Amos Komenský (Comenius).[12]

Though not the object of any concerted interest, Denmark was thus not an unknown entity in Bohemia. From the 1840s onwards, the Czech national movement turned from an uncritical adoration of everything Slavic to a stronger emphasis on the lot of small nations in Europe, whether Slavic or not (a Czech "secret society" active in Prague from 1844 to 1848 was named Repeal, with reference to the Irish example). Such perceptions also found expression in Czech reactions to the war of

1864. In the war, Prussia was seconded by Austria, which, in a sense, rendered Danes at war with Czechs. The Czech press, however, never turned against the Danish "enemy," criticizing instead British and French diplomacy or – with increasing intensity from the summer of 1864 – Prussian aggression and expansiveness. It also made analogies to Hungary's position within the Hapsburg Monarchy or even to the Czech-German rivalry in Bohemia (Hojda 1996).

At the turn of the century, Czech interest in the lot of the Danish minority in Schleswig, and in Danish affairs in general, increased significantly. This was not the least thanks to the indefatigable efforts of the already mentioned Arnošt Kraus. In 1898, he addressed the minority issue in an article in the progressive philosopher T.G. Masaryk's (1850–1937) journal *Naše doba* (*Our Era*). Kraus describes how the promise of the Peace of Prague in 1866 of a referendum in Schleswig had been broken, and how the national minorities in the German Empire, including the Danes of Schleswig, were ill-treated. In 1899, he followed up on this by translating Georg Brandes's article "Danskheden i Sønderjylland" (the Danes of Southern Jutland) into Czech (Hojda 1996, 78). Kraus, who taught Germanic philology at the Czech university in Prague, saw the Danes not merely as victims of German aggression but as nothing less than "the most eminent among the small nations on the planet," (Kraus 1908, 2) primarily due to their remarkable achievements in the field of popular education. Grundtvig would surely have agreed.

Kraus's journeys to Denmark had made him familiar with the Folk High Schools, which he describes in detail in several books and pamphlets. He credits Grundtvig for formulating the basic educational principles of these schools and for finding the pupils and supporters that could transform his visions into reality. His account of the birth and development of the Folk High School movement is thorough and detailed, and it highlights the Danish efforts to compensate for the loss of Schleswig-Holstein through domestic "inner" mobilization. Kraus argues that the egalitarian spirit and the emphasis on activism and moral character formation in the Folk High Schools were major factors in explaining Danish economic and spiritual progress since the terrible defeat of 1864 (Kraus 1908, 99–115).

Egalitarianism and self-help though the education of the broad popular masses and the improvement of their lot resonated well with large segments of the Czech national movement at the turn of the century, including the Social Democrats. It thus made good sense when Kraus once compared Grundtvig to Jan Kollár, both in terms of the obvious similarities in the philosophies and aspirations of the two Protestant clergymen and as a way of making the former accessible to a broader domestic public.[13] Unlike the two, however, Kraus had a strong general sympathy for small nations regardless of their racial affiliation. This is well illustrated in the following quote, which concludes a paragraph on the growth of the Grundtvig-inspired folk high school movement in Norway, Sweden, and Finland: "Happy, educated Finland next to the lands of the wretched, oppressed Latvians and Estonians demonstrates very nicely what the difference is between the Scandinavians and the Germans as carriers of culture; it is a difference like between light and darkness; sadly, over all of them expands a great power, which brutally crushes them all, and that power is, we confess with shame, Slavic" (Kraus 1908, 112).

Kraus was by no means alone in propagating Scandinavian culture among the Czechs at the turn of the century, and he was not the author of the lengthy entry (approximately seven hundred words) on Grundtvig in the monumental Czech encyclopaedia *Ottův slovník naučný* (28 vols., Prague 1888–1909). With rich references to Danish and other primary and secondary sources, the entry covers Grundtvig's biography, theological thought, writings on history, patriotism and political activities in 1848, and, later, and his contributions to the creation of a system of folk high schools in Denmark and Scandinavia (*Ottův slovník naučný* 1886, 539). Its author (using the signature "HKa") was Hugo Kosterka (1867–1956), a translator with a passionate interest in contemporary Scandinavian literature (Ibsen, Strindberg, Hamsun, etc.). While accounting loyally for Grundtvig's life and work, Kosterka thus sought to bring Czech and Scandinavian culture together on a very different platform – that of literary modernity.[14] Both trends – the interest in Danish society and in its avant-garde culture – remained present in Czech society beyond the collapse of the Hapsburg Monarchy in 1918 as yet another testimony to the affinity of outlooks of both these neighbours of Germany.

NOTES

1 Hroch's model led Lorenz Rerup to argue that the Danes of the kingdom formed a great nation, whereas the Danes in the Duchy of Schleswig are to be included under the small, incomplete ones, sadly without reflecting

further on the consequences of assuming the existence of two distinct nations by the same name (Rerup 1993, 21; cf Hroch 1985, 8, 117–24).

2 The idea that Russia/the Slavs belonged to the North of Europe was also common in Germany and France until after the Napoleonic Wars, when their relocation to the East on the mental map of Europe began in earnest (Lemberg 1985). August von Schlözer's (1735–1809) *Allgemeine Nordische Geschichte* (1771) thus defines the Slavs as undoubtedly northern people and offers favourable accounts of their history (Baár 2010, 120–1). Lelewel's *Edda* book is an adapted Polish translation of Paul-Henri Mallet's *Introduction à l'Histoire de Dannemarc* (3 vols. Copenhagen, 1758–77), another example of the transnational travelling of ideas among national awakeners.

3 The essay, "A Word to the Brave and Highly Educated Bohemarius" appeared in the journal *Prvotiny*. Jungmann echoes Lamentations 3:45.

4 Inevitably, Fichte and Jahn had similar concerns about the pernicious influence of everything French.

5 The Budeč project actually got further than Grundtvig's plans, but it collapsed for lack of sufficient funding in 1847.

6 Compare with Wolff (1995). In Lelewel's case, after 1831, these practices followed from bitter necessity when he had to go into exile after the failed Polish uprising. Still, the point to make is that a transnational European public, and writings addressed to it, did not disappear with the advent of nationalization.

7 N.F.S. Grundtvig, "Verdens-Historien 12 (i Danske Forening 1855 Mai 2)" [World History 12 (in the Danish Union 1855, May 2], reprinted in Vind (1999, 595–602 [quotes pp. 599 and 602]). See also Vind (1999, 407–9, 464).

8 In his *En Reise fortalt i Breve til mit Hiem* [A journey narrated in letters to my home] (1817–18) Adam Oehlenschläger notices the presence of Bohemian speakers in the province, and, although he found the present failure of the Bohemian Slavs to thrive in their German surroundings fully understandable, he speculated that, in five hundred years, we would find "Poland, Bohemia, Hungary, Russia blossoming and the other languages in hibernation" (Hougaard 1971, 15). Oehlenschläger was the only Danish traveller to make such observations about the Czechs before 1843.

9 Bowring was the author and translator of *Specimens of the Polish Poets* (1827), *Serbian Popular Poetry* (1827), *Poetry of the Magyars* (1830), *Cheskian Anthology* (1832), and so on. On Bowring and the Czech national movement, see Macura (1995, 110–12).

10 In a postscript to the third volume of his *World History*, covering the eighteenth and nineteenth centuries, Grundtvig makes no mention of the Polish uprising of 1830 (in sharp contrast to his extensive discussion of events in Greece) or of the national movements in the Hapsburg Empire in 1848 and later.

The literature on German and Western European attitudes towards Russia and the Slavs is enormous. See, for example, Groh (1988); Liulevicius (2009); and Malia (1999).

11 Kraus, a secular Czech Jew, died of tuberculosis in Theresienstadt.

12 On Müller, see *Lexikon české literatury: Osobnosti, díla, instituce, Díl 3/II: P – Ř* [Dictionary of Czech literature: Persons, works, institutions, vol. 3/II: P – Ř] (Prague: Academia 2000), 372–3. Müller had translated H.C. Andersen's novel *Improvisatoren* into Czech in 1851 (some translations of short stories had appeared in 1848), which suggests that he possessed some command of Danish, although it is possible that he translated the novel from a German version published in nearby Regensburg as *Der Improvisator* in 1849.

13 The comparison is mentioned in Pokorný (2003, 17), with reference to a Kraus text of 1907 to which I have not had access. The interest in education for the masses and in the Danish experiences in this field was not confined to the Czechs of the Hapsburg Empire. The geologist Eduard Reyer (1849–1914), professor at the University of Vienna, published *Handbuch des Volksbildungswesens* (Handbook of institutions of adult education) (Stuttgart, 1896) and wrote the Introduction to Ernst Schultze's *Volkshochschulen und Universitäts-Ausdehnungs-Bewegung* (Folk high schools and the university-expansion movement) (Leipzig, 1897), both with solid references to Denmark.

14 See Kadečková (1995) on Kosterka and the Czech-Scandinavian connections in general. Kadečková makes the poignant observation that part of the unprecedented expansion of a hitherto marginal literature into the centre of European attention was due, in large part, to the escape from the province of many of its protagonists. Also, the Scandinavians had no fear of translation or of reaching their European audiences through German.

REFERENCES

Abrahamowitz, F. 2010. *Grundtvig. Danmark til lykke* [Grundtvig: A blessing for Denmark]. Copenhagen: Informations forlag.

Baár, M. 2010. *Historians and Nationalism: East-Central Europe in the Nineteenth Century*. Oxford: Oxford University Press.

Bugge, P. 2002. "'Land und Volk' – oder: Wo liegt Böhmen?" [Land and people – or: Where is Bohemia?]. *Geschichte und Gesellschaft* 28 (3): 404–44.

– 2009. "'Something in the View Which Makes You Linger': Bohemia and Bohemians in British Travel Writing, 1836–1857." *Central Europe* 7 (1): 3–29.

Drews, P. 1990. *Herder und die Slaven: Materialien zur Wirkungsgeschichte bis zur Mitte des 19. Jahrhunderts* [Herder and the Slavs: Contributions to the history of his reception up to the middle of the 19th century]. Munich: Sagner.

Groh, Dieter. 1988. *Rußland im Blick Europas* [Russia in Europe's eyes]. Frankfurt am Main: Suhrkamp.

Grundtvig, N.F.S. 1862. *Haandbog i Verdenshistorien efter de bedste Kilder: Et Forsøg, Anden Deel* [Handbook on world history based on the best sources: An attempt, part two], 2nd ed. Copenhagen: Karl Schønberg.

– 1905. *Nik. Fred. Sev. Grundvig's Udvalgte Skrifter* [Selected writings of Nik. Fred. Sev. Grundtvig]. Vol. 2. Copenhagen: Gyldendal.

– 1908. *Nik. Fred. Sev. Grundtvig's Udvalgte Skrifter* [Selected writings of Nik. Fred. Sev. Grundtvig]. Vol. 7. Copenhagen: Gyldendal.

Hojda, Z. 1996. "Dánská válka roku 1864 a její ohlas v Čechách" [The Danish war of 1864 and its reverberation in Bohemia]. *Acta Universitatis Carolinae – Philosophica et historia 3, Studia historica XLIV* [Records of Charles University – philosophy and history 3 – historical studies XLIV], 69–80.

Hougaard, C. 1971. *Tjekkoslovakiet i Danmarks spejl* [Denmark in Czechoslovakia's mirror]. Odense: University Press of Southern Denmark.

Hroch, M. 1985. *Social Preconditions of National Revival in Europe: A Comparative Analysis of the Social Composition of Patriotic Groups among the Smaller European Nations*. Cambridge: Cambridge University Press.

– 2007. *Comparative Studies in Modern European History: Nation, Nationalism, Social Change*. Aldershot: Ashgate.

Jedlicki, J. 1999. *A Suburb of Europe: Nineteenth-Century Polish Approaches to Western Civilization*. Budapest: Central European University Press.

Jørgensen, T. 1993. "Reflections on Grundtvig and Germany." *Grundtvig Studier* 44 (1): 91–104.

Kadečková, H. 1995. "Skandinavský fin de siècle z českého pohledu" [The Scandinavian fin de siècle from a Czech point of view]. In *Moderní revue 1894–1925* [Modern review 1894–1925], ed. Otto M. Urban and Luboš Merhaut, 112–29. Prague: Torst.

Kořalka, J. 2007. *František Palacký, 1798–1876: Der Historiker der Tschechen im österreichischen Vielvölkerstaat* [František Palacký, 1798–1876: The historian of the Czechs in the Austrian multinational state]. Vienna: Verlag der Österreichischen Akademie der Wissenschaften.

Kraus, A. 1902. *První výlet českých rolníků do Dánska* [The first expedition of Czech farmers to Denmark]. Prague: Čas.

Kraus, A. 1908. *Dánsko, jeho hmotná a duševní kultura* [Denmark, its material and spiritual culture]. Prague: J. Otto.

Lemberg, H. 1985. "Zur Entstehung des Osteuropabegriffs im 19. Jahrhundert: Vom 'Norden' zum 'Osten' Europas" [On the emergence of the concept of Eastern Europe in the 19th century: From "the North" to "the East" of Europe] *Jahrbücher für Geschichte Osteuropas* [Yearbooks for the history of Eastern Europe], 33: 48–91.

Lexikon české literatury: Osobnosti, díla, instituce, Díl 3/II: P – Ř [Dictionary of Czech literature: Persons, works, institutions, vol. 3/II: P–Ř]. 2000. Prague: Academia.

Liulevicius, V.G. 2009. *The German Myth of the East: 1800 to the Present.* Oxford: Oxford University Press.

Macura, V. 1995. *Znamení zrodu: České národní obrození jako kulturní typ* [Sign of the birth: The Czech national awakening as a cultural type]. Jinočany: H&H.

Malia, M. 1999. *Russia under Western Eyes: From the Bronze Horseman to the Lenin Mausoleum*. Cambridge: Harvard University Press.

Mallet, P-H. 1756. [1758–77]. *Introduction à l'Histoire de Dannemarc* [Introduction to the history of Denmark]. Copenhagen: Claude Philibert.

Ottův slovník naučný, Desátý díl. Gens – Hedwigia [Otto's encyclopaedia, vol. 10. Gens – Hedwigia]. 1896. Prague: J. Otto.

Pokorný, J. 2003. *Lidová výchova na přelomu 19. a 20. století* [Popular education on the threshold of the 19th and 20th centuries]. Prague: Karolinum.

Pynsent, R. 1994. *Questions of Identity: Czech and Slovak Ideas of Nationality and Personality*. Budapest: Central European University Press.

Rerup, L. 1993. "Grundtvig and 19th Century Nationalism." *Grundtvig Studier* 44 : 16–26.

Reyer, E. 1896 *Handbuch des Volksbildungswesens* [Handbook of institutions of higher education]. Stuttgart: Cotta.

Rieger, F.L., ed. 1863. *Slovník naučný: Díl tretí: F – Chyzice* [Encyclopaedia: Volume 3: F – Chyzice]. Prague: I.L. Kober.

Schultze, Et. 1897. *Volkshochschulen und Universitäts-Ausdehnungs-Bewegung* [Folk high schools and the university-expansion-movement]. Leipzig: Freund.

Vind, O. 1999. *Grundtvigs historiefilosofi* [Grundtvig's philosophy of history]. Copenhagen: Gyldendal.

Vodička, F., ed. 1948. *Boj o obrození národa: Výbor z díla Josefa Jungmanna* [The struggle for the revival of the nation: Selections from the work of Josef Jungmann]. Prague: F. Kosek.

Walicki, A. 1994. *Poland between East and West: The Controversies over Self-Definition and Modernization in Partitioned Poland*. Cambridge, MA: Harvard University Press.

Wolff, L. 1994. *Inventing Eastern Europe: The Map of Civilization on the Mind of the Enlightenment*. Stanford, CA: Stanford University Press.

– 1995. "Voltaire's Public and the Idea of Eastern Europe: Toward a Literary Sociology of Continental Division." *Slavic Review* 54 (4): 932–42.

Zacek, J.F. 1970. *Palacký: The Historian as Scholar and Nationalist*. The Hague: Mouton.

14

Crisis of Religion and Nineteenth-Century Spiritual Reform: Varieties of Nation Building in Grundtvig and Emerson

TROELS NØRAGER

What does it mean to contribute to nation building? In the perspective adopted in this chapter, it entails developing a notion of a country's purpose and destiny and, thereby, promoting a common, national identity and stronger social bonds. By comparing two leading nineteenth-century figures who made substantial contributions to nation building, Denmark's Nikolai Grundtvig (1783–1872) and the United States's Ralph Waldo Emerson (1803–82), I intend to show how interesting parallels emerge, despite vast differences in national context and conditions.[1] Differences apply as well to the two personalities in question. In fact, had Grundtvig and Emerson known each other, they would no doubt have regarded each other as antipodes rather than as fellow travellers: all through his life, Grundtvig took pride in calling himself "an old-fashioned Christian," whereas Emerson adopted an increasingly "heretical" attitude and, late in his life, supported the establishment of the Free Religious Association. Admittedly, then, the primary justification for comparing them stems from the history of *reception*, which has elevated both men to the status of national icons, a process beginning while the two were still alive. Is the view of posterity simply wrong, then? No, but posterity creates (and recreates) their national past from a variety of desires and interests, one being a need to establish a canon of founding fathers. How this was done in the case of Grundtvig and Emerson could make a fascinating story, but one that is another's to tell.

Instead, I make a quasi-Hegelian argument – namely, that, despite all their differences, the reform agenda of Grundtvig and Emerson reveals surprising parallels due to the spirit of the times working behind their backs (so to speak). My argument proceeds in three steps. First, I demonstrate how they both engage in cultural diagnosis in order to establish the need for radical reform, notably in two areas: religious life and popular education. The remedy for the perceived cultural crisis can be summarized in one word: "spirit." Second, I make a case for seeing their proposals for religious reform as a way of translating traditional religion into different forms of "civil religion." I hasten to add that this interpretation makes no claim to match their respective self-understanding at the time; what I try to make plausible is that it makes good sense from a contemporary nation-building perspective. Third, I show how "spirit" is not least at work in their proposals for educational reform and how this was envisaged to strengthen the ties between individual and community.

CULTURAL DIAGNOSIS: SECULARIZATION AS THE CRISIS OF TRADITIONAL RELIGION IN MODERNITY

As perceptive commentators of the cultural and political developments in their respective countries, both Grundtvig and Emerson engage in cultural diagnosis and critique, which play a prominent role in their writings. What they witness is nothing less than an important part of the process of secularization. "Secularization," as is well known, is a multilayered concept; here, I take it to mean roughly what Taylor (2007) describes as the last of three different meanings – namely, as a shift in "the conditions of belief."[2] Already in the mid-eighteenth century, Hume had struck a serious blow to Christian belief, and from around 1820 German scholars' historical criticism of the Bible reached the theological circles of Denmark and the United States, shaking the traditional foundation of Christianity and causing a wave of scepticism and doubt, particularly among intellectuals (Wilson 1999).

Like so many of his contemporaries, Grundtvig had been shocked not only by the French Revolution but also by the July Revolution in 1830. In combination with increasing and widespread demands for a constitution, this formed a serious challenge to Grundtvig, who was only a rather late and hesitant supporter of democracy. In his writings of the 1830s there are many different expressions for his conviction that something is rotten in the state of Denmark – something that needs to be corrected. Thus, he can say that "the world is out of joint" and that we need "a rescue from this great shipwreck" (Broadbridge, Warren, and Jonas 2011, *School for Life* [hereafter SFL] 55). An even more dramatic image is used in the following quotation, in which Grundtvig makes it quite clear that he considers *education* the proper means to save society from the abyss:

> And who can doubt that we in the North are at present standing on the edge of a bottomless abyss? Nowhere has it been felt so deeply and for so long that it is education, general education, that is lacking, and that it is education that can save us. However, we need to distinguish true and useful education from the false and empty kind, and thus it is no wonder that so far we have constantly been in error over the proper educational means. This must drive every Nordic man who sees it to attempt even what is irrational in order, if possible, to put our peoples on a better track. (*SFL* 176)

Part of what is needed, according to Grundtvig, is a national *awakening*; Grundtvig had perceived that this was already in its beginnings around Europe, and, by casting himself in the role of seer and prophet, warning his people, he contributed decisively to the course of events. To be more specific, we see how he hoped to harness and channel the energies and resources of the people into an idea of what constitutes the "common good" of a nation, thus avoiding revolutionary unrest and instability.

The fact of increasing secularization is reflected in Grundtvig's realization that "the age of the church" had been eclipsed by "the age of the school." But how did this insight affect Grundtvig as an orthodox minister of the state church? At this point an interesting parallel to Emerson emerges: having realized that traditional religion is in a crisis, both distance themselves from the religion of their forefathers, although in Grundtvig's case this move is accompanied with feelings of deep ambivalence. In his educational writings the criticism of the "old" religion surfaces in a context in which Grundtvig accuses the forefathers of having religiously legitimized rote learning in the "black" school, or the "school for death":

> After the school had laid us in the grave, or at least deformed our healthy human nature and eroded our vitality, our forefathers apparently consoled themselves with the thought that it was only the body that was being killed, only our completely depraved human nature that was being maltreated. As long as we had learned our scripture and catechism as well as the next man, we had obtained a title-deed

> to eternal life. As for temporal death, far from separating us from it, it was precisely the only road and desirable bridge *towards* that eternal life. I realise that this superstition with a Christian appearance is a long way from either oppressing or comforting many people in our time. (SFL 196)

An important part of Grundtvig's diagnosis of the times is his reaction to the political situation, that is, the demand for democratic constitutions and assemblies. Although there is a popular image of Grundtvig as a father of Danish democracy, scholars have long since recognized that he in fact opposed democracy. In this he was far from alone at the time. In fact, as Jeppe Nevers (2011) has recently shown, "democracy" was a negative term designating "mob rule," which was a general fear in the wake of the French Revolution. In terms of political philosophy, Grundtvig was inspired by the contractarian view that civil society rests on a fundamental agreement on the common good.[3]

To sum up: in his diagnosis of the times, Grundtvig uses strong words ("shipwreck," "abyss") to convey his conviction that Danish society is heading for disaster due to disintegration. The background comes from more than one source: religiously, he sees that the church has lost much of its former power to create strong social bonds and that the forefathers' pilgrimage view of this life was no longer worth believing; philosophically, he faults German idealism and its celebration of reason and individual autonomy for contributing to the problems; and finally, politically, he fears that the increasing demands for constitutional democracy will weaken rather than strengthen both state and civil society. Perceiving that he lives in a time of transition, Grundtvig warns against what he regards as two equally terrible scenarios: on the one hand, an elitist democracy without public legitimacy and, on the other, an anarchic democracy in the form of mob rule.

The cultural critique of the early, transcendentalist Emerson is a reflection of his newly found spiritual revelation, centring on the soul, on spirit, and on the moral sentiment. Let us see how this unfolds by exemplifying, first, his general diagnosis of the time and then looking deeper into the causes of the maladies as well as the proposed cure.

In his "Lectures on the Times" (1841–42) Emerson (1971, 167) puts forward his view that the times "have their root in an invisible spiritual reality." Already in this statement, indicative of Emerson's idealism, we get a first feel of what is going to be the overall argument: we have lost or perverted our connection to this reality, and we need to rediscover it. Until this happens, we are confronted with dire consequences in the entire range of our experience: the world "lacks unity," complains Emerson in *Nature* (1836), it lies "broken and in heaps," "because man is disunited with himself" (Emerson 1971, 43). The reason for this is not always quite clear in Emerson. In "The American Scholar" (1837), in what might look like Emerson's variant of the Fall, he states that man has "wronged himself" and "has almost lost the light that can lead him back to his prerogatives" (Emerson 1971, 65). What are these prerogatives? They are inherent in Emerson's doctrine "that man is one," or a microcosm, a particular incarnation of Universal Man. But instead, he complains, men today are called "the mass" and "the herd." Compared to Grundtvig, we find in Emerson a more pronounced individualism. Part of Emerson's critique is directed at the superficial way in which most people live, seeking money or power. This makes him characterize them as "sleep-walking," and here, quite literally, he wants to act as their awakener: "Wake them, and they shall quit the false good and leap to the true, and leave governments to clerks and desks" (ibid.).

Emerson's primary diagnosis of the time, however, points (as we have seen in Grundtvig) to a profound crisis of faith. Thus, in the "Divinity School Address" (1838) he not only points to the need for "new revelation" but also informs his audience of "the sad conviction, which I share, I believe, with numbers, of the universal decay and now almost death of faith in society" (Emerson 1971, 84).[4] The following statement from "The Young American" (1844) can be said to sum up Emerson's cultural critique: "The people, and the world, is now suffering from the want of religion and honor in its public mind. In America, out of doors all seems a market; in doors, an airtight stove of coventionalism ... I find no expression in our state papers or legislative debate, in our lyceums or churches, specially in our newspapers, of a high national feeling, no lofty counsels that rightfully stirs the blood" (Emerson 1971, 239).

The causes: the faults of historical Christianity have resulted in "a decaying church and a wasting unbelief" (Emerson 1971, 88). All of the crisis, however, should not be attributed to the errors of historical Christianity. Like Grundtvig, Emerson sees clearly that what our forefathers believed is no longer credible: "Certainly there have been periods when, from the inactivity of the intellect on certain truths, a greater faith was possible in names and persons. The Puritans in England and America, found in the Christ of the Catholic Church, and in the dogmas inherited from Rome, scope for their austere piety, and their longings for civil freedom. But their creed is passing away, and none arises it its room" (ibid.).

Let us see now how Emerson proposes to remedy this troubled situation. To those gathered for his notorious "Divinity School Address" he offered the following answer: "And now, my brothers, you will ask, What in these desponding days can be done by us? The remedy is already declared in the ground of our complaint of the Church. We have contrasted the Church with the Soul. In the soul, then, let the redemption be sought" (Emerson 1971, 89). But just pointing to "the soul," how is that supposed to remedy anything? Here we must remind ourselves that "soul," for Emerson, is the seat of the moral sentiment acting according to a law, which corresponds to the laws of nature (cf. Hallengren 1994). Without this law, so we must understand the argument, religion, morality, and society in general degenerates and decays.

CIVIL RELIGION AS THE SPIRIT OF A NATION

Both Grundtvig and Emerson had read extensively about the French Revolution; in Emerson's case part of this reading involved his friend Thomas Carlyle's famous book on the subject. Their reactions to this decisive event, however, had to differ: in the pre-constitutional monarchy of Denmark, the royalist Grundtvig was terrified by the prospect of disintegration and mob rule. In the democratic republic of the United States, where a political culture of individual freedom was in its early beginnings, Emerson realized that traditional Calvinism was bankrupt; however, at the same time he was ambivalent about the blessings of market economy and the division of labour. In fact, we need to emphasize the vast difference between the new and young republic of the United States, faced with the task of constructing its founding myth, and the age-old monarchy of Denmark where, the task (so vigorously adopted by Grundtvig) was rather to revitalize the core elements of a long-standing tradition.[5]

The core problem here, of course, is the relation between the individual and the community. In order for a society or nation to be stable over time, you need to have strong, interconnecting ties that are regularly invigorated. Without being aware of it, or adopting it as a fully fleshed-out strategy, both Grundtvig and Emerson bought into the idea of civil religion, historically going back to Rousseau but made useful for sociological analysis through the seminal article by Robert Bellah (1967). The paradox I want to highlight is that the solutions propagated by our two protagonists display remarkable similarities.

The challenges facing the early republic of the United States, where market economy and increasing individualism were rapidly dissolving traditional forms of life, have been admirably described and analyzed in Alexis de Tocqueville's *Democracy in America* (1835) (Tocqueville 1969). For one thing, Tocqueville is quite clear about the need to balance the concern of the individual as well as that of the community. For another, he has intriguing sections in which he discusses the important role of religion in relation to the problem of combining freedom and equality. Thus, in a chapter entitled "How Religion in the United States Makes Use of Democratic Instincts," we find the following interesting reflections:

> For my part, I doubt whether man can support complete religious independence and entire political liberty at the same time. I am led to think that if he has no faith he must obey, and if he is free he must believe.
>
> The great usefulness of religions is even more apparent among egalitarian peoples than elsewhere ...
>
> The greatest advantage of religions is to inspire diametrically contrary urges. Every religion places the object of man's desires outside and beyond worldly goods and naturally lifts the soul into regions far above the realm of the senses. Every religion also imposes on each man some obligations toward mankind, to be performed in common with the rest of mankind, and so draws him away, from time to time, from thinking about himself. That is true even of the most false and dangerous religions.
>
> Thus religious peoples are naturally strong just at the point where democratic peoples are weak. And that shows how important it is for people to keep their religion when they become equal. (Tocqueville 1969, 444ff.)

To understand how the reform agenda of Grundtvig and Emerson amounted to something like civil religion, we need to look at a particular cognitive figure operative in the sermons, essays, and poems of both men – namely, the two-world motive, which can be traced all the way back to Plato. In its religious variant, this is the idea that each individual has a divine origin and, despite the Fall, a partly divine nature by virtue of which she is able to communicate with the unseen world. Now romanticism, which heavily influenced both Grundtvig and Emerson, is just a (partly) secularized version of this idea: the transcendent spirit manifests itself in the dynamic unfolding of immanent nature. The point here is that the two-world motive offers a way to bridge the threatening chasm between individual and community: by virtue of what is common (i.e., spiritual nature) the individual can be connected to the community, and salutary infusions from above can energize both. The fact that this powerful idea is operative in both Grundtvig and Emerson points to what distinguishes them from many reform movements of the time, notably in France.

One of the characteristic features of Grundtvig and Emerson is precisely that they managed to distill or concentrate the meaning and destiny of a people, and thus we have come to know and celebrate them as major forces in defining what is, respectively, the "Spirit of America" and the "Spirit of Denmark." They accomplished this not just by drawing upon a notion of spirit pervasive in Romanticism and German Idealism but also by casting themselves in the role of sage, seer, and poet.[6]

Still, "spirit" may appear today as an extremely vague and fluffy notion. What is noteworthy about Grundtvig and Emerson, however, is that, despite their heavily idealistic commitments, they were both convinced that spirit is an actively working force producing very real effects. Thus, we are justified in juxtaposing them as representatives of a spiritual realism.[7] In the final section, I demonstrate how the idea of "spirit" is operative in their ideas of education, which they both considered a primary area of reform.

SPIRITUAL EDUCATION AS A BRIDGE BETWEEN INDIVIDUAL AND COMMUNITY

My basic claim in this section is that attempts to meet the challenges of the "age of the school," to use Grundtvig's expression, may properly be regarded as forms of national awakening and reform and, thus, as significant contributions to nation building. In the case of Grundtvig, his views of enlightenment and education may be regarded as yet another application of his demand for a "living" religion, which perhaps signals his most important parallel to Emerson. Grundtvig's first move, in attempting to set matters right, is to distinguish between "false" and "genuine" enlightenment. Echoing his general and frequently occurring criticism of eighteenth-century rationalism, he notes that the false version has its background in the French Revolution, and he complains that its one-sided eulogy of "Reason" is propagated by the German philosophy of his time.

The false enlightenment is dangerous to the state because it places the individual and its reason and autonomy at centre stage. Contrary to this, the genuine enlightenment represents a more organic view, aimed at contributing to a harmonious relation between the individual and the community:

> However, a genuine enlightenment extends itself to the whole of human life, shows the deep coinherence between the life of the individual, the nation, and the whole human race, and develops a way of thinking that is desirable for all social relations. Such an enlightenment, the state must by no means leave to its own devices, i.e. leave it to the individual, scattered householders, and to teachers who will always do their best to disseminate it in their local circles. This genuine enlightenment the authorities must take a fatherly responsibility for at all levels of education, from the common people to the erudite scholars, if the state is to be rescued and to blossom instead of perishing from "enlightenment." (SFL 83ff.)

Spirit, the invisible power, is closely linked to another core concept in Grundtvig – namely, life – since spirit may be said to create or foster life by way of the spoken word. This basic notion has two consequences for his idea of true education: (1) it must be based on narrative and lively conversation rather than on dead books, and, (2) learning, in order to be truly practical, must start with life. In fact, the whole purpose of general education is to make the individual fit for life. In this sense, Grundtvig's educational ideas clearly give priority to practice over theory.

The young Emerson's notebooks display a pronounced interest in rhetoric and ideals of eloquence. He looked for this in his teachers at Harvard, but his primary role model was Boston Unitarian minister William Ellery Channing (1780–1842), who, in many ways, formed a bridge from Unitarianism to Transcendentalism. From Channing, Emerson also inherited the idea of education as self-culture.[8] As an American version of the idea of *Bildung*, which Goethe personified, the concept of self-culture is the core theme of Emerson's lectures. It is the frame of reference within which to grasp the meaning of his recurrent emphasis on "self-reliance" and "character."[9] In the words of Field (2001, 486), Emerson "envisioned his message of self-culture as the intellectual complement to Americans' headlong pursuit of material prosperity. As a national idealist prophet, Emerson believed himself to be the harbinger of the nation's next giant step toward greatness." And a few pages later he concludes that "Emerson devoted the bulk of his mature life to calling people from their material pursuits. Prosperity was nothing more than a means to spiritual and cultural ends. In all of his lectures and essays, Emerson never departed from the theme of self-culture and the singular value of education" (492).[10]

Having pointed to the German-romanticist elements of self-culture, we should not overlook its deeper, theological background. To Unitarian liberal theology (and certainly to Emerson) the essence of religion is morality, and the scriptural authority behind this idea is Jesus's admonishing his disciples with the words: "Therefore you are to be perfect, as your heavenly Father is perfect" (Mathew 5:48). Inspired by this, philosopher Stanley Cavell (2003) coined the term "Emersonian moral perfectionism" (see also Saito 2005). But let us turn now to the more practical consequences of these ideas.

To the widespread call for reform in all areas of life, Emerson (1971, 174) once again points to the moral sentiment as the only real solution: "For the origin of all reform is in that mysterious fountain of the moral sentiment in man, which, amidst the natural ever contains the supernatural for men. That is new and creative. That is alive. That alone can make a man other than he is. Here or nowhere resides unbounded energy, unbounded power." This, we could say, is a crucial step in what Emerson would see as "educating the spirit."[11] A similar requirement holds for the teacher, for only the person "on whom the soul descends" can teach (cf. 84). Still, in Emerson's view, we should all be open to "ecstasy" or "divine illumination" (145), and the "finished man" is nothing less than a mediator between the "spiritual" and the "actual" world (159).

Part of the influence of romanticism is manifest in Emerson's fondness for the notion of "Genius," which he distinguishes from mere "talent" (cf. Emerson 1971, 134). In his later essays, however, it is noteworthy that Emerson's effort to educate the spirit shifts to an interest in fostering "Character." Obviously, "character" is closely connected with Emerson's focus on private integrity, self-reliance, and the moral sentiment; but, as Thomas Augst (1999, 90) reminds us, something more is involved, and modern scholars have difficulty in "appreciating the degree to which general knowledge about character, of the sort retailed by Emerson in his later lectures, constituted a practical civic pedagogy concerned with the epistemological, social, and ethical challenges of democracy under modern capitalism." And, although it is hard to miss the tone of elitism in several of Emerson's texts, Augst nonetheless directs our attention to the important fact that Emerson (in this respect much like Grundtvig) tried to flesh out an egalitarian idea of civic agency and virtue. In the words of Augst: "When Emerson ... sought to analyze and respond to the conditions of market culture, he understood the practice of character in business as providing an egalitarian alternative to an elitist, aristocratic tradition of European civic education. It was not by reading but through attention to their own experience that individuals would learn the skills and capacities they needed to undertake citizenship in a democracy" (94).

In Grundtvig's educational writings, the idea of Folk High Schools figures prominently. In light of the importance of the lyceum movement (from the 1830s) for general, public education in the United States, and since we have numerous testimonies to the fact that Emerson was one of its most popular lecturers, I believe that we are entitled to see the lyceums as a parallel to the Danish Folk High Schools.[12] Thus, I think that Buell (2003, 293) is quite correct in calling Emerson a pioneer in adult education. Turning to Grundtvig's ideas of spiritual education, we find a curious combination of conservative and liberal, even progressive, elements. The conservative element, which was intended to forestall the constitutional process, was obviously doomed to fail. But at the same time we may grant that Grundtvig has an important point when he emphasizes that political participation can be dangerous if a people is not properly educated (numerous contemporary examples of this spring to mind). And, as a part of this, we should not overlook the fact that his focus on history (the heroic deeds of the past), poetry, and national songs has made a strong contribution to nation building by fostering a love of the nation.

With regard to the more progressive aspects of the Folk High School, I would point in particular to the idea of a mutual learning process, a conversational interaction between teachers and students based upon Grundtvig's core idea of "the living word." At least to some extent this ideal became a reality in the Folk High Schools, and I believe a case can be made for seeing this feature as having played an important role in the process of developing a democratic culture, a deliberative democracy. Is there a parallel to this in Emerson? Not directly, of course, since his political and cultural context was markedly different from that of Grundtvig. Nonetheless, we may wonder whether his gospel of self-reliance, of love of nature and poetry, may not have had similar effects. But, of course, such effects and assumed consequences are elusive and can at most be considered worthy of a degree of plausibility.

Having considered some of the major differences between Grundtvig and Emerson, let us conclude by summing up the similarities in their contributions to nation building. Most important, I believe that we should focus on their common conviction that "the age of the church" (to use Grundtvig's expression) is coming to an end. But this is only the more negative half of the story. The other half is their agreement that religion or worship is nonetheless necessary to society. Hence, their call for a new and truly *living* religion, although in trying to solve this task, they took the idea in rather different directions.

Basic to both thinkers is a genuinely *positive* religious anthropology claiming that human nature is not depraved, but, by virtue of being created in the image of God, the vessel of divine energies and destined to fellowship with God. Since part of God's creation was the gift of spirit, a core idea in Grundtvig and Emerson is the *indwelling of spirit* in all humans. Emerson may well have taken this idea too far for Grundtvig's liking, or, put differently, Grundtvig would no doubt have strong reservations about the pantheistic and mystical tendency in some of Emerson's more bold formulations. Be that as it may, the important thing is that they shared a basically theological idea of Spirit as creative, divine energy manifesting itself in nature, language, history, and poetry. And it would no doubt be hard to find a better statement of their basic agreement on this point than Emerson's statement (quoted earlier in this chapter) to the effect that only by new infusions of the Spirit may we hope to achieve reforms.

CONCLUSION

Although Emerson had already given up his ministry in 1832, the idea of being a preacher remained essential to his self-understanding.[13] The other, perhaps even more important, part of his identity involved being a poet, just as was the case with Grundtvig. Hence, we are justified in concluding our brief comparison by saying that Grundtvig and Emerson were *poet-preachers* following a calling to serve as nineteenth-century reformers and national awakeners. In this respect, and with the benefit of historical distance, we may see them as different representatives of an enlightened counter-enlightenment, which is reflected in the often paradoxical mix of Enlightenment and Romantic ideas in their writings. Both men strove to accomplish a spiritual reform centring on the Christian virtues of faith, hope, and the sentiment of love, as Emerson formulates it in "Man the Reformer" (cf. Sacks 2008, 111ff.).

Why do we still remember and revere them? Grundtvig and Emerson were great men, yes, but this does not go far enough to explain our continued fascination and attraction. I believe we come closer to the core of the matter by realizing that they chastized us but, at the same time, elevated us by insisting that we may each communicate directly with the divine and receive life-giving energy by way of Spirit. Is it necessary to add that this dialectic is a Christian figure of thinking (law versus gospel)? If this is the aspect of the preacher, we should not overlook or forget the poet, or, to be more specific, the importance of conveying a message in a certain form. Both Grundtvig and Emerson were acutely aware that *what* is said cannot be separated from the *way* it is said. Perhaps, then, it is not least by their poems and the poetry in their writings that they have managed to touch, stir, and influence our sense of national identity and of belonging to a community (cf. Baunvig, chap. 11, this volume).

NOTES

1 I am indebted to Ove Kaj Pedersen for inspiration and helpful comments to this abridged version of a much longer first draft.

2 Taylor (2007, 3) points to "a move from a society where belief in God is unchallenged and indeed, unproblematic, to one in which it is understood to be one option among others, and frequently not the easiest to embrace." Secularity 3 (i.e., in its third meaning), in other words, "puts an end to the naïve acknowledgment of the transcendent, or of goals or claims which go beyond human flourishing" (21).

3 For more on Grundtvig as a political thinker, see Korsgaard (2012); and Dalsgaard (chapter 15, this volume).

4 A similar note is struck in Emerson's (1971, 157) lecture "Man the Reformer" (1841), in which he states: "I see at once how paltry is all this generation of unbelievers, and what a house of cards their institutions are."

5 Interestingly, Grundtvig was no admirer of the new American nation. Thus, in a late addition to his world history, in 1869, he discusses "Naturalism" as the cultural feature threatening to destroy European civilization. And it is this same spirit that he considers responsible for the (according to Grundtvig) illegitimate establishment of the American republic. Thus, he characterizes the revolt in 1776 as a "foolhardy, childish, and spiteful breach of the eternal laws of history" (cf. Nyborg 2012, 129).

6 Like Emerson, Grundtvig was well versed in German idealist philosophy. More than Emerson, who eagerly adopted Coleridge's romantic transformation of the Kantian concepts "Understanding" and "Reason,"

Grundtvig was ambivalent towards, but primarily critical of, Kant, Fichte, and Schelling because he saw the ideas of autonomy and reason as a threat to Christian faith.

7 Danish bishop Hans L. Martensen (1808–84) used this expression to characterize the core of Grundtvig's thinking (cf. Johansen 1948, 182).

8 Buell (1973, 90) opines that, to the transcendentalists, self-culture meant "roughly, the total growth of one's intellectual-moral-spiritual faculties, the ultimate in liberal education. Their literary source for this idea was Goethe; but essentially it was another of Unitarianism's legacies to the movement, formulated most memorably by Dr. Channing, for whom the idea was the quintessence of the Unitarian principle that religion consists chiefly in the improvement of the character." Interestingly, Channing's 1838 lecture on "Self-Culture" was translated into Danish (*Om Selvopdragelse og Dannelse*) and published in 1866.

9 There is a vast scholarly literature devoted to the concept of self-reliance that I cannot go into here. Suffice it to say that some, notably George Kateb (1995), try to separate it from its religious underpinnings, while others argue that self-reliance is actually God-reliance.

10 Buell (2003, 293), however, has a valid point when he comments: "Because Emerson's favorite topic in academic speeches was self-reliant self-fashioning, we easily overlook the extent to which pedagogy itself interested him. Though he hated his stint as a teenage schoolmaster, for most of his adult life he was active in a multitude of volunteer school and university projects. His younger daughter, Edith, recalled that her father's 'interest and sympathy about every detail of school affairs and school politics' was 'unbounded.'"

11 In an early lecture from 1837 Emerson declares: "The great object of education should be commensurate with the object of life. It should be a moral one; to teach self-trust ... Thus would education conspire with the Divine Providence" (quoted in Mott 2010, 153).

12 The economic aspects of lecturing in the lyceums is explained at length by Emerson in a letter to Carlyle dated 30 April 1835 (see Carlyle and Emerson 1888, 55ff.).

13 In a letter to Carlyle (2 November 1837) Emerson explains how he regards preaching in the lyceum as his proper calling: "I find myself so much more and freer on the platform of the lecture-room than in the pulpit, that I shall not much more use the last; and do now only in a little country chapel at the request of simple men to whom I sustain no other relation than that of preacher. But I preach in the Lecture-Room and then it tells, for there is no prescription. You may laugh, weep, reason, sing, sneer, or

pray, according to your genius. It is the new pulpit and very much in vogue with my northern countrymen" (Carlyle and Emerson 1888, 137).

REFERENCES

Augst, T. 1999. "Composing the Moral Senses: Emerson and the Politics of Character in Nineteenth-Century America." *Political Theory* 27 (1): 85–120.

Bellah, R.N. 1967. "Civil Religion in America." *Dædalus* 96 (1): 1–21.

Broadbridge, E., trans. and ed., C. Warren and U. Jonas, co-eds. 2011. *The School for Life: N.F.S. Grundtvig on Education for the People*. Aarhus: Aarhus University Press.

Buell, L. 1973. *Literary Transcendentalism: Style and Vision in the American Renaissance*. Ithaca: Cornell University Press.

– 2003. *Emerson*. Cambridge, MA: The Belknap Press of Harvard University Press.

Carlyle, T., and R.W. Emerson. 1888. *The Correspondence of Thomas Carlyle and Ralph Waldo Emerson, 1834–1872*. Vol. 1. Boston, MA: Ticknor and Company.

Cavell, S. 2003. *Emerson's Transcendental Etudes*. Stanford, CA: Stanford University Press.

Emerson, R.W. 1971. *The Collected Works of Ralph Waldo Emerson*. Vol. 1: *Nature, Addresses, and Lectures*. Cambridge, MA: The Belknap Press of Harvard University Press.

Field, P.S. 2001. "'The Transformation of Genius into Practical Power': Ralph Waldo Emerson and the Public Lecture." *Journal of the Early Republic* 21 (3): 467–93.

Hallengren, A. 1994. *The Code of Concord: Emerson's Search for Universal Laws*. Stockholm: Almqvist and Wiksell International.

Johansen, S. 1948. *Grundtvigs Erindringer og Erindringer om Grundtvig* [Grundtvig's recollections and recollections of Grundtvig]. Copenhagen: C.A. Reitzel.

Kateb, G. 1995. *Emerson and Self-Reliance*. Thousand Oaks, CA: Sage.

Korsgaard, O. 2012. *Grundtvig*. Copenhagen: DJØF.

Mott, W.T. 2010. "Education." In *The Oxford Handbook of Transcendentalism*, ed. J. Myerson, S.H Petrulionis, and L.D. Walls. New York: Oxford University Press.

Nevers J. 2011. *Fra skældsord til slagord: Demokratibegrebet i dansk politisk historie* [From invective to slogan: The concept of democracy in Danish political history]. Odense: Syddansk Universitetsforlag.

Nyborg, O. 2012. “Grundtvig og naturalismen” [Grundtvig and naturalism]. *Grundtvig Studier* (vol. 63) : 109–44.
Sacks, K., ed. 2008. *Emerson: Political Writings (Cambridge Texts in the History of Political Thought)*. Cambridge: Cambridge University Press.
Saito, N. 2005. *The Gleam of Light: Moral Perfectionism and Education in Dewey and Emerson*. New York: Fordham University Press.
Taylor, C. 2007. *A Secular Age*. Cambridge, MA: The Belknap Press of Harvard University Press.
Tocqueville, A. de. 1969. *Democracy in America*. New York: Harper Perennial.
Wilson, A.N. 1999. *God's Funeral: A Biography of Faith and Doubt in Western Civilization*. New York: Ballantine.

15

Community and Individuality: Grundtvigian and Kierkegaardian Protestantism in Denmark

MATIAS MØL DALSGAARD

INTRODUCTION

The Danish priest Carl Koch, who was born in 1860, five years after the death of Søren Kierkegaard and twelve years before the death of N.F.S. Grundtvig, once recounted: "Someone told me that he had seen Grundtvig and Kierkegaard walking together along Østergade [a street in central Copenhagen]. Grundtvig progressed, steady and broad; Kierkegaard, playfully mobile, at one moment on one side and the next moment on the other side of his companion – all during vivid conversation. Then they arrived at the gate that Grundtvig was heading towards; he tipped his hat; Kierkegaard bowed deeply and took off his hat with great reverence" (Holm 2009, cover, my translation).

This account, which might or might not be historically correct, is one of the few that we have of a direct encounter between Grundtvig and Kierkegaard, two contemporary intellectual giants in mid-nineteenth-century Copenhagen. Grundtvig (1783–1872) was twenty years older than Kierkegaard (1813–55) and already a celebrated writer, priest, and Danish church father during the years of Kierkegaard's intellectual formation. Thus, the picture of a self-confident, elderly Grundtvig walking along Østergade with a young, eager, and gesticulating Kierkegaard by his side seems plausible. But the picture symbolizes more than mere difference in age: it symbolizes two different positions in the intellectual and Christian life of nineteenth-century Copenhagen. Despite having suffered long periods of censorship by, and being marginalized from, the established church and authorities in his early life, during his lifetime Grundtvig became the epicentre of the church and social movement labelled "Grundtvigianism." Kierkegaard never became the centre of any popular movement but, rather, remained at the fringes of the establishment. His theology and writings gained significant attention and caused public commotion and scandal, but they remained the voice of the individual and of individual faith as opposed to the established church and religion. "Kierkegaard, playfully mobile, at one moment on one side and the next moment on the other side of his companion": this was Kierkegaard's position in Copenhagen – the restless, doubting, individual believer.

If a person's funeral can be seen as his or her last statement, the funerals of Grundtvig and Kierkegaard show the great differences in their positions on Christianity and public and intellectual life in general. Grundtvig received the funeral of a statesman, one of the largest in Danish history. Allegedly, more than three hundred Danish priests participated, and Grundtvig's Norwegian follower and later Nobel Prize winner Bjørnstjerne Bjørnson gave a famous speech inspiring the future life of the Grundtvigian movement (*Den Store Danske*). Kierkegaard's funeral, on the other hand, attracted a relatively large crowd – reportedly around one thousand persons. But, according to the then bishop of Zeeland, H.L. Martensen, a representative of the established church, this crowd consisted of "young people and obscure persons. No notabilities were present" (Garff 2000, i, my translation). Not only were no notabilities present, but a young follower of Kierkegaard, his nephew Lund, caused great scandal when, during the ceremony, he stepped forth with Kierkegaard's writings and the Gospel in his hands, protesting against the church for taking possession of the body of his deceased uncle (ii–iii).

Kierkegaard was scandalous, while Grundtvig became the epicentre of a broad Danish Christian and cultural movement. Later, Kierkegaard became world famous as philosopher, theologian, and writer, and he obtained a central position within twentieth-century Danish theology. Grundtvig, despite being a central figure in Danish Christianity, remains relatively unknown outside of Denmark. His thoughts and writings have been far less exportable than Kierkegaard's. This is most likely so because the nation-building dimension of his work is aimed at building not just any nation but, specifically, the Danish nation. In Kierkegaard's writings we find no interest in nation or nationality. Kierkegaard's writings on Christianity and existence are not tied to any notion of "nation" or "people" and are thus exportable. Hence, although, over the last two hundred years, Grundtvig and Kierkegaard are the two most influential figures in Danish theology, they have very different backgrounds.

TWO VOICES OF DANISH PROTESTANTISM

In comparing Grundtvig and Kierkegaard I argue that, despite significant differences in their understandings of Christianity, the individual, and society, they also share certain fundamental traits. The differences are related to their differing notions of the role of culture and community in the life of the individual Christian. In particular, it is the notions of nation and nationality that set the two thinkers apart. Kierkegaard stresses individual faith while Grundtvig stresses a shared faith and the imagination of the community. However, underneath these differences Kierkegaard and Grundtvig share a radical notion of individual spiritual freedom, and it is this that governs their theologies and styles of writing.

What Grundtvig and Kierkegaard have in common I label "Danish Protestantism." Dogmatically, both Grundtvig and Kierkegaard operate within the framework of Lutheran theology; however, within this framework, in style and thought, they both emphasize individual and spiritual freedom. My notion of Danish Protestantism does not imply that thoughts similar to those of Grundtvig and Kierkegaard cannot be found outside of Denmark; rather, it attempts to show that their conflicting thoughts and theologies have features in common – features that are easily overlooked and that can help us to understand how Protestantism has taken a particular shape in Denmark. My concern is how Danish Protestantism developed and expressed dialectic notions of human freedom and shared belonging that are both individually liberating and socially binding.

It should be noted that my focus is on "the self" rather than on the institutional dimensions of Danish Protestantism. What I am concerned with is the level of self that Charles Taylor, for example, investigates in *Sources of the Self* (Taylor 1989): What are the pictures or ideas of the human being, of society, and of the divine that shape the basic notions of self in Grundtvig and Kierkegaard? What pictures of "good" or "true" Christian living are governing the thoughts and writings of the two thinkers? And what notions and feelings of self are evoked in their writings?

CONFLICTING NOTIONS OF INDIVIDUAL AND SOCIETY

Uniting Grundtvig and Kierkegaard under "Danish Protestantism" is not without its problems. The Grundtvigian and Kierkegaardian branches of Christianity have traditionally viewed each other with great animosity. Adherents of Grundtvig have tended to dislike Kierkegaard and vice versa,[1] and, in their own texts, Grundtvig and Kierkegaard criticized, if not mocked, each other (Holm 2009).

This mutual animosity is not simply a result of politics or misunderstandings. Grundtvig's and Kierkegaard's visions of Christianity conflict with each other. Or to put it differently: Grundtvig and Kierkegaard cannot be liked at the same time. The pictures of good or true Christian living that they present tend to cancel each other out. An increase in affection for one picture leads to a decrease in affection for the other. Grundtvig offers a Christianity of shared enthusiasm and imagination, whereas Kierkegaard offers a Christianity of individual responsibility, of fear and trembling. A mocking 1847–48 journal entry by Kierkegaard clearly shows how their visions of true religious life collide. In the perspective of the stern, individual Christianity of Kierkegaard, Grundtvig's enthusiastic and imaginative Christianity lacks the true virtues of Christian living: "Grundtvig does not know of the piety of the quiet suffering (which is the right piety). Grundtvig is and will always be noisy, even in eternity I will find him disagreeable … Grundtvig is a yodeling fellow [*jodlende friskfyr*] or a roaring blacksmith" (Kierkegaard 1997–2012, 20:290, my translation).

Grundtvig views Christianity as a collective practice carried out in culture and congregation, whereas Kierkegaard views any sort of collectivity (in the name of Christianity or not) with great suspicion.[2] For Kierkegaard the collective is primarily a place to hide from individual responsibility: it is never in itself a true source of Christian or ethical living. Grundtvig, on the other hand, sees Kierkegaard's attack on established religious practice as purely negative and as lacking a positive notion of Christian and spiritual life on earth (Grundtvig 1909, 9:417ff.). Accordingly, Grundtvig and Kierkegaard have had rather different audiences and followers. Whereas "Grundtvigianism" has been a broad and influential movement within practical Danish church and school life, Kierkegaard has primarily been read within the academy and by individual devotees. Kierkegaard thus became the major source of inspiration for the Danish strand of dialectical theology known as

Tidehverv (change of times), a strand that was never for the masses but only for the intellectual elite in Danish theology.

The differences in Grundtvig's and Kierkegaard's views on true Christian living are reflected in their conceptions of nation and nationality. Contrary to Kierkegaard, Grundtvig develops a positive notion of nation, or people, within his theology. To Grundtvig Christianity must take place in – and thus depend upon – a national language and tradition. The popular spirit of a nation (*folkeånd*), which thrives on language and tradition, is the foundation for the development of Christian spirit (Grundtvig 1909, 9:82; Thaning 1963). National spirit and Christian spirit mutually reinforce each other. It is, however, crucial for Grundtvig to defend himself against the allegation that he conflates nationality and Christianity. According to him, nationality and Christianity coexist but pertain to two different dimensions of life. Christianity is a "heavenly guest" in the earthly home of the people.[3] Nevertheless, in Grundtvig's thought the notions of nationality and Christianity stand in an inherently dynamic relationship to one another and the one cannot fully be understood without the other. This is evident, for instance, in his popular hymn "Den signede dag" (the blessed day), the last stanza of which begins "Så rejse vi til vort fædreland, dér ligger ej dag i dvale" (We journey unto our fatherland, where day is not frail nor fleeting) (*Den danske salmebog* 2002, 402).[4] *Fædreland* (fatherland) is the Danish word for native country or homeland, but, in the hymn, its metaphorical meaning is the kingdom of heaven. The notion of fatherland in this instance informs our understanding of heaven, which, in turn, throws a heavenly light upon, or provides an uplifting spirit to, the concrete fatherland.

Kierkegaard, as mentioned, rejects any notion that nationalism has relevance for Christianity, which he sees has having taken a step forward from the nationalisms of Judaism and paganism (Holm 2009, 134; Tudvad 2010). Christianity presents a universal gospel to the individual, and celebrating or even thematizing the national within Christianity represents a lapse into a pre-Christian worldview. Kierkegaard mocks Grundtvig's interest in Old Norse literature, which to Grundtvig, is a central source of the Danish national spirit but which, to Kierkegaard, is nothing but "Old Horse."[5] The national myths celebrated by Grundtvig have no reality or moral relevance in Kierkegaard's universe.

These different perceptions lead to very different forms of engagement with national politics. Kierkegaard's engagement in politics is basically confined to a few critical remarks on "the masses." He remained anti-democratic, observing the democratic movement and take-over of government in the 1840s with great scepticism (Garff 2005). And he never engaged in any "national causes" or in any "mobilization of the people." Kierkegaard was in favour of the monarchy, and in this he never wavered. The people were dangerous not so much as a political force but, rather, as a category. The problem with "the people," or with government by the people, was not so much that the majority would rule but that, upon becoming part of a "people," the individual would start caring about the wrong things. For the religious mind, people were a distraction. Kierkegaard, for instance, writes in the *Postscript*: "Of all kinds of government, the monarchy is the best. More than any other it favors and preserves the quiet imaginations and innocent madness of the private person. Only democracy, the most tyrannical kind of government, obliges everyone to positive participation ... Is it tyranny that one person wants to govern so that the rest of us do not have to? No, but it is tyranny that everybody wants to govern" (Kierkegaard 1997–2012, 7:563, my translation). It is Kierkegaard as priest, as "shepherd of the souls," not as politician who warns against the people. He warns against the people becoming politicized. Had Kierkegaard been familiar with the statement by his famous contemporary, that religion is the opium of the people, he might have concurred – and responded that the people is the opium of the soul.

Grundtvig, too, was hesitant to embrace democracy as a mode of government. But his position was less adamant than Kierkegaard's, and, over the years, he developed a favourable view of democracy. Grundtvig's initial scepticism was guided not so much by a principled opposition towards democracy as such but, rather, by pragmatic reasoning. For instance, in 1834 Grundtvig stated that the peasants were not yet ready to govern either themselves or the country. For this they needed education. But Grundtvig saw the solution to this situation as the education of the peasants, not a principled opposition to a democratic government run by the peasants (Korsgaard 2011). Throughout his life, the many different stances and statements Grundtvig makes regarding democracy seem to reflect pragmatic circumstances rather than principled positions for or against democracy. As far as Grundtvig was concerned, the basic aim was to mobilize, spiritually awaken, and educate "the people." And, to the extent that democracy could serve this aim, it could be a legitimate mode of government.

SHARED NOTIONS OF FREEDOM

The Lutheran Heritage

Despite conflicting visions of Christian living, the thoughts and works of Grundtvig and Kierkegaard do have fundamental similarities. Both men maintain a Lutheran "negativity" at the core of their thought and writing, and this negativity, in turn, produces their choice of writing style as well as their visions of individual freedom and sociality.

With a reference to Luther, Kierkegaard (1997–2012, 13:46, my translation) in the 1851 text *Judge for Yourself!*, states: "Faith is an unquiet thing." This Lutheran statement could have issued from either Kierkegaard or Grundtvig. They both vehemently criticize notions of Christianity that reduce faith to a quiet thing. Both attack the Christianity of safety – that is, versions of Christianity in which the living and passionate nature of faith comes under the yoke of a rationalized or institutionalized notion of grace or justification. Unsurprisingly, they both – being good Lutherans – applaud Luther's break from the justification industry of the sixteenth-century papal church (Grundtvig 1909, 9:415). But this Lutheran stance does apply only to an easily criticized church of the past. Grundtvig and Kierkegaard criticize the established church and religion of their own time as well. They are both highly critical of the concept of a state church that, in effect, turns Christian life into a matter of being a citizen of the Christian state. Kierkegaard, in both his philosophical and theological texts, mocks and criticizes the bourgeois Christianity of his time, and Grundtvig agrees with Kierkegaard that being Christian cannot be reduced to a matter of mere "Christian citizenship" and regular church attendance (Grundtvig 1909, 9:417).

Similarly, Grundtvig and Kierkegaard both attack the various strands of enlightenment rationalism. Philosophically, Kierkegaard delivers the most elaborate attack in his criticism of Hegelian speculative philosophy (cf. Stewart 2003). It is the underlying premise of Kierkegaard's critique of Hegel that faith and Christian living are not a matter of speculation – that is, that existence and thinking belong to two different categories. See, for instance, *Concluding Unscientific Postscript* (Kierkegaard 1997–2012, 7) and *Fear and Trembling* (Kierkegaard 1997–2012, vol. 4). In the Hegelianism of his time, Kierkegaard saw a tendency to reduce Christian existence to a matter of intellectual reflection and, thus, a tendency to reduce the content of faith to human understanding. Faith is part of the here and now, not a theory that exists outside the present moment. Grundtvig takes a similar stance against the rationalism of his time. Philosophically, his stance is less sophisticated than Kierkegaard's, and it is aimed at adversaries other than Hegelian speculation. However, in general, Grundtvig criticizes attempts to turn questions regarding the truth of Christianity into scientific or scholarly endeavours. In 1825, after he came to the conclusion that the life of the church and congregation rather than the text of the Bible is Christianity's true, continuity-establishing core (Grundtvig's so called great discovery, or *mageløse opdagelse*), he attacked the "exegetical papacy" of the theologians of his time. The truth of Christianity is not owned by the scholarly trained theologians; rather, it belongs to everybody through religious service and, first and foremost, through the statement of the Creed.

At the core of Grundtvig's and Kierkegaard's attacks on rationalism lie their notions of, respectively, paradox and enigma. Kierkegaard develops his notion "paradox of faith" by showing how faith involves a leap beyond the straightforward or scientifically comprehensible. Grundtvig insists on the notion of enigma (*gåde*) when discussing human and, therefore, religious life (see, for example, Korsgaard 1997). These notions are not identical. Paradox is an epistemological term while enigma is a mythic or poetic term. The two notions do, however, influence Grundtvig's and Kierkegaard's authorships in comparable ways. While insisting on the notions of paradox and enigma at the core of human and religious life, they both develop styles of writing that assume that true religious living cannot be a matter of finite theory. Since – at the core of religious living – there is no theoretical truth to be learned, both Grundtvig and Kierkegaard develop writing styles that are poetic and performative rather than descriptive. In other words, they develop writing styles that invite the reader to follow the (imaginative) movements of faith rather than dogmatic or theoretical truths.

The Use of Poetic Style

In an unpublished text, Grundtvig once stated that he did not know of any question more difficult than the question about the borderline between literal and figurative, or prosaic and poetic, speech (Thyssen 1991, 194). This points to his weakness as well as to his strength as a thinker and writer. It is very difficult to translate Grundtvig's theology into other languages, and this is primarily because he offers no theology in the strict sense of the word. Grundtvig's theology is poetic, inviting the reader to view him- or herself as part of the religious, historic, and national visions that his writings provide. His major work on Nordic mythology, for instance, is as much a piece of mythology as it is a work on mythology (Grundtvig 1909, 5:376ff.). This quality of Grundtvig's writing may be viewed as a product of his notion of enigma. If, at the end of life, there is enigma rather than finite theory, then teaching the religious and worldly fundamentals of life should set in motion a living imagination rather than provide finite answers to fundamental questions. Grundtvig's hallmark struggle for the "living word" as opposed to the "dead word" shows itself in his writings (see, for instance, Grundtvig 1909, 9:407ff.).

Kierkegaard's writings have similar qualities. Kierkegaard is often referred to as the poet-philosopher – the philosopher whose writings are closer in style to literature than to philosophy. Neither as a philosopher nor as a theologian does Kierkegaard deliver any systematic or steadfast theory. His concern as a writer is not the communication to the reader of any objective truth but, rather, the reader's subjective appropriation of truth. He thus develops a whole range of writer-pseudonyms, which, in different perspectives and with different literary styles, approach the themes and existential challenges of Christian living. In his unpublished *The Dialectic of the Ethical and the Ethical-Religious Communication*, Kierkegaard reflects on this mode of "indirect communication." Referring to Socrates, Kierkegaard states: "My achievement with the writer-pseudonyms has been the discovery of the maieutic within Christianity" (Dalsgaard 2007, 59, my translation). Socrates practised his so-called maieutic method within the field of philosophy and epistemology; Kierkegaard practises his within the field of Christianity and existence. The aim of his method is not to give the reader finite answers to Christian questions but, rather, to provoke a subjective appropriation of and adherence to Christian ideals.

It could be claimed that Grundtvig's and Kierkegaard's theologies are truly Lutheran in that they both insist that human rationality falls short of God's rationality (Dalsgaard 2012). The notions of paradox and enigma do not in themselves make Grundtvig and Kierkegaard stand out from traditional Lutheran theology. In this sense, there is nothing particularly Danish about Grundtvig and Kierkegaard. It is not in theology, as such, that we find the defining characteristics of our "two odd Danes" vis-à-vis Lutheran theology but, rather, in the aesthetic consistency with which they present and develop the paradoxical and enigmatic dimension of Christian life. They produce a Christianity of radical spiritual freedom – not only in theory but also in practice. They consistently produce an "open," or "living," Christianity. This defining trait, I argue, sets their theology apart as a specifically Danish version of Lutheran Protestantism.

In fact, when Grundtvig's and Kierkegaard's visions of Christian life differ it is due to conflicting notions of human nature rather than to conflicting notions of Christianity. For both, Christianity adds a dimension of radical freedom, spirit, and paradox/enigma to human life. But the two thinkers conceive of human nature so differently that their descriptions of Christian life also differ radically. For Grundtvig, human nature begins with the people, or the congregation, whereas for Kierkegaard it begins with the subject, or the individual. But in both cases the role of Christianity is to "uplift," or "awaken," what is naturally given to a new and truer life. For instance, in his brief but concise text on "people and Christianity" (*Folkelighed og Christendom*) Grundtvig describes how the people or the national cultures "in our days awaken within Christianity and stand up against what is foreign [i.e., unnatural] with light and might" (Grundtvig 1909, 985). For his part, Kierkegaard (1997–2012, 9:278), in his major work on Christian ethics, *Works of Love*, describes how Christian love gives courage (*frimodighed*) – that is, helps the individual find the courage to be and to rejoice in being his or her natural self. For Kierkegaard it is the individual self that is waiting for the uplifting "light and might" of Christian love.

CONCLUSIONS AND PERSPECTIVES

Despite conflicting notions of human nature, both Grundtvig and Kierkegaard advance a notion of Christianity that is freedom-oriented, that is of the gospel rather than of the law. In order to see how peculiar this notion is, one might compare it with the North American Puritan Calvinism analyzed by Max Weber and Charles Taylor (Taylor 1989; Weber 2001). To the Puritan Calvinist the question of who belongs to the chosen people remains central. Who is part of God's plan and what moral code of conduct expresses this plan?[6] In Grundtvig and Kierkegaard the question of who belongs to the chosen people does not come up. 'The people' is simply there – the people or the individuals of nineteenth-century Denmark – and what is at stake is the spiritual or existential state of that people.

It has been observed (Gundelach, Iversen, and Warburg 2008) that Denmark represents a paradoxical case, displaying, on the one hand, a very high degree of religious, cultural, and ethnic homogeneity and, on the other hand, a very undogmatic and non-moralistic Christianity. I offer no further discussion of differences between various versions of Protestantism and Protestant cultures. However, in order to understand the call for radical freedom in the Danish Protestantism of Grundtvig and Kierkegaard, it is crucial to keep in mind that this call occurs within a relatively homogeneous culture and society. This call for freedom should not be confused with a call for moral lawlessness. It is a call for spiritual freedom within the realms of a stable law-abiding society. The aim is not to identify the chosen people but, rather, to (Christianly) free the spirits of the people who are there.

Hence, Grundtvig and Kierkegaard share a strong emphasis on spiritual freedom. This emphasis is shared within the framework of Lutheran theology and within a relatively homogenous culture and ethos. But what remains a question of conflict between the two Danish giants and their followers is whether spiritual freedom is a task primarily for "the people" or for "the individual believer."

NOTES

1 Compare with, for instance, Jan Lindhardt's (2002, 10ff) description of the troubled relationship between the Kierkegaardian Johannes Sløk and the more Grundtvigian Hal Koch.

2 Grundtvig thus identifies the true signs of a "living Christianity" as confession, preaching, and hymn in the mother tongue of the Christian community (Grundtvig 1909, 9:408). Kierkegaard, on the other hand, would never call any specific practice a true sign of Christianity. Consider, for instance, his mocking of the notion of a "believing congregation" in the *Concluding Unscientific Postscript* (Kierkegaard 1997–2012 [1846], 7:124). To Kierkegaard, Christian life and belief is individual and subjective (i.e., without any knowable "true signs").

3 See, for instance, the text "Folkelighed og Christendom" from 1847 (Grundtvig 1909, 9:80–8). The notion *folkelighed* is notoriously difficult to translate into English. "Folk" means "people," and *folkelighed* points to the popular and traditional life of the people. When I use the term "nation" this can be misleading in that *folkelighed* does not (necessarily) involve any sense of nationalism. *Folkelighed*, as Grundtvig originally used it, is an inclusive rather than an exclusive notion. It positions the traditionally low culture of the people (which, to Grundtvig, primarily meant the farmers) as the high, or true, culture of the nation.

4 Translation by Rolf Færch at www.danishmission.net.

5 In 1844 Kierkegaard, in his journal, refers to Grundtvig as *denne ølnordiske Kæmpe* (Kierkegaard 1997–2012 [1844], 18:220). *Ølnordisk* means "beer-Nordic" and plays on the Danish word *oldnorisk*, which means "ancient Nordic" or "Old Norse." "Old Horse" is my, probably dismal, attempt at an English translation of Kierkegaard's wordplay.

6 Compare with, for instance, the opening lines of a sermon from 1684 by the Boston minister Samuel Willard: "The reason why the Children of God are so little regarded here in the world; it is because the world knows not who they are, not what they are born unto: their great glory for the present is within" (Dutkanicz 2005, 112). Whereas Willard, in these lines, stresses the invisibility of God's works, a clear distinction between those who are chosen (the Children of God) and those who are not is in place. See also Taylor (1989).

REFERENCES

Dalsgaard, M.M. 2007. "Kærlighed og meddelelse: Et etisk forsvar for den andens fravær i Kierkegaards tænkning" [Love and communication: An ethical defence of the other's absence in Kierkegaard]. In *Kierkegaardiana* 24, ed. T.A. Olesen, R. Purkarthofer, and K.B. Soderquist, 49–67. Copenhagen: C.A. Reitzel.

– 2012. *Det protestantiske selv: Kravet om autenticitet i Kierkegaards tænkning* [The Protestant self: The requirement for authenticity in Kierkegaard's thinking]. Copenhagen: ANIS.

Den Danske Salmebog [The Danish hymnbook]. 2002. Det Kgl. Vajsenhus: Copenhagen.

Dutkanicz, D., ed. 2005. *Sinners in the Hands of an Angry God and Other Puritan Sermons*. Mineola, NY: Dover.

Garff, J. 2005. *SAK: Søren Aabye Kierkegaard – En biografi* [SAK: Søren Aabye Kierkegaard – A biography]. Copenhagen: Gads Forlag.

Grundtvig, N.F.S. 1904–09: *Grundtvigs Udvalgte Skrifter* [Grundtvig's selected writings], vols. 1–10. Copenhagen: Nordisk Forlag.

Gundelach, P., H.R. Iversen, and M. Warburg, eds. *I hjertet af Danmark* [In the heart of Denmark]. Copenhagen: Hans Reitzels Forlag.

Holm, A. 2009. *To samtidige: Kierkegaards og Grundtvigs kritik af hinanden* [Two contemporaries: Kierkegaard's and Grundtvig's criticisms of each other]. Copenhagen: ANIS.

Kierkegaard, S. 1997–2012. *Søren Kierkegaards Skrifter* [Søren Kierkegaard's writings], vols. 1–27. Copenhagen: Gads Forlag.

Korsgaard, O., ed. 1997. *En Orm – En Gud: Om mennesket i verden* [A worm, a god]. Odense: Odense Universitetsforlag.

– 2011. "Grundtvigs syn på demokrati, 1831–1866" [Grundtvig's views on democracy, 1831–1866]. Aarhus: Danmarkshistorien.dk, Aarhus Universitet.

Lindhardt, J. 2002. *Johannes Sløk: Modernismens teolog* [Johannes Slok: The theologian of modernity]. Frederiksberg: ANIS.

Stewart, J. 2003. *Kierkegaard's Relation to Hegel Reconsidered*. Cambridge: Cambridge University Press.

Taylor, C. 1989. *Sources of the Self*. Cambridge: Cambridge University Press

Thaning, K. 1963. *Menneske først: Grundtvigs opgør med sig selv* [Human first: Grundtvig's showdown with himself]. Copenhagen: Grundtvigselskabet, Gyldendal.

Thyssen, A.P. 1991. *Grundtvig og den grundtvigske arv* [Grundtvig and the legacy of grundtvigianism]. Frederiksberg: Anis.

Tudvad, P. 2010. *Stadier på antisemitismens vej: Søren Kierkegaard og jøderne* [Stages on the way to anti-Semitism: Soren Kierkegaard and the Jews]. Copenhagen: Rosinante.

Weber, Max. 2001. *The Protestant Ethic and the Spirit of Capitalism*. London: Routledge Classics.

PART FIVE

Transmission

16

Grundtvig's Idea of a People's High School and Its Historical Influence

OVE KORSGAARD

THREE PHASES IN THE BUILDING OF THE DANISH NATION

Danish history from 1848 to 1945 tells the story of how three classes – the civil service, the peasantry, and the working class – were, by turns, the motive power that built the Danish nation-state. The civil servants gathered together as a political grouping in "the National Liberals," which, however, was not a party in the modern sense. The peasants joined the Left Party, which is now the Danish Liberal Party (or *Venstre*, in Danish). And the working class formed the Social Democratic Party. In cultural terms, the educated citizenry made up the core of the National Liberal network, the Grundtvigian movement made up that of the left, and the workers movement made up that of the Social Democratic Party.

Politically, the civil service officials were only dominant for a brief period, from 1848 to 1864. They nevertheless formed a kind of alliance with the old landed gentry that came back to power following Denmark's disastrous military defeat to Germany in 1864. This alliance managed to prevent the left from taking over the government until 1901, but it could not stop the peasantry from taking the lead in economic business and civil society. Under the government of the landed gentry from 1864 to 1901 the peasantry won an economic and cultural influence that was exceptional in the European context. In the power vacuum that arose after the fall of the National Liberals, the cultural shock wave of the peasantry – that is, popular Grundtvigianism – was the only movement that could fill the gap; the workers movement had yet to see the light of day.

Table 16.1 Movements involved in building the Danish nation, 1848–1945

	1848–1864–1901	*1901–1929*	*1929–1945*
Classes	Civil Service officials Landed gentry	The peasantry	The working-class
Political parties	National Liberals Right	Left Radical Left	Social Democrats Radical Left
Cultural movements	Educated citizenry/ 1864 Grundtvigian movement	Grundtvigian movement/Labor movement	Labor movement/ Grundtvigian movement

Left enjoyed only a brief period in power and occasionally had to cede it – first to the breakaway party, the Radical Left (now the Social Liberal Party) formed in 1905 and, later, to the Social Democrats from 1924 to 1926. In 1929, the latter finally assumed power in its own right and, in close collaboration with the Social Liberal Party, became the party behind the formation of the Danish nation-state in the 1930s. This happened under a symbolic refrain that held that liberal democracy should become social democracy and the liberal state a welfare state – even though the phrase "welfare state" was not used until after the Second World War.

The dominant class structure, the political parties, and the cultural movements involved in building the Danish nation between 1848 and 1945 are illustrated in table 16.1.

GRUNDTVIG'S IDEAS FOR A PEOPLE'S HIGH SCHOOL

Grundtvig's entrance onto the political stage and the development of his ideas for a People's High School were very much incited by political events in Denmark and the rest of Europe in the 1830s and 1840s. In particular, the 1830 July Revolution in Paris reverberated throughout Europe, leading to disturbances in Holland and Poland, and even in Denmark. In November 1830 a young Danish civil servant in the German Chancellery, Uwe Jens Lornsen, published a twelve-page booklet that attracted great attention. In *Ueber das Verfassungswerk in Schleswigholstein* (On the Constitution in Schleswig-Holstein) Lornsen argues that the duchies of Schleswig and Holstein should have a free constitution and share only "kings and enemies" with Denmark. Simultaneously, the German Confederation was pressuring King Frederik VI to make good on his 1814 promise to introduce a States General for Holstein. When he finally did so in 1831 and 1834, four consultative provincial assemblies were set up in Denmark and the duchies: two in Denmark (at Roskilde and Viborg) and one each in Schleswig (in the city of Schleswig) and in Holstein (in Itzehoe).

The establishment of these assemblies contributed very much to Grundtvig's development of his ideas for a People's High School. Grundtvig gradually came to realize that this pre-democratic institution could benefit the country in general, that is, if its members had better opportunities to receive an education and, hence, enlightenment. But this required a new kind of high school, a *People's High School*, based on the *people's* language. The idea of a People's High School was first advocated in 1831, in Grundtvig's first real political work, *Political Considerations, with a Glance at Denmark and Holstein*. It is no coincidence that he developed his educational philosophy and his political philosophy side by side in the same work, for the building of any society involves the building of the personality, both that of the individual and the of the nation. While Rousseau developed the link between political and educational philosophy in his classic works of 1762, *The Social Contract* and *Emile*, Grundtvig merely intimated this link in his *Political Considerations*; however, it was an intimation that, over the following twenty years, he expanded into a full-blown philosophy.

Grundtvig formulated the revolutionary idea that one could become an enlightened and educated person through the *language of the people*. This ideal – inspired by Herder – led him to direct a long and vehement attack on the academic schooling of his time, which demanded Latin as the entry ticket to education and a good career. Since attendance at the Latin schools was limited to a small minority, the link between Latin and education inevitably opened up a major divide between "the educated elite" and "the common people." As Grundtvig (2011, 65) writes, he was attempting to "link the culture of the educated to that of the people."

Grundtvig's ambition was to establish a large People's High School in Sorø that was to be a teaching establishment for the adult youth of Denmark. As the opposite pole to the Latin-based education of the academic elite, the People's High School was to contribute to the development of a "Danish" education. Once Grundtvig had come to the conclusion that Danish was a perfectly suitable language for education, he led a frontal attack on the dominant cultural tradition that regarded Latin as a prerequisite for cultural education. In so doing he clashed with the National

Liberal politician J.N. Madvig, who, in 1848, as minister of education, rejected Grundtvig's plan for a People's High School in Sorø.

THE EDUCATED CITIZENRY

While Grundtvig was inspired by Herder's *people's* nationalism, the National Liberals were strongly influenced by Hegel's *state* nationalism and the attendant idea that the will of the people should be administered by the educated elite. In reality, the National Liberals sought a kind of elite democracy, with themselves in the driver's seat. However, after Denmark's defeat by Prussia in 1864 the educated citizenry lost its political and cultural legitimacy, a fact that was decisive in the formation of nationalist sentiment in Denmark. In contrast to the National Liberals, the Grundtvigians did not link the concept of the people to the "state" but, rather, to "civil society." In the Danish context this meant that what belonged to the people became more or less synonymous with what did *not* belong to the state (at least in the liberal tradition).

The weakening of the educated citizenry and the strengthening of the Grundtvigians after 1864 was decisive for the building of the Danish nation. In his classic work *The Decline of the German Mandarins* the American historian Fritz K. Ringer (1969) documents how the German-educated citizenry of Germany was a significant factor in the development of German cultural nationalism. This citizenry consisted primarily of civil servants (such as priests, jurists, professors, senior teachers, and doctors), and, throughout the nineteenth century, it built up a position based more on cultural learning than on aristocratic traditions or economic and political power. For the German bourgeoisie *Bildung* (self-cultivation) was the central cultural concept, drawing a front line between "culture" and "civilization." *Bildung* had to do with *inner* cultivation as opposed to civilization, which had its roots in a rationalist utilitarianism. As bearers and stewards of a German *Geist* the academically educated citizenry served very much to legitimize the authority of the German state. This explains the marked difference that arose between Denmark and Germany with regard to popular education, even though a strengthening of the national cultural interest was a theme common to both.

In contrast to Germany, in Denmark the linking of political power to the academic elite was destroyed, as we have seen, by the events that led to the national disaster of 1864. Whereas the German academics stepped up their efforts to legitimize the state as the core of the German nation, their Danish colleagues lost their legitimacy as bearers of the state's identity. A number of their leaders doubted that Denmark even *had* a future as a nation. This was particularly true of the prime minister, D.G. Monrad, the man who came to personify the disaster. After Denmark's defeat to Germany he immigrated to New Zealand, shattered by feelings of defeat and a fear of destruction.

Nevertheless, the educated citizenry of Denmark attempted to make its presence felt *after* 1864. In 1870, the National Liberal professor H.N. Clausen almost begged the Danish people to accept the form of education dispensed by the universities. He ended a speech in connection with the king's birthday with the words: "I cannot leave this rostrum, which bears the words 'In Spirit and Truth', without adding one prayer more – for our people: that they may become more and more worthy of help from above, and better and better at using that help, when the time of help arrives" (Clausen 1870, 14). In other words, by allowing themselves to be guided by professors lecturing from their university platforms, the rest of the population would gain a share in the clear light that emanated from men of education.

Although for the rest of the century the educated citizenry continued to enjoy considerable influence, it cannot be compared with the influence that their German counterparts exercised over the German state. In Denmark it was Grundtvigian ideas on education that came to exert increasing influence, making their mark on the development of civil society in the form of free schools, free churches, and free organizations. In Grundtvigian thought, freedom and voluntary service are two sides of the same coin. In the final analysis, freedom cannot be *guaranteed* by the state; rather, it must be *ensured* by the people. The shift from state to civil society was not only ideological: it was also dictated by the fact that, right up until 1901, the landed gentry and the king had sufficient power to prevent the left from gaining power.

Professor Lundgreen-Nielsen (1992, 173) summarizes the consequences of Grundtvig's social philosophy and its focus on Danish elements as opposed to the German academics' focus on German elements: "All those factors that in Germany led from Herder and Fichte to the disasters under Wilhelm II and Hitler, led in Denmark to the emergence of the *people's high school*, cooperative movements and parliamentary and popular culture based on discussions and compromises – ideally always with respect for the minority."

THE GRUNDTVIGIAN MOVEMENT

Grundtvig never realized his own plan for opening a People's High School in Sorø. In 1844, however, the first of its kind opened in Rødding in South Jutland, and, over the next few years, several more were established around the country, though not all of them were inspired by Grundtvig's ideas. Among the most important men to develop this new kind of school was Christen Kold, who, as a young teacher, had been dismissed for refusing to teach a number of catechism texts by rote learning. In 1851, he opened a People's High School for young adults and a year later a free school for children – both based on storytelling as an educational method. For him the core of teaching was emotionality – that is, "the teaching of the heart." The core of his educational philosophy was Herder's idea that a pupil should find his or her authentic self. For this to happen, according to both Grundtvig and Kold, we must take as our starting point the language that we learned at our mother's knee. Both men insisted that the language of the peasant could form the basis of education; indeed, it was better for this purpose than Latin.

Kold's People's High School left its mark on posterity. However, it was not until after Denmark's military defeat by Prussia and Austria and the loss of Schleswig/Holstein in 1864 that the People's High Schools inspired by Grundtvig and Kold began their comprehensive expansion and became the school's prototype. From 1865 to 1872 no fewer than fifty new schools opened, the vast majority on the lines set down by Grundtvig and Kold. When Schleswig was lost to the Germans, Rødding People's High School moved north of the new border to the village of Askov. It reopened in 1865 as Askov People's High School and became the model, and the leading, high school in Scandinavia – a true cultural stronghold in Denmark. The other Nordic countries also established high schools, the first in Norway in 1864, then in Sweden in 1868, and then in Finland in 1889.

Nearly all the People's High Schools set out to do two things: (1) to give young boys and girls from the country a *people's* education, the purpose being to integrate them into a national and democratic community and (2) to give them training in agriculture and housekeeping to enable them to improve conditions on the land. The archetypal example of this interplay between culture and training occurred at the first great public meeting at Askov in 1865, where three talks were given: one on Nordic mythology, one on the South Jutland/Schleswig question, and one on horses that contract bone spavin. The same people heard about the world of the Nordic gods, the national issue with Germany, and veterinary measures to combat spavin.

After 1864 the Grundtvigians projected an impressive self-awareness. As the movement advanced, more than ever the "popular" became understood as a counterpoint to the state. Grundtvigians criticized the state educational system (the common school, the Latin school, and the university), hoping to create an alternative, more "popular," system with private schools (for children) and People's High Schools (for young adults). By the time of the 1864 defeat, Grundtvig's "popular" elite, desiring the people's enlightenment, had begun to found a vast number of Grundtvigian private schools and People's High Schools. According to Grundtvigianism, the public school could not, due to its ties to the state, be regarded as truly popular. Only the "free" school could be popular. By virtue of this liberal streak, the notion of the popular had become almost synonymous with what was outside the state. And, in this manner, in Denmark the notion of the popular came to be equated with the liberal notion of "voluntarism." Freedom and the volunteer spirit are, in both traditions, two sides of the same coin. Freedom cannot ultimately be guaranteed by the state; only the people can secure freedom. And that can happen only if they have a foundation in "popular" and "civil" society. Open associations were seen as a sign of a voluntary social solidarity, which, in turn, was seen as the ideal for a grander popular and national society.

THE GRUNDTVIGIAN CULTURAL REVOLUTION

In 1870, the United Left Party was founded as a peasants' party in opposition to the landed gentry and the National Liberals. The United Left established a close relationship with the People's High Schools and the left in a faction still known as People's High School Left. Grundtvig died two years after the party's foundation, but he was barely in his grave before the United Left split into two factions: the Grundtvigian Right and the Grundtvigian Left. Already in 1875 Frederik Hammerich, professor of church history, had published *Grundtvig and the United Left: An Account and a Testimony*, while the following year Pastor Niels Lindberg published *Grundtvig's Political Standpoint*. Hammerich claims that Grundtvig was opposed to the United Left, while Lindberg argus that Grundtvig's views harmonized with those of the new party. The disagreement might almost be said to be a constituent principle in "Grundtvigianism" to this day. It blazed up in the politically turbulent year of 1883 when the Friends of Grundtvig were meeting to celebrate the centenary of his birth. Prior to the event many from the Grundtvigian Right were worried that politics and the various claims on Grundtvig would overshadow the meeting. Their worries were confirmed when the Grundtvigian Left demanded that the People's High Schools commit themselves to the political struggle for parliamentarism. Further tensions were felt with the establishment of People's High Schools based on ideological or religious foundations other than those of Grundtvig and Kold. However, the tensions in these rivalries gradually gave way to an acceptable co-existence – until the 1960s.

The political struggle from 1864 to 1901 was dominated by a single major constitutional question: Was it the king or the people (i.e., the elected Parliament) who chose the government? The Left Party, which was often split into factions, argued with increasing emphasis that Parliament was the highest authority in the land. The Right Party, on the other hand, still wished to keep the executive power well away from the legislative branch. Similar conflicts took place in a number of European countries, but few saw such a tenacious struggle as Denmark. The clash over parliamentary government continued right through to 1901, but it was in the 1870s and 1880s that it was at its most heated – over the question of national defence. The Right Party employed a section in the new Constitution on provisional laws that allowed the king to issue his own provisional laws in special circumstances. The parliamentary speaker, Chresten Berg, led the Left Party's fight against the government and was himself the focal point at the well-attended political meetings that the party held across the country, especially in the summers from 1882 to 1884. In the 1884 election the Left Party won a major victory and Berg anticipated an imminent change of government. But it was not to be. The king continued to support the right-wing government despite the massive left majority in Parliament. Instead of becoming prime minister, Berg was arrested in 1885 after a public meeting in Holstebro at which the chief of police felt that he had been harassed. Berg was subsequently sentenced to six months imprisonment on a prison diet. On his release in 1886, he was carried in triumph from his constituency in Kolding the twenty-nine kilometres to Askov People's High School.

Historians continue to debate the significance of the People's High Schools for political developments in the last three decades of the nineteenth century. Most of them agree that the schools were a precondition for what has been called the Grundtvigian cultural revolution in Denmark. This had an enormous effect on the growth of civil society and also exerted an influence on the capitalist market economy in Denmark. The movement towards internationalization in the 1870s – the first step towards globalization – meant that Danish agriculture was exposed to very tough competition. Cheap grain, mainly from the United States, had gained a foothold in the European markets, thanks to technological developments such as the railway and the steamship. The growing crisis in Danish agriculture gave rise to the demand for protection through customs duties; however, the more dynamic response was to move from vegetable production to stock-rearing. The decision required new research and new knowledge as well as agricultural reforms and a new distribution system. A particular problem concerned whether to build up the new "agro-industry" on a capitalist basis – as urban industrial production was doing – or opt for cooperative principles. For the most part, Danish farmers opted for the latter, organizing their dairies, slaughterhouses, and the distribution network into wholesale cooperative societies. The emphasis on empowerment at the People's High Schools and the general improvement in popular education has often been regarded as central to farmers' choosing the cooperative model (see Hjermitslev, chap. 19, this volume).

In the twentieth century, the Danish People's High Schools and the cooperative movement became internationally known. They inspired, among other things, a series of reform movements in Eastern Europe in the interwar period. But there were a number of countries where the farmers were *not* included in the move to democracy and nation building. When the liberal principle of "the people's right to decide" was accepted at the peace treaty of Versailles in 1919–20 as an international principle, the peasants of many European kingdoms in Europe suddenly became citizens of new republics, but these did not thereby become stable democracies – on the contrary. With the exception of Czechoslovakia, the peasants were *not* integrated into functional democracies in Central and Eastern Europe (Müller 2011). Their integration in Denmark was far from being solely due to Grundtvig, but his constant insistence on the necessity of education during this process without doubt laid the corner-stone.

THE LABOUR MOVEMENT

The Social Democrats' view of "people," "nation," and "democracy" was clarified through the experience of the First World War. The leading Social Democrat, Frederik Borgbjerg, was the first to formulate the ideological platform that the party could draw from the conclusion of the war – namely, that national solidarity comes before international solidarity. The nation should not be seen as a stage of historical development that belonged to the past but, rather, as the basis for the realization of democracy and socialism. The linking of the two was crucial to the concept of "nation" that the Social Democrats gradually developed in the interwar period, and it was also the basis of its entire program: *a strategy of peaceful reform on a democratic basis*. One element in this strategy – inspired by the successful Grundtvigian People's High Schools – was the establishment of workers' colleges, whose ideological profile differed from that of the Grundtvigians. The first such college opened in Esbjerg in 1910. Its driving force was the editor I.P. Sundbo, who, in his youth, had spent three winters at Askov People's High School. On the national question he differed from the Grundtvigian position in being an ardent internationalist. Thus, in 1912, he urged the Danish-minded workers in South Jutland to vote for the German Social Democrats instead of for the Danish-national caucus.

In 1930, the Workers' Educational Association, founded in 1924, took over the Grundtvigian People's High School in Roskilde and turned it into a Workers' High School. The symbol-laden inauguration took place on Whit Monday 1930. A crowd of several thousand listened to a prologue written by a later prime minister, H.C. Hansen, and read by another prime minister-to-be, Hans Hedtoft. The current prime minister, Thorkild Stauning, then gave a speech in which he emphasized how the working class had been vilified and scorned because it lacked education and culture, and how this would still be the case had not the workers set up their *own* educational structures. Next came the principal, Hjalmar Gammelgaard, who spoke of how Grundtvig's ideas on education and democracy had helped to create the very first People's High Schools. Now was the time, he added, for the Workers' High Schools to "give their service to a new phase in the democratic development." Such schools should, of course, impart skills and satisfy the thirst for knowledge; however, first and foremost, they should "seek to build a higher arch over the workers' lives and endeavors." They should help the worker to understand that one can also live "a worthy life in the cottage as much as in the castle." Grundtvig's genial foresight was to confront liberalism's individualism by arguing "that human life can only reach its fulfillment in community" (Gammelgaard 1960, 61ff). The forms of community to which Grundtvig had referred were national and religious; now it was just as natural to refer to the social and the international. The final speaker was the Social Democrat minister of education Frederik Borgbjerg, who prayed that the best of Grundtvig's ideas might live on at the Workers' High School. The socialist anthem *Internationale* ended the day.

It was the Social Democratic government of 1929 that laid out the strategy for the growth of a democratically founded "welfare state." After the election the party teamed up with the Social Liberal Party in the so-called Stauning-Munch government to form the longest-serving administration of the century – from 1929 to 1940. In the same period all the totalitarian ideologies – communism, fascism, and Nazism – subscribed to the main objective in political democracy: "the people." The Italian political philosopher Giovanni Gentile called fascism the most valid form of democracy for the fascist state is "a state of the people, and as such, the democratic state *par excellence*" (quoted in Müller 2011, 106). Furthermore, it was not only the Nordic Social Democrats who stressed social welfare. Soviet communism and German National Socialism had distinct ideas about the welfare state. The combination of socialism and nationalism was a common element in Stalin's communism, Hitler's National Socialism, and among leading Nordic Social Democrats, but only in the Nordic version were these elements combined with democracy.

In 1933, in his book *Pest over Europa* (Plague across Europe), the Danish Social Democrat Hartvig Frisch was the first to draw a frontline against the three ideologies mentioned above, denouncing them all as a threat to democracy. He was particularly interested in the position of the working class in the ideological struggle, squeezed as it was between communist agitation on the one side and fascist and Nazi propaganda on the other. "Every democrat who wishes to take a stance on the problem must realize that this cannot be done academically as a theoretical choice between democracy and dictatorship. The problem is actually to do with the position of the working class in society and its relationship to the other social classes" (Frisch 1993, 10). So it was not just the consciousness of the farmers that was the object of the struggle but also that of the workers. As an antidote to the totalitarian ideologies Frisch points to the Nordic democracies. It was the farmers who "created the political democracy – that honor is theirs. It is the workers' movement that has built on this basis and laid the foundation of 'social democracy'" (13). Hartvig Frisch dedicated his book to Prime Minister Thorvald Stauning, whose home in Kanslergade has acquired mythological significance in Danish history. On 30 January 1933, the very same day that Hitler came to power in Germany, "peasants and workers," the Liberal Party, the Social Liberal Party, and the Social Democrats signed an agreement – the so-called Kanslergade Agreement – on the implementation of reforms to deal with the social and economic crisis that had followed in the wake of the Wall Street Crash in 1929. With Hitler's election Germany chose to tackle the crisis differently.

With Hitler at the German helm the fight for possession of the "nation" and the "people" intensified. Hitler defined the "people" in racial terms: the primary task of the state was to keep the race pure, and this necessitated moving some "peoples" and killing other "peoples" in order to reconstruct Europe on racial principles. The concept of *fuehrer* further degraded the people from being sovereign holders of power to being devotees of a mentor. One of those who expounded this text was the German philosopher Martin Heidegger, who became a Nazi Party member in 1933 and was appointed principal of Freiburg University. In his work he points to the problem, found in all democracies, of "the community's consciousness of its will" – a problem that could only be solved when the will of the *fuehrer* and the will of the people are regarded as twin concepts. According to Heidegger, a community only arises when the leader transforms the people into a company of followers.

Crucial to the positive moves in Denmark was the energy with which, in the interwar years, the Social Democrats threw themselves into the uncompromising struggle for possession of "the people" both figuratively and literally. Borgbjerg and Stauning both knew how dangerous it would be to cede possession of this concept to the totalitarian ideologies; accordingly, their strategy was to distance themselves from the Nazis' definition of "the people" by forging indissoluble links between the "social," the "national," and the "democratic."

The strategy took shape in the new party program, which had the appropriate slogan "Denmark for the People." It was here that "the people" became a core concept in Social Democrat ideology, and it was here that the frontlines were drawn: "We totally oppose the attempt to deprive the people of their right to self-determination. We are fighting against the movement towards dictatorship that bears the name of communism, and we are fighting the various forms of fascism that are now appearing in Denmark ... [W]e will continue to cooperate with nations that rest on democracy's foundations, first and foremost with the Nordic peoples, whose social and political views coincide with the Danish people's traditions, views, and will" (quoted in Reeh 2006). With regard to the concept of "the people of Denmark" – as well as of the other

Scandinavian countries – social democracy has managed to win out against other interpretations by making it the basis of a *social* democracy.

In a 1933 celebration of the 150th anniversary of Grundtvig's birth Frederik Borgbjerg made a speech praising him as a bulwark against anti-democratic currents: "He was a true son of the century of Enlightenment and an 'apprentice to the Germans' ... [B]ut it was not Bismarck's and Hitler's Germany he supported ... The reason why the Danish people cannot be infected by nazism and fascism is not least Grundtvig's mighty effort to educate the people" (Borgbjerg 1933). Borgbjerg points out that Grundtvig was an ardent supporter of free democracy and the broadest franchise possible.

In 1935, prime minister-to-be Hans Hedtoft argued that the Social Democrats should look at the concept of the nation with a fresh pair of eyes. Rather than reject national sentiments as suspect, they should accept them: "Not only were they facts of life; denying them would be like denying they existed. Over the past 20 years in European politics this fatherland-feeling has proved that it is capable of moving millions of people's souls, also within the working-class." Hedtoft pointed out that, after the First World War, German social democracy had been fraught with a series of gruelling theoretical discussions between one wing, which supported *Staatsbejahung* (state acceptance), and another, which supported *Staatsverneinung* (state rejection): "We know the result of this. In Denmark this conflict has not been particularly widespread. The attitude has been positive: 'Walk its path till justice wins the war / and only use the law to change the law.' If you want to practice politics, you cannot avoid the national basis" (Hedtoft-Hansen 1993, 75ff).

A NATIONAL COMPROMISE

The German occupation of Denmark on 9 April 1940 resulted in a strengthening of Grundtvig's position as a national figure around whom the people rallied. On 8 September 1940 – Grundtvig's birthday – the Grundtvig Church in Copenhagen was consecrated. Nine days later the Royal Theatre premiered Kaj Munk's play, *Egelykke*, the subject of which was the young Grundtvig. The following day Professor of Church History Hal Koch began a series of lectures on Grundtvig at Copenhagen University. The queue for the first of these was described in the daily paper *Berlingske Tidende* (1940) as follows: "The Studiegaard yesterday afternoon provided the prelude to a sensational premiere. Three broad queues stretched up to the entrances to the university annex, two from the street, and the third and biggest, consisting of young students, up to the Studiegaardens door." There was far too little seating for an audience of over five hundred, so the subsequent lectures had to be duplicated.

In the fall of 1940, Koch was asked to be the president of the newly established Danish Youth Association (*Dansk Ungdomssamvirke*), whose aim was to counter the impact of Nazism on young Danes. Nazism and fascism confronted Koch with a question: What was supposed to keep Danish society together? When the anti-democratic ideologies were advocating for national-cultural values it was necessary, according to Koch, to focus on political-democratic values. He stipulated that the aim of the Danish Youth Association should be to politicize Danish youth. In this way Koch dissociated himself from the common view of the "cultural" as unifying and the "political" as dividing. "When it comes down to it, it is the political that ties us together" (Koch 1942, 16). That is to say, a democratic ethos.

Koch regretted that the People's High School "ha[d] not acquired the 'political' character that Grundtvig had originally intended." What Grundtvig had wanted was to create "a civic, political school for the youth of the land, without regard to differences of faith or opinion" (Koch 1942, 46). In Koch's view, Grundtvig's intentions were best realized in his view of confirmation, whereby he distanced himself from the centuries-old tradition of church confirmation in favour of a civic confirmation "for all the youth of the country, whatever religious community they belonged to" (47). On this point Koch followed Grundtvig and pointed to history and civic education as the two subjects that ought to constitute the core of a civic catechism (54).

Hal Koch became one of the great ideologues in the building of the welfare state after the Second World War. In his view, the financial crisis of the 1930s had been a vital factor in the advance of totalitarian systems and the crisis of democracy. For this reason he did not believe that a political democracy could last without a concomitant social and economic democracy. By emphasising the connection between the national, social, and democratic questions, Hal Koch contributed to the formation of "a national compromise" between the two powerful social movements of Grundtvigianism and the workers movement. Many of the political controversies that had characterized the period from 1920 to 1940 were minimized considerably thanks to the war's need for collaboration. Because of this there was strong political agreement to solidify democracy, and this was to be done through democratizing new areas of society. After the Second World War the national compromise was instrumental in creating the ideological foundation for the construction of the Danish welfare state on both socialist and liberal principles. Welfare and Danishness became one and the same: to be Danish was to identify oneself with the Danish welfare system.

It should be noted that the Danish welfare system was also built by referring to Grundtvig and, especially, to his 1820 poem entitled "Far Higher Are Mountains," in which he summarizes his social philosophy in two lines: "In this lies our wealth, on this tenet we draw: / that few are too rich, and still fewer too poor". It should also be noted that Grundtvig the legend has had far more influence on the continuation of nation building than has Grundtvig the man.

REFERENCES

Berlingske Tidende. 1940. "Det skulle Grundtvig have set!" [Grundtvig should have seen that!]. 18 September.

Borgbjerg, F.J. 1933. *Social-Demokraten*, 8. September 1933.

Clausen, N.H. 1870. *Det videnskabelige Livs Forhold til det borgerlige Frihedsliv* [The academic life's relationship to the bourgeois life of freedom]. Copenhagen: G.E.C. Gad.

Frisch, H. 1993 [1933]. *Pest over Europa* [Plague across Europe]. Copenhagen: Forlaget Fremad.

Gammelgaard, H. 1960. *Taler og artikler* [Speeches and articles]. Arbejdernes Oplysningsforbund.

Grundtvig, N.F.S. 2011 [1832]. "Nordic Mythology." In *The School for Life: N.F.S. Grundtvig on Education for the People*, trans. and ed. E. Broadbridge, co-ed. C. Warren and U. Jonas. Aarhus : Aarhus University Press.

Hedtoft-Hansen, H. 1993. "National og International" [National and international]. Foredrag for DSU-ledere I 1936 [Lectures for DSU-leaders in 1936]. In *Danskernes identitetshistorie* [The history of Danish identity], ed. T.B. Jensen, 74–7. Copenhagen: C.A. Reizels Forlag.

Koch, Hal. 1942. *Dagen og Vejen* [The day and the road]. Copenhagen: Westermann.

Korsgaard, Ove. 1997. *Kampen om lyset: Dansk voksenoplysning gennem 500 år.* [The struggle for enlightenment: Danish adult education over 500 Years]. Copenhagen: Gyldendal.

Lundgreen-Nielsen, F. 1992. "Grundtvig og danskhed" [Grundtvig and Danishness]. In *Dansk Identitetshistorie III* [The history of Danish identity III, ed. Ole Feldbæk, 9–187. Copenhagen: Reitzels Forlag.

Müller, Jan-Werner. 2011. *Contesting Democracy.* New Haven, CT: Yale University Press.

Reeh, N. 2006. *Religion and the State of Denmark*. Copenhagen: KUA.

Ringer, F.K. 1969. *The Decline of the German Mandarins*. Cambridge, MA: Harvard University Press.

17

Grundtvigianism as Practice and Experience

ANDREW BUCKSER

One of the stories told about Peter Larsen Skræppenborg, a nineteenth-century Danish lay preacher, recounts his first encounter with the writings of N.F.S. Grundtvig. According to the story, Skræppenborg was staying with a friend on one of his periodic travels around Denmark, and, as they sat by the fire after dinner, the friend handed him a copy of one of Grundtvig's recent sermons. Skræppenborg read a few pages, leaped to his feet, and dashed out of the house, running barefoot into the falling snow. The friend, alarmed, ran to the door. "What's the matter?" he called. Skræppenborg shouted back, in a frenzy of excitement, "Your ceiling is too low in there, and I have to jump for joy!"

I heard this story on the Danish island of Mors (population twenty thousand) in 1990, when I was doing fieldwork with a Grundtvigian congregation there as part of my dissertation research in cultural anthropology (Buckser 1996a). Skræppenborg had been one of Grundtvig's earliest emissaries in this part of northwest Jutland, and his followers had subsequently established what remains the largest independent Grundtvigian congregation in Denmark. I was a bit sceptical of its historicity – charismatic figures like Skræppenborg attract stories like this one – but it did seem to me to capture the intense emotionality that Grundtvig's work evoked among his followers in the region. Perhaps a more reliable account comes from one of Skræppenborg's own letters, telling of the time he first read Grundtvig's influential sermon, *The Church's Retort (Kirkens Genmæle)*:

> The first time I really came to love old Grundtvig was when I first got a chance to read *Kirkens Genmæle*. Oh, I must have jumped two or

> three feet off the ground. Had you stood in a corner and looked on, you might well have laughed at me. But how could my weak sinner's body resist, when my heart became so light that it jumped in the air and took my legs along with it? And if I had had old Grundtvig there on the spot, I would have said to him, "You lied, old fellow, when you tried to fool us into thinking that the written word is just a dead letter! For if your written words can set such life in a lump of flesh like me that I can't even keep my legs still, what can't you imagine that Our Lord's written word can do?" (Schrøder 1991, 100)

Many of his listeners shared his reaction, and, in the second half of the nineteenth century, a Grundtvigian awakening electrified the countryside of northern Mors. Grundtvigian ministers read his sermons to packed churches across the island, religious meetings proliferated in homes and meeting houses, and theological debates animated local political and organizational life. A panoply of Grundtvigian social institutions sprang up, ranging from "free butchers" and "free bakers" to newspapers, recreational organizations, and political groups. In 1871, followers erected their own sizable church, the Church of Ansgar (*Ansgarskirken*), in the village of Øster Jølby. A decade later, following their increasingly radical Grundtvigian minister, they left the state church altogether and formed the Mors Island Free Congregation (*Morsø Frimenighed*). Their passion for Grundtvig's message divided villages and families, shaping the social contours of the island well into the twentieth century.

Almost 150 years have passed since the movement began, and the debates that raged among its founders have long since passed into history. Grundtvigianism is not a radical movement on Mors these days but a familiar element of local tradition; the questions about under-age communion and clerical independence that produced firestorms in 1871 are all but nonsensical to the current inhabitants of Øster Jølby. Yet the church still stands, and its large and active membership still sees itself as a key centre of Grundtvigianism in Denmark. They think this, in part, because of their theological outlook, which, though it has changed somewhat over time, remains inspired by what they see as the essential elements of Grundtvig's thought. Even more so, however, they think this because of a continuity of experience, a sense in which the practice and aesthetic of the congregation remain rooted in Grundtvigian culture. The hymns they sing, the societies they join, the exercises they do, and the environment that surrounds them maintain a continuity with Grundtvigian practice, one that gives them a tangible, emotional connection to Grundtvig long after writings like *Kirkens Genmæle* have lost their impact.

This chapter discusses this element of Grundtvigianism – Grundtvigianism as practice and experience – as a supplement to the more ideologically focused chapters that comprise most of this volume. Of course, Grundtvigianism began as an ideological movement, and its impact on Danish politics, religion, education, and culture derived largely from the power of Grundtvig's theological and social argument. For most of its early adherents, however, Grundtvigianism was as much a matter of experience as of intellect, emerging out of participation in a community animated by a particular set of practices and aesthetics. The extraordinary spread of Grundtvigianism in the late nineteenth century, often among people with little understanding of the debates then raging about national identity, cannot be fully understood without an appreciation of this dimension of the movement. Such an understanding can also illuminate the continuing power of Grundtvigianism in places like contemporary Mors, where the ideological disputes of the nineteenth century have long since become moot.

Grundtvigianism was a complex movement, and Grundtvig himself was both long-lived and extraordinarily productive. A brief chapter like this one can do little more than suggest the rich variety of Grundtvigian practice and aesthetics. I try to provide a flavour of this dimension of the movement, however, by discussing two aspects of Grundtvigian practice as they have manifested themselves on Mors. These examples are to some extent specific to Mors, and it would be inaccurate to present them as representative archetypes of Grundtvigian practice. They share a family resemblance with practices elsewhere in Denmark, though, and they offer a sense of the enduring appeal of Grundtvig more than a century after his death.

THE BUILT ENVIRONMENT AS RELIGIOUS PRACTICE

However abstract its ideas, however otherworldly its theology, religion always involves action taken on a very concrete level, using instruments and structures created by human hands. The construction of these concrete elements both reflects and, in turn, shapes the nature of the religion's ideological discourse. A cathedral does not serve merely as a neutral space within which Catholic services can take place; the architecture itself figures strongly in the ritual, lending a sense of grandeur, awe, and historical depth to the service that a hotel conference room could not. In a Quaker meetinghouse, conversely, the simplicity and plainness of the surroundings connote an ethic of humility and worldly engagement. On Mors, the built environment for Grundtvigian worship evokes a different sort of feeling, one closely connected with the islanders' understanding of the meaning of Grundtvigianism. Its architecture celebrates the distinctiveness and vitality of rural communities generally and of the Mors Grundtvigians in particular. It constitutes a palpable presence in the organization's social and ritual life, one that ties contemporary religiosity with the origins of the community and the folk tradition.

This role manifests itself vividly in the Church of Ansgar, which remains the centre of congregational worship a century and a half after its inception. The erection of the church was an act of remarkable audacity in the late nineteenth century – not so much because it asserted the independence of the Grundtvigians from the state church as because of the size and complexity of its construction. Village churches in this part of Jutland usually trace back to the eleventh or twelfth centuries, and their modest size and simple construction reflect the scale of rural life at the time. Most are small stone rectangles with a few vaulted windows on each side; some have square towers at one end, others simply a wooden overhang for the church bell. The churches in Øster Jølby and surrounding villages are among the more modest. The designers of the Church of Ansgar, by contrast, envisioned something grand, a large brick structure with a vaulted ceiling, a tall tower, and elaborate ornamental brickwork. They wanted a statement of the rising power and status of the rural free farmers who made up the backbone of the Grundtvigian movement on the island and for whom Grundtvigianism embodied a rebellion against the urban power centres represented by the state church. Mors Grundtvigians connected their religious and cultural efforts to the assertion of rural empowerment; just as the Folk High Schools challenged a model of education dominated by urban elites, so the builders of the Ansgarskirke rejected an architectural tradition that reserved beauty and elegance for the cathedrals in Viborg and Copenhagen.

The project clearly exceeded both their technical abilities and their financial resources, but they managed it surprisingly well. Their unlikely success figures in the many stories that circulate about its construction, which emphasize the triumph of rural pluck over the obstacles in its path (Begtrup 1934; Buckser 1996a, 111–14; Fisker 1971). The walls, for example, were designed without a real knowledge of the structural requirements of buildings that size. They were only a third as thick as needed to support the weight of the structure; unable to afford enough bricks for solid walls, moreover, the builders made hollow ones filled with loose flint from a nearby quarry. They discovered the errors only after the walls were completed, when the head mason decided to finally read an architectural book about church construction. His solution was to throw the book away. He admitted that this did not actually improve the walls; they stayed up, however, and the story of their endurance became a testimony to the power of rural ingenuity (see Fisker 1971, 26).

Among the people impressed by the church was the aging Peter Larsen Skræppenborg, who visited Mors during the construction. He glimpsed the edifice from his carriage as he approached Øster Jølby and, according to local accounts, leaped to his frail feet and danced ecstatically with delight. He also donated the altar painting, a striking Dahlsgaard that depicts Bishop Ansgar conducting a baptism. The scene reinforces an emphasis on the Danish folk that runs throughout the congregation's symbolism – it features not Christ but Ansgar, the Apostle of the North, and the foundational event it depicts is the arrival of Christianity in Denmark. Other aspects of the built environment echo this theme. Carved ears of wheat ornament the massive granite baptismal font, a tribute to the local agriculture; the pulpit is shaped like a flower; and a rooster rather than a cross crowns the steeple. Surrounding the church, as is the case with most Danish churches, is a cemetery, where the graves of the local heroes of the movement remain as permanent reminders of the group's history. Most of them follow the Grundtvigian practice of using inscribed round boulders, rather than rectangular headstones, to mark the grave. Members described the practice as a way to emphasize the connection of the individual to the land, the rootedness of identity in the rocks and stones of the island.

The congregation's other built environments carry many of the same themes. Across the street from the church, for example, stands the Eight-Sided Meeting House, where Grundtvigian community activities have taken place since the 1870s. These include the meetings of Grundtvigian social organizations, political associations, and cultural groups; they have also housed Grundtvigian gymnastics, one of the community's most popular activities in the twentieth century (see Eichberg, chap. 18, this volume). Like the church, the meeting house is a conspicuously splendid building for its purpose, with far more space and light than the meeting houses in most Danish villages. The church's parsonage, likewise, is a large and well-built structure with abundant meeting space and tasteful furnishings. It also contains something particularly appealing to me as a researcher – a large and secure vault for the storage of congregational archives, records, and memorabilia. Not all religious groups in Denmark set great store by archives: the members of Mors Island's Inner Mission movement, for example, have kept only the most minimal historical records, and, during my time there, they offered very little access to them (see Buckser 1996a, 152–86). This practice reflects their general focus on the next world as opposed to this one, a sense that the past is something to be liberated from, not dwelt upon. As one of them put it to me, "We're not here to read history, we're here to make history." For the Free Congregation, by contrast, the reading and celebration of history is integral to religious experience. For Grundtvigians, the folk heritage is a central element of the individual self, and learning about it is a key part of the self-awareness necessary for Christian awakening. They have built this notion into their environment, surrounding members with reminders of the power of folk culture and the ongoing presence of their own history. As they engage with religious practice and community life, members of the Free Congregation experience a continual restatement of underlying tenets of the movement.

EXPERIENCE AND THE AESTHETICS OF WORSHIP

Grundtvigian religiosity on Mors, as in most Lutheran congregations in Denmark, is centred on worship rituals held in the church. Other observances do exist, from individual prayer to home religious study, and in its early days home meetings were a defining feature of the Grundtvigian movement. Such activities have rarely played a large role on Mors, however, and the tide of self-conscious secularism that dominates contemporary Scandinavia has washed most of them away (see Buckser 1996b). For most of the island's Grundtvigians today, religious experience revolves mainly around the Sunday services and lifecycle rituals conducted in the Church of Ansgar. These rituals bear a strong resemblance to those in most Danish Lutheran churches and, indeed, to mainline Protestant worship in much of the modern West.

Services take place in the church's main sanctuary, a large vaulted rectangular hall with the congregants seated in rows of pews facing an altar at one end. Sunday rites include the singing of hymns, readings from the scriptures, and a sermon by the priest, along with a communion ceremony at the altar rail. A studied formality pervades the service, one very much in keeping with the understated politeness that characterizes much

Danish social interaction. Activities follow a predictable order of service, with songs and readings chosen from a uniform hymnal. Congregants sit quietly in their pews for most of the service, raising their voices only for hymns and group prayers sung in stately unison. Readers, including the priest, speak calmly and quietly, with minimal gestures. As in most Danish churches, the effect of the ritual is to stress the group over the individual, contemplation over expression, commonality over debate.

The Grundtvigian character of the services stands out in two primary ways. One involves the music, which relies heavily on Grundtvig's own work as a hymnist; the other is an emphasis on congregational control of the liturgy. To take the music first: for all of Grundtvig's contributions to Danish theological and political debate, his hymns remain indisputably the most enduring, influential, and widely read of his writings. The power of this work is difficult to convey to an Anglo-American reader, in part because of the different place of hymns in Danish worship. Danish churchgoers sing more hymns than do North American churchgoers. Few of the hymns in a typical North American hymnal have more than four or five verses, and churches frequently abbreviate them; in Denmark, many hymns have ten or more verses, and congregations sing them all the way through. Grundtvig's hymns tend to be particularly long, so that singing them involves an engagement with his thought not normally found in North American services. A Grundtvigian hymn constitutes a small theological treatise on its own, probably the most extended theological argument most Danes encounter on a regular basis.

Even more difficult to convey, however, is the extraordinary beauty and power of Grundtvig's poetry. Denmark has a long tradition of great hymnists, including Thomas Kingo, Hans Adolf Brorson, and Bernhard Severin Ingemann; however, at his best, Grundtvig towers above them all. His hymns combine grandeur with intimacy, themes of salvation and spiritual grace with references to the concrete minutiae of everyday life in Denmark. They do so with an uncanny fluidity of language and imagery, producing arresting visual and emotional images in smooth, unlaboured metre. And the spiritual image they paint is vividly alive, envisioning faith as something joyous and uplifting – not the submission of penitents to an exacting judge but the acceptance by children of a loving parent's embrace. All great poetry suffers in translation; Grundtvig's suffers more than most because of the immediacy of his references to the rural life of nineteenth-century Denmark. To the ears of my informants on Mors, however, Grundtvigian hymns represented a singularly beautiful and exuberant aesthetic experience.

I first encountered this experience in the fall of 1990, during a visit to a Sunday service in Øster Jølby. The island of Mors lies high in the north of the Jutland peninsula, a large irregular oblong wedged into an inland waterway known as the Limfjord. It remains largely rural 140 years after Skræppenborg's death; the village of Øster Jølby, like most of its rural settlements, consists of a cluster of low houses and small shops along a two-lane road, with farms spreading out on either side. My own home was in Nykøbing, the market town on the eastern shore of the island, and I had taken an early bus to travel the twenty or so kilometres out to the service. It was a lovely ride across rural roads, with an autumnal landscape bathed in the indescribably crisp light of September in high latitudes. I would have been hard put to express the beauty of the experience. As it turned out, I didn't have to – I arrived a bit late for the service, and as I entered the congregation had just launched into hymn 677, a Grundtvig carol set in the autumn. The text of the hymn reads as follows:[1]

Nu falmer skoven trindt om land og fuglestemmen daler; alt flygted storken over strand ham følger viltre svaler.	Now the forest fades around the land and the songs of birds diminish the stork has flown over the sea, and the inconstant swallows follow him.
Hvor marken bølged nys som gyld Med aks og vipper bolde der ser man nu kun sorten muld og stubbene de golde	Where the field waved in the breeze like gold with ears of wheat and swaying buds all one sees now is the blackened mud and the golden stubs of the stalks.
Men i vor lade, på vor lo, der har vi nu Guds gaver, der virksomhed og velstand gro i tøndemål af traver.	But in our barns, up in our loft, there we now have God's gifts, there industry and prosperity grow in barrels full of the harvest.
Og han, som vokse lod på jord	And He, who let grow on the earth

de gyldne aks og vipper
han bliver hos os med sit ord,
det ord, som aldrig glipper.

the golden ears and buds
He remains with us through His word,
that word, that never fails us.

Ham takker alle vi med sang
for alt, hvad han har givet,
for hvad han vokse lod i vang
for ordet og for livet.

Let us all thank him with song
for everything he has given,
for what he let grow in the fields,
for His word and for life itself.

Da over os det hele år
sin fred han lyser gerne,
og efter vinter kommer vår
med sommer, korn, og kerne.

For over us throughout the year
his peace shines down upon us,
and after winter spring will come,
with summertime, crops, and seeds.

Og når engang på Herrens bud
vort timeglas udrinder,
en evig sommer hos vor Gud
i Paradis vi finder.

And when in time, by the Lord's command,
our hourglass is emptied,
an eternal summer, home with our God
we will find in Paradise.

Da høste vi, som fugle nu,
der ikke så og pløje,
da komme aldrig mere i hu
vi jordens strid og møje.

Then we will harvest as the birds do now
who never sow or till,
then no more will we call to mind
the strife and discontent of the world.

For høsten her og høsten hist
vor Gud ske lov og ære,
som ved vor Herre Jesus Krist
vor Fader ville være!

For the harvest here, and the harvest there,
praise and honor be to our God,
who by our Lord Jesus Christ
will be a Father to us!

Hans Ånd, som alting kan og ved
i disse korte dage

May His Spirit, that can do all and knows all
in the short days of this season

med tro og håb og kærlighed	through faith and hope and love
til Himlen os ledsage!	lead us to Heaven!

(Kirkeministeriet 1978, 643–5)

As always with translated poetry, it is difficult to convey the beauty of the language – the economy with which Grundtvig paints a picture of rural Denmark, the intricate interplay between agricultural and religious language, the subtle use of seasonal imagery as a metaphor for spiritual transformation. The evocative fit between the metre and the soaring melody, likewise, defies written description. In the context of the service in the Ansgarskirke, however, the emotional impact of the hymn was palpable. It created a powerful awareness of the season, a sense of unity between the spiritual experience of the service and the natural landscape that surrounded it. It momentarily dissolved the walls between the service and the world outside, rooting Grundtvig's Christianity in the intimately familiar world of fields and farms through which all of the parishioners had come to the ritual.

Like much of Grundtvig's poetry, the impact of "Now the forest fades around the land" derives in part from its connection to the seasonal round of Danish life. As a northern country, Denmark experiences a particularly dramatic variation in its seasons, between warm summers when the sun barely sets and long, dark, cold winters. The holidays marking those seasons are celebrated exuberantly, particularly the month-long winter festival culminating on 24 December with Christmas Eve (*juleaften*). Singing makes up an important part of these festivities, and Grundtvig's songs remain among the most popular, even in an increasingly secular age. Their popularity reflects the sense of joy and the concrete imagery that pervade his work. His Christmas hymns draw on images from the seasonal landscape, as in perhaps his most-sung carol:

Dejlig er den himmel blå	Delightful is the blue of the heavens
lyst det er at se derpå	looking on them is a joy
hvor de gyldne stjerner blinke	how the golden stars blink
hvor de smile, hvor de vinke	how they smile, how they beckon
os fra jorden op til sig	us from the earth up to them
os fra jorden op til sig	us from the earth up to them

(Kirkeministeriet 1978, 118–19)

They also posit a particularly warm and intimate relationship between believers and the divine, one that neatly complements the ethic of *hygge*, which pervades the season in Denmark. The striking role reversal in "Strange to Tell" (*Forunderligt at sige*), evoking the infant Jesus in the manger, shows this vividly:

Selv spurven har sin rede,	Even the sparrow has his nest,
kan bygge der og bo	where he can build and dwell
en svale ej tør lede	neither need a swallow go searching
om nattely og ro –	for nightly rest and peace –
de vilde dyr i hule	the wild animals in their dens
har hver sin egen vrå	each have their own corner;
skal sig min Frelser skjule	then must my Savior hide
i fremmed stald på strå?	in the straw of a stranger's barn?
Nej, kom jeg vil oplukke	No, come, I will open up
Mit hjerte, sjæl og sind	my heart, soul, and mind
ja, bede, synge, sukke	yes, pray, sing, sigh,
kom Jesus, kom herind. –	come, Jesus, come within. –
Det er ej fremmed bolig	This is no stranger's residence;
du den har dyre købt	you have purchased it at a high price
her skal du hvile rolig	here shall you rest peacefully
i kærligheden svøbt.	swaddled in love.

In this carol, God Himself has need of *hygge*, the sense of enveloping community and intimate belonging so central to the Danish self-concept and so particularly celebrated around Jul. And the connection of believer to deity is personalized enough to permit at least the intimation that He finds *hygge* in his flock, that the warmth of Danish souls in this season can give shelter even to the Almighty. Grundtvig's poetry provides an intimate and viscerally compelling connection of the divine to the seasonal world of Denmark.

On Mors, the congregation links this aesthetic to a distinctively congregationalist approach to liturgy. Since its inception, the congregation has used ritual variation to emphasize its independence from the larger world – an independence its members associate with the rural empowerment implicit in Grundtvig's notion of the folk. The church's founding priest, Rasmus Lund, was neither a charismatic speaker nor a prominent theological writer; his persistence in ritual nonconformity, however, made him a national figure in the late nineteenth century (see Begtrup

1934; Buckser 1996a; Fisker 1971). He initially broke from the national church on the issue of under-age communion. Lund had deep objections to the rite of confirmation, the ceremony for fourteen-year-olds that entitled them to take part in the Eucharist. Following Grundtvig's approach to ritual, he disputed the legitimacy of a rite that reflected high church regulations rather than the practice of the Apostles. He asserted, moreover, that local ministers rather than distant bishops should decide when children had the spiritual maturity for the ceremony. Beginning around 1880, therefore, he began administering communion to a number of eleven to thirteen-year-olds. The regional bishop ordered Lund to stop; in 1882, after Lund openly defied the order, the bishop dismissed him from the priesthood. The majority of the congregation followed Lund out of the church, resigning their state affiliation and reincorporating as the Mors Island Free Congregation. Like Lund, they expressed this decision not through argument but through ritual action, joining him at the altar rail in an electrifying and wholly extralegal service the following week.

In the century that followed, an aesthetic of independence and anticlericalism became a recurrent feature of the group's liturgical practice, one that its members connected directly to their Grundtvigian origins. As late as the 1980s, for example, under the leadership of priest Erik Lau Jørgensen, the congregation was experimenting with the reformulation of one of its most basic rituals, baptism (Buckser 1996a, 124). Like all Danish Lutheran churches, the Free Congregation practises infant baptism, which includes sprinkling the child with water to indicate its incorporation into the Christian community. A central part of the ritual involves a recitation of the Apostles' Creed. The priest asks the child three questions relating to the basic beliefs of the church, to which a godparent responds affirmatively on her or his behalf. This creed has a particularly strong significance in Grundtvigianism since it traces its origins to the early Christian congregations; Grundtvig regarded the practices of these congregations as a better guide to Christ's teachings than the New Testament, which first appeared long after Jesus's death.

Prior to his ordination, Lau Jørgensen himself regarded the creed as all but untouchable, a bedrock element of Grundtvigian ritual. When he became priest in 1975, however, he discovered a strong undercurrent of resentment towards it among his parishioners. Many of them argued that it violated the freedom of conscience that lay at the heart of Grundtvig's thought: How could they force members to affirm a set of beliefs, when the essence of Grundtvigianism lay in the individual's free acceptance of grace? An individual's beliefs might change and evolve over a lifetime; the key element of membership, they contended, lay not in a commitment to particular beliefs, but in a commitment to the community of believers. After a long period of research and discussion, Lau Jørgensen came to agree, and he drafted a new ritual formulation still used today. The new language does not question the child about faith; rather, it lists the elements of the Apostles' Creed, states that they represent the beliefs of the congregation, and asks the child if, knowing this, he or she wishes to become a member.

The concrete impact of this change is slight, but its symbolic weight is considerable. In making the change, the congregation asserted its freedom not only from church authorities but also from an unquestioned obedience to the writings of Grundtvig himself. The action accorded with the congregation's general approach to ritual, one that emphasizes both individual freedom of conscience and the moral sovereignty of the folk. As it wends its way through individual services and the ritual year, the conduct of religious practice restates the independence of the rural community that members experience as an essential element of Grundtvigianism.

Taken together, then, the aesthetics of religious ritual impart a distinctive flavour to Grundtvigian practice on Mors, rooting religious experience in a particular vision of the moral community. It is a vision of the divine as attuned to the physical world, embedded in the landscape and seasonal round of the Danish countryside. It ties the divine intimately to the local world and the individual believer, painting a picture of a kind, benevolent, and very personal deity. It clothes that vision, moreover, in music and poetry of surpassing beauty, a beauty that itself is rooted in the distinctive linguistic and natural environment within which its adherents live. It is this experience of practice, as much as any of Grundtvigianism's ideological or theological positions, that binds the members of the Mors Island Free Congregation to their church.

Grundtvigian practice today differs significantly from that of the nineteenth century, on Mors and elsewhere. Not only have ritual details shifted over time but the everyday behaviour associated with membership has changed its character. An early feature of the Free Congregation, for example, was an emphasis on propriety that bordered on the oppressive; determined to combat any suggestion that their nonconformity extended to moral and social behaviour, members watched each other vigilantly for signs of moral weakness. Such actions would have been hard to imagine in the late twentieth century, particularly as Grundtvigians had come to define themselves in opposition to the ascetic moralism of the Inner Mission. Just as Grundtvig's followers have selectively emphasized and reinterpreted different parts of his theological writings, so have they continually revised the practical and experiential dimensions of the movement.

Like Grundtvigian ideology, however, Grundtvigian practice has retained some key features over its lifetime, features that foster a continuity of experience between contemporary followers and the heady days of the nineteenth-century awakening. These include a variety of practices that valorize the rural, the local, and the congregational, placing symbolic and practical emphasis on the folk community that Grundtvig situated at the heart of the Christian experience. They also include an emphasis on freedom, particularly freedom of conscience. And everywhere, they include the use of Grundtvig's words in rite and song, infusing worship and daily life with his distinctive poetic vision. A century and a half after Skræppenborg's first encounter, the soaring beauty of that vision still inspires a distinctive transcendent experience, instilling in its hearers a sense of community with the past and each other and perhaps, now and then, the urge to run out into the snow and jump for joy.

NOTES

1 Translations of hymns by the author. I would like to thank Edward Broadbridge for his very helpful suggestions on the translations. Broadbridge's (2009) own renditions of Grundtvig's hymns, which are much more poetic and melodically faithful than the necessarily literal ones here, may be found in his *Hymns in English*, published by Kongelige Vajsenhus Forlag.

REFERENCES

Begtrup, H. 1934. Dansk Menighedsliv i Grundtvigske Kredse [Danish congregational life in Grundtvigian circles]. Copenhagen: G.E.C. Gads.

Broadbridge, Edward. 2009. *Hymns in English*. Copenhagen: Det Kongelige Vajsenhus' Forlag.

Buckser, A. 1996a. *Communities of Faith: Sectarianism, Identity, and Social Change on a Danish Island*. Providence, RI: Berghahn Books.

– 1996b. "Religion, Science, and Secularization Theory on a Danish Island." *Journal for the Scientific Study of Religion* 35 (4): 432–41.

Fisker, P. 1971. Morsø Frimenighed, 1871–1971 [Morsø free congregation, 1871–1971]. Nykøbing: Morsø Frimenighed.
Kirkeministeriet. 1978. *Den Danske Salme Bog* [The Danish hymnbook]. Copenhagen: Det Kongelige Vajsenhus' Forlag.
Schrøder, L. 1991. *Peter Larsen Skræppenborg*. Copenhagen: Lohses Forlag.

18

The Popular Voicing of Sport: Comparative Aspects of Grundtvigian Movement Culture

HENNING EICHBERG

Grundtvig was influential not only directly, through words, actions, and inventions, but also indirectly through practical and oral channels, the Grundtvigian movement, free congregations, gymnastic associations, cooperatives, and People's High Schools. Sport and movement culture show how practical Grundtvigianism affected Danish everyday life, down to the personal, bodily level. This happened in a way that would probably have surprised Grundtvig.

GRUNDTVIGIAN *FOLKELIG* GYMNASTICS IN CONTEXT

In Denmark, the world of sport is marked by the impact of Grundtvigian gymnastics. So-called *folkelig* gymnastics made people meet in voluntary associations and in large summer meetings (*stævne*), singing and playing together, mostly in a non-competitive way. The "popular" model can be compared with Swedish Lingian gymnastics, German *Turnen*, Slavic *Sokol* gymnastics, Gaelic sport in Ireland, the Highland Games in Scotland, Glima in Iceland, and, more generally, with folk sport in different parts of the world. And yet, Danish *folkelig* gymnastics was unique in that it combined Lingian Swedish gymnastics with a people's movement based on voluntary self-organization.

A common denominator of the diverse national sporting activities (most of them having their roots in a nationalist romanticism) and the Grundtvigian approach was nation building through bodily movement. Or folk building.

However, the rise of Danish *folkelig* gymnastics and sport did not derive from Grundtvig. Grundtvig himself did not initiate any sport-like practice. If he had done so, he would eventually have favoured combat over gymnastics. That is why, with an ironic undertone, Korsgaard (1986b) imagines "Grundtvig as boxer." Furthermore, Danish *folkelig* gymnastics are not a continuation of ancient Nordic practices, as they could be interpreted if looked at through a nationalist romantic lens (Engelstoft 1801). Instead, modern Danish *folkelig* gymnastics are a result of complex effects of the Grundtvigian movement, which, since the nineteenth century, has combined bodily movement, personal development, and national identity. And one can see some spill-over from this Grundtvigian movement in other Danish sport movements, such as bourgeois sport and workers sport.

FROM RIVALLING FOLK MOVEMENTS TO MODERN SPORT

What characterizes Danish sport is the fact that it originated in popular movements from different social milieux. Modern Danish sport culture involved, from its very beginning in the nineteenth century, a complex mix of three class-related elements – rural farmers culture, urban bourgeois culture, and workers culture. During the twentieth century, this initial profile was supplemented by new reform movements, cultural radicalism, and welfare culture. All these gave different, and sometimes contradictory, impulses to the Danish practice and understanding of sport. And, in different ways, they were related to Grundtvigian impulses.

First, the main source of Grundtvigian cultural influence was the Danish *farmers culture* of the nineteenth century. It was socially based on a class of landowners who had developed a liberal-democratic self-consciousness and a social practice of their own – in contrast to the aristocratic ruling class, on the one hand, and Copenhagen's bourgeoisie, on the other. The farmers founded rural producers cooperatives, People's High Schools (*folkehøjskoler*), and local assembly halls. Continuing some traits from the revivalist religious movements of the 1820s, the rural milieu, with its spiritual, emotional, and educational impulses, became the cradle of a special type of gymnastics. These gymnastics were adopted from the Swedish-Lingian system in the 1880s and eventually transformed into the Danish popular (*folkelig*) sport found in voluntary associations. They contrasted with German Turner gymnastics and the more paramilitary Danish rifle movement as well as later English competitive sport. They started at People's High Schools, which integrated the new movement activities into the construction of "the whole human being," to express it in Grundtvigian terms. Gymnastics played a central and controversial role in the national-democratic policy of education around 1900, when the majority party, the farmers' Left Party, finally gained power (Korsgaard 1982, 1986a).

The second source of sport in Denmark was the urban *bourgeois culture* of Copenhagen and, soon afterwards, that of other towns as well. Following the English model, middle-class people – mostly men and only a few women and young people – met in socially exclusive clubs, taking over British patterns of achievement and competition. It can be asked whether the local clubs of that time, with their specialized activities, could really be regarded as a proper "movement." When, in 1896, a minor group of well-dressed men founded the Danish Sports Federation, they were mostly interested in common rules of competition and in amateur rules, which distanced non-bourgeois people from sport. On the political level, they were "non-political," with undertones of national liberalism and royalist conservatism. At first, this umbrella federation, represented by military officers, medical doctors, businessmen, and lawyers, did not catch the interest of the majority of local clubs. However, when, in the early twentieth century, sport became a mass movement, the Danish Sports Federation gradually developed more elements of a *folkelig* movement, such as common symbols, rituals, and a health-related ideology.

The third source of sport in Denmark was the *workers culture*. Indeed, this is what enabled sport to become a mass movement. Part of the workers culture milieu was connected with social democracy and its cultural initiatives – "peoples' houses," socialist scouts, cultural associations, and socialist People's High Schools (which combined the Grundtvigian idea of a People's High School with cultural socialism). Workers sport in Denmark, however, failed to develop a lasting alternative to bourgeois competitive sport. The Danish Workers Sport Association lasted for only a few years (1931–37) as a separate body before joining the Danish Sports Federation. As social democracy became increasingly hegemonic and reformist, it favoured corporative structures and sport for all rather than socialist sport. A special feature of workers sport was the "Festivals of Professions," which mixed sports with carnival-like folk competitions such as tug-of-war (Hansen 1993). Today, the Danish Workers Sport Association organizes social and integrative sports, with special focus on elderly people, immigrants, and disabled people.

After 1900, some new reform movements supplemented the sport picture with youth movements, alternative health movements, and outdoor activities (*friluftsliv*). As an open-air movement, sport now obtained a new profile and a new mass character. Cultural radicalism, which appeared between the two World Wars, added further innovations. It connected functionalism and technological enthusiasm with jazz, boxing, expressive gymnastics, and nudism, valuing sport as an aesthetic event. Some cultural radicals distanced themselves from Grundtvig, while others, like Martin Andersen Nexø, translated Grundtvigian inspirations into socialist ideas. Later, this radicalism found particular expression in the work of the Situationist artist Asger Jorn (1964), who designed a huge project consisting of ancient and folk art in the North and that explicitly referred to Grundtvig. Jorn's (1962, 37–8) proposed "triolectic" game of football with three sets of goal posts (the point being to avoid the dualist war-like configuration of soccer) was an original and "weird" Neo-Grundtvigian approach, which still has a certain international appeal.

At the same time as these reform movements, urban social democratic administrations developed a welfare system, including "culture for the people" (Julius Bomholt). In the name of social consensus, the cultural struggle was downgraded and a new type of welfare culture institutionalized the workers movement. Welfare policy supported people's tourism (*Dansk Folkeferie*), laid out urban people's parks with sport facilities, opened the green natural environments of the countryside for outdoor activities, and supported sport for all, especially municipal sport and company sport, in the spirit of health for all (*folkehygiejne*). The Grundtvigian term "folk," or "people," entered into welfare-democratic discourse. From the underground of this welfare culture – with its protest against authoritarianism – the youth revolt of 1968 expressed a sort of Neo-Grundtvigianism with hippie undertones.

HØJSKOLE SPORT: FROM ENTERTAINMENT TO EDUCATIONAL IDEA

People's High Schools have historically played a central role in the diffusion of popular gymnastics in Denmark. The close connection between the Free High Schools and sport is particular to Denmark. As a space of alternative education, the "school for life" had an important impact on sport, depicting it as "sport for life" and "popular sport" (*folkelig idræt*). Sport as *folkehøjskole* activity was, however, marked by the fact that the connection between the school and sport was originally unintended. Nevertheless, in the long run it followed a certain educational logic, which developed and alternated through five historical periods.

First Historical Period: Intermediary Spaces

In the first historical period, when the first *folkehøjskoler* were established (beginning in Rødding in 1844), sport had no place within the concept of education. Students were taught through lectures and some manual labour. But elements of body culture entered into their daily practice as a break in daily routines. It was for practical purposes that gymnastics and exercises of the "Danish" type, similar to German *Turnen*, were here and there introduced – as healthy exercise and compensation for sitting while learning, as a joyful change and as entertainment. Body movement in Grundtvigian People's High Schools was not present as a subject of its own, and it was not related to "popular enlightenment": it developed in the intermediary spaces between "real" subjects.

Second Historical Period: "The Whole Human Being"

In the second historical period, the place of body culture changed when physical exercises became integrated into *højskole* education in the 1880s. It is here that Grundtvigianism really began to influence body culture. The process started in the People's High School in Vallekilde on the isle of Zealand. In 1884, under its headmaster Ernst Trier, students began to train in Swedish Lingian gymnastics, and a group of teachers was sent to Sweden in order to learn this system in more detail. Subsequently, Danish *folkehøjskoler* began, one by one, to introduce Lingian gymnastics.

This change happened at a time of inner tensions, when Denmark was threatened by a civil war between the majority of democratic farmers (the Left Party) and the ruling minority of aristocrats and landowners (the Right Party). Instead of turning to military confrontation, People's High Schools and popular gymnastics became part of a peaceful cultural revolution, which finally overthrew the right-wing dictatorial regime. This contributed to the non-militaristic (or even anti-militaristic) agenda of Danish *folkelig* gymnastics. The choice of (left-wing) gymnastics was a choice against the military policies of (right-wing) revanchism. And yet the *folkelig* milieu was also nationalist, but in another way, referring, as it did, to Nordic identity in confrontation with the German Reich.

On the level of practice, lectures, joint singing, and gymnastics constituted the characteristic triad of *højskole* education. Together they formed "the whole human being." Ernst Trier (1884) expresses the philosophy of gymnastic Grundtvigianism in a famous speech at the opening of Vallekilde gymnastic hall in 1884: "Gymnastics shall promote what is divine in the human being – what distinguishes the human being from the animal."

The spiritual vision of education through gymnastics was both noble and pretentious. However, the actual practice of gymnastics was rather tawdry and routine, being derived from rank-and-file military-like exercises. Traditional patterns of discipline and control were, however, not turned towards militarism but, rather, towards self-discipline and self-control as part of personal development. And both *folkehøjskoler* and *folkelig* gymnastics contributed to the change of political power in Denmark. In 1901, parliamentary democracy became a reality. Thus, bodily movement and social movement were linked together in *højskole* gymnastics.

A third element in this combination of movements was the farmers cooperative movement. Between 1880 and 1900, a strong network of associations developed in the fields of production and consumption. This cooperative movement – being the economic wing of the democratic revolution in Denmark – received an important impetus from the People's High Schools, from the cultural wing. And *folkelig* gymnastics in the villages came to link the idea of *folkelig* self-organization to the idea of practical economic cooperation.

From the end of the nineteenth century, the range of the People's High Schools became more varied. A gap opened between more positivistic and natural-scientific orientations and more "mythological" orientations. Also, *højskoler* that were based on more orthodox Christian beliefs ("Inner Mission") were founded. And, at the beginning of the twentieth century, the rising workers movement opened socialist People's High Schools. There is, however, very little known about the role of gymnastics and sports in these other types of *højskoler*.

Third Historical Period: Gymnastic and Sports High Schools

In the 1920s and 1930s, a third historical period of *højskole* development began. With the realization of parliamentary democracy in 1901, the democratic agenda of the People's High Schools lost its sharpness. And, with the return of South Jutland to Denmark in 1920, national ambitions were also saturated. New forms of *højskole* were needed. Important elements of this quest for a new orientation were bodily activities and movement culture.

People's High Schools that specialized in gymnastics and sports were established and expressed new currents of educational and cultural reform, first in Ollerup in 1920 and Snoghøj in 1925, and later in Gerlev in 1938, Vejle in 1943, and Viborg in 1951. With gymnastics, for the first time a "special" field of activities was placed at the centre of *højskole* education. The leader of a gymnastic team, *delingsfører*, became a social figure of particular character, important for generations of "bodily Grundtvigians," and the *højskole* became the place for their education. At some People's High Schools, this innovation was achieved to the disadvantage of the spiritual message, which had been at the centre of the classical Grundtvigian People's High School. This was the case in Ollerup, the school of Niels Bukh, who became the most famous Danish gymnastic leader – and a controversial pro-Nazi right-winger (Bonde 2003).

However, the shortcomings of this school were critically remarked by a Japanese observer, the young Shigeyoshi Matsumae (1987). After travelling through Denmark in the 1930s, he contrasted the lack of spirituality in Ollerup with the spiritual atmosphere surrounding gymnastics in Snoghøj and Askov, where the attempt was to combine physical activity with spiritual culture and democratic nationalism. In Snoghøj, female gymnastics was closely connected with the Grundtvigian philosopher Jørgen Bukdahl, who regularly lectured at this People's High School. Bukdahl launched the idea that body culture needed a "point outside" to give movement a deeper meaning. This "point outside" was, for Bukdahl (1943), "popular enlightenment." The "point outside" became a famous phrase in Danish popular sport.

After the Second World War, sport became a broader leisure activity among the population, but, generally, the People's High Schools turned more towards literature and democracy. In this phase, a gap opened between "the book" and "the physical." Sport did not play any important role in the self-understanding of the *højskoler*. In their program, sport was associated with leisure and entertainment. The process of specialization, however, continued, and new Sports High Schools were established in Sønderborg in 1952 and in Århus in 1970. On the other hand, sports organizations started to build their own system, which involved specialized courses outside those taught at the People's High Schools.

Fourth Historical Period: Neo-Grundtvigianism

In a fourth historical period, from the 1960s onward, the People's High School and the classical gymnastic Grundtvigianism were questioned and redefined in new and often conflicting ways. A driving force behind this change was the youth movement of 1968, which, in a revolutionary gesture, gave birth to a Neo-Grundtvigianism. The People's High Schools were now challenged by new types of grassroots movements on the outside and by generational conflicts on the inside. New types of People's High Schools were opened. There were new *højskoler* that were related to ideological currents and known as "red" People's High Schools; there were Tvind schools, which were engaged in solidarity work in the Third World; and there were new spiritual *højskoler* whose programs included meditation. Other schools were established for special groups, such as women, elderly people, and disabled persons. Further types of People's High Schools specialized in certain disciplines, such as arts, theatre, music, or sport. Sport entered into an anti-authoritarian and anti-capitalist agenda: "The private is political!" Centres of Neo-Grundtvigian body culture opened in Gerlev (under headmaster Ove Korsgaard), in Viborg, and in Køng (founded in 1978). New games, new forms of meditation, expressive gymnastics, anti-authoritarian pedagogy, hippie culture, sport as personal development – cultural struggle reappeared.

Youngsters from new urban milieux, which earlier had been distant from the rural People's High Schools, now began to enter the *højskole*. Side by side with long courses that lasted several months, short summer courses became popular. The latter courses were often more specialized than the former and appealed to middle-aged participants. The links between the People's High Schools and working life – which had traditionally been of a rural character – loosened, and the *højskole* became more leisure-oriented, sometimes even seen as an alternative to "the world of capitalist labour."

This educational shift changed the balance between literature, which to this point had been central, and the creative arts. The *højskole*, which so far had mainly been teaching young farmers, became an aesthetic People's High School centred around music and arts. From here, the step towards a body-focused *højskole* was not so very far. The new significance of arts, music, sports, and psychology weakened the role of the lecture and the study circle in favour of the workshop, of "doing things together." Education for life, *livsoplysning*, was close to both leisure education and critical-alternative education. Under both, sport could find an important place; however, under each it was also reinterpreted and changed. Sport entered into a connection with the new "body subjects," *kropsfag*, that developed during the 1970s, with the new social movements pertaining to protest and civil innovation. In some schools, competitive sport became secondary to "sport for life," which was adapted to the values of popular gymnastics from earlier periods. Body culture appeared as alternative education and personal development.

Fifth Historical Period: The 1980s and 1990s

In the fifth historical period, during the 1980s, the tendency of specialization continued with the founding of new Sports High Schools in Ålborg in 1982, Nordjylland in 1986, Odsherred in 1993, and Midtvestjylland in 1994. Some tendencies pointed back to discipline-oriented education, and the significance of the market was strengthened, too. One talked about "individualization" and disciplinary "competences" and included fashionable sports, as was the case at the new *højskole* in Oure in 1989. The social movements of the 1970s, which had promoted new humanistic innovations inside the People's High Schools, became weakened.

Among the ninety-eight People's High Schools that existed in 1999, thirty-one had a general character, eleven were schools of sport, and the rest specialized in other areas. This specialization made it more and more difficult to identify a comprehensive vision of "sport in popular education" – and of "*folkelig* education" more generally. Some attempted to adapt the People's High School curriculum to fashionable sports, propagating a "sport without Grundtvig," while others wanted to go back to "the classical Grundtvigian" *højskole* based on history, literature, and philosophy – without the focus on body or sport.

After one hundred years of development, in the 2000s, *højskole* sport was confronted with a problem that was the opposite of that faced in the 1880s: activities were now rich and diverse but the common vision had become blurred.

SPORT FOR LIFE: THE TRANSFORMATION OF SPORT BY *HØJSKOLE* EDUCATION

Did Grundtvigian body culture "win" after all? No – and yet, the impact on sport of Grundtvigian spirituality and People's High Schools has given Danish sport more new profiles. The Grundtvigian contribution was to make evident which qualities could be featured in sport for life and which in sport for social and personal development.

The qualities of sport: Sport has "enlightening" qualities that are fairly diverse – dance and expressive activities, fight and competition, meditative movement, games and play, outdoor activities. Each of these implies its own psychology of movement. The dialogical principle of Grundtvig's "living word" (*levende vekselvirkning*) is enlarged to encompass the mimetic principle of dialogue between body and body.

Community of action: Through popular sports, people develop their common rhythm, *fællesskab*. *Højskole* is a field of common action and voluntary commitment. Sport can contribute to building self-confidence – "I can!'" But the condition is that the activity must not discriminate between the "abled" and the "disabled" as this would make losers out of all those who are not at the top of the achievement hierarchy. This is *folkelig* sport's contribution to living democracy: one body, one vote.

Joint singing: Danish popular sport is a movement that involves singing, which is connected with the Danish *højskole* as a singing high school. Popular sports – represented by the Danish Gymnastic and Sports Association – have a songbook of their own, and the same is true for the Peoples' High Schools, with their *Højskolesangbogen*. People sing songs from a broad range of genres, from folk ballads to Grundtvig's psalms and patriotic songs to pop, rock, and international songs – African folk, African-American spirituals, the Beatles. Joint singing is usual at the more official meetings of sport associations, at the national festivals of sports, and at the opening of *højskole* lectures. Ever since the beginning of modern democracy, social movements have involved singing.

Wholeness: Popular sport is a practical way of understanding the social, philosophical, aesthetic, and religious dimensions of human life (Korsgaard 1986b). These qualities are under threat due to the routine and stress of everyday life. But *højskole* sport is a way to re-establish wholeness, consciousness, and practical innovation.

Variety: The students can use their *højskole* stay to test different sports side by side, thus experimenting with "other" types of movement. Specialization is not at the centre. This coincides with the general tendency among young people to choose "one's own sport" with a flexibility that one does not find in specialized traditional organizations. *Højskole* sport also had some impact on the development of new sports clusters such as martial arts (e.g., judo and other budo, capoeira, stunt), traditional games, outdoor life, body therapies, yoga and relaxation, movement communication, body theatre, cricket, and parkour.

Choice: For a People's High School, activities are always a result of a choice. They are never fixed, as in a university course or in the course plan of sport organizations, which let one know exactly which sports are the "real" ones. In a *højskole*, one never knows this for sure. On a very practical level, the People's High School has to test and query the "market" again and again: Which sports appeal to our students? In this climate, the practice of play and various games could thrive, and, in 1999, the International Playground, *Legepark*, was opened at the Gerlev High School, the emphasis being Grundtvigian (Møller 2010). And yet, the personal choice of "one's own" sport is not individualistic; rather, it is a matter of togetherness (*fællesskab*).

Social encounter: Meeting the "other" sport is connected with meeting other people, the "other" social personality: *Højskole* is a social meeting. The lack of educational hierarchy in the People's High Schools contributed to this social opportunity.

Culture of democracy: The People's High Schools have an important impact on sport as a democratic practice: "Do it yourself" – and do it together with the others. A key phrase in people's education is: *Vil du tænde, må du brænde* (If you want to set something on fire, you must burn yourself). This "burning," playing on the Grundtvigian metaphors of fire, warmth, light, and *folkelig* enlightenment, is a driving force behind voluntarism and civil society. That is why foreign students, especially from "new" developing democracies in Eastern Europe, have entered Danish *højskoler* – combining bodily movement and learning about democracy.

FOLK SPORTS: RIGHT WING AND LEFT WING ...

The Grundtvigian movement created an understanding of "the *folkelig*" in sports that, when compared with that of other countries, is unusual. The term "folk sport" has been used in various countries, and often with nationalist romantic undertones similar to those in Denmark – and yet with distinct connotations. Folk sports and the terminology of "folk" were in some cases attached to a particular ideology, whether right-wing nationalism, as in German *völkisches Turnen*, or left-wing socialism or communism, as in Italian *sport popolare*.

Grundtvig was well aware of these broader political dimensions of body culture, which he observed in the case of German gymnastics.

German *Turnen*, as a popular movement, was started by *Turnvater* Friedrich Ludwig Jahn and his national revolutionary students (Becker and Bernett 1979). In his lectures *Mands Minde* (1838), Grundtvig spoke vividly about Jahn's *Turner* gymnasts, which he translated as "swingers" (*Svingere*). They represented Germany's "great merits for freedom and enlightenment in the new Europe which we always should recognise whatever we'll object against the German way of thinking" (Grundtvig in Korsgaard 2012, 92–100). Jahn, whom Grundtvig referred to as a "giant nature" (*Kæmpenatur*), had engaged German youth for the liberation of their country, but he also filled them with a "deep contempt for all [things] foreign," as Grundtvig critically remarked. And yet Grundtvig's sympathy was clearly on Jahn's side when he talked about the ban that the reactionary Metternich system had instituted against *Turner* gymnastics (ibid.).

What Grundtvigian gymnastics have in common with German *Turner* gymnastics as well as with the Slavic *Sokol* movements of the nineteenth century (Blecking 1991) is the assumption that gymnastic exercises are at the centre of identity-building. Other models of "popular sport," like the Scottish Highland Games (Jarvie 1991) and the Breton games, were organized around traditional competitions and games. Further forms of "folk sport," such as Glima in Iceland and Schwingen in Switzerland, had indigenous forms of wrestling at their centre. An important and basic difference between Grundtvigian gymnastics, on the one hand, and German *Turnen* and Slavic *Sokol*, on the other, concerned the bodily militarism that marked the latter.

MOVEMENT, DIVERSITY, AND VOICING

The significance of Grundtvigian body culture raises questions touching on the relation between personality and movement, and the significance of *stemning* (voicing).

The Role of Personality in Relation to Culture and Movement

The main interpretations of sport and gymnastics try to find the origin of these practices either in certain rules that were established by bureaucratic organizations (as in competitive sport) or in the ideas of founders such as Friedrich Ludwig Jahn (German *Turner* gymnastics), Pehr

Henrik Ling (Swedish gymnastics), Miroslav Tyrš (*Sokol* gymnastics), and Pierre de Coubertin (Olympic sport). The history of Grundtvigian movement culture challenges these assumptions.

Jahn wrote *Deutsches Volkstum* (1810) and *Deutsche Turnkunst* (1816), which provided ideas to both the nationalist and the gymnastic movements. Pierre de Coubertin formulated national-pedagogical ideas for Olympic sport. But the case of Grundtvig shows that the step from ideas to social practice is not so simple. Grundtvig did not write on sports or gymnastics, yet he became important for Danisk *folkelig* sports. Grundtvig's influence worked outside written literature. Even his *højskole* writings may have been of minor significance beside the real impetus provided by the People's High Schools in Denmark.

Thus, there is not one straight line that leads from a historical founder to subsequent and current social practice, as is often postulated by traditional historiography: "From Jahn, Coubertin, or whoever to..." What happens between ideas and social realities is a matter of curves rather than straight lines. Discontinuities of this type may be seen in the move from non-sporting Grundtvigianism to gymnastic Grundtvigianism (Trier 1884), the later differentiation between Bukh in Ollerup and Bukdahl in Snoghøj, and then the emergence of body-cultural Neo-Grundtvigianism (Korsgaard in Gerlev). It was only in hindsight that Grundtvig was credited with so much influence.

The Grundtvigian sports movement demands a closer look at the term "movement." In Danish, as in many languages, the word *bevægelse* has a threefold meaning, oscillating between bodily movement, psychic-emotional movement, and social movement. So far, research has underplayed the connection between these three dimensions. For the most part, sociological literature treats movements as though they are just organizations based on ideas and on mobilizing resources (della Porta 1999; Raschke 1985; Snow, Soule, and Kriesi 2004). However, in contrast to this top-down view, movements develop from below, involving doing, singing, and atmosphere.

The Significance of Stemning

Folkelig body culture is marked by what in Danish is called *stemning*, or voicing. This voicing can also be characterized as energy or atmosphere, as mood or "spirit." *Stemning* is a world of feelings, connecting individual emotions within a collective atmosphere. It represents the "warm" side of people's lives. The contradiction between warmth and coldness constitutes an important element in the Grundtvigian understanding of life. Grundtvig also used the word "heart" to characterize this dimension of human life as well as "school" and "nation." "Heart" and *stemning* were indeed central concepts of German romanticism. They also contribute to understanding the Grundtvigian term "spirit," which is more and other than an abstract religious or philosophical idea. Spirit is connected with the *gejst* of *begejstring* (emotional exaltation), with the spirit of "spiritus," high and jag (i.e., intoxication), and with the *ånd* of *åndedræt* (breathing). All these express experiences of an energetic, bodily, and emotional character.

In line with terms such as "aura," "charisma," "resonance," and "magnetism," voicing has a deep material meaning for people's bodily practice. *Stemning* connects social movement, emotional movement, and bodily movement. The People's High School is *stemning*, as is people's sport (*stævne*). *Stemning* is an important element of the "material basis" that is the crux of people's lives.

As the Grundtvigian and *højskole* headmaster Hal Koch expressed it, the human being is fundamentally a *stemningsvæsen*, a voicing being. This "warm" quality is not simply an idealistic construction, and it cannot be reconstructed in abstract philosophical or scientific terms. Nor is it simply metaphorical. But human energy is – as the history of Grundtvigian movement culture shows – a material power in people's social life. It comes under the category of bodily materialistic understanding (Eichberg 2010).

Last but not least, the connection between *stemning* and popular movement contributes to the theory of democracy. It is tempting to explore the connections between Grundtvigian practice and voicing in sport – and the remarkable significance of equality and mutual trust (*tillid*) in Danish culture. The connection between equality and trust may be regarded as a matter of national pride, as it was expressed in Grundtvigian patriotic songs with all their "warm" voicing. They were literally electrifying democracy.

REFERENCES

Becker, H., and H. Bernett, eds. 1979. *Internationales Jahn-Symposium Berlin 1978* [International Jahn Symposium Berlin 1978]. Cologne: Brill.

Blecking, D., ed. 1991. *Die slawische Sokolbewegung: Beiträge zur Geschichte von Sport und Nationalismus in Osteuropa* [The Slavic Sokol movement:

Contributions to the history of sport and nationalism in Eastern Europe]. Dortmund: Forschungsstelle Osteuropa an der Universität.

Bonde, H. 2003. *The Battle of Youth: Niels Bukh and the Creation of Modern Gymnastics. 1880–1950*. Copenhagen: Museum Tusculanum.

Bukdahl, J. 1943. "Dansk Idræt" [Danish sport]. In *Idræt: Vor Tids store Folkeopdrager* [Sport: The great folk educator of our time], vol. 2, ed. K. Krogshede, 333–5. Odense: Arnkrone.

della Porta, D., and M. Diani. 1999. *Social Movements: An Introduction*. Oxford: Blackwell.

Eichberg, H. 2010. *Bodily Democracy: Towards a Philosophy of Sport for All*. London: Routledge.

Engelstoft, L. 1801. *Om den Priis, Oldtidens Skandinaver satte på Legemsøvelser, mest med Hensyn til Nationalopdragelsen: Et Indbydelsesskrift til den offentlige Examen i det Schouboeske Institut* [About the value, the ancient Scandinavians attributed to physical exercise, mostly concerning national education: A book of invitation to the public examination at the Schouboe Institute]. Copenhagen: N.p. Reprint Oslo 1981.

Hansen, J. 1993. "'Fagenes Fest": Working-Class Culture and Sport." In *Körpersprache: Über Identität und Konflikt* [Body language: About identity and conflict], ed. K. Dietrich and H. Eichberg, 97–129. Frankfurt/Main: Afra.

Jarvie, G. 1991. *Highland Games: The Making of the Myth*. Edinburgh: Edinburgh University Press.

Jorn, Asger. 1962. *Naturens orden* [The order of nature]. Valby: Borgens.

– 1964. *Ting og polis* [Thing and polis]. Valby: Borgens.

Korsgaard, O. 1982. *Kampen om kroppen: Dansk idræts historie gennem 200 år* [Struggle about the body: 200 years of Danish sport history]. Copenhagen: Gyldendal.

– 1986a. *Krop og kultur: Andelsbøndernes gymnastik mellem almuens leg og borgerskabets sport* [Body and culture: The gymnastics of co-operative farmers between peasants' game and bourgeois sport]. Odense: Odense Universitetsforlag.

– 1986b. *Kredsgang: Grundtvig som bokser* [Struggle in the circle: Grundtvig as boxer]. Copenhagen: Gyldendal.

– 2012. *N.F.S. Grundtvig*. Copenhagen: Jurist- og Økonomforbundets Forlag.

Matsumae, S. 1987. *In Search of the Culture of Scandinavia*. Tokyo: Tokai University Press.

Møller, J. 2010. *Med leg skal land bygges* [With play, shall country be built]. Gerlev: Bavnebanke.

Raschke, J. 1985. *Soziale Bewegungen: Ein historisch-systematischer Grundriß* [Social movements: A historical-systematical outline]. New York: Campus.

Snow, D.A., S.A. Soule, and H. Kriesi, eds. 2004. *The Blackwell Companion to Social Movements*. Oxford: Blackwell.

Trier, E. 1968 [1884]. "Tale ved indvielsen af Vallekilde Højskoles Gymnastikhus" [Lecture for the inauguration of the gymnastic hall of Vallekilde High School]. In *En højskolevinter* [A high school winter], ed. R. Skovmand, n.p. Copenhagen: Gad.

19

Windmills, Butter, and Bacon: The Circulation of Scientific Knowledge among Grundtvigians in the Decades around 1900

HANS HENRIK HJERMITSLEV

It is well documented that the followers of N.F.S. Grundtvig played a seminal role in the Danish nation-building process, including the forming of national identity and democratic modernization. Hence, the Grundtvigian movement took a central part in the national, religious, and cultural enlightenment of the rural population in Denmark in the nineteenth and early twentieth centuries (Korsgaard 2006; Østergård 2006). In line with this perspective, existing historiography has primarily focused on the Grundtvigian People's High Schools and their program of liberal education, emphasizing the role of history and literature in the formation (*dannelse*) of the Danish people (Hjermitslev 2010; Korsgaard 2010).

However, the focus on the formative aspects of the teachings at the People's High Schools has resulted in a misleading downplaying of the scientific, technical, and vocational education at these schools. This chapter demonstrates that, in spite of the sceptical attitude among many Grundtvigians towards traditional education and natural science, in the decades around 1900 the People's High Schools were major players in the dissemination of scientific knowledge to rural youth. Thus the teaching of agriculture and other scientific and vocational subjects went hand in hand with the formation of hearts and minds. As a result, the rural population in Denmark reached an educational level unparalleled in most other countries, and this paved the way for rapid agricultural and economic development in the decades around 1900.

I place the Danish case in a comparative perspective and focuses on two aspects of the circulation of scientific knowledge among Grundtvigians. First, I analyze the teaching of natural science at the People's High Schools and then demonstrate how the People's High School teachers K.C. Knudsen in Karise and Poul la Cour in Askov popularized scientific and technological knowledge in Grundtvigian circles. Second, I discuss the impact of the Grundtvigian People's High Schools and agricultural schools on the development of the cooperative movement, the introduction of scientifically based agricultural practices, and the swift transition of Danish agriculture from crops to butter and bacon as the primary export commodities in the 1880s.

TEACHING THE NATURAL SCIENCES AT THE PEOPLE'S HIGH SCHOOLS

The authority of Grundtvig lived on after his death in 1872, and this meant that, if one wished to legitimize innovative ideas in Grundtvigian circles, the chance of success would be significantly improved if one's ideas could be backed by arguments drawn from Grundtvig's writings. Grundtvig's ideas were a synthesis of idealistic philosophy of history, Christianity, nationalism, and liberalism. He understood history as a teleological process and as the unfolding of the Creator's plan, in which the peoples of the North were regarded as one of God's chosen people. According to Grundtvig, all knowledge was rooted in a specific people with its unique language and culture, and at a specific time in history. Therefore, history and literature were primary to his vision of liberal education, while practical and vocational training and natural knowledge were secondary. Grundtvig's views on the natural sciences are complex and much debated among historians. In this context, it suffices to note that he was critical of the abstractions of contemporary natural philosophy, which he feared would alienate people from their daily endeavours, discredit their common sense, and shake their religious faith (Hjermitslev 2010, 2011, 2012; Korsgaard 2010, 2011; Malone 1940; Pedersen 1990).

Grundtvig's reservations about academic learning and the natural philosophy of his day, and his distinction between the "dead letters" of traditional education and "the living word" found in Danish literature and Nordic myths, were fundamental for Grundtvig's followers, who established an alternative to the existing educational system in rural areas. Thus, from the middle of the nineteenth century hundreds of free primary schools, People's High Schools, agricultural schools, and colleges of education were founded by Grundtvigians (Korsgaard 2006; Østergård 2006).

The People's High Schools were the most profiled Grundtvigian institutions. They proliferated after the Danish defeat to Prussia and Austria in the Second Schleswig War in 1864, and their numbers reached seventy-five in 1890. The vast majority of the People's High Schools supported Grundtvig's educational program, while a minority of them were based in either rationalistic or evangelical principles. The People's High Schools were boarding schools for young people from the age of eighteen and offered five months of education to men during winter and three months of education to women during summer. The students experienced an intense life at the schools, with classes from 8:00 AM to 8:00 PM six days a week and joint activities in the evening and on Sundays. From 1864 to 1920, the People's High Schools received around 250,000 students (i.e., around 15 percent of the rural youth), of which three-quarters were sons and daughters of peasant-farmers. Strongly influenced by Grundtvig, the schools were based on liberal principles. Thus, in general they did not offer any exams or diplomas but, rather, saw it as their duty to enlighten the students in terms of historical awareness, national identity, and democratic citizenship. The primary didactic means to this end were storytelling, lectures, discussions and, community singing (Hjermitslev 2010; Korsgaard 2006).

In accordance with Grundtvig's ideas about national and spiritual formation, the fundamental subjects at the People's High Schools consisted of various historical disciplines such as Danish history, world history, and literary history, which took up between one-fourth and one-half of the schedule. This, however, left plenty of room for the teaching of other subjects. Among the students and their parents there was a strong demand for useful knowledge that could strengthen their future vocations as independent farmers and housekeepers. Principals at the People's High Schools thus saw it as a pecuniary necessity to offer classes in basic subjects such as writing and arithmetic. In this way, the People's High Schools functioned as a kind of senior school and as a supplement to the students' seven years of primary education (Hjermitslev 2010, 117–18).

Alongside the historical lectures and the practical writing and arithmetic classes, most of the People's High Schools offered a wide range of scientific and vocational subjects. Like in the state schools, the students were offered classes in biology, geography, and physics, often with an emphasis on topics relevant to becoming farmers and housekeepers. These classes were supplemented by practical subjects relevant to rural youth. The male students were taught the basic principles of accounting, surveying, and levelling, agricultural chemistry, and agricultural geology, while the female students were educated in useful subjects such as home economics, needlework, dairying, household chemistry, and health (Hjermitslev 2012).

In sum, the schedule at the People's High Schools was divided into three more or less equally large elements: (1) lectures on history and literature, which were seen as the fundamental, formative subjects; (2) basic classes in writing and arithmetic; and (3) scientific and practical subjects relevant to agriculture (moreover, gymnastics and community singing were compulsory subjects at a majority of the People's High Schools). However, as Ove Korsgaard points out, the historical narrative of the Danish People's High School movement focuses on the first element in order to confirm its identity as a "school for life," that is, an institution devoted to spiritual and national formation, while the other two elements are downplayed in an attempt to distance the People's High Schools from traditional and technical education (Korsgaard 2010).

In Sweden, by contrast, a rationalistic rather than a humanistic concept of formation dominated the People's High Schools, and therefore scientific subjects were more easily included in the educational ideology than they were in Denmark, where principals and teachers were reluctant to emphasize the scientific and practical value of the schools since it could make it difficult to legitimize their connection to the Grundtvigian educational program (Hjermitslev 2010; Lundh Nilsson 2010). Moreover, Grundtvig's reservations about natural science and its materialist and atheist potential did not make things easier for teachers interested in profiling natural science at the schools. In reality, however, the People's High Schools offered daily classes in the natural sciences, and, even though the principals at the schools were reluctant to inform students about the use of textbooks, which were often associated with the "dead letters" of traditional education, there is evidence that many People's High Schools used textbooks in classes such as arithmetic, surveying, agricultural chemistry, and agricultural geology. Moreover, more than two-thirds of the People's High Schools had equipment for physical and chemical experiments (Skovmand 1944, 257–63). Thus, no doubt, the People's High Schools played an important part in disseminating mathematics and scientific knowledge, especially of agriculture, to rural youth (Hjermitslev 2010).

THE "PHYSICAL HIGH SCHOOL" IN KARISE

While a majority of People's High Schools focused on lectures on history and literature supplemented by the teaching of basic skills and subjects relevant to agriculture and house economics, two schools launched a strong scientific program: Karise People's High School on Zealand and Askov People's High School in Jutland. In Karise the principal from 1879 to 1910, K.C. Knudsen, established what was commonly called "the physical high school," while in Askov, the physicist Poul la Cour introduced an ambitious mathematics and physics program when, in 1878, Askov established an advanced course for second- and third-year high school students. The cases of Knudsen and la Cour are illuminating since they highlight the precarious relation to natural science in Grundtvigian circles.

Like many other People's High School teachers, K.C. Knudsen was educated at Blaagaard College of Education in Copenhagen. He started his career as a teacher at Emdrupgaard People's High School before taking up positions as teacher and later principal in Karise. Here he gave the school a strong scientific profile. The male students had five physics classes a week (most People's High Schools only offered three weekly classes at this time), and he established a laboratory, an observatory, and a large collection of scientific instruments, which he used in his natural science classes. Knudsen focused on the practical application of scientific discoveries, and he purchased an X-ray machine that was used by many doctors in South Zealand. Moreover, Knudsen challenged Grundtvigian ideology by giving his students exams (Hjermitslev 2010, 124–5).

However, Knudsen was a devout Christian and acknowledged his Grundtvigian legacy. Six lectures on history was part of the schedule, and, according to one biographer, Knudsen endorsed Grundtvig's vision of enlightening the rural population while, at the same time, opening the students' eyes to "the wonderful world of nature" (Martekilde and Grønborg 1919, 34, my translation). Knudsen's interest in science was stimulated by contacts with professors at the University of Copenhagen. Frequently, professors from Copenhagen lectured in Karise. Among the visitors were Professor of Philosophy Harald Høffding and Professor of History Kristian Erslev. They both played an important part in the establishment of university extension in 1899. Initially, the university extension movement was based on cooperation between university academics and People's High School teachers, but, as early as 1902, the joint venture collapsed due to ideological differences between radical and positivist circles in Copenhagen and Grundtvigian idealists in the People's High Schools. University extension was primarily aimed at the workers in the large towns and in the city of Copenhagen, and it was regarded as a scientific alternative to the spiritual enlightenment of the People's High School movement (Andersen 2007). Thus, Knudsen's close contacts with university professors and his attempt to build a bridge between the university and the People's High School placed him in a precarious situation and marginalized him from mainstream Grundtvigianism (Hjermitslev 2010, 125).

In the late 1890s, Knudsen was involved in the pioneering work of illuminating the local cooperative dairy with electric lightning, and, from 1901 to 1911, Karise hosted a state-sponsored course in physics aimed at country teachers. The course took place during fourteen days in August and attracted no fewer than 475 teachers altogether. By contrast, the number of regular students was modest. During Knudsen's reign from 1879 to 1910, 684 students were enrolled in Karise, and when Knudsen resigned, "the physical high school" was not able to survive. In 1922 it closed, and two years later the building burned down. However, Knudsen's collection of scientific instruments was not lost in the fire. In 1912, he handed the collection to Askov, another People's High School with a strong scientific program (Hjermitslev 2010, 125; Vleuten 1998, 45).

LEGITIMIZING MATHEMATICS AND SCIENCE IN ASKOV

While the school in Karise remained in a marginal position in the Grundtvigian high school movement, since its establishment in 1865, Askov People's High School was one of the most influential schools. The principal, Ludvig Schrøder, was widely regarded as the leader of the People's High School movement, and Askov received much attention when, in 1878, he launched an extended People's High School with advanced courses for second- and third-year students. Schrøder realized that it was necessary to include natural science classes in the schedule, and he regarded the physicist, inventor, and deputy director of the Danish Meteorological Institute, Poul la Cour, as the right person to teach the natural sciences in a non-materialistic way that did not violate the Christian atmosphere and the Grundtvigian ideology of the school. Thus, la Cour was hired as a safeguard against positivism and atheism, with which Grundtvigians often associated modern science. Since the literary critic Georg Brandes proclaimed the so-called "modern breakthrough" in 1871, Grundtvigians were engaged in a two-front war against classical education, on the one side, and Brandesian free thought, on the other (Hjermitslev 2010, 126).

In order to legitimize the natural sciences as core subjects in an anti-scientific Grundtvigian context, la Cour realized during his first years in Askov that they had to be regarded as more than just useful and practical: they had to be perceived as formative. Following Quentin Skinner (2002, 149–50), an "innovating ideologist" such as la Cour was "obliged to march backwards into battle" by applying to his innovative ideas terms with a positive speech act potential. In a Grundtvigian context, few terms had a more positive speech act potential than "historical," which was closely linked to the Grundtvigian concept of formation. Thus, in his attempt to legitimize mathematics and physics as core subjects at the extended People's High School, la Cour worked on combining the analytical element of the natural sciences with a historical perspective. Principal Schrøder, who was widely regarded as the authoritative interpreter of Grundtvig's philosophy of history, supported la Cour's innovative approach to mathematics and natural science and accepted a relatively ambitious scientific program. The advanced course was spread over two winters, from October to April, and included eight weekly mathematics classes and two weekly physics classes (Hansen 1985, 118–21; Hjermitslev 2010, 126–7; Schrøder 1892).

In 1881 la Cour completed a manuscript entitled *Historisk Mathematik* (Historical mathematics). The work functioned as a textbook and was sold in Askov. It was organized in a historical way and dealt with mathematics in different cultures in different historical epochs. In line with Grundtvig, la Cour outlined the spiritual development of humankind. La Cour focused on the Greeks, the Egyptians, and, especially, the Hindus, who were regarded as the masters of algebra and, according to Grundtvig, the future seventh Christian congregation. In this way, La Cour's work fulfilled two purposes: (1) the students were able to learn since they came to understand the problems and the contexts out of which mathematics had developed, and, at the same time, (2) the historical approach made it possible for la Cour to legitimize mathematics as a formative subject (Hjermitslev 2010, 127; la Cour 1881). Indeed, a positive review in *Højskolebladet* (The high school magazine) indicated that la Cour succeeded in legitimizing mathematics and natural science in a Grundtvigian context: "this book breaks fresh ground for a new school of thought within scientific education. That is, to implement Grundtvig's educational vision in the scientific subjects in order to apply them to a healthy, formative education so that they can be part of the struggle for real, popular enlightenment" (quoted in Hjermitslev 2010, 127, my translation).

Repeatedly la Cour argued his case in popular lectures and in Grundtvigian journals. In the 1880s, for example, la Cour explained his didactical vision in the Askov mouthpiece *Historisk Månedsskrift* (Historical monthly). La Cour (1883, 104) emphasized that a historical approach to mathematics "is a small part of the general teaching of history" and therefore can function as "a very useful means of formation" (98, my translations). La Cour also explained his historical approach to the teaching of physics. He distanced his didactical method from traditional education and "encyclopaedic formation" and argued that the aim of his teaching was to let "the students' thoughts follow the same path as the one mankind has walked." In this way, the teaching of physics would be relevant to the student's own life and his or her personal development (la Cour 1884, 56, 53, my translation).

In 1896 and 1897 la Cour and his colleague Jacob Appel's textbook *Historisk Fysik* (Historical physics) was published in a series of installments, available via subscription, by the large publishing house Nordisk Forlag. The work was quite successful in terms of circulation, and editions were issued until 1966. In their work, la Cour and Appel (1896–97) outlined the history of physics by focusing on the discoveries of individual scientists. In the first decade of the twentieth century, la Cour became one of the most widely read popular science writers in Denmark. From 1903 to 1904 his work *Menneskeaandens Sejre* (Victories of the human spirit), co-authored by physicist Helge Holst, was published by Nordisk Forlag in the exceptionally popular book series *Frem* (Forward), which sold up to 100,000 copies each week. *Menneskeaandens Sejre* was a work on the history of technology, and it reflected a general belief in science and technology as vehicles for progress and wealth. This enthusiasm and optimism connected to technological inventions was popularized by la Cour and shared by many of his fellow Grundtvigians, who were eager to exploit the potential of new inventions such as X-ray machines, telephones, diesel engines, electric lightning, and, most important, various agricultural machines (Andersen and Hjermitslev 2006; Hjermitslev, Andersen, and Kjærgaard 2006, 363–8; la Cour and Holst 1903–4).

During the 1880s, Askov Extended People's High School witnessed the successful implementation of la Cour's ideas of scientific education.

Besides la Cour's classes in mathematics and physics, the students were offered chemistry and agricultural zoology and botany. This strong scientific profile did not put off the students and their parents, which indicates that la Cour was successful in legitimizing the teaching of mathematics and natural science in Askov. The school received around one hundred students each winter, of which one-third were second- or third-year students, and, as early as 1885, women were allowed to join the advanced courses. When Jacob Appel joined the staff in 1890 scientific education was upgraded at Askov. New instruments were bought for the physics laboratory, and second-year students could choose a natural science side, which included no fewer than sixteen classes of mathematics, physics, and chemistry. This move did not result in a decrease in the number of applicants: in the 1890s, the number of students during winter reached 150, with one-fifth of them being second-year students. In 1897, however, the number of mathematics and science classes decreased due to la Cour's work with windmills and electricity, which occupied most of his time from then until his death in 1908. As principal from 1906 to 1928, Appel remained faithful to la Cour's vision of integrating the natural sciences with the ideology of formation at Askov. However, in the second quarter of the twentieth century, the mathematics, physics, and chemistry classes were gradually replaced by humanistic subjects, and, since then, the natural sciences have been marginal at Askov and at most of the other People's High Schools in Denmark (Hjermitslev 2010, 129–30).

In 1891, Poul la Cour initiated an experimental research program concerning the electrical exploitation of wind power. When he arrived at Askov, la Cour was already known for his inventions of telegraphic devices, and when, in 1891, he received a small grant from the state, his career as an inventor was back on track. An experimental windmill was built, and, together with Appel, he began to work on optimizing the windmill and finding an effective way to store wind energy. Government funding continued during the 1890s, which, around 1900, resulted in a remarkable situation of la Cour's being the Danish scientist who received the largest government subsidies. However, the investment in him paid off: in 1895, the rooms of Askov People's High School were illuminated by electricity produced by wind power; in 1898, a large experimental windmill was ready for use; and, in 1902, la Cour converted the windmill to a DC power station that supplied the electricity for a pioneering local electricity system in the village of Askov. By 1903, the local system supplied more than four hundred lights and a handful of electro motors.

Ninety-two percent of the energy was produced by the windmill, while a petrol engine was used as a back-up unit in periods without wind. Thus, around 1900, Askov was the powerhouse of Danish research on electrification (Hedal 1993; Vleuten 1998, 83–8).

While la Cour was focusing on the technological challenges facing wind electricity in the 1890s, in 1902 he turned his attention to the electrification of rural Denmark. At this time many towns witnessed a rapid development of central electricity systems, but the state and the municipalities did not engage in the electrification of rural areas. La Cour regarded electricity supply as a condition of economic development. In order to avoid having people and industry migrate to urban areas where they could find electricity, he saw it as his task to provide a suitable solution for the rural population. He suggested a decentralized system in which villages established local supply systems while isolated farms invested in autoproduction systems. Both systems could rely on wind energy supplemented by a gas or diesel engine. The primary aims were to supply electric lighting for private homes, farms, and industrial sites, such as cooperative dairies and slaughterhouses, and to provide electromotors for driving the threshing machines and other farm appliances (Hedal 1993; Vleuten 1998, 83–8).

In order to boost his technological and political agenda, la Cour established *Dansk Vind Elektrisitet Selskab* (Danish society of wind electricity) in 1903. It published its own journal, which argued the cause of rural electrification, and it provided inexpensive consultant and projecting work for people planning to establish a local supply system. In the period from 1903 to 1912, when the society ended its consultant work and focused on disseminating knowledge of electricity, la Cour and his associates in the society designed a total of 131 village systems. Moreover, in 1904, the society launched a three-month education program for rural electricians in Askov. The course included both theory and practice and was headed by la Cour until his death. No fewer than 230 rural electricians graduated from Askov and disseminated knowledge of electricity and its practical applications to all parts of rural Denmark. The society was dissolved in 1916 due to the development of an internal combustion engine, which largely did away with windmills, while the education of rural electricians continued until 1919 (Hedal 1993, 100–2; Vleuten 1998, 83–8).

Historians estimate that la Cour and *Dansk Vind Elektrisitet Selskab* played a decisive role in the electrification of rural Denmark (Hedal 1993, 105; Vleuten 1998, 88). In 1923, the number of village supply systems in Denmark reached 358, of which 264 were owned by cooperative societies. By contrast, forty-five of the seventy-one large town supply systems had municipal ownership (Vleuten 1998, 67). This indicates that, while the public sector took the lead in the towns, it was the efforts of independent groups of people in civil society, often connected to the People's High School movement, that modernized the rural areas of Denmark. As in the agricultural sector in the 1880s and 1890s, this was primarily achieved through cooperative organization. In 1907, a Danish farmer emphasized the importance of the People's High School movement to the technological development of the country: "Surely it can rightly be argued that pupils of the Danish folk high school and the agricultural schools have been the mainstay of the well-run Danish farm and smallholding ... It is likely, that the pupils of these schools may open a passage, first for the small power stations, later for the utilization of bigger ones in the practical life of the country; surely they are having a double task of throwing 'Light on the country'" (Hedal 1993, 109). Compared to Denmark's neighbouring countries, the 1902 take-off of rural electrification in Askov was very early. By the time Denmark reached 177 village systems in 1910, the electrification of rural areas had hardly even begun in Norway, Sweden, and the Netherlands, and this process only started in Great Britain after the First World War (Hedal 1993, 107; Vleuten 1998, 67).

SCIENTIFIC AND VOCATIONAL EDUCATION AT THE GRUNDTVIGIAN SCHOOLS: THE CASE OF AGRICULTURE

The strong focus on the teaching of the exact sciences found at Karise and Askov was exceptional. At the vast majority of the People's High Schools the primary scientific subjects were related to agriculture. The teaching of agricultural chemistry, geology, biology, and botany was part of the schedule of the male winter courses at around two-thirds of the schools. These lectures focused on theory as most of the students had practical experience in the form of their daily work on farms. Theory was thus regarded as an inspiration, which could strengthen their vocation when they returned to their rural homes. In the 1880s, the average number of agricultural classes increased from four to eight per week. The reason for this increase seems to have involved developments within the agricultural sector (Hjermitslev 2010, 118–19).

In the late 1870s, Danish agriculture experienced a crisis due to competition from North America and Russia as well as due to German agricultural protectionism. Cheap cereals flooded the European market and Danish farmers, who primarily relied on the export of vegetable products, saw it as necessary to change priorities. In the 1880s, this resulted in Danish agriculture's primary export commodities swiftly transitioning from crops to butter and bacon. The effective transformation of Danish agriculture was closely linked to the contemporary introduction of scientifically based agricultural practices initiated by national and local agricultural societies and the Royal Agricultural College, which was established in 1858 in Copenhagen. Thus, when the crisis occurred in the late 1870s, networks for disseminating innovative knowledge of agriculture already existed. In the decades around 1900, agricultural journals and research stations mushroomed, agricultural exhibitions took place all over the country, experts lectured in community houses, and agricultural advisors visited societies and individual farms. As a result, Danish agriculture succeeded in establishing a close link between research and practice – a link unparalleled in other countries at this time (Andersen and Hjermitslev 2006).

Through teaching and public lectures on agricultural topics, the People's High Schools played an important role in this effective dissemination of agricultural knowledge. Generally, the agricultural teaching at the People's High Schools was handled by well-qualified graduates from the Royal Agricultural College. Furthermore, many teachers established agricultural research stations and were involved in the process of making Danish agriculture more competitive (Hjermitslev 2010, 118–19).

THE COOPERATIVE MOVEMENT

The success of Danish agriculture from the 1880s was not only due to the effective dissemination of technology and scientifically based methods. In addition, farmers launched a new form of agricultural organization: in 1882, the first cooperative dairy was established in Hjedding in Western Jutland. The cooperative organization soon proved to be competitive compared to traditional private and estate dairies, and, in 1909, there were no fewer than 1,163 cooperative dairies in Denmark, more than half of which had been established before 1890. Likewise, beginning in 1887 cooperative slaughterhouses mushroomed in Denmark. Both dairies and slaughterhouses focused on the British market, primarily offering high-quality butter and lean bacon. In 1900, Danish butter exports alone accounted for around 9 percent of the national income. The cooperative movement was based on democratic principles and was headed by a self-conscious class of liberal peasant-farmers who positioned themselves against conservative-leaning big landowners and urban capitalists during the constitutional struggle from the 1870s to 1901, when the liberal majority in the two houses of Parliament finally took over government. The cooperative organization, especially within the dairy business, had many technological and economic advantages compared to other forms of production (such as private and capitalist enterprises). Hence it achieved the gains of large scale production and offered the possibility of investment in new technological equipment while, at the same time, ensuring the quality of milk and animal deliveries and offering a yearly dividend to the producers (Henriksen 1999; Henriksen, Lampe, and Sharp 2011; Henriksen and O'Rourke 2005; O'Rourke 2006).

In sum, the combination of the effective diffusion of scientifically based agricultural methods and technological inventions such as the automatic cream separator in 1878, on the one hand, and cooperative organization, on the other, resulted in a successful Danish agricultural sector that remained the primary export industry until after the Second World War. Thus, the success of Danish agriculture in the decades around 1900 paved the way for economic growth and was decisive in the development of modern Denmark.

Historians have debated why cooperatives did better in Denmark than in other countries that had more or less similar economic and agricultural conditions (e.g., Ireland). Ingrid Henriksen and Kevin O'Rourke make a convincing case when they argue that Denmark's key advantage was its homogenous population, which had a large number of middle-sized farms and a rural population that shared a common value system. Thus, compared to other countries, Denmark was a relatively religiously, ethnically, and economically homogenous nation-state. Homogeneity generated social capital and trust, which was one of the necessary conditions for the establishment of cooperatives. Two factors were crucial in the development of a homogeneous population and thus in Danish nation building: (1) the land reforms from 1788 to 1814, which resulted in a large class of freeholders, and (2) the loss of the German-speaking territories in 1864, which meant that Danish language and culture became omnipresent in the state (Henriksen 1999; O'Rourke 2006).

Like the People's High School movement, the cooperative movement was part of a general mobilizing of the rural population in the second half of the nineteenth century. Among Grundtvigian historians it is commonplace to explain the development of the Danish cooperative system by referring to the People's High School movement. However, while it seems to be evident that the People's High Schools played an important role in the diffusion of agricultural knowledge, it is not possible to establish a causal link between them and the cooperative movement: the schools did not teach cooperative principles and, unlike other countries, such as Canada and Ireland, the aim of the Danish cooperatives was purely economic rather than political, cultural, or religious. Moreover, cooperative producers were not exclusively Grundtvigian farmers but included farmers and smallholders with evangelical and radical leanings (Bjørn 1971; Lipset 1967; O'Rourke 2006).

In his detailed study of the relation between the People's High School movement and the cooperative movement, Claus Bjørn identifies no significant correlation between the pioneers of the cooperative movement and People's High School teachers and students. However, he concedes that education and enlightenment achieved at People's High Schools might have provided the students with the tools necessary for engaging in the establishment of local cooperative dairies. Furthermore, Bjørn argues that people connected with the Grundtvigian movement in general, including People's High Schools but also free primary schools, lecture societies, community houses, and free evangelical-Lutheran congregations, seem to have played an important role in the establishment of cooperative enterprises, at least in some areas of the country (Bjørn 1971).

AGRICULTURAL SCHOOLS

Unlike the People's High Schools, another institution influenced by Grundtvigian ideas, the agricultural schools, played a direct and active role in the development of cooperative dairies. Hence, the agricultural schools educated dairymen and milk producers in innovative methods, and some of the leading advocates of cooperative dairies were teachers and principals at the agricultural schools (Bjørn 1971, 17–20).

The agricultural schools were a direct offspring of the People's High School movement. In 1867, the older brother of Poul la Cour, Jørgen Carl la Cour, opened an agricultural school based on the same principles as the People's High Schools. La Cour's ambition was to combine Grundtvig's ideology of formation through history and literature with a ten-month theoretical education in agriculture. During the 1870s and 1880s, a handful of agricultural schools were established, resulting in a total of seventeen agricultural schools in 1919. In the period from 1867 to 1920 approximately forty-five thousand students visited the schools, which regarded themselves as part of the Grundtvigian movement and included historical and literary lectures and community singing in their schedules (Hjermitslev 2010, 121–4).

The agricultural schools had a huge impact on the rapid diffusion of scientific knowledge from research institutions to farmers. In particular, the teaching of animal husbandry and dairying was important to Danish agriculture during the transition in the 1880s. The diffusion of useful scientific knowledge from the agricultural schools was not restricted to students. The teachers, of whom a majority were former People's High School students and graduates from the Royal Agricultural College, were eager to popularize their knowledge in lectures and in print. The most efficient channel of information was the journal *Vort Landbrug* (Our agriculture), which was launched in 1882 by a group of teachers at the agricultural school in Tune on Zealand with the explicit purpose of diffusing knowledge from the agricultural schools to ordinary farmers. During the 1880s, *Vort Landbrug* was the primary advocate of dairy cooperatives in Denmark. Meanwhile, the principal at the agricultural school in Ladelund near Askov in Southern Jutland, Niels Pedersen, a former Askov student and teacher, travelled the country agitating for the cause of cooperative dairies. During the pioneering years in the early 1880s, Pedersen also functioned as a consultant for farmers interested in establishing cooperative dairies, and he launched the first theoretical education of dairymen. Small wonder that Bjørn claims that Pedersen was "the midwife to the cooperative dairy movement" (Bjørn 1971, 18; Klitmøller 2008).

In comparative perspective, the influence of the People's High Schools and the agricultural schools on the modernization of Danish agriculture in the decades around 1900 is particularly remarkable since these independent, locally based institutions initiated by farmers were specific to Danish (and somewhat to Norwegian and Swedish) rural culture. Thus, in North America, Britain, and Ireland, where the transformation from traditional methods to scientifically based methods in agricultural practice were much slower than in Denmark, the dissemination of agricultural knowledge was dominated by less successful, top-down and state-controlled initiatives such as agricultural colleges (Adelman 2009;

Cochrane 1993; Kett 1994; Klitmøller 2008; O'Rourke 2006; Orwin and Whetham 1964).

CONCLUSION

In spite of ideological concerns due to Grundtvig's reservations about the natural sciences and the traditional education of his day, the Grundtvigian movement and, especially, teachers at the People's High Schools and the agricultural schools played an important role in the dissemination of scientific knowledge to the rural population in the decades around 1900. The diffusion of technological innovations such as a decentralized electricity supply system and an automatic cream separator for cooperative dairies had a profound and lasting impact on the development of modern Denmark. Hence, the Grundtvigian movement contributed not only to political and cultural nation building but also to technological modernization and economic growth in late nineteenth- and early twentieth-century Denmark.

REFERENCES

Adelman, J. 2009. *Communities of Science in Nineteenth-Century Ireland.* London: Pickering and Chatto.

Andersen, C. 2007. "For arbejderen, universitetet og videnskaben: Gerson Trier og Kristian Erslev i Folkeuniversitetet 1898–1918" [For the worker, the university and science: Gerson Trier and Kristian Erslev in the university extension movement, 1898–1918]. *Slagmark* [Battlefield] 50: 66–80.

Andersen, C., and H.H. Hjermitslev. 2006. "Videnskab på landet" [Science in the country]. In *Dansk Naturvidenskabs Historie 3: Lys over Landet* [History of Danish science 3: Light on the country], ed. P.C. Kjærgaard, 251–60. Aarhus: Aarhus University Press.

Bjørn, C. 1971. "Folkehøjskolen og andelsbevægelsen" [The people's high school and the cooperative movement]. *Årbog for dansk skolehistorie* [Annual of Danish school history]: 7–28.

Cochrane, W.W. 1993. *Development of American Agriculture: A Historical Analysis*, 2nd ed. Minneapolis: University of Minnesota Press.

Hansen, H.C. 1985. *Poul la Cour: Grundtvigianer, opfinder og folkeoplyser* [Poul la Cour: Grundtvigian, inventor and public educator]. Askov: Askov Højskoles Forlag.

Hedal, H. 1993. "Early Rural Electrification in Denmark: A Reaction from People outside the Town Establishment." In *European Historiography of Technology*, ed. D. Christensen, 91–110. Odense: University of Southern Denmark Press.

Henriksen, I. 1999. "Avoiding Lock-In: Cooperative Creameries in Denmark, 1882–1903." *European Review of Economic History* 3: 57–78.

Henriksen, I., and K.H. O'Rourke. 2005. "Incentives, Technology and the Shift to Year-Round Dairying in Late Nineteenth-Century Denmark." *Economic History Review* 58: 520–54.

Henriksen, I., M. Lampe, and P. Sharp. 2011. "The Role of Technology and Institutions for Growth: Danish Creameries in the Late Nineteenth Century." *European Review of Economic History* 15: 475–93.

Hjermitslev, H.H. 2010. "Naturvidenskabens rolle på de danske folkehøjskoler, 1864–1920" [The role of science at the Danish people's high schools, 1864–1920]. In *Två sidor av samma mynt? Folkbildning och yrkesutbildning vid de nordiska folkhögskolerna* [Two sides of the same coin? Nation building and skills training at the Nordic people's high schools], ed. A. Nilsson and F. Lundh Nilsson, 111–38. Lund: Nordic Academic Press.

– 2011. "Protestant Responses to Darwinism in Denmark, 1859–1914." *Journal of the History of Ideas* 72: 279–303.

– 2012. "Mellem dannelse og nytte: Et perspektiv på folkehøjskolernes historie" [Balancing formation and vocation: A perspective on the history of the people's high schools]. In *Hvorfor skal hverdagen ligne en slutspurt: Højskolen til debat 2012* [Why should everyday life look like a final spurt: Debating the high school in 2012], ed. B.A. Popp-Madsen, R.D. Henriksen, and H.R. Christensen, 125–40. Aarhus: Klim.

Hjermitslev, H.H., C. Andersen, and P.C. Kjærgaard. 2006. "Populærvidenskab og folkeoplysning" [Popular science and public education]. In *Dansk Naturvidenskabs Historie 3: Lys over Landet* [History of Danish science 3: Light on the country], ed. P.C. Kjærgaard, 345–74. Aarhus: Aarhus University Press.

Kett, J.F. 1994. *The Pursuit of Knowledge under Difficulties*. Stanford: Stanford University Press.

Klitmøller, L. 2008. *Som en skorsten: Mejeribrugets uddannelser i Danmark, 1837–1972* [Like a chimney: Courses in the dairy sector of Denmark, 1837–1972]. Sønderskov: Landbohistorisk Selskab.

Korsgaard, O. 2006. "The Danish Way to Establish the Nation in the Hearts of the People." In *National Identity and the Varieties of Capitalism: The Danish Experience*, ed. J.L. Campbell, J.A. Hall, and O.K. Pedersen, 133–58. Copenhagen: DJØF Publishing/McGill-Queen's University Press.

– 2010. “Den rene højskole som ideal: Den urene som praksis” [The pure high school as ideal: The unpure as practice]. In *Två sidor av samma mynt? Folkbildning och yrkesutbildning vid de nordiska folkhögskolerna* [Two sides of the same coin? Nation building and skills training at the Nordic people’s high schools], ed. A. Nilsson and F. Lundh Nilsson, 19–36. Lund: Nordic Academic Press.

– 2011. “Om Grundtvigs udviklingslære – og noget om Darwins” [On Grundtvig’s theory of evolution – and something on Darwin’s]. *Grundtvig Studier* 62: 124–55, 172.

la Cour, Poul. 1881. *Historisk Mathematik* [Historical mathematics]. Kolding: Konrad Jørgensens Bogtrykkeri.

– 1883. “Om historisk mathematik og fysik” [On historical mathematics and physics]. *Historisk Månedsskrift* [Historical monthly] 1: 96–104.

– 1884. “Om historisk mathematik og fysik” [On historical mathematics and physics]. *Historisk Månedsskrift* [Historical monthly] 2: 51–9.

la Cour, P., and J. Appel. 1896–97. *Historisk Fysik* [Historical physics], vols. 1 and 2. Copenhagen: Nordisk Forlag.

la Cour, P. and H. Holst. 1903–4. *Menneskeaandens Sejre* [The victories of the human spirit]. Copenhagen: Nordisk Forlag.

Lipset, S.M. 1967. *Agrarian Socialism: The Coöperative Commonwealth Federation in Saskatchewan*. Berkeley: University of California Press.

Lundh Nilsson, F. 2010. “Den svenska folkhögskolans yrkesinriktade utbildninger, 1868–1940” [The vocational training at the Swedish people’s high schools, 1868–1940]. In *Två sidor av samma mynt? Folkbildning och yrkesutbildning vid de nordiska folkhögskolerna* [Two sides of the same coin? Nation building and skills training at the Nordic people’s high schools], ed. A. Nilsson and F. Lundh Nilsson, 81–110. Lund: Nordic Academic Press.

Malone, K. 1940. “Grundtvig’s Philosophy of History.” *Journal of the History of Ideas* 1: 281–98.

Martekilde, J., and Andr. Th. Grønborg. 1919. *Karise Højskole: Dens Historie og Virksomhed igennem 50 Aar* [Karise High School: Its history and activity throughout 50 years]. Copenhagen: Richard Steenbecks Bogtrykkeri.

O’Rourke, K.H. 2006. “Late Nineteenth-Century Denmark in an Irish Mirror: Land Tenure, Homogeneity, and the Roots of Danish Success.” In *National Identity and the Varieties of Capitalism: The Danish Experience*, ed. J.L. Campbell, J.A. Hall, and O.K. Pedersen, 159–96. Copenhagen: DJØF/McGill-Queen’s University Press.

Orwin, C.S., and E.H. Whetham. 1964. *History of British Agriculture, 1846–1914*. London: Longmans.

Østergård, U. 2006. "A Big Small State: The Peasant Roots of Danish Modernity." In *National Identity and the Varieties of Capitalism: The Danish Experience*, ed. J.L. Campbell, J.A. Hall, and O.K. Pedersen, 51–98. Copenhagen: DJØF Publishing/McGill-Queen's University Press.

Pedersen, K.A. 1990. "Grundtvigs natursyn" [Grundtvig's view of nature]. *Grundtvig Studier* 41: 66–104.

Schrøder, L. 1892. *Meddelelser fra den udvidede Folkehøjskole i Askov, 1869–1892* [News from the extended people's high school in Askov, 1869–1892]. Askov: Askov People's High School Library.

Skinner, Q. 2002. "Moral Principles and Social Change." In *Visions of Politics*. Vol. 1: Regarding Method, ed. Q. Skinner, 145–57. Cambridge: Cambridge University Press.

Skovmand, R. 1944. *Folkehøjskolen i Danmark, 1841–1892* [The people's high school in Denmark, 1841–1892]. Copenhagen: Det Danske Forlag.

Vleuten, E. van der. 1998. "Electrifying Denmark: A Symmetrical History of Central and Decentral Electricity Supply until 1970." PhD diss., University of Aarhus.

20

An Ongoing Influence: The Political Application of Grundtvig's Ideas in the Debate on Danish Society, 2001–09

ESBEN LUNDE LARSEN

In this lies our wealth, on this tenet we draw:
that few are too rich, and still fewer too poor
"Far Higher Are Mountains" (Grundtvig 1820)

In this chapter I investigate how and why the ideas of the Danish theologian, politician, and poet N.F.S. Grundtvig (1783–1872) were used by Danish politicians in the Danish public debate from 2001 to 2009, and what effect these ideas have on nation building in today's Denmark. My investigation is threefold. First, I look at Grundtvig's historical role in the Danish political debate to indicate examples of his influence and to compare them with examples from other famous Danes from the Danish Golden Age Literary and Artistic Tradition. Second, I look at how Danish politicians used Grundtvig's ideas in the Danish debate from 2001 to 2009. Third, I explain why Danish politicians use Grundtvig's ideas and why they fall into specific categories.

A LONG TRADITION

In Danish society there is a well-established tradition for referring to Grundtvig in all kind of debates as well as across party lines. Here I mention examples from the two major parties, the Social Democratic Party (*Socialdemokraterne*) and the Danish Liberal Party (*Venstre*).

The Danish Liberal Party has a close ideological connection with Grundtvig and his liberal thinking, and when the United *Venstre* was founded in 1870 by Sofus Høgsbro (1822–1902) and Frederik Bojsen (1841–1926), Grundtvig was thought of as one of its core ideological fathers. This thinking continued and, since Grundtvig's death in 1872, numerous politicians from *Venstre* have referred to him as their source of inspiration. In the 1990s, the first Danish prime minister from *Venstre*, I.C. Christensen (1856–1930), was a student at Grundtvig's high school, Marienlyst. Klaus Berntsen (1844–1927), also from Venstre and the longest-serving MP in the Danish Parliament as well as prime minister (1910–13), grew up in a Grundtvigian environment and successfully fought for the revision of the Danish Constitution (1915) and the abolition of privileged rights to vote for positions on the *Landsting*.[1] The Danish prime minister Erik Eriksen (1902–72) grew up in one of the most central Grundtvigian environments in Denmark, Ryslinge on Fyn.

There are two central contemporary politicians from *Venstre* who were inspired by Grundtvig: (1) the former Danish prime minister and current secretary general of NATO, Anders Fogh Rasmussen, who thinks of himself as Grundtvigian and who often refers to Grundtvig's ideas about freedom (Birkelund 2008, 18–20) and (2) the former Danish prime minister and current chairman of *Venstre*, Lars Løkke Rasmussen, who also refers to Grundtvig as one of the most central fighters for freedom of speech and freedom of religion in Denmark (Rasmussen 2011).

In the 1930s the famous minister of education, Frederik Borgbjerg (1866–1936) from the Social Democrats, gave a speech on the occasion of Grundtvig's 150th birthday in which he paid tribute to Grundtvig not only for his understanding of enlightenment and education but also for his understanding of freedom. During the Second World War the Social Democratic thinker Hal Koch (1904–63) gave a number of Grundtvig-focused lectures at the University of Copenhagen, where he used Grundtvig's ideas to warn the Danish population against Nazism and fascism. After the youth rebellion of 1968 many endorsed Grundtvig's thinking, especially on the political left and in the critical cultural movement that followed that rebellion. The famous Danish left-wing author Ebbe Kløvedal Reich published the novel *Frederik* in 1972, in which Grundtvig was portrayed as a spokesman for a popular movement that sought to overthrow capitalism (Reich 1972). And at the election for a new chair of the Social Democratic Party in 2005, the chair and candidate Helle Thorning-Schmidt, now prime minister of Denmark, referred in her election speech to Grundtvig's famous word in the poem "Far

Higher Are Mountains" (1820): "In this lies our wealth, on this tenet we draw: / that few are too rich, and still fewer too poor" (Birkelund 2008, 15–18).

Grundtvig's position in Danish political-mental imagery is massive compared to other important Danish thinkers. During the period from 2001 to 2009, in Parliament various MPs referred to Grundtvig no fewer than 221 times. Compared to this the Danish author and poet Hans Christian Andersen (1805–75), who wrote more than 150 fairy tales and who played a central part in the Danish Golden Age Literary and Artistic Tradition, was referred to fifty-one times. The theologian and existentialist philosopher Søren Kierkegaard (1813–55), who wrote critical texts on Christianity, morality, ethics and philosophy of religion, and who is known for works such as *Angst*, *The Absurd* and *The Works of Love*, was referred to twenty-one times. Meanwhile, the author, politician, and radical thinker Edvard Brandes (1847–1931), who founded the Danish radical newspaper *Politiken* in 1884 and was minister in the Danish government for several years, was referred to four times.

While some of the influential Danes from the Danish Golden Age Literary and Artistic Tradition are not so strongly represented in the political debate today, Grundtvig's ideas and their practical application continue to resonate in Danish society. His influence on the aims and methods of "the people's education" still mark discussions and celebrations at every level. Not least, his radical definition of freedom for everybody, "for Loki as well as for Thor," colours everyday life in Denmark.

Grundtvig is very present in practical policy in the following areas:

- Independent kindergartens, primary schools, continuation schools, and care homes based on Grundtvig's thought and in Grundtvig's spirit. These are Grundtvigian in the sense of being "free-spirited," free of religious and political influence, publicly financed by the municipalities and yet, paradoxically, private (self-owning) institutions.
- Discussions of freedom, liberal thinking, and Danishness draw on Grundtvig's use of these concepts. He first employed the phrase "liberal mind" (*frisind*) in his literary testament, presenting it as the goal of all his work (Grundtvig 1907 [1827], 170; Kjær 1974).
- Hymns and songs by Grundtvig are widely sung – in churches, at school assemblies, at political party meetings, and at gatherings of many of the associations, societies, and clubs in Denmark.
- The focus on cultural upbringing (*dannelse*) is still central to the debate on the purpose of education in present-day Denmark. The tradition is

coloured by Grundtvig's educational writings in the 1830s and by his ideals of enlightenment for all.

Danish politicians associate themselves with Grundtvig as a significant point of reference, partly when they recount the formation of Denmark as a modern society and partly when they argue for present-day policies. The Grundtvig "narrative" appears: in discussions of the extent and the cost of freedom for all; in definitions of what is "Danish" and "un-Danish"; in concerns for the people's life and culture (*folkelighed*); and in debates linked to the Constitution, such as the current one on state and church. The concepts that Grundtvig either introduced or borrowed and incorporated into his thinking are still broadly accepted by Danish society in both its organization and its self-image.

While Grundtvig is very present in daily politics in Denmark, he is not very present in political science or political theory at Danish universities. Professor Ove Korsgaard (2012, 66–8) notes that Grundtvig is absent in reference works and syllabi in political science because he is not a systematic theorist and because political science works with the state and its institutions and not with the concepts of "people" and "nation." By extension it will be interesting to see how long Grundtvig's ideas will be present in the Danish debate if a new generation of political scientists is not familiar with his work. Also, in what light will Grundtvig's ideas and concepts be presented? Not all Danes refer to Grundtvig in positive terms.

There are politician and debaters who think of Grundtvig as a nationalist and as a liberalist without any social policy. As one example, consider the interview given by the former minister of foreign affairs, Villy Søvndal, to the left-wing daily *Information* (30 July 2008) on the subject of Grundtvig's understanding of the song "Far Higher Are Mountains" (*Langt højere bjerge*). Here Søvndal criticizes Grundtvig for his national self-assertiveness, which, according to Søvndal, leads to anxiety and to the fact that Danes marginalize themselves while the members of other nations do not. As another example, consider the interview given by the Danish social-democratic debater and author Henning Tjørnehøj to the conservative daily *Berlingske* (4 June 2005), in which Tjørnehøj rejects the argument that Grundtvig is the main ideologue behind the Danish welfare system. Tjørnehøj finds Grundtvig overtly anti-social and cynical when it comes to the poor and lower classes in eighteenth-century Denmark.

GRUNDTVIG AS NATION BUILDER

I begin this section by defining "building," "building a society," and "building a nation," all of which are linked to Grundtvig as nation builder. I use "building" to refer to the transferring of Grundtvig's work and stimuli into ideas, institutions, and organizations that can be proved to have derived from Grundtvig's influence. These include the church, the school system, and political institutions. Today, the concept of building is employed in history, political science, and other social sciences to analyze how and why ideas and institutions have come into being.

"Building a society" involves creating feelings of interdependence and solidarity among citizens who understand and formulate their own interests in light of community or national interests. Building a state, on the other hand, entails creating political institutions and defining their power relations. Individuals are granted citizenship and certain rights (personal, financial, and political).

"Building a nation" requires citizens who have rights in a state and who are granted a national identity, whereby they consider themselves as part of that nation, whatever their origin (Pedersen 2010).

I follow Professor Ove Kaj Pedersen (2010) in drawing distinctions between (1) Grundtvig the person and Grundtvig the works, (2) analyses of Grundtvig's work (interpretation), and (3) Grundtvig and Grundtvigianism (effect). I focus primarily on (1) and (2), and only secondarily on (3). The category of Grundtvig the person and Grundtvig the works has to do primarily with his view of freedom, which is the absolute precondition for ideas, activity, and the building of institutions and organizations. We are not talking about unlimited freedom to do everything but, rather, freedom for the common good. A number of Danish politicians associate themselves with this promotion of freedom for both the individual and Danish society in general, particularly when the church or the school is being debated.

Analyses of Grundtvig's work (interpretation), his concepts of "Danishness" and "the people's culture," are realized through creating a feeling of interconnectedness, a sense of social cohesion. Within this framework individuals are free to promote their own interests – for this is in the national interest, says Grundtvig – but not at the expense of others. These interests include their education and enlightenment, which bring with them increasing duties and responsibilities as people acquire a sense of nationhood. A number of our politicians draw on Grundtvig here, not least in debates on what constitutes present-day "Danishness" and "Danish culture."

As for Grundtvig and Grundtvigianism (effect), Grundtvig barely distinguishes between building a society and building a nation; the concepts melt into one another. But he is very conscious of the difference between "state" and "society/nation." From the middle of the 1830s he downplays the concept of state in favour of the concepts of people and nation. Grundtvig is not a supporter of strong institutions that support a "state" consciousness.

A NEW TURN

Over the best part of a hundred years, Denmark built its society on the above tenets, with a faith in the welfare of the community balanced against the welfare of the individual – even as Christianity was declining under the influence of secularization. After the Second World War the application of Grundtvig's ideas to Danish society saw a gradual but decisive change – away from the religious and towards the social and political. The freedoms that were taken for granted were challenged from various sides, including the freedom of the press (e.g., pornography and the Mohammed cartoons) and the freedom of worship (the building of mosques and temples "in Grundtvig's fatherland").

With the election of a center-right government in 2001 (which held power until 2011), the debate on Danish values and their cohesive power took a new turn. The social welfare model was accused of being *too* social, of neglecting the need for individual responsibility in favour of a state-subsidized equality drive. Politicians from left and right still employed Grundtvig's ideas to argue their case, but there was no longer any consensus on their thrust, only on their lasting importance.

The survey I look at is limited to the period from 27 November 2001 to 5 April 2009, during which Anders Fogh Rasmussen was prime minister of Denmark. The politicians' use of Grundtvig from 2001 to 2009 is documented in the Danish PhD dissertaion entitled *Frihed for Loke saavelsom for Thor: N.F.S. Grundtvigs forståelse af begrebet "åndelig frihed" i historisk og aktuelt perspektiv* (*Freedom for Loki as well as for Thor: N.F.S. Grundtvig's understanding of the concept of "spiritual freedom" in a historical and contemporary perspective*) (Larsen 2012).

This period was marked by new directions in Danish politics and included the above-mentioned debate on cultural values initiated by

Fogh Rasmussen in his 2002 New Year Address. During these seven and a half years, Grundtvig was cited time and again as a reference point – by left and right alike.

It is fascinating to look at the way in which certain Danish politicians have drawn on Grundtvig to bolster their case, and it is to this that now turn. First, however, I provide a list of these politicians.

Left

- Villy Søvndal (b. 1952), Socialist People's Party, MP since 1994. Party chair (2005–12). Minister of foreign affairs, 2011–13.
- Pernille Vigsø Bagge (b. 1975), Socialist People's Party, MP since 2005. Floor leader since 2011.

Centre-Left

- Christine Antorini (b. 1965), Social Democrat Party, MP since 2005, current minister of children and education since 2011.
- Svend Auken (1943–2009), Social Democrat Party (1971–2009). Former minister of labour and minister of environment and energy. Party chair (1987–92).

Centre-Right

- Margrethe Vestager (b. 1968), Social Liberal Party, MP since 2001. Former minister of education and church affairs. Minister of economic and home affairs 2011–14.
- Marianne Jelved (b. 1943), Social Liberal Party, MP since 1987. Former minister of economic affairs and Nordic cooperation. Floor leader since 2011. Minister of culture and church affairs since 2012. Member of Parliamentary Presiding Committee.

Centre-Right

- Lars Løkke Rasmussen (b. 1964), Liberal Party, MP since 1994. Former minister of home affairs, health, and finance. Party chair since 2009. Prime minister 2009–11.
- Anders Fogh Rasmussen (b. 1953), Liberal Party, MP (1975–2009). Former minister of tax and economy. prime minister (2001–09), general secretary of NATO 2009–14.
- Birthe Rønn Hornbech (b. 1943), Liberal Party, MP since 1990. Former minister of refugees, immigrants and integration, and church affairs.
- Bertel Haarder (b. 1944), Liberal Party, MP since 1977. Former minister of education and research, integration, Europe, development, church affairs, and Nordic cooperation. Former Euro MP.

Right

- Per Stig Møller (b.1942), Conservative People's Party, MP since 1984. Former Minister of Environment, Foreign Affairs, Cultural and Church Affairs. Chairman of Conservative People's Party 1997–98.
- Søren Krarup (b. 1937), Danish People's Party, MP 2001–11. Former Vice-Chairman of Nationality Committee, Member of Church Affairs Committee, and party spokesman for nationality and constitution issues.

Politicians use Grundtvig's thoughts and concepts because Grundtvig, in the eyes of many Danes, has something positive to contribute. They identify with his quotes, songs and hymns, and ideas of freedom and culture. It is expedient for politicians to take advantage of this identification. Politicians also use Grundtvig's terms and phrases out of context, without necessarily subscribing to the original meaning of these terms, because doing so resonates with the audience.

HARNESSING GRUNDTVIG, 2001–09

There is considerable variation in the way politicians hitch their horses to Grundtvig's wagon during this period – in *what* they say, *how* they say it, and *why* they say it. Two groups are visible. The members of the first group employ Grundtvig as a natural part of their argument in the social debate and even place him on their agenda, often as a corrective measure against what is happening in society. They include Svend Auken, Marianne Jelved, Birthe Rønn Hornbech, Bertel Haarder, Anders Fogh Rasmussen, and Søren Krarup. The members of the second group tend to be more reactive, responding rather than initiating, for instance when approached by journalists or by various Grundtvigian institutions. They comprise, from left to right: Pernille Vigsø Bagge, Villy Søvndal, Christine Antorini, Margrethe Vestager, and Per Stig Møller.

The various political traditions in Denmark give rise to various attitudes towards Grundtvig. Especially after the change of government in 2001, he has been cited both as a source of great wisdom and as a Danish chauvinist with tunnel-vision. From both sides of the chamber, politicians have found it expedient to draw on Grundtvig in support of their views, and occasionally he is quoted selectively, or even completely out of context, in an ad hoc manner. Consider again, for example, the interview given by former minister of foreign affairs Villy Søvndal to the left-wing *Daily Information* (30 July 2008) on the subject of Grundtvig's song "Far Higher Are Mountains" (*Langt højere bjerge*), the gist of which is that Danes are not made for mountain-climbing but for keeping their feet on flat ground. The most important moral Søvndal draws from the song is the idea of equality and solidarity, even though Grundtvig does not argue for equality in the social sense but, rather, for equal dignity for all (a consequence of his Christianity). We see a similar pattern in Prime Minister Anders Fogh Rasmussen's praise of Grundtvig's concept of freedom, even as the number of new parliamentary laws, government orders, and circulars affecting individual freedoms rose by 66 percent in the period between 2001 and 2010.[2] Finally, when discussing the same song in *Daily Information* (3 August 2008), the then minister of environment and energy, Svend Auken, argued that it represents Grundtvig's vision of Denmark as a "country of community" (*fællesskabets land*) in which no one goes to the dogs because the community is the guarantor of the individual's welfare. At the same time, Auken criticizes Grundtvig's opposition to social help and welfare measures.

What politicians actually say about the influence of Grundtvig's ideas falls into three categories: (1) freedom, including freedom of religion and worship; (2) the Danish people's culture and the country's system of government; and (3) the link between Danishness and the concept of freedom. All three of these were challenged during Fogh Rasmussen's period in government (2001–09).

It is no coincidence that these topics were discussed with reference to Grundtvig between 2001 and 2009. During this period, as a result of stricter immigration legislation, Denmark had strong debates on immigration and Danish values. It also had strong debates on democracy and democratic rights as a result of the 11 September 2001 attacks in the United States, wars in Iraq and Afghanistan, and the Danish cartoon crises of in 2006. When politicians have to provide answers in the context of value-oriented debates, a lot of them look back to the starting point for this sort of thinking. And in Denmark that starting point is often Grundtvig.

THREE DANISH POLITICIANS

I turn now to the way in which three Danish politicians employed their knowledge of Grundtvig in the period between 2001 and 2009, with a particular view to the concept of Danishness. They are Svend Auken, a Social Democrat; Søren Krarup from the Danish People's Party; and Bertel Haarder of the Liberal Party. See above for their positions on the political spectrum.

The headline in Svend Auken's above-mentioned interview in *Information* is "Where Few Are Too Rich and Still Fewer Too Poor" – a line from Grundtvig's "Far Higher Are Mountains." Auken argues that this, in practice, leads to a system of redistribution, which is one of the aims of the welfare state. He admires the song for providing an authentic flavour of Denmark, but, at the same time, he notes that it walks a tightrope between self-satisfaction and "idyllic Danishness." In a period of increasing internationalization he finds it quite natural that Danes wish to explore their origins. However, while accepting the fact that knowledge of our history is healthy, Auken (2008) criticizes the Danish government and the Danish People's Party for their misuse of the concept of Danishness: "because by and large the present parliamentary majority is built on this ... nationalism – to such a degree that all of us who love our country and all things Danish and share Grundtvig's love of it now and again find it distasteful. They use 'Danish' to poke others in the eye and discriminate against them." Auken goes on to deal with the problem of Danishness in relation to Christianity. According to him, Danishness has "to a considerable degree been mixed up with being Christian. That is as far away from Jesus as it is possible to get."

In his advocacy of Denmark as a "land of community" Auken emphasizes the importance of Grundtvig: "Denmark is a land of community. No one must be left to themselves or be allowed to go to the dogs in a country where the community is the guarantor of the individual's welfare. This vision of society ... no one has expressed better than Grundtvig in "Far Higher Are Mountains" (*Information*, 3 August 2008). Auken draws a parallel between the situation in Grundtvig's time and that of today: "The community ensures that everyone gets an education and has a decent state of health. That's not something that the individual needs to deal with. On the other hand, within the community there is plenty of room for good individual achievements. That's why we've come so far as a society" (ibid.).

In 2006, Søren Krarup, MP for the Danish People's Party, published *Systemskiftet: I kulturkampens tegn* (Changing government: In the sign of the cultural clash) (Krarup 2006). He describes how, at the 2001 election, the Danes rejected changing of Danish society from a nation into an "immigrant country," and he argues that it was Grundtvig's grasp of "the people's spirit" that contributed to this resistance. Krarup understands what it was that caused "the people's reaction, the instinctive, spontaneous 'no' to changing Denmark from a nation into an immigrant country, the popular rejection of a political correctness that would make us historyless, rootless, and spiritless. Let me simply say with Grundtvig, 'The people's spirit' ... The change of government in 2001 is the nation's answer" (10). In addition to "the people's spirit" Danish society rests on a spiritual foundation that is still worth building on: "We call the mid-nineteenth century the golden age of Danish culture, for in the streets of Copenhagen wandered the spiritual giants, Grundtvig, Kierkegaard ... who made Denmark a spiritually great power. Danish culture then had a shared quality. Its foundation was what Grundtvig called Christianity and Danishness. And in all its simplicity this shows how from the beginning of our history Christianity has been the Danes' spiritual foundation, which in turn has taught the Danes to take care of their own, their country, and their people" (13).

Two years later Krarup wrote an open letter on Danishness and freedom to the Danish daily newspaper the *Jutland Post* (27 May 2008), in which he follows Grundtvig in linking spiritual freedom, Danishness, and Christianity. He is concerned with the limits of freedom in Danish society, and he draws on Grundtvig as freedom's true defender. Krarup (2008) is against turning Denmark into a multicultural society and argues, with Grundtvig, that only by accepting that in Denmark the culture is *Danish* can the country speak of "freedom" – especially from Islamic culture, which includes "sharia and Islamic customs, honor killings, suppression of women, uniformity of family life, and demands for purity and injunctions against impurity."

Krarup (2008) emphasizes how Grundtvig "fought for civil freedom, but did not dilute his own opposition to making all cultures equally good and equally legitimate in Denmark." It was Grundtvig who roused his countrypeople to think and feel *Danish*: "As a member of parliament he [Grundtvig] provoked consternation and ire with his clear, no-nonsense views. The Germans should be allowed to be German in Germany, but in Denmark we were Danish and should hold firm to that" (ibid.)

Grundtvig is portrayed as a role model in the battle for Danishness, someone who, "as the fearless champion of Danishness, openly rejected anything that was hostile to Danishness." A typical example of a politician quoting Grundtvig occurred in the second reading of the bill to change the right to Danish nationality on 28 May 2009, from Søren Krarup (2009) of the Danish People's Party, who, prefacing his remarks with "Let me quote Grundtvig," said:

> "To a people all belong who
> recognize themselves as such,
> those who speak the mother-tongue,
> who for their fatherland burn much."
>
> To be part of the Danish people is to say that this is my people; you acknowledge your affiliation to the Danish people and are at the same time able to speak their language, and, as Grundtvig says, identify with their history, ... To quote Grundtvig again, you must have a heart-relation to the people called 'Danish' and which you call your own. Then you are an integrated part of the Danish people.

In the daily newspaper *Kristeligt Dagblad* (Christian daily), 18 July 2003, Bertel Haarder (2003) of the Liberal Party explained the present-day significance of Grundtvig's idea of freedom as a prerequisite for Danishness: "Grundtvig's view of international exchanges was that the freedom we ourselves demand to enjoy must also extend to others." This has practical consequences for Haarder as a government minister: "it means among other things that discussions on the Muslim demands for the right to the veil, to shower curtains and daily prayers does not enflame the minister! There must be room for this in the name of freedom of religion." Grundtvig saw freedom as a condition for the cohesion of Danish society, but, even though he took a broad view of freedom, there had to be some limits: "Grundtvig said that there was freedom to say everything, also from the pulpit. On the other hand there was no freedom to hurt even a single hair of a heretic's head. The mouth was free, but the hands were tied."

Grundtvig's importance for Danishness and self-understanding is indisputable, according to Haarder:

> If we are in any way to explain the peculiarity of the Danes in relation to others, we cannot by-pass Grundtvig. This goes for his liberal thought, his educational policies, his ideas on local government, and his distrust of centralized power unless it shared out money ... Grundtvig was also ... a strong contributor to the development of the Danes' national feeling. Grundtvig knew what schooling was to be used for: namely, that the coming generation should have a share in a common culture of books, pictures, hymns, and songs. And with the People's High School came the idea that education was for the whole people, not just for the Copenhagen elite. This is still the core

element in Danish culture, and any talk of this culture being changed is superficial. The most important points are still valid.

Haarder praises Grundtvig's understanding of being rooted in one's own culture, "where not everything is equally good": "Freedom requires rootedness, whereas rootlessness does not presuppose freedom. Some Grundtvigians have simply opened up the barn door in the name of liberalism – not freedom – and argued that everything was equally good, or equally unimportant."

The following year, in *Kristeligt Dagblad* (20 January 2004), Haarder (2004) states that the legacy of Grundtvig has at all times since exerted a pervasive influence on the creation of Danish society and its institutions, and that Grundtvig's philosophy continues to be a significant part of social thinking: "I really do hope that we don't throw Grundtvig's philosophy overboard. Without his ideas on the necessity of popular education, his thoughts on the people's community, and their shared cultural experiences committed to history, literature, songs and hymns, in art and culture, there would be no People's High School." In relation to national feeling, Haarder underlines the fact that Grundtvig was nationally *aware* but was *not* a nationalist; indeed Grundtvig's awareness of "the minority" had significance for Danish society: "The fantastic thing about Grundtvig's ideas is that at no time does he become imperialist. At no point does he state that the Germans ought to become Danes. And it has always been the Grundtvigians that have led the way when it has been a matter of giving rights to other national minorities."

These are typical examples of how Danish politicians use Grundtvig's ideas in different ways and from different political perspectives. What is interesting is that these three politicians, operating from three different political perspective, manage to make Grundtvig their own. This is mainly due to the fact that, through his long life, Grundtvigchanged his views and moderated his concepts.

Therefore, when we look at the political application of Grundtvig's ideas in the period between 2001 and 2009, there can be no doubt that they continue to exercise considerable influence even today. This is particularly true of his concept of freedom, which underpins everything he said and did. Grundtvig helped to bring about a democratic Denmark characterized by spiritual *freedom*: freedom of faith, freedom of expression, and freedom of conscience for the individual, but always for the purpose of the common good. Moreover, his concepts of "the people's culture" and "Danishness" remain central to Danish self-understanding, as demonstrated by their continuing application in the Danish Parliament. They continue to be instrumental in building a society in which the feeling of cohesion, of "togetherness," is the primary element of national identity.

NOTES

1 The *Landsting* was the Danish Upper Chamber until 1953, when the bicameral system was abolished.

2 This is according to the head jurist of the centre-right think tank CEPOS, Jacob Mchangama (2012, 44).

REFERENCES

Auken, Sv. 2008. Hvor få har for meget og færre for lidt [Where few are too rich, and still fewer too poor]. In *Dagbladet Information* [Daily information], 3 August.

Birkelund, R. 2008. *Frihed til fælles bedste* [Freedom for the common good]. Aarhus: Aarhus Universitetsforlag.

Grundtvig, N.F.S. 1820. Langt højere bjerge så vide på jord [Far higher are mountains elsewhere on the earth]. In *Sange til den 10de April 1820* [Songs for the 10th of April 1820]. Copenhagen: Seidelin.

– 1907 [1827]. "Skribenten Nik. Fred. Sev. Grundtvig's Literaire Testamente" [The writer Nik. Fred. Sev. Grundtvig's literary testament]. In *Grundtvig, N.S.F. Udvalgte Skrifter. Bd. 5* [Selected works, vol. 5]. Copenhagen: Nordisk Forlag.

Haarder, B. 2003. "Frihedsrettigheder er universelle" [Freedoms are universal]. *Kristeligt Dagblad* [Christian daily], 18 July.

– 2004. "Striden til verdens ende" [Controversy to the world's end]. In *Kristeligt Dagblad* [Christian daily], 20 January.

Kjær, H. 1974. *Tolerance eller frisind* [Tolerance or liberalism]. Fredericia: Lohses Forlag.

Korsgaard, O. 2012. *N.F.S. Grundtvig*. Copenhagen: Jurist- og Økonomforbundets Forlag.

Krarup, S. 2006. *Systemskiftet: I kulturkampens tegn* [Changing government: In the language of the culture-clash]. Copenhagen: Gyldendals Forlag.

– 2008. "Den vigende Haarder" [The declining Haarder]. In *Jyllands-Posten* [Jutland post], 27 May.

– 2009. "Forslag til folketingsbeslutning om dobbelt statsborgerskab" [Proposal for a parliamentary resolution on dual citizenship]. 28 May. http://www.ft.dk/samling/20081/beslutningsforslag/B55/beh2/12/forhandling.htm?/samling/20081/beslutningsforslag/B55/beh2/12/forhandling.htm.

Larsen, E.L. 2012. *Frihed for Loke saavelsom for Thor: N.F.S. Grundtvigssyn på åndelig frihed i historisk og aktuelt perspektiv* [Freedom for Loke as well as for Thor: N.F.S. Grundtvig's vision of spiritual freedom in historical and contemporary perspective]. Copenhagen: Det Teologiske Fakultet.

Mchangama, J. 2012. *Fri os fra friheden* [Free us from freedom]. Copenhagen: Gyldendal.

Pedersen, O.K. 2010. *Grundsvig som samfundsbygger* [Grundtvig as nation builder]. http://grundtvigcenteret.au.dk/fileadmin/www.grundtvigcenteret.au.dk/nyheder_og_arrangementer/arrangementsarkiv/Grundtvig_som_samfundsbygger/Ove_K_Pedersen.pdf.

Rasmussen, L.L. 2011. "Frihed og fællesskab: Arven efter Grundtvig" [Freedom and community: The legacy of Grundtvig. In *Fri, friere, Grundtvig* [Freedom, freer, Grundtvig], ed. H.G. Jensen, E.L. Larsen, and B.S. Larsen. Copenhagen: Vartov.

Reich, E. Kløvedal. 1972. *Frederik*. Copenhagen: Gyldendal.

21

The Economic Consequences of the Size of Nations: Denmark in Comparative Perspective

JOHN L. CAMPBELL AND JOHN A. HALL

Queen Gertrude advised her son to "cast thy knighted colour off / and let thine eye shine like a friend on Denmark." We do not have Hamlet's problems, find little that is rotten in the state of Denmark, and certainly regard ourselves as friends of the country. This is scarcely surprising: we have now spent large chunks of our lives in Copenhagen and have accordingly been drawn ever more into understanding the political economy and culture of Denmark, seen in comparative and historical terms. Explaining the research journey that we have taken and have yet to complete is an idiosyncratic way of addressing the title of this chapter, and we hope that it will prove to be illuminating.

THE SOCIOLOGY OF SIZE AND NATION

Let us begin with two memories. The initial responses that we received in the 1970s when asking about the character of Danish politics all stressed factors to do with social class, seen as the underpinning of social democracy. There is of course truth here, as Ove Korsgaard's second chapter in this volume makes clear. But the image that was often presented to us, probably as the result of a measure of Marxist-like influence in both popular and academic life, suggested a society of great conflict, torn apart by visceral hatreds. It did not feel like that to us. Danes seemed to be Danes, highly similar and blessed with a huge consensual background that kept conflict within bounds. Perhaps we felt this because of basic knowledge of the factors that created really vicious conflict within the deeply divided societies of Europe. What mattered there was the layering of conflicts, to use Dahrendorf's (1959) expression – above all the way in which class factors in combination with nationalities problems could create real social dynamite, as Ernest Gellner (1983) so brilliantly demonstrates. Hence Bernard Shaw (1907, xxxiv–xxxv) helps us understand Denmark: "A healthy nation is as unconscious of its nationality as a healthy man of his bones ... But if you break a nation's nationality it will think of nothing else but getting it set again. It will listen to no reformer, to no philosopher, to no preacher, until the demand of the Nationalist is granted." To put it bluntly, the Danes had forgotten the national homogeneity of their society and were unaware of how much this influenced their politics. The likelihood that a consensual background mattered made us suspicious of the claim made in the late 1970s by Michael Porter (1990), the guru of the Harvard Business School, that Denmark was on the rocks, bound to decline, adrift in a sea of conflict. Conflict there was, but one sensed that Danes would, in the end, pull together. After all, had not previous crises been resolved over beer and smorrebrod?

Our initial attempt to understand Denmark, through a series of working seminars organized in conjunction with Ove Pedersen, led to *National Diversity and the Varieties of Capitalism: The Danish Case* (Campbell, Hall, and Pedersen 2006), a book containing a series of chapters on many elements of contemporary Denmark. We were particularly encouraged to find ourselves in the midst of scholars who did take the national question in Denmark seriously. The views of Uffe Østergård and Ove Korsgaard were immediately important, and they are well represented in this volume. It is worth noting the difference in the emphases. Østergård's analysis of the move from a multinational composite monarchy to a homogeneous nation-state contains an element of regret, not least as he follows John Ruskin in noting that "golden ages" of cultural flowering often have as their base complex societies in which all sorts of people interact in unpredictable ways. In contrast, Korsgaard seems to have a more positive view of the power of fraternity created by national solidarity. But the contribution of the Irish economic historian Kevin O'Rourke (2006) is, if anything, more important still. The most striking finding in his subtle and careful account of the way in which the Danes replaced the Irish in the English butter market concerns social homogeneity. The best way for the Danes to make money, especially given the influence of Grundtvigianism, was to set up cooperatives and, in so doing, to improve their product. The Irish case was wholly different: money could be made in the courts, claiming back land held by

Protestant English aristocrats. Homogeneity seemed to be linked to efficiency, national conflict to a lost market.

With these factors in mind we began to think about the economic consequences of the size of nations. It seemed to make sense to join together two literatures that had ignored each other, to their mutual disadvantage. The classic account of the economic performance of small advanced capitalist democracies remains that of Peter Katzenstein (1984, 1985). He notes that small European states were likely to have relatively few natural resources, which made them dependent on the external world. Furthermore, a limited domestic market necessitated involvement in international trade so that economies of scale could be achieved. Moreover, the behaviour of small and large states differed in the world polity: the great could bend the rules of the international political-economic game to their own advantage, whereas the puny had no option but to manouevre within rules that they could hardly influence. In general, smallness translated into vulnerability vis-à-vis international political and economic forces. Paradoxically, this very vulnerability lay behind the success of small countries. Shared fear created the capacity to limit internal conflict, to plot and plan, and to cope with international vulnerabilities by designing policies allowing small states to swim in the seas of larger international social forces. Crucially, small size allowed all interested parties to gather around a single table and to work together. This led Katzenstein (1985, chap. 1) to appreciate social arrangements in small states that provided great capacities for learning and flexibility, specifically (1) a centralized system of interest groups, (2) voluntary coordination of conflicting objectives through continuous political bargaining, and (3) an ideology of social partnership expressed at the national level.

Comparative political economists have written a great deal about the first two points but little about his suggestion that an ideology of social partnership is also important (e.g., Hemerijck, Unger, and Visser 2000; Hicks and Kenworthy 1998; Smith 1992). Where does such an ideology of social partnership come from? What are its roots? How does it work? In all fairness, these questions were not central to Katzenstein's agenda. His basic point is that this ideology stemmed from collectively held perceptions of vulnerability associated with the nation-state's small scale. However, he also notes briefly that the degree to which nation-states were ethnically homogeneous affected how they reacted in response to such perceptions (Katzenstein 1985, chap. 4). He did not pursue this second point in great detail, but others have.

Ernest Gellner's contribution seems crucial. His focus, in part because of his own experience of the collapse of the small nation-states of Central Europe during the interwar period, is on the vulnerability and economic development of nations (Gellner 1973, 1983; Hall 2010). He makes two specific points in this regard that are pertinent for our purposes. First, societies that are deeply divided ethnically often cannot cooperate and, as a result, cannot coordinate their political or economic activities because the different sides want different things. Similarly, the ability to endure sacrifice for the sake of the nation often results from the sort of strong national sentiment found among people with a common culture. All of this led Gellner (1983, chaps. 3, 6) to conclude that a common culture emanating from ethnic homogeneity was often a precondition for economic success. This is an argument that has resurfaced in various forms among those who today see links between nationalism, social capital, national economic prosperity, and globalization (e.g., Bates 2008; Helleiner and Pickel 2005; Putnam 2007). The point is that ethnic homogeneity and the nationalism that often stems from it can provide the critical social foundation for the ideology of social partnership that Katzenstein suggested was crucial for small states. Second, one way to develop the common culture needed for cooperation and sacrifice is to provide people with a common educational background that instills a strong sense of national identity. For Gellner the rigid status barriers – often based on ethnic differences – that prevented occupational mobility in preindustrial times had to be reduced in order to expand opportunities for everyone and, in turn, help to forge a common national identity, not to mention labour market flexibility, upon which industrialization and economic performance depended. Central to the removal of such barriers was the rise of mass education and the widespread cultivation of human capital among all ethnic groups. Arguably, a common educational background, elevated human capital, and strong national identity can enhance people's capacities to learn and respond flexibly to a wide variety of challenges, not just those in the labour market. Hence, for Gellner (1983, chap. 3) common education can, to a degree, counterbalance problems otherwise associated with ethnic heterogeneity and improve economic performance accordingly.

These theoretical considerations led to a description of Denmark's social formation (Campbell and Hall 2010). Absorbing secondary sources allowed us to describe the creation of a notably homogenous nation-state and to suggest that the success of its political economy likely resulted from this very fact. Differently put, we were writing wholly in the spirit of this conference, *avant la lettre*, and would have done much better had we been aware of its findings! But this particular piece of work moved in a slightly different direction, speculating about Finland, Ireland, and Switzerland – that is about countries whose small size combined with national homogeneity to form a political economy capable of swimming with notable success inside international capitalist society. We ended very firmly with a point that can usefully be stressed here as well. To say that this political economy has advantages in the modern world is not – not for a moment – to suggest that the rest of the world should move in this direction. We issued no call for downsizing and offered no mandate for ethnic cleansing. Description stood above prescription.

FROM THEORY AND DESCRIPTION TO NUMBERS

There is a large difference between being suggestive, on the one hand, and nailing down a hunch with detailed empirical investigation, on the other. In order to move forward we decided to apply, as is now popular, a mixed-methods approach combining statistical analysis designed to detect a general linkage with case studies that could go beyond this – as our work to that point had not done – by specifying the mechanisms that allow size and solidarity to so positively affect economic performance.

The statistical exercise took a great deal of time. The data used to specify ethnic fractionalization were dated, defective, and badly in need of improvement. Accordingly, the first paper that we produced was a new dataset for postwar OECD countries (Patsiurko, Campbell, and Hall 2012). In particular, this involved constructing various so-called "fractionalization" indexes – that is, measures of how ethnically, linguistically, and religiously homogeneous or heterogeneous the OECD nations were in 1985 and 2000. In addition to simply improving on already existing fractionalization indexes, we were interested in seeing how homogeneous the OECD countries actually were on these dimensions and how much homogeneity varied within and across countries and over time. We were also interested in beginning to explore whether this variation was associated with national economic performance. The results were intriguing.

At the aggregate level ethnic and religious homogeneity decreased significantly but linguistic homogeneity did not change much at all among the OECD countries. Moreover, there were some surprising changes within countries as well. Notably, Belgium and the Netherlands became more ethnically diverse by 2000, while the Czech Republic and Slovakia became more ethnically homogenous by 2000 after the Velvet Revolution divided them into independent nation-states in 1992. Whether these changes were due to substantive population changes or new ways of counting population subgroups is sometimes difficult to determine, but we have reason to believe that the former is certainly at work thanks, in part, to increased migration facilitated by globalization and European integration. In any case, we also discovered through multiple regression analysis that ethnic fractionalization – our most robust predictor – was inversely related to growth at statistically significant levels. Put differently, the more ethnically homogeneous a country was the stronger its economic performance as measured by its average GDP growth rate. This is consistent with what others have found worldwide (e.g., Alesina et al. 2003; Easterly and Levine 1997).

However, these results gave rise to two questions: (1) Does a country's size matter? and (2) Would the statistical effect of ethnic fractionalization be nullified if we accounted for the possibility that, in some countries, ethnic diversity might not undermine cooperation (and thus economic performance) if ethnic groups were systematically incorporated into political decision making? In other words, was ethnic diversity less important in countries where steps had been taken to institutionalize the political participation of major ethnic groups? To address these issues we wrote a second paper expanding on the quantitative analysis in the first (Patsiurko, Campbell, and Hall 2013). The results were again interesting but contained two surprises.

Consider ethnic fractionalization. We appreciate that ethnic diversity is a tricky variable. All sorts of nominal differences can be passively present in a society. What may matter, however, is the degree to which inhabitants of a country perceive that their ethnic differences are salient politically. Hence, building on the multiple regression model from the previous paper we added into our analysis a time sensitive measure of "ethnic political exclusion," developed by Wimmer and his colleagues (Min, Cederman, and Wimmer 2010). Ethnic political exclusion is the percentage of the total national population that is excluded from the executive branch of government due to ethnicity. To our knowledge this is the only quantitative measure of ethnic political salience that is available for the OECD countries. The results surprised us. We expected that controlling for ethnic political exclusion in the analysis would essentially wipe out the statistical significance of our initial ethnic fractionalization variable. But it did not. As in our first quantitative analysis we found that ethnically homogeneous countries still tended to have stronger rates of economic growth during the period in question than did ethnically heterogeneous countries. Moreover, the ethnic political exclusion variable did not prove to be a good predictor of growth.

We think we can explain these results. To begin with, researchers who have found this to be significant in other analyses include developing as well as developed countries, many of which, notably several in Africa, are highly heterogeneous and very far removed from norms and institutions of liberal democratic governance. Accordingly, there is more opportunity for ethnicity to be politically and economically salient (e.g., Bates 2008; Posner 2005). Second, there may be some limitations to the ethnic political exclusion data we used insofar as it only measures ethnic groups' relations with the executive branch of government. It says little about representation in political parties or legislatures per se and nothing about unions, civic associations, and citizenship rights more broadly. It may very well be the case that the reason the nominal ethnic fractionalization variable outperforms the more substantive ethnic political exclusion variable in our analysis is that it captures some of these additional mechanisms.

The second surprise was that country size was not a statistically significant predictor of national economic growth. We measured size in terms of population and land mass. It may be possible, again, to suggest why this is so. First, it is important to recognize that the survival strategies of small nation-states vary according to the condition of the world political economy within which they have to live. The widespread protectionism of the 1930s was disastrous for these countries, which have ever since argued for free trade regimes and thus economic openness. In contrast, the late twentieth-century and early twenty-first-century world is rather peaceful in the OECD. Accordingly, land mass is not crucial when an increasingly global economy allows access to raw materials and markets through trade. Similarly, a large population is not crucial when the global economy permits outsourcing and enables workers to move rather easily into and out of countries as needed (as seen, for instance, in Switzerland and Ireland).

Second, however, our results show that the more open an economy is to trade, the stronger its economic growth. The results are statistically significant. Following conventions in the literature, we measured trade openness as imports and exports as a percentage of GDP. Some researchers, including Katzenstein, argue that trade openness is a good proxy for nation-state size and so would object to our conclusion that size did not matter. But caution is required here. The statistical effect of trade openness was quite small. Furthermore, even if trade openness is correlated with size, it cannot be reduced to it. Large countries as well as small ones may pursue policies that facilitate free trade. And we also wondered whether the effect of size on growth might manifest in more indirect ways that transpire over longer periods of time than those we were able to analyze. Indeed, our analysis concerned only the very recent past, the period between 1985 and 2007. It would be wonderful if we could extend our analysis backward to earlier historical periods. But, due to the lack of good historical data on ethnic composition and other important variables, this is not possible. The point is that we need to think more about the nature of nation-state size and what it means for economic performance. One potentially fruitful way to do this would be to develop qualitative historical analyses of key national cases.

CASE ANALYSIS

We began looking at all of these issues through the lens of the Danish case. Then we turned to quantitative analysis to see whether our argument was generalizable. Now we are turning back to specific cases but in a substantially more detailed and systematic way. We have started studying how a sample of small nation-states has managed the onset of severe economic crises. Specifically, we are examining how Denmark, Ireland, and Switzerland (and perhaps Finland) responded to the stagflation crisis of the 1970s and early 1980s and then the financial crisis of 2008. To a significant degree the analysis is be based on in-depth interviews with key actors who were intimately involved in coping with these crises (e.g., top-level politicians, state officials, and business leaders). What follows is a preliminary interpretation of data not yet fully digested. But, so far, the data do seem to support our theories. Let us explain with reference to the Danish interviews regarding the 2008 financial crisis.

Denmark suffered a financial crisis in 2008, as did many countries, although in Denmark it was not as severe thanks to the legal restrictions limiting the opportunities for banks to deal in asset-backed securities, credit default swaps, and other complex derivative investments that wrought havoc worldwide. Nevertheless, several Danish banks ran into trouble, and the government moved swiftly to control the crisis by passing a series of so-called "Bank Packages." These involved, for instance, the state guaranteeing all bank accounts, forcing bank bond and stockholders to take steep financial loses – that is, to incur "haircuts" – and ramping up regulations on the banking and financial services industry.

What is relevant here is how these decisions were made through a consensus-based political process that very much conforms to our models and theoretical expectations. First, just about everyone agreed that the situation was dire due to the fact that Denmark was a *small country* with its own currency and therefore subject to the whims of internationally mobile capital. Put differently, unless the system was shorn up fast, Denmark ran the risk of suffering a serious bout of capital flight. Everyone realized that Denmark's small size made it vulnerable and gave it only limited room to manoeuvre. Second, and also related to Denmark's small size, virtually all of the economists involved in the decision making were trained at either of two university economics departments – Copenhagen University and Aarhus University. Hence, not only did they all share a common paradigmatic view of the situation but they also tended to know each other personally, which facilitated a modicum of trust among them. Indeed, during our interviews we repeatedly heard that, because Denmark is a small country, decision makers tend to know each other well, engage in negotiations of various sorts over and over, and thus develop a sense of trust, which bolsters tendencies for cooperation, compromise, and consensus making on a wide range of issues.

Putting all of this into historical perspective the former CEO of one major bank explained that Denmark is a small country that learned its lesson about vulnerability as early as 1864, when it famously lost a war with Prussia and, with it, substantial territory – a lesson in small-size vulnerability, he explained, that financial, business, and political elites have never forgotten and that still spurs them towards cooperating for the sake of the country. This view was amplified by a senior official from the Confederation of Danish Employers, who told us that, thanks to the strong sense of national vulnerability virtually all Danes, regardless of their political affiliation, share a belief in prosperity, egalitarianism, and a healthy welfare state. He said that, at heart, everyone – even most members of the business community – are social democratic. Indeed, we heard on several occasions that everyone continued to accept the importance of long-standing and rather generous Keynesian-style automatic stabilizers as a way of dampening swings in the business cycle. In short, a rapid consensus-oriented response to the 2008 financial crisis was facilitated by Denmark's perception of small-state vulnerability combined with a strong sense of solidarity and trust borne from face-to-face familiarity and being accustomed to handling its economic problems through repeated episodes of negotiation.

Two caveats are in order. One is that the proclivity for consensus making was reinforced by the fact that, since the mid-1980s, the political parties began to set aside their ideological differences and turn more towards pragmatic politics brought about by the need to deal with an earlier crisis – stagflation and fiscal imbalance during the 1980s. In particular, we learned that the Social Democratic Party's ties to the labour movement had worn thin during this period, such that its views on key issues began to resemble those of the centre-right parties. This became readily apparent in 1982, when, without an election, a Social Democratic government voluntarily turned over the reins of power to a centre-right coalition simply because it believed that, at that moment, the opposition was in a better position to manage the country's economic problems.

The second caveat concerns cultural homogeneity. Nobody told us during our interviews that compromise and consensus-making was premised on the fact that Danes are a very homogeneous group of people. But, as it turned out, this silence was much like the dog that did not bark in the famous Sherlock Holmes tale. This became apparent in a few interviews when people began to speak about recent concerns about the immigration of people from northern Africa and various Muslim countries. Indeed, the xenophobic Danish People's Party emerged thanks to this issue and formed the lynchpin of a centre-right coalition government during the first decade of the twenty-first century. Some of our interviews told us that immigration, as catapulted into the political arena by the People's Party, had undermined consensus-making in politics around some issues, such as welfare reform and, of course, immigration policy. The sensitivity of the issue became apparent during our interview with a senior official from the Confederation of Danish Employers when he preferred not to comment about how its membership stood on the issue. The point, however, is that the Danish consensus model, which served so well during the financial crisis, was premised in part on the country's cultural homogeneity – a condition that some perceive as changing in ways to the point that it has begun to subvert traditional consensus making.

CAUSAL MECHANISMS

Our results so far are promising in terms of supporting our argument that small size and cultural homogeneity afford countries certain advantages in coping with their economic problems, especially as globalization proceeds to unfold. And our intention going forward is to pay increasing attention to the important causal mechanisms whereby small size and cultural homogeneity may or may not translate into cooperation, trust, consensus formation, and, in turn, relatively strong economic performance. So far we have in mind several such mechanisms, some of which we allude to above.

One is *social capital* – that is, informal personal connections that facilitate trust and cooperation. We heard during several interviews that this is an important mechanism that helps decision makers reach agreement. A former Social Democratic finance minister explained that, because of Denmark's small size, people know each other and, regardless of who wins or loses, often go for drinks and conversation following negotiations. Moreover, these people are involved in repeated negotiations, with the result that trust emerges simply due to a constantly repeated scenario. In other words, people learn to trust each other not only because they know each other through repeated dealings but also because they know that, if they violate people's trust in one negotiation, they will not be trusted in subsequent negotiations and their bargaining position will be weakened accordingly.

But social capital comes in other forms as well. We acknowledge the brilliant discussion of the micro-mechanisms at work in the Danish economy offered by Kristensen and Sabel (1997). They demonstrate the direct linkage between Grundtvigian institutions and the craft tradition of the Danish economy, present in both agrarian and urban life. Danes change employment more than do other Europeans, and their high level of skill has allowed the country to prosper in small niche markets at the higher end of the product cycle. It is worth making a point here about the Danish "flexicurity" system described by Madsen (2006). One way of looking at this system is as a support for the skill of Danish workers. But another equally sensible way of looking at it, as is often the case, is to see it as much a consequence as a cause, as an expression of the nature of Denmark's social formation.

Another mechanism is *cultural capital*. Cultural capital is that set of beliefs and common understandings that binds people together. For instance, the shared historical knowledge of vulnerability, such as that learned at the hands of the Prussians in 1864, is an integral part of Danish culture and it helps forge a common national identity. Another example is the shared belief in the value of a strong welfare state, automatic stabilizers, and the like. Recall that most Danes hold social democratic principles dear regardless of their political party affiliation. And, at a more limited level, there exists a common cultural capital among economists trained at the same few universities – a phenomenon similar to that acquired by the political and administrative elites in France who pass through the Grandes Écoles, notably the Ecole Nationale d'Administration.

A third mechanism that appears in our interviews is the revolving door that facilitates *professional mobility* in this small country. One reason there is such high familiarity among Danish elites is that, over the years, many have worked in the same organizations. Notably, many of the top economic elites began by being trained in the two top economics departments and then getting jobs in the Ministry of Finance, after which they moved on to other positions. We were told in one interview that one reason that the Ministry of Finance, National Bank, Danish Financial Stability Company (*Finansiel Stabilitet*), and Danish Financial Supervisory Authority (*Finanstilsynet*) could easily agree and reach consensus on how to handle the 2008 financial crisis was the high degree of occupational mobility among this set of public organizations.

Finally, it is impossible not to believe that institutions matter too, and one of these the *proportional representation* electoral system. After all, this system forces compromise on politicians who, for much of the twentieth and twenty-first centuries, have had to form coalition governments since only very rarely has a single party garnered a clear majority in any national election. This, of course, is also one reason that the Danish People's Party was able to fight above its weight during the early 2000s – its participation was deemed necessary in order to form a centre-right government. In this historically exceptional case, however, proportional representation may have served to undermine rather than to reinforce consensus making, which further bolsters our point that we need to pay further attention to detailed historical case studies in order to adequately sort out the important mechanisms by which small, culturally homogeneous nation-states manage economic crises.

Another institutional factor concerns the extensive *system of negotiations* through which virtually all important policy decisions are made in Denmark. Perhaps the most notable are the extensive labour market negotiations that involve the Ministry of Finance and peak business and labour associations. However, Denmark also relies heavily on a vast array of ad hoc commissions that are staffed in large measure by experts but that operate in close contact with social partners (Campbell and Pedersen forthcoming, chap. 5). The reliance on expert commissions is reflected in how the 2008 financial crisis was handled. We learned from a senior official at the agency regulating the banking industry that, because the issues involved were highly technical and very complicated, most decisions were made through negotiations among the Ministry of Finance, the Danish Financial Stability Company, the Danish Financial Supervisory Authority, and the Danish National Bank. The political parties recused themselves from participating for fear of letting politics undermine quick and effective decision making during the crisis.

CONCLUSION

Our arguments regarding how Denmark handled its financial crisis are preliminary. But what we have learned in our interviews so far is consistent with our theoretical approach as well as with the results of our quantitative analyses. We think that our research proves that the legacy of Grundtvig is alive, retaining its structural role as the basis of the success of Denmark's political economy.

A first point is obvious: the Grundtvigian legacy is somewhat troubled. Due to immigration, in part mandated by limited fertility, Denmark is no longer as homogeneous as it once was. The numbers are not especially large, but they have nonetheless, as noted, turned Danish politics upside down. Interesting questions arise. Is it possible for Denmark to remain flexible if new Danes are not fully integrated? To put the matter in a repulsive way: Is national social democracy, excluding minorities, actually possible? Alternatively, is it the case that Denmark will be able to assimilate immigrants – that is, to become a civic nation – given that, in light of its homogeneous background, multiculturalism is not really an option? We know that immigrants wish to get in and that it is possible for them to leave their own communities (Schmidt and Jakobsen 2004; Shakoor and Riis 2007). But we also know that there are few "out marriages," that it is hard for immigrants to enter the host society in the most important way. But there is nothing special about Denmark in this regard: a similar set of social patterns is visible in another homogeneous nation-state – Switzerland (Wimmer 2002). And a final thought applies equally to all such countries. The ability to adapt flexibly may no longer be the crucial ingredient to economic success that it once was. Innovation may now matter more, and that precious quality may benefit from a rich and diverse pool of talent.

A second point is that, in our own research, Denmark remains very much under scrutiny. One point that concerns us particularly is that of Denmark's uniqueness within the general category of the small and nationally homogeneous advanced states. Not all countries of the type that concern us have done as well as has Denmark. Does Grundtvigianism give a bite to the mechanisms, noted above, that are missing elsewhere? The brilliant article by Kristensen and Sabel (1997) seems to suggest this. They show that the Grundtvigian emphasis on popular education led to technical innovation both in agriculture and in crafts, with interesting flows between them as particular individuals moved back and forth between the country and the city. Further, we must ask: Does Grundtvigianism underlie mechanisms that we have failed even to recognize?

REFERENCES

Alesina, A., A. Devleeschauwer, W. Easterly, S. Kurlat, and R. Wacziarg. 2003. "Fractionalization." *Journal of Economic Growth* 8: 155–94.

Bates, R. 2008. *When Things Fell Apart: State Failure in Late-Century Africa*. New York: Cambridge University Press.

Campbell, J.L., J.A. Hall, and O.K. Pedersen, eds. 2006. *National Diversity and the Varieties of Capitalism: The Danish Case*. Montreal and Kingston: McGill-Queen's University Press.

Campbell, J.L., and J.A. Hall. 2010. "Defending the Gellnerian Premise: Denmark in Comparative and Historical Context." *Nations and Nationalism* 16 (1): 89–107.

Campbell, J.L., and O.K. Pedersen. Forthcoming. *The National Origins of Policy Ideas: Knowledge Regimes in America, France, Germany and Denmark*. Princeton, NJ: Princeton University Press.

Dahrendorf, R. 1959. *Class and Class Conflict in Industrial Societies*. London: Routledge and Kegan Paul.

Easterly, W. and R. Levine. 1997. "Africa's Growth Tragedy: Politics and Ethnic Divisions." *Quarterly Journal of Economics* 112: 1203–50.

Gellner, E. 1973. "Scale and Nation." *Philosophy of the Social Sciences* 3: 1–17.

– 1983. *Nations and Nationalism*. Oxford: Blackwell

Hall, J.A. 2010. *Ernest Gellner: An Intellectual Biography*. London: Verso.

Helleiner, E., and A. Pickel, eds. 2005. *Economic Nationalism in a Globalizing World*. Ithaca, NY: Cornell University Press.

Hemerijck, A., B. Unger, and J. Visser. 2000. "How Small Countries Negotiate Change." In *Welfare and Work in the Open Economy*, vol. 2, ed. F. Scharpf and V. Schmidt, 175–263. New York: Oxford University Press.

Hicks, A., and L. Kenworthy. 1998. "Cooperation and Political Economic Performance in Affluent Democratic Capitalism." *American Journal of Sociology* 103: 1631–72.

Katzenstein, P.J. 1984. *Corporatism and Change*. Ithaca, NY: Cornell University Press.

– 1985. *Small States in World Markets*. Ithaca, NY: Cornell University Press.

Kristensen, P.H., and C. Sabel. 1997. "The Small-Holder Economy in Denmark: The Exception as Variation." In *World of Possibilities: Flexibility and Mass Production in Western Industrialization*, ed. C. Sabel and J. Zeitlin, 344–80. Cambridge: Cambridge University Press.

Madsen, P.K. 2006. "How Can It Possibly Fly? The Paradox of a Dynamic Labour Market in a Scandinavian Welfare State." In *National Identity and the Varieties of Capitalism: The Danish Experience*, ed. J.L. Campbell, J.A. Hall, and O. Pedersen, 321–55. Montreal and Kingston: McGill-Queen's University Press.

Min, B., L.-E. Cederman, and A. Wimmer. 2010. "Ethnic Exclusion, Economic Growth, and Civil War." Unpublished manuscript, Department of Sociology, University of California, Los Angeles.

O'Rourke, K. 2006. "Late Nineteenth-Century Denmark in an Irish Mirror: Land Tenure, Homogeneity and the Roots of Danish Success." In *National Diversity and the Varieties of Capitalism: The Danish Case*, ed. J.L. Campbell, J.A. Hall, and O. Pedersen, 159–96. Montreal and Kingston: McGill-Queen's University Press.

Patsiurko, N., J.L. Campbell, and J.A. Hall. 2012. "Measuring Cultural Diversity: Ethnic, Linguistic and Religious Fractionalization in the OECD." *Ethnic and Racial Studies* 35 (2): 195–217.

– 2013. "Nation-State Size, Ethnic Diversity and Economic Performance in the Advanced Capitalist Countries." *New Political Economy* 18 (6): 827–44.

Porter, M. 1990. *The Competitive Advantage of Nations*. New York: Free Press.

Posner, D.N. 2005. *Institutions and Ethnic Politics in Africa*. New York: Cambridge University Press.

Putnam, R. 2007. "E Pluribus Unum: Diversity and Community in the Twenty-first Century–The 2006 Johan Skytte Prize." *Scandinavian Political Studies* 30 (2): 137–74.

Schmidt, G., and V. Jakobsen. 2004. *Pardannelse blandt etniske minoriteter i Danmark* [Dating among ethnic minorities in Denmark]. Copenhagen: Socialforskningsinstituttet.

Shakoor, T., and R.W. Riis. 2007. *Tryghed blandt unge nydanskere* [Comforts and worries among Danish ethnic minority youth]. Copenhagen: Tryg Fonden.

Shaw, G.B. 1907. "Preface for Politicians." In *John Bull's Other Island and Major Barbara: Also How He Lied to Her Husband*, n.p. London: Constable.

Smith, M. 1992. *Power, Norms, and Inflation: A Skeptical Treatment*. New York: Aldine de Gruyter.

Wimmer, A. 2002. *Nationalist Exclusion and Ethnic Conflicts. Shadows of Modernity*. Cambridge: Cambridge University Press.

Conclusion

OVE K. PEDERSEN

GRUNDTVIG AS PARADOX

In *The Origins of Political Order* Francis Fukuyama entitles one of his chapters "Getting to Denmark." In this chapter he says it all: How can other countries become like Denmark – that is, "stable, democratic, peaceful, prosperous, inclusive, and [having] extremely low levels of political corruption" (Fukuyama 2011, 14–19)? To his unreserved praise of Denmark Fukuyama adds the following: "Most people living in rich, stable, developed countries have no idea how Denmark itself got to be Denmark – something that is true for many Danes as well" (14). By way of explanation he writes: "The struggle to create modern political institutions was so long and so painful that people living in industrialized countries now suffer from a historical amnesia regarding how their societies came to that point in the first place" (ibid.).

His choice of the phrase "historical amnesia" is both purposeful and imprudent – at least in the case of Denmark. He is right to argue that every independent nation, including the Danes, writes its own history and draws on narratives to create a "happy memory" (Ricoeur 2004, 412) of a historical community that rarely, if ever, corresponds to the realities of the past (Anderson 1991, 200–6). But "historical amnesia" is not synonymous with historical ignorance, nor has it led to the Danish people having "no idea how Denmark got to be Denmark." Quite the contrary. For the Danes have managed precisely to create and to disseminate a common narrative for themselves to this effect. The point is that amnesia is not an absence of knowledge but, rather, its opposite: a joint understanding of history so widespread and broadly accepted that there is barely room for any alternative (Hettne, Sörlin, and Østergård 2006, chap. 6).

This is where N.F.S. Grundtvig comes into the picture. There are few others whose life and work have been accorded so great an influence on the history of the Danish nation as those of Grundtvig. There are equally few whose influence on present-day political matters is so often underlined (Larsen, chap. 20, this volume). For most Danes, Grundtvig is the father figure and the constant reference point for an understanding of the birth of the Danish nation. And yet few have studied his specific influence on the Danish nation and nationalism, and even fewer have studied him as a nation builder (Feldbæk 1992a, 1992b; Lundgreen-Nielsen 1992). This is what makes him a paradox. His influence on Danish theology and the national Lutheran Church is studied by theologians; his role in forming the national identity is studied by historians; his hymns and poems are studied by literary experts. But he is all too seldom seen as a *political* figure (Bjørn 2007; Dam 1983; Damsholt, chap. 7, this volume), and this despite being regarded by his contemporaries as one of the most deprecated participants in the national political debate. Also, it must not be forgotten that Grundtvig was a member of the Constitutional Assembly (1848), of the Lower House of the first democratic parliaments (1849–58), and later of the Upper House (1866) (until the age of eighty-two).

GRUNDTVIG AS A LEGEND

When the Centre for Grundtvig Studies first commissioned *Building the Nation*, there was no doubt that Grundtvig was a legend, an "icon of the nation" (Smith, chap. 2, this volume). However, at subsequent conferences and seminars, there have been a number of surprises, first with regard to how little we actually know about the role of legends in nation building, and, more important, with regard to how much room such legends take up in the narrative of a nation's birth. A further surprise has been the difficulty of achieving an impartial approach to Grundtvig as a person, writer, and legend. His position in Danish historiography has proved to be so substantial that we have had our work cut out to establish a methodical distance between ourselves and Grundtvig as our subject. Why should this be so? Can it be that no systematic study of the creation of the Danish nation and the Danish state has ever been carried out in lieu of the narratives that place Grundtvig in a legendary founding role? Or is it perhaps because scholarly studies in theology, history, and literature have merely contributed to the creation of this narrative? Here, the claim is that no basic study has been carried out to examine *why* the Danish state and the Danish nation "look" the way they do today. Instead, there are narratives that can be seen as *components in the process* whereby the Danish nation has been built and a Danish identity has been constructed.

Of course the above claim is slightly exaggerated. There has been wide and deep research into both Grundtvig and the history of the Danish nation and Danish nationalism. And of course it is difficult, if not impossible, to draw a distinction between a scholarship that creates narratives and a scholarship that leads to knowledge. Nevertheless, I argue that this book's contribution points to something typical: namely, that there is no generally acknowledged approach to studying one's own national identity or how, impartially, to methodologically implement such an approach. In this sense *Building the Nation* is exemplary in demonstrating the methodological and theoretical tensions that accompany the attempt to question one's own national identity.

RESEARCH INTO NATIONALISM

International research into how nations and nationalism are created took off after the Second World War (Böss, chap. 3, this volume; Hettne, Sörlin, and Østergård 2006, chap. 3; for Denmark, see Bjørn, Grant, and Stringer 1994; Feldbæk 1992a, 1992b). But whereas this research has continued to gather speed internationally, in Denmark it came to a stop in the 1990s. The question of Danish nationalism and national identity, including Grundtvig's role as a legend, remained merely a project in process (Jensen 1995). It is with this in mind that *Building the Nation* reintroduces international research on nationalism and national identity into the question of the role of icons, of the towering historical personalities. Our hope is to gain insight into both the extent to which Denmark has found a specific way to create a state, a nation, and a society, and the degree to which personalities such as Grundtvig have played a role in this. In order to achieve this we have formulated what may be called "the four basic questions" for the study of nationalism:

1 What is the historical context for nation building?
In Denmark's case this is understood to be the position that the Danish state occupied in the European arena from the 1650s until the

end of the nineteenth century as well as developments in commerce and trade, urbanization and technology, and the relationship between state and citizen during this period.

2 What is the historical process by which nations are built?
This includes: the wars and negotiations between state leaders; the political confrontations in the individual countries; the social movements that, in this context, became organized; and the ideological, religious, cultural, and political clashes to which they gave rise.

3 What is unique about – or common to – the building of any nation?
Such comparisons raise the question of the extent to which context, process, and personality have influenced events in historical situations, and why there have been certain states that were able to establish themselves as nations, and certain nations that were able to establish themselves as states.

4 What significance should be attached to "the unique" in present-day understandings? This includes: the vitality of democracy, the sovereignty of the state, and the homogeneity of the population. By "significance" I mean the possible connections between historical events and present-day institutions as well as the role of narratives in present-day understandings of community, identity, and history.

It is within this framework, and through a comparison between countries and over time, that Grundtvig's person (his life), Grundtvig's activity (his oeuvre), and the narratives about him (his historical effect) must be tested. Were his life and work unique? Or did the narratives about him make them so? Did he exert a personal influence on the building of the Danish nation? Or was this the effect of the narrative? All told, it is the life, the work, and the effect that I refer to as "the legend of Grundtvig," thus raising the issue of a single individual and his role in the building of a nation. Against this background, and based on the contributions of this book and the discussions that have preceded it, I formulate five theses about Grundtvig. They have to do not so much with the questions that are asked and answered in this book as with those that are not asked but only hinted at. I advance these five theses in order to inspire further studies.

First Thesis

In the narratives of "how Denmark became Denmark," the many military defeats in the nineteenth century play a particular role. The same goes for the narrative about the person Grundtvig and his role during the transition from martial failure to national success. The wars were against England, 1801–14 (loss of Norway) and against Prussia in the First and Second Schleswig Wars, 1848–51 and 1864 (loss of Schleswig-Holstein). Also included is Denmark's neutrality in the First World War, the reunion of North Schleswig with Denmark in 1920, the occupation by German forces beginning in 1940, the creation of the welfare state after the Second World War, and the heated debates about Danish integration into the European Economic Community and, later, the European Union. This sequence constitutes the narrative of how a medium-sized European empire becomes one of Europe's smallest but also most successful states.

However, behind the defeats lies a different narrative – namely, that of how the will power of various leaders reconstructed the nation internally to become one of the world's most homogeneous nations (Hettne, Sörlin, and Østergård 2006, chap. 5; Østergård 1997). Writers of Danish history usually draw a direct line from Denmark's loss of its territories to its construction as a nation. (Bregnsbo and Villads Jensen 2004). But the writers often fail to remember that the Danish absolute monarchy was one of the most tenacious of all and that, with the transition to limited constitutional monarchy in 1848–49, Denmark became perhaps the most centralized European state of all.

Thus, parallel to the narrative of a weak state runs the story of a strong state founded at the Reformation in 1536, reinforced by the introduction of absolutism in 1660, strengthened by the promulgation of the Danish Law in 1683, and subjected to a long period of reforms from the mid-eighteenth century right up to modern times. This gives rise to the first thesis: it is the double narrative of external defeat and internal capacity for reform that opens up opportunities for Grundtvig the person.

While the loss of territories creates the conditions for him (and others) to formulate the narrative of one state, one people, one nation, under one God, the strong state creates the conditions for him (and others) to participate in the narrative: namely, by building a nation within the borders of an existing, though changeable, state – and doing so with dutiful respect for the absolute monarchy.

Grundtvig lived in turbulent times and within a context of contradictory developments. The importance of both must not be forgotten. The Swedish wars of the sixteenth century and the English wars of the early nineteenth century left Denmark bankrupt in 1813. With the loss of Norway (to Sweden), and an ongoing conflict over the duchies of

Schleswig and Holstein, the question became whether or not Denmark could survive as a unitary state (*Helstat*). It is in this context that a burgeoning nationalism challenged the unitary state, arguing that the state would become stronger if it limited itself to the territories in which Danish alone was spoken. By way of response the absolute monarchy succeeded in centralizing all authority within the contracted territory. Simultaneously, it reformed state finances and money matters in general, while allowing freedoms to both citizenry and peasantry and loosening the cities' monopoly on trade and markets (Pedersen 2013), thus, at the beginning of the nineteenth century, creating one of the strongest states on the European scene.

Second Thesis

Outside Denmark there has been limited philosophical interest in Grundtvig (Dalsgaard, chap. 15, this volume). Even in Denmark only a few studies place him among the ranks of the Enlightenment philosophers (Birkelund 2008; Korsgaard 2012; Vind 1999). To foreigners he is unknown; to Danes he is a legend, though not a philosopher. Yet this is the second thesis: Grundtvig is also a political philosopher, although his place among the philosophers of Enlightenment must also take into account the double context of the weak and the strong state in which he functioned.

Grundtvig was extremely well-read – in church writings, in the history of religion, in Nordic mythology and Old English manuscripts, and in the classical and Enlightenment philosophers. He was inspired by German idealism (Øhrgaard, chap. 10, this volume); French and American republicanism (Damsholt, chap. 7, this volume; Nørager, chap. 14, this volume; Baunvig, chap. 11, this volume); British liberalism (Birkelund 2008, 75–132; Vind, chap. 12, this volume); and partly also by Slavonic nationalism (Bugge, chap. 13, this volume). In many ways Grundtvig was a poly-historian. He read and interpreted recent European history but always with the aim of arguing for a *reformist* way to enlightenment. On the one hand, he opposed revolution (Damsholt 2000; Damsholt, chap. 7, this volume), on the other hand, he was appalled by the massive economic and social inequalities that he witnessed in England as a result of industrialization, free trade, and market liberalism. Between the radical philosophers of France and the moderate economists of Britain he chose a third way, what Jonathan Israel (2010, 116–23) calls "the revolution of the mind." For Grundtvig it is education, cultural and vocational, that will make all individuals – of whatever class or rank – the equal of their fellow beings and facilitate the transition from absolute government to the people's government.

Arguing against the moderate British economists, Grundtvig advocated social and economic equality. He appears not to accept Adam Smith's rationale that success in business is a sign of a divine gift to the individual (Israel 2010, 111). Arguing *with* the moderates, Grundtvig supports the continuation of the absolute monarchy. Arguing *against* the radical French philosophers, he condemns violent rebellion against the Church and the King, and he spurns rationalism as a replacement for religious faith. Arguing *with* the radicals he holds that a person's freedom of faith and expression and his or her cultural and vocational education should furnish him with an insight into the equal dignity of all people and the experience that education is an instrument to demolish the pyramid of privileges and monopolies in society (Nørager, chap. 13, this volume). Also, in *contrast* to both the moderates and radicals, Grundtvig assigns much greater priority to the general good. Everything that creates a framework of dignity for the individual is more important than the actual person, just as the community is more and different than the sum of its individuals. He draws logical connections between freedom of faith and expression as a precondition for education, and he favours open debate as a prerequisite for defining "the common good" (Damsholt, chap. 7, this volume). In so doing, Grundtvig also obliges all and each to submit their will to the general will – for this, in his opinion, is essential to the creation of the common good. He links individual freedom to the common freedom to realize what they all share – namely, the Danish four-leaf clover: King, People, Fatherland, and Mother-Tongue (Korsgaard 2012, 22).

This is why Grundtvig may be understood as a *political* philosopher. His philosophy differs from the French and, in particular, the German academic tradition, with its emphasis on systematic conceptual constructions (Øhrgaard, chap. 10, this volume; Damsholt, chap. 7, this volume). Even more conspicuously, Grundtvig is a polyglot: he uses poetry and hymns, history and myth, sermons and lectures, among his communication strategies. Like Kierkegaard, his writing style is rich in images and poor in concepts (Dalsgaard, chap. 15, this volume), while his works are persuasive rather than conclusive. This second thesis therefore requires us to read him as a *political philosopher* and to see him in the context of the Enlightenment's confrontation between moderates and radicals while, at the same time, acknowledging that his philosophy is more poetic than it is academic. This also allows us to see how his theology relates to the creation of his political ideas.

Third Thesis

It is uncommon to include Danish history in the European history of revolutions and counter-revolutions of the late eighteenth and nineteenth centuries. In Danish historiography the slow transition from autocracy to democracy has become the narrative of how Denmark managed to dismantle absolute monarchy without civil war or revolution. It is equally uncommon to present Grundtvig as a political leader. Nor *is* he one, if we compare him with Robespierre in France or Paine in America. And, in comparison with the academic philosophers of the Enlightenment, he is far from an elitist. Yet the third thesis reads as follows: Grundtvig is also a political leader, occupying a third position between the revolutionaries and the elitists, and, on this account, he should therefore be written into the European history of revolutionary and reformist leaders.

Grundtvig is a revolutionary – though with reservations. He supports the education of the common people but will not allow them political authority until they are duly enlightened – so he is not initially in favour of democracy (Korsgaard, chaps. 9 and 16, this volume; Damsholt, chap. 7, this volume). He is a utopian – though with reservations. Grundtvig can imagine the responsible citizen morally bound to realize the general good, but he cannot imagine an ideal form of government. He is also a reformist – though with reservations. He defends the emancipation of the peasantry from adscription and the citizenry from subordination, and he champions the empowerment of all citizens through popular education, but not so that servants, day labourers, and women to enjoy the rights given to peasants, citizens, and husbands (Damsholt, this volume) The third thesis is this: if we combine all Grundtvig's merits, we can see him as a political front man – with no power to enforce political decisions; with no authority to represent church, rank, or king; and with no influence other than the spoken and written word made public through his own efforts and at his own risk.

But Grundtvig is a man who also appears to pursue the same conscious strategy over decades in arguing for a "civil religion" (Nørager, chap. 14, this volume) without necessarily relinquishing faith as a foundation for existence; a man who criticizes scholarship without necessarily overlooking the opportunities for science to contribute to the education of the common people (Hjelmslev, chap. 19, this volume); a man who taunts the elite of his day without necessarily distancing himself from elite knowledge and status (Korsgaard, chap. 9, this volume); and, finally, a man who founds newspapers, occupies official posts, and goes in and out of parliamentary politics, depending, apparently, on what best serves his own political cause (Damsholt, chap. 7, this volume). If Grundtvig is a political "leader," it is because he is a *pragmatic reformist*. He takes the long view, lays out strategies, but has no utopian goal.

Fourth Thesis

In the narrative of Danish history, Grundtvig's role is indispensable. This is not the case with Grundtvigianism, however (Fabricius Møller 2005). People rarely make a distinction between Grundtvig as a person and the popular movements that were established in his name from the end of 1864 until after the Second World War. Confusing Grundtvig the person with Grundtvigianism, his historical effect, enables some to speak of him as a "nation builder." From this confusion arises the fourth thesis: it is Grundtvigianism, together with other movements, that builds the Danish nation and creates the national identity, but it is neither coincidental nor insignificant that this occurs in Grundtvig's name and through his inspiration as a political leader.

The "godly assemblies" promoting a religious revival began in the 1820s, but it was not until the end of the following decade that they were linked to Grundtvig to form the basis of the Grundtvigian movement (Korsgaard 1997, 149–70). Beginning in the 1840s a number of Lutheran congregations in Denmark, while still remaining within the national church, began to choose their own pastors rather than accepting the appointed ones – an arrangement that was finally legalized in 1868. These so-called "free choice congregations" appointed pastors of Grundtvig's persuasion, and, in 1839, Grundtvig himself became pastor at Vartov Church, attracting many worshippers from outside his parish. Even more came to his "Friends' Meetings," which he began at his home in 1863 and which continued until 1893 (long after his death in 1872). As the People's High School movement grew in the 1860s and 1870s, the foundations were laid for creating greater public awareness through newspapers, meetings, reading circles, and church activities in the Grundtvigian spirit. In the 1890s, this began to manifest itself in associations of high schools, free schools, and continuation schools; shooting and gymnastics circles; temperance societies; and farmers associations. The term "Grundtvigian" is not usually applied to this movement until after the defeat to Prussia in 1864; however, all along it was clearly Grundtvig's strategy for spiritual revival and popular education that was the motivating power behind the development of a haphazard local initiative into a social movement (Damsholt, chap. 7, this volume; Korsgaard 1997, 2005).

Yet Grundtvig himself was not the master builder. Others built the structures. People such as Christian Flor, founder of Røddinge People's High School and the newspaper *Danne-Virke* [The Dane-work]; Christen Kold, founder of Ryslinge People's High School and inspirer of other such schools (Korsgaard, chap. 16, this volume; Eichberg, chap. 18, this volume); Ernst Trier, founder of Vallekilde People's High School, builder of a local gymnasium centre, and originator of the concept of "the whole person" (Eichberg, chap. 18, this volume; Korsgaard 2004). There are other names, but the list is not so important. Of more significance is the fact that Grundtvigianism never became an *organization* with a leadership, a secretariat, and an address; rather, it became a *political jousting field*, a field of differing interpretations, where individuals and organizations turned their attention to one another and made routine contact, usually because they were engaging in open debate regarding the proper interpretation of everything from Lutheran theology to Grundtvig's definition of popular society or national community. Grundtvigianism therefore appears to have formed the foundation for a people's movement in keeping with the increasing interest in a particular set of problems that never lost sight of Grundtvig and his strategy for creating a *community of the people.*

There were three stages in this process of trending towards a social movement. The first came with the establishment of a public sphere through newspapers and parish hall meetings, later supplemented by local congregations, goal-oriented meetings, and, finally, solid organizations. The second stage came with disagreements regarding not only theology, including the warring revival movements (Sanders, chap. 4, this volume), but also regarding how to deal with the common people, including altercations on the purpose, character, and curriculum of the burgeoning People's High Schools (Korsgaard, chap. 16, this volume). The third and most important phase came after the First World War, when the socialist movement linked working-class interests to an acceptance of the nation as the framework for a people's society (Korsgaard 1997, 2004). This coupling "of the national, the democratic, and the socialist idea," in which "the nation [was] seen not as a stage in a historical development but as a starting-point for the realization of democracy and socialism" (Korsgaard 2004, 418), created a historical ideological compromise between Grundtvigianism and the socialist workers movement, and laid the groundwork not only for a social movement referencing Grundtvig but also for the Danish father figures of social democracy, in particular Frederik H. Borgbjerg and Thorvald Stauning.

This, therefore, is the fourth thesis: it is neither Grundtvig as a person who builds the Danish nation nor Grundtvigianism alone; rather, it is a historical compromise between the Grundtvigians and the socialist workers movement. And yet Grundtvig is a recurrent point of reference for many people, including many socialists. It is thus the political jousting field that creates the momentum for the social movement that, in time, links persons, institutions, and organizations in the effort to place people and nation, nation and democracy, before the individual's own interests.

Fifth Thesis

Grundtvig is not a democrat (Korsgaard, chaps. 9 and 16, this volume; and Damsholt, chap. 7, this volume). On the other hand, the issues of democracy and democratization are central to the organization of a welfare state. Again Grundtvig is a major point of reference, only this time within the framework of the compromise mentioned above, and now including new combatants in the form of socialists, social democrats, liberalists, and conservatives across political parties (Lunde Larsen, chap. 20, this volume). The debate is crucial to the actual organizing of the welfare state, which gives rise to the fifth and final thesis: the welfare state is organized with its basis in a number of ideas about the community of the people and the individual's moral obligation to this community; it is the welfare state that makes Danish nationalism a mass nationalism.

The "welfare state" can be included in the narrative of the centralist state power that has the capacity to reform itself (Pedersen 2011, 2014) as well as in the narrative of how the common good is given priority over the individual's interests. In particular, the coalition between the Social Democratic Party and the Social Liberal Party – both influenced by the historical compromise of the 1930s – play an important part in the establishment of a welfare state financed by taxes that pay for free welfare benefits as a prerequisite for the individual's moral obligation to the common welfare (Pedersen 2011).

The fifth thesis therefore holds that the welfare state continues the nationalist project while simultaneously turning it into a mass nationalism. This is buttressed by a progressive tax system and is characterized by the distribution of universal welfare rights and the promotion of an education system geared to making every member a fellow citizen in a popular democracy. During this period Grundtvig gradually becomes a legendary figure. His name and work are cited in national debates and as justifications for law-making. He becomes the object of scholarship, and his influence is discussed by writers of history, theology, and literature, and, later, of the history of ideas, until finally he is portrayed as a legend (Kløvedal Reich 1972).

BUILDING A NATION

The five theses cited above have been occasioned by the project of building a nation. They are doubtless neither certain nor safe in providing the distance or the neutrality I have sought in my contribution to analyzing "how Denmark became Denmark." Equally, they may provide the launch pad for a new way of looking at Denmark. To what extent they may give rise to new scholarship or a new narrative is not within my ability to assess. Yet the link between mass nationalism and Grundtvig as a legend does touch on a problem that has long been central to research into nationalism: Does the state arise before the nation or does the nation arise before the state (Bugge, chap. 13, this volume)?

The radical French philosophers believed that a state was a *precondition* for a nation, and they therefore argued that a state takeover was needed before the people could be educated to understand the nature of freedom under a nation. By contrast, the German philosophers (Øhrgaard, chap. 10, this volume) believed that a German nation was the precondition for the creation of a state, which would be formed from many duchies. Grundtvig the legend tells a more complex story: not only that the nation can be built "from below," within the existing state, but also that this process can lead to an awakening of the citizenry and thus to the *reform* of the state. In this context we can see the *creation of a society* as a path to the *creation of a welfare state* via the *formation of a nation*. We can also see Grundtvig as a political leader choosing a strategy whose consequences he could neither foresee nor have the wherewithal to pursue. Nevertheless, the fact that he chooses to accept the opinion-guided monarchy (Damsholt, chap. 7, this volume) – and that it is Grundtvigianism that establishes the public sphere, the institutions, and the organizations – does mean that, in Denmark, nation building has its own peculiar character. First, *society building* is a prerequisite for building a nation-state. This involves educating citizens to understand themselves not only as self-governing and self-loving but also as morally obliged to the community – be that a people, a nation, or a state. Second, *nation building* occurs as a result of society building because it equips the many and the self-governing with a common language, a common history, and possibly a common faith, all of which enables them to understand the community to which they are morally obliged and the common good they are to realize. Third, *state building* involves establishing political institutions that have the capacity to distribute common rights to all and also to protect these common rights.

This is how Grundtvig became a legend – how his person and work became the political jousting field that, even today, is at the heart of the narrative of "how Denmark became Denmark."

REFERENCES

Anderson, B. 1991. *Imagined Communities. Reflections on the Origin and Spread of Nationalism.* London: Verso.

Birkelund, R. 2008. *Frihed til fælles bedste: En Oppositionel stemme fra fortiden – Om Grundtvigs frihedsbegreb* [Freedom for the common good]. Aarhus: Aarhus University Press.

Bjørn, C. 2007. *Grundtvig som politiker* [Grundtvig as a politician]. Copenhagen: Anis.

Bjørn, C., A. Grant, and K.J. Stringer, eds. 1994. *Nations, Nationalism and Patriotism in the European Past.* Copenhagen: Academic Press.

Bregnsbo, M., and K. Villads Jensen. 2004. *Det Danske Imperium: Storhed og Fald* [The Danish empire: Rise and fall]. Copenhagen: Aschehoug.

Dam, P. 1983. *Politikeren Grundtvig* [Grundtvig the politician]. Copenhagen: Aros.

Damsholt, T. 2000. *Fædrelandskærlighed og borgerdyd* [Patriotism and civic virtue]. Copenhagen: Museum Tusculanum.

Fabricius Møller, J. 2005. *Grundtvigianisme i det 20. Århundrede* [Grundtvigianism in the 20th century]. Copenhagen: Vartov.

Feldbæk, O., ed. 1992a. *Dansk Identitetshistorie III: Folkets Danmark, 1848–1940* [The history of Danish identity III: The people of Denmark, 1848–1940]. Copenhagen: C.A. Reitzels Forlag.

– 1992b. *Dansk Identitetshistorie IV: Danmark og Europa, 1940–1990* [The history of Danish identity IV: Denmark and Europe, 1940–1990]. Copenhagen: C.A. Reitzel.

Fukuyama, F. 2011. *The Origins of Political Order: From Prehuman Times to the French Revolution*. London: Profile Books.

Hettne, Björn, S. Sörlin, and U. Østergård. 2006. *Den globala nationalismen: Nationalstatens historia och framtid* [Global nationalism: The history and future of the nation-state]. Stockholm: SNS Förlag.

Israel, J. 2010. *A Revolution of the Mind: Radical Enlightenment and the Intellectual Origins of Modern Democracy*. Princeton, NJ: Princeton University Press.

Jensen, B.E. 1995. "Dansk identitetshistorie" [The history of Danish identity]. *Historisk Tidsskrift* [Historic journal] 16 (4): 75–98.

Kløvedal Reich, E. 1972. *Frederik: En folkebog om N.F.S. Grundtvigs tid og liv* [Frederik: A popular book on the life and times of N.F.S. Grundtvig]. Copenhagen: Gyldendal.

Korsgaard, O. 1997. *Kampen om lyset: Danish voksenoplysning gennem 500 år* [The struggle for enlightenment: Danish adult education over 500 years]. Copenhagen: Gyldendal.

– 2004. *Kampen om folket: Et dannelsesperspektiv på Dansk historie gennem 500 år* [The struggle for the people: An educational perspective on Danish history over 500 years]. Copenhagen: Gyldendal.

– 2005. *Oppositioner til Ove Korsgaards disputats: Kampen om folket: Fra Rune Slagstad, Peter Kemp og Ove K. Pedersen* [Opposition to Ove Korsgaard's thesis: The battle for the people: From Rune Slagstad, Ove Kemp, and Ove K. Pedersen]. Copenhagen: Institut for Pædagogisk Filosofi, Aarhus University.

– 2012. *N.F.S. Grundtvig: Statskundskabens klassikere* [N.F.S. Grundtvig: As a Political Thinker]. Copenhagen: Jurist- og Økonomforbundets Forlag.

Lundgreen-Nielsen, F. 1992. "Grundtvig og danskhed." In *Dansk Identitetshistorie III: Folkets Danmark, 1848–1940* ["Grundtvig and Danishness." In *The History of Danish Identity III*], ed. O. Feldbæk, 9–87. Copenhagen: C.A. Reitzels Forlag.

Østergård, U. 1997. "The Geopolitics of Nordic Identity – From Composite States to Nation States." In *The Cultural Construction of Norden*, ed. Ø. Sørensen and B. Stråth, 25–71. Oslo: Scandinavian University Press.

Pedersen, O.K. 2011. *Konkurrencestaten* [The competition state]. Copenhagen: Hans Reitzels Forlag.

– 2013. *Markedsstaten* [The market state]. Copenhagen: Hans Reitzels Forlag.

Ricoeur, P. 2004. *Memory, History, Forgetting*. Chicago: University of Chicago Press.

Vind, O. 1999. *Grundtvigs Historie Filosofi* [Grundtvig's philosophy of history]. Copenhagen: Gyldendal.

Contributors

KATRINE BAUNVIG received her doctorate from Aarhus University in 2013 for her work on Durkheim and Grundtvig. She is a postdoctoral fellow at the Grundtvig Center at the same university, integrating methods from digital humanities into Grundtvig studies.

MICHAEL BÖSS is associate professor of history and social studies at Aarhus University and director of the Match Points Conference Series. His research concerns Irish, Danish, and Canadian history. His most recent book is *Republikken Danmark* (2011).

ANDREW BUCKSER is the dean of arts and sciences and professor of anthropology at the State University of New York in Plattsburgh. He is the author of *Communities of Faith: Sectarianism, Identity, and Social Change on a Danish Island* (1996).

PETER BUGGE is associate professor of Czech and European studies at Aarhus University. He has published extensively on Czech and East European history of the nineteenth and twentieth centuries.

JOHN L. CAMPBELL is the Class of 1925 Professor of Sociology at Dartmouth College and professor of political economy at the Department of Business and Politics at Copenhagen University. His most recent book is (with co-author Ove K. Pedersen) *The National Origins of Policy Ideas: Knowledge Regimes in the United States, France, Germany and Denmark* (2014).

MATIAS MØL DALSGAARD has a doctorate in philosophy. He is the author of *The Protestant Self: The Demand for Authenticity in*

Kierkegaard's Thought (2012) and *Don't Despair: Letters to a Common Man* (2014).

TINE DAMSHOLT is associate professor of European ethnology at the Saxo Institute, University of Copenhagen. Her current research concentrates on citizenship ceremonies within European states.

HENNING EICHBERG is a cultural sociologist and historian at the University of Southern Denmark specializing in the study of body culture and sport. His most recent book is *Bodily Democracy: Towards a Philosophy of Sport for All* (2010).

FRANCIS FUKUYAMA is Olivier Nomellini Senior Fellow at the Freeman Spogli Institute for International Studies and professor of political science at Stanford University. He is the author of many books including *The Origins of Political Order* (2011) and *Political Order and Political Decay* (2014).

JOHN A. HALL is the James McGill Professor of Comparative Historical Sociology at McGill University in Montreal. His most recent books are *Ernest Gellner* (2011) and *The Importance of Being Civil* (2013).

HANS HENRIK HJERMITSLEV is assistant professor of social science at University College, South Denmark. His research focuses on the circulation of scientific knowledge in nineteenth- and twentieth-century Scandinavia. He is the co-author of *The History of Creationism in Europe* (2014).

JASON O. JENSEN is a doctoral student at McGill University. His research concerns types of political crises and the costs of financial crises.

UFFE JONAS has researched the philosophy, cosmology, and spirituality of Grundtvig for a quarter century, and currently works at the Grundtvig Study Center as an editor and commentator on Grundtvig's writings in English. His most recent book is *The Sun at Midnight* (2014), a study of Grundtvig's cosmology.

OVE KORSGAARD is professor of education at Aarhus University. Among his many books is the classic treatment of Danish national identity, *Kampen om folket* (2004)

ESBEN LUNDE LARSEN is a member of the Danish Parliament and an associate research fellow at the Institute of South East Asian Studies. His current research focuses on American, Singaporean, and Danish views on the nature of civil society.

TROELS NØRAGER gained his doctorate in theology and is now associate professor of ethics and the philosophy of religion at Aarhus University. His most recent book is *Taking Leave of Abraham: An Essay on Religion and Democracy* (2008). His current research concentrates on the religious views of Emerson.

PER ØHRGAARD is professor of German and European studies at the Copenhagen Business School. He is the author of many books on German literature and history.

UFFE ØSTERGÅRD was formerly the director of the Danish Center for Holocaust and Genocide Studies and is now professor of European and Danish history in the Department of Business and Politics at Copenhagen Business School. He is the author of many books on national identities within Europe.

OVE K. PEDERSEN is professor of comparative political economy in the Department of Business and Politics at Copenhagen Business School. His most recent book is (with co-author John L. Campbell) *The National Origin of Policy Ideas: Knowledge Regimes in the United States, Germany, France, and Denmark* (2014).

HANNE SANDERS is professor of history at Lund University. She is a specialist in the relations between religion, nationalism, and secularization, together with the significance these have for people's everyday lives; she has an especial interest in borders between states.

ANTHONY D. SMITH is professor emeritus of nationalism and ethnicity at the London School of Economics. He is the author of classical works on nationalism, most recently *Ethno-symbolism and Nationalism* (2009).

OLE VIND gained his doctorate from Copenhagen University, and has taught at Grundtvig's Folk High School north of Copenhagen since 1976. He writes regularly about intellectual history and the history of ideas.

Index

An italic *t* following a page reference indicates a table.